Edinburgh For Under Fives

a handbook for parents

5th Edition
by local members of the National Childbirth Trust

Published by Edinburgh for Under Fives

Editors	: Marion Donohoe and Kate Blackadder
Cover Design	: Ann R Paterson
Cover Artwork	: Gill Waugh (Art Dept.)
Cartoons	: Douglas Bruton and Fred Volans
City Centre Map	: Forbes Mutch and Mark Blackadder
Area Map	: Neil McLeish and Philip Hunsley
Index	: Marion Donohoe

ISBN 0 9512397 4 0

1st Edition	1987 Reprinted 1987
2nd Edition	1989
3rd Edition	1991
4th Edition	1993
5th Edition	1995

Printed by D. & J. Croal Ltd., Haddington

Editorial and Publishing Committee:
Kate Blackadder, Sheila Capewell, Marion Donohoe, Carolyn Sellars

Co-ordinator: Philip Hunsley

Research Team:
Caroline Argo, Senga Bate, Kate Blackadder, Rosemarie Bland, June Campbell, Sheila Capewell, Carolyn Clark, Alison Connelly, Lorna Conway, Marion Donohoe, Janet Gent, Jill Gillard, Siobhan Gilliland, Liz Hardy, Deborah Harris, Ann Hubbard, Philip Hunsley, Alison Hyde, Siân Jarman, Vivienne Miller, Jane Millican, Chris Pattison, Lesley Rankin, Julie Robertson, Beth Rutherford, Jane Sanders, Carolyn Sellars, Mary Soulsby, Jane Tupper, Naomi Visscher, Patricia Watson.

ACKNOWLEDGEMENTS:
Margaret Barbier, Cato, Maggie Corr, Eric Donohoe, Margaret Flaherty, Adam Gillard, Nige Gillard, Kathy McGlew, Elizabeth McLeod (Play Development Officer,EDC), Jon Mengham, Rosemary Mutch (WRVS), Sarah Robertson, Brenda Rowans, Willie Rutherford, Carolyn Warlock, Jane Watson, Dave Watson.

Special thanks to: Bill Main of Brown, Scott & Main, Chartered Accountants; David Robertson, Paris Steele & Co., W.S., North Berwick; Colin Redpath of Allingham & Co, Solicitors.

FOREWORD

Anticipation of Rosie's birth was enhanced by wandering effortlessly around maternity and nursery departments and stopping to admire gorgeous babies in the supermarket as their mothers calmly shopped. I dreamed of outings with my baby — the fun we'd have! Reality came as a shock. Difficult access, nowhere to change nappies, were a couple of problems I encountered. Why hadn't anyone warned me? How did parents cope?

Thankfully it is getting easier to take tots out and about and guides like Edinburgh for Under Fives are a wonderful starting point for mums and dads alike. Planning a busy family's life is certainly helped — be it planning a party or playgroup, and your choice is more informed by having the facts at your fingertips.

Edinburgh can be proud of its achievements in pioneering provision for children and making sure their voice is heard. Edinburgh for Under Fives has become like a parent's bible and one which I'll certainly use when visiting Scotland's capital.

Lorraine Kelly and Rosie aged — 15 months.

INTRODUCTION

Welcome to the fifth edition of Edinburgh For Under Fives. As well as revising and updating the existing entries, we have added a section on supermarkets, as they have been responding to the specific needs of customers with children.

We have been delighted by the warm reception the fourth edition received, as with the earlier editions, and by the many letters of congratulations, thanks and encouragement. We have continued to note an increasing awareness of the need to make the City more accessible and welcoming for children and are pleased to find that many shops now have public toilets and feeding and changing rooms.

The presentation of 'Child Friendly Edinburgh' awards by Edinburgh District Council has helped highlight the needs of parents of young children and it is encouraging to find the range of establishments that make children welcome is increasing. This year the criteria for gaining an award were such that we felt it was more suitable to indicate the award of Child Friendly Edinburgh, so look out for the award as you peruse the new edition.

Many people have contributed to the book in many ways. All the researchers are parents of young children, who have experience of the day to day problems (and joys) of living in Edinburgh and we thank them for putting their experiences on the page.

We hope this book will provide information and inspiration and help to make life for families in Edinburgh, whether permanent or visiting, easier and more enjoyable.

If you have any comments, suggestions or contributions on the book or would like to help in the research for future editions you can write to **Edinburgh for Under Fives, PO Box 012345, Edinburgh, EH9 2YB.**

The information in the book was correct, to our knowledge, at the time of going to press and the views expressed are not necessarily those of the contributors or the National Childbirth Trust.

We cannot be held responsible for any errors or omissions.

Contents

MAP   vi-vii

Child Friendly Edinburgh viii-ix

SHOPPING   **1**
Department Stores   2
Shopping Centres and Markets 7
Supermarkets   10
Maternity Wear   12
Baby and Children's Clothes 14
Schoolwear   19
Kilts   20
Dancewear Shops   21
Make Your Own   21
Children's Shoes   23
Nursery Equipment including
Repairs   25
Toy Shops, Special Gifts and
Doll Repairs   27
Outdoor Toys   31
Bicycle Shops   31
Outdoor and Ski Shops 36
Buying Children's Books 38
Bookshops   39
Secondhand Goods   43
Chemists with Extended Hours 44
Hairdressers   46
Recording the Event   49
Creches While Shopping 50

TOILET STOPS   **50**

SHOPPING FROM HOME **52**
Children's Books   52
Clothes   52
Food   54
Shoes   54
Toys   54
Miscellaneous   55
Party Plan   55

HIRING   **57**
Bicycles   57
Cake Tins   57
Clothes   57

Equipment   57
Inflatables   58
Skis   59
Toys   59
Video Cameras   59
Miscellaneous   59

EATING OUT   **60**
In Central Edinburgh   62
In East Edinburgh   73
In North Edinburgh   73
In South Edinburgh   75
In West Edinburgh   79
Pubs   81

BIRTHDAYS & CELEBRATIONS **83**
The Venue   83
Children's Parties at Home 87
Catering and Cakes   88
Entertainment   89

PRE-SCHOOL PLAY &
EDUCATION   **91**
Parent and Baby Groups 92
Parent and Toddler Groups 92
Playgroups, Home Playgroups 97
Private Nurseries   107
Nursery Schools and Nursery
Classes in Primary Schools 116
Independent Schools   118
Looking Forward to Starting
School   119
Special Schools   119
Local Play Organisations 119

CHILDCARE   **120**
Childminders   121
Childcare in Your Own Home 122
Children's Centres and
Day Care   123
Organisations involved in
Childcare   123
Professional Help with
Childcare and Babysitting 124
Babysitting Circles   125

LIBRARIES   **126**

TOY LIBRARIES	**132**	**PLAYGROUNDS & PARKS**	**208**
		Adventure Playgrounds	218
ACTIVITIES FOR CHILDREN	**135**	Playbus	218
Art	135		
Dance	135	**WALKS & COUNTRY PLACES**	**219**
Gymnastics	138		
Music	141		
Reading	142	**TRAVEL & TRANSPORT**	**233**
Skating	142	On Foot	234
Swimming	142	Cycling	235
Playcentres	151	Travel by Car	235
		Bus Transport	237
		Taxis	239
ACTIVITIES FOR PARENTS	**154**	Travel by Train	240
Centres Offering a Variety		Air Travel .	242
of activities	155		
Women's Groups		**WELFARE**	**246**
and Parents Centres	158		
Sources of Information			
on Adult Classes & Training	160	**HEALTH CARE FACILITIES**	**253**
Adult Classes & Training		Emergencies	253
Courses	161	General Practitioner (GP)	
Sports and Leisure	166	Services	253
		Alternative Medicine	253
		Maternity Units	255
PLACES TO VISIT	**174**	Antenatal Care	255
Art Galleries	175	Registration of Birth	256
EDINBURGH AREA MAP	**176**	Post-Natal Support and	
		New Babies	257
Museums	177	Feeding	259
Historic Places	179	Post Natal Depression	260
Animals in the City	182	Children's Hospitals	
Boats, Planes and Trains	185	and Wards	260
Theatres and Cinemas	186	Dental Care	262
		Problem Solving	262
OUT OF TOWN TRIPS	**190**		
East Lothian	190	**INDEX**	**265-275**
Midlothian	192		
West Lothian	193	**CRISIS LINES**	**278**
Borders	195		
Central	196		
Fife	196		
Strathclyde	197		
Tayside	198		
ANNUAL EVENTS	**200**		
SOURCES OF INFORMATION	**205**		

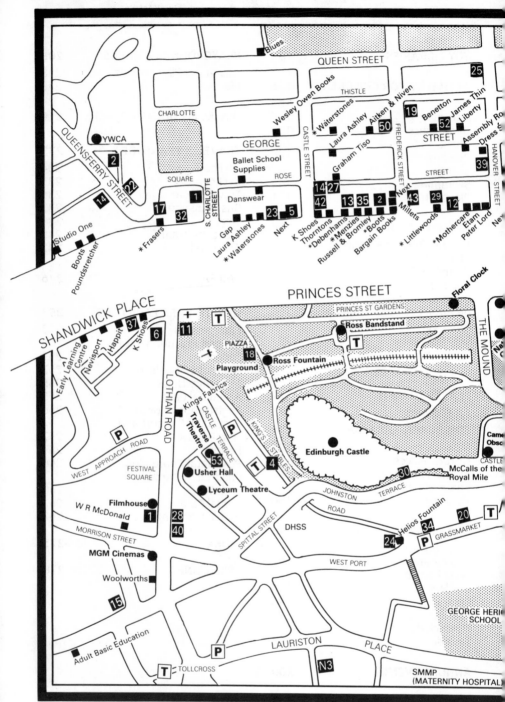

QUEEN STREET

Blues

25

CHARLOTTE

Wesley Owen Books

THISTLE

*Waterstones

Laura Ashley   Aitken & Niven

19   Benetton   James Thin
                Liberty

52   Assembly Ro

Dress &

YWCA

GEORGE

CASTLE STREET

FREDERICK STREET

STREET

HANOVER STREET

QUEENSFERRY STREET

Ballet School
Supplies

Graham Tiso

50

STREET   39

2

ROSE

14 27

43   29   12

22

SQUARE

S. CHARLOTTE STREET

Danswear

14   1

42   13 35   2

Next

Millets

17   32

23   5

K Shoes
Thorntons
*Debenhams
*Menzies
Russell & Bromley

*Boots
Bargain Books

*Littlewoods   *Mothercare
                Etam
                Peter Lord

Studio One

Boots
Poundstretcher

*Frasers

Gap
Laura Ashley
*Waterstones

Next

PRINCES STREET

Floral Clock

SHANDWICK PLACE

37

6

+

11

T

PRINCES ST GARDENS

Ross Bandstand

THE MOUND

Na

Early Learning Centre
Nevisport
Happit
K Shoes

PIAZZA

18

Playground

Ross Fountain

T

Kings Fabrics

LOTHIAN ROAD

CASTLE TERRACE

Traverse Theatre

P

KING'S STABLES

Edinburgh Castle

Came
Obsc

P

WEST APPROACH ROAD

FESTIVAL
SQUARE

53

T   4

CASTLE

Usher Hall

30

McCalls of the
Royal Mile

Filmhouse

Lyceum Theatre

JOHNSTON   TERRACE

W R McDonald

1

MORRISON STREET

28

40

SPITTAL STREET

DHSS

ROAD

Helios Fountain

20   T

24   34   P   GRASSMARKET

MGM Cinemas

WEST PORT

Woolworths

15

GEORGE HERI
SCHOOL

Adult Basic Education

P

LAURISTON   PLACE

SMMP
(MATERNITY HOSPITAL)

T   TOLLCROSS

N3

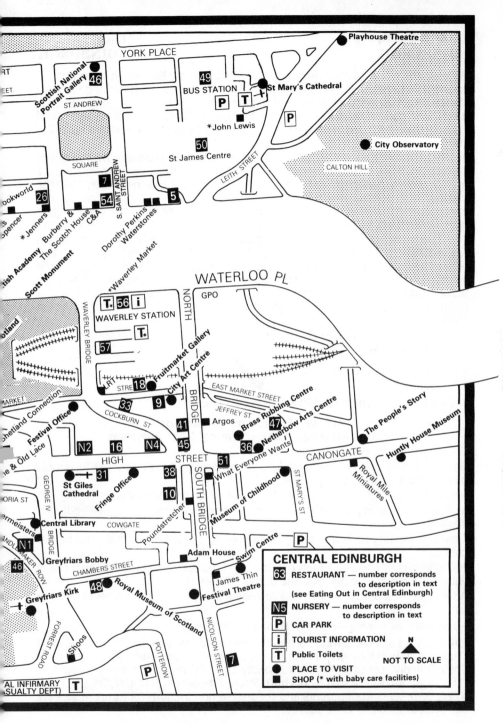

York Place
Playhouse Theatre
Scottish National Portrait Gallery **46**
St Andrew
Bus Station **49**
P T St Mary's Cathedral
*John Lewis
P
City Observatory
Square
St James Centre **50**
Calton Hill
Leith Street
Bookworld **26**
*Spencer
Scottish Academy
*Jenners
Burberry & The Scotch House
C&A **54**
S. Saint Andrew Street
7
Dorothy Perkins
Waterstones **5**
*Waverley Market
Scott Monument
*Scotland
Waverley Bridge
Waterloo Pl
GPO
T. **56** i
Waverley Station
T.
57
North
Market
Shetland Connection
Art Street **18**
Fruitmarket Gallery
City Art Centre
33
9
Festival Office
Cockburn St
East Market Street
Jeffrey St
Argos
Brass Rubbing Centre
The People's Story
41
47
Netherbow Arts Centre
Huntly House Museum
Shetland Connection
Lace & Old Lace
N2 **16** N4
45
36
What Everyone Wants
Canongate
Royal Mile Miniatures
High Street
51
St Mary's St
George IV Bridge
St Giles Cathedral **31**
Fringe Office
38
10
South Bridge
Museum of Childhood
Victoria St
Central Library
Cowgate
Poundstretcher
P
N1
Bridge
Candlemaker Row
Greyfriars Bobby
Chambers Street
Adam House
Swim Centre
46
James Thin
Festival Theatre
Greyfriars Kirk **48**
Royal Museum of Scotland
Forrest Road
Shoos
Nicolson Street
7
Potterow
P
Al Infirmary (Sualty Dept) T

CENTRAL EDINBURGH

63 RESTAURANT — number corresponds to description in text (see Eating Out in Central Edinburgh)

N5 NURSERY — number corresponds to description in text

P CAR PARK

i TOURIST INFORMATION

T Public Toilets

● PLACE TO VISIT

■ SHOP (* with baby care facilities)

N
NOT TO SCALE

vii

Child Friendly
EDINBURGH

Child Friendly
EDINBURGH

People often ask where the inspiration for Child Friendly Edinburgh came from — predictably that's not easy to determine. It developed as initiatives and research showed that the needs of parents and children when 'out and about' were not being met. It was consolidated in 1994 when Edinburgh District Council set up a Child Friendly Unit in recognition of the many issues affecting children and families in the city.

In 1992 the first Child Friendly Guide and Awards were produced by Edinburgh District Council's Public Relations Department. All entries were nominated by members of the public and visited by District Council staff and children. By 1993 the number of entries in the guide has almost doubled — an indication of both improvements in businesses and an increased awareness of the need to give positive feedback to those improving their welcome to children and their carers.

The Child Friendly Unit produced a new guide in June 1995. Although still relying on nominations from parents and children, it is different from previous guides. This edition awards symbols to premises to indicate in which ways a place is child friendly. This is because we were sometimes asked why certain places were included in the previous guides — perhaps because they did not have facilities for nappy changing, or were not especially sympathetic towards tired or bored children.

Entries which have gained a Child Friendly Edinburgh award are denoted throughout the book by this symbol:

The categories in which symbols were awarded are:

Access Environment Attitude
Toilet/Changing Facilities Eating Play Provision

Criteria within the categories include:

Doors and main aisles wide enough for a double buggy; lifts wide enough for double buggy where necessary.

No smoking policy; healthy snacks if available; high level of cleanliness.

Staff are welcoming, friendly and understanding to children; breastfeeding is allowed.

Clear sign-posting of facilities; nappy-change area available to male and female carers.

Half portions or children's menu, bottle and food warming facilities; high chairs with restraints; own baby food and drinks permitted.

A safe play area or toys or activities provided; play provision available to children with disabilities.

A complete list of recipients is given on the next page.

Full details of all award winners, and the criteria for awards are given in the Child Friendly Edinburgh Guide. To obtain a copy of it or its companion guide 'How to be Child Friendly' contact the Child Friendly Unit, Strategic Services Department, Edinburgh District Council, 6 Cockburn Street, Edinburgh, EH1 1NY, Tel. 0131 529 4276. Comments from parents and children or nominations for future guides are also welcome, to the same address.

Child Friendly
EDINBURGH

EATING OUT AND PUBS
The Bridge Inn, Ratho
Ratho Park Brewer's Fayre
Giuliano's
The In-Filling Coffee Shop
The Abercorn
Bar Roma
Bethany Homemaker Cafe
Burger King
Cafe St James
Carlton Highland Hotel
Cavaliere Restaurant, Dalkeith
Coronation Inn, Gorebridge
Fairmile Inn
Fat Sam's
Garfunkel's
Gennaros
Harry Ramsden's
Hawes Inn, South Queensferry
Holiday Inn Garden Court
Kalpna
Khushi's
La Rusticana
Lauriston Farm
Maharajah's
Mamma'a American Pizza Company
McDonalds
Mr Mario's
Omar Khayyam
Pasquales
San Marco
Starbank Inn
The Sycamore Tree
The Terrace Cafe, Royal Botanical Gardens
The Tiffin
Up the Junction

SHOPS
John Lewis Partnership
Boots
Gyle Shopping Centre
Bruntsfield Cards
Cameron Toll Shopping Centre
Clark's Shoe Shop, Cameron Toll
Clark's Shoe Shop, Musselburgh
Clark's Shoe Shop, Princes St
Disney Store
James Thin, South Bridge
Jenners
John Menzies, Princes St
Klownz Hair Ltd
Leigh Thomas Hairdresser
Marks and Spencer
Raeburn Pram Centre
Scotmid, Leith Central
Shoos
Toys 'R' Us
Waverley Shopping Centre

PLACES TO VISIT
Gorgie City Farm
The Royal Museum of Scotland
Edinburgh Zoo
Children's Adventure Tours
Bird of Prey Centre
Bufferfly and Insect World
Brass Rubbing Centre
City Arts Centre
Huntley House Museum
Museum of Childhood
The People's Story
Scottish National Gallery of Modem Art
The Writer's Museum

LEISURE AND SPORT
Gracemount Leisure Centre
Little Marco's
Leo's
Ainslie Park Leisure Centre
Caledonian Cycle Route
Calton Centre
Clambers
Claremont Health Club
Fettes Village
Koko's Children's Leisure Centre
Leith Waterworld
McLeod Street Sports Centre
Meadowbank Sports and Leisure Centre
Megabowl, Kinnaird Park
Scotland Yard Adventure Centre
South Queensferry Coarse Angling Club
St Bride's Community Centre
Roseburn to Leith Railway Path

LIBRARIES
Balgreen
McDonald Road
Newington
South Queensferry
Stockbridge

MISCELLANEOUS
Macadam's, Solicitors, Charlotte Sq
J P Optometrist, Gt Junction St
Ellersly House Hotel
Abbey National Building Society, Morningside Rd
Ben Doran Guest House, Mayfield Gdns
Edinburgh House Guest House, McDonald Rd
Family Care, Castle St
The Herald House Hotel, Grove St
National and Provincial Building Society, South Charlotte St
One Parent Families Scotland, Gayfield Sq
Trotter's Opticians, George St

THE NATIONAL CHILDBIRTH TRUST

Formed over thirty years ago, the NCT is Britain's best-known charity concerned with education for pregnancy, birth and parenthood. It is run by, and for, parents, through its network of 350 Branches and Groups all over the UK. There are three NCT Branches in Edinburgh.

'New Generation' is the quarterly magazine of the NCT which covers new discoveries and initiatives in the fields of pregnancy, birth, parenthood and infant feeding, as well as the current activities of the NCT nationwide. Locally, each Edinburgh Branch publishes a quarterly newsletter.

The principal aim of the National Childbirth Trust is to help parents achieve greater enjoyment and satisfaction in parenthood, and with that in mind the Edinburgh Branches provide the following:

- Antenatal classes
- Support with breastfeeding
- Hire scheme for electric breast pumps
- Friendly support for new mothers through contact with other mums living locally
- Visits to schools and colleges to talk about being a parent (our children go along too)
- The NCT's own range of maternity wear and baby equipment (MAVA bras, nightdresses, swimsuits) and also Ameda battery and mini-electric breast pumps
- Information leaflets on a variety of topics relating to pregnancy, birth, infant feeding and weaning and parenthood
- The books 'NCT Your Choices for Pregnancy and Childbirth' by Helen Lewison, 'NCT Get into Shape after Childbirth' by Gillian Fletcher and the 'NCT Book of Breastfeeding' by Mary Smale
- Working Mothers' Group and Postnatal Exercise Classes

Further details of these services are provided in the relevant sections of 'Edinburgh for Under Fives' eg Shopping p13 and Health Care Facilities p256, p257 and p259. For more information please contact:
    The NCT Office
    Stockbridge Health Centre
    1 India Place
    Edinburgh EH3 6EH
    Tel: 225 9191
The office is open Mon-Fri 9-12noon.

The National Childbirth Trust is a registered charity no. 801395

Shopping

"IF WE CAN'T USE YOUR TOILETS HAVE YOU GOT A MOP?"

Shopping with small children requires an entirely different approach from shopping on your own. Not only do you have to discover good sources of maternity, baby and children's equipment and clothes, but when accompanied by little ones, timing, access and toilet stops are of utmost importance. In this section you will find some ideas of where to shop for yourself and your children's needs, and all the information you need to plan a less stressful experience. As with any expedition (shopping with children is no longer a 'trip') planning is the key and knowing the easiest entrance and dept locations can lessen some of the hassle.

Feeding and changing rooms are now considered a standard requirement in large dept stores and shopping centres. They are available to male and female carers, although if they are combined changing/feeding rooms it would be sensible for fathers to ask an assistant to check the room (some breastfeeding mothers may feel uncomfortable with strangers sharing the facility).

These rooms should be separate from customer toilets, but it is an advantage to be near the toilets, especially if you also have an older child with you. The standard of parent and baby rooms in the centre of Edinburgh is generally high, but should you find them lacking in facilities, or not clean, it is worth mentioning this to a manager or supervisor (some rooms have a comments book) as it is only

1

through such information that store managers are aware of customer requirements.

Urgent toilet stops for young children and expectant mums can be a great problem when shopping. We carry out the research by questionnaire, so if an entry indicates that use of a staff toilet is permitted, insist about using it, as it is the store's declared policy, no matter what an assistant may think! Generally you will have more success if you ask a more mature assistant who understands the consequences of a refusal. (see cartoon) See also Toilet Stops p54.

Use the store guides in large shops to get to where you are going. Make note of changing rooms, toilets, restaurants convenient for this trip and it is wise to set a time limit — children do get bored. One tip from an experienced shopping Mum is to always carry a snack/carton of juice in your handbag; it always buys you a little extra time.

Information to help you use this chapter:

● Most city centre shops have late night shopping on Thur. Some stores open at 9.30 am on Tues or Wed due to staff training.

● Tues or Wed is half-day closing in the suburbs.

● Many stores open later and longer in the summer or during the Festival, and Sunday trading at Christmas, and in suburban shopping centres is almost standard practice.

● We have used 'baby' to describe clothes for under 2s and 'children's' for over 2s.

● Where we have listed shops with several branches, the description generally refers to the main branch and you may find that other smaller branches do not have the same choice of goods.

● Shops which have received a Child Friendly Edinburgh Award are indicated. See pviii.

DEPARTMENT STORES

Large shops are responding to customer demand and parents are seeing improvements in access and child friendly facilities. Shops do change their layout fairly often, so check the information by using the store guide. If you have something to return, ask as soon as you enter the store for the correct procedure. You may be directed to a Customer Service Desk.

Aitken & Niven
77 George St
225 1461
Mon-Sat 9-5.30

Access: Two entrances from George St both with a few steps up. Left to menswear, right other to shoe dept. Traditional, quality shop in Edinburgh's prestigious George St. A fitting room could be made available for feeding and nappy changing.

Ground: Children's shoes see p23.

1st: School wear see p20.

2nd: Restaurant.

Toilets.

Argos
Unit 2/5 North Bridge (opposite Scotsman offices)
558 1474
Mon-Sat 9-5.30; Thurs 9-7.30; Sun 12.30-4.30

Also at Kinnaird Park, Newcraighall Rd
657 3754
Mon-Fri 9-8; Sat 9-6; Sun 10-5

Clean easy shopping. Free catalogue to take away and choose purchases at leisure. Many items on display. Quote catalogue no. to cashier and goods are collected from the stockroom for you. 16 days to return goods if not satisfied. Good value.
See also Nursery Equipment p25, Toyshops p27 and Bicycles p35.

BhS

64 Princes St
226 2621
Mon, Wed 9-5.30; Tues 9.30-5.30; Thurs 9-8; Fri, Sat 9-6; Sun 12.30-5

Access: Good from Princes St with central escalators giving access to all floors. Small lift halfway along left handside. From Rose St through restaurant, escalator down to Ground floor.

Basement: Children's clothes, *see* p15; lighting — stocks night lights, dimmers etc; some toys; linens.

Rose St level: Restaurant *see* Eating Out p62.

Feeding and changing room, toilets: on 1st, upstairs from Restaurant, no lift access. Toilet for the disabled on restaurant level.

Boots the Chemist
101 Princes St
225 8331
Mon-Wed 9-5.30; Thurs 9-7; Fri, Sat 9-6

Also at 48 Shandwick Pl, St James Centre, North Bridge, Cameron Toll and the Gyle (open Sun) and suburban locations (*see* Phone Book). *See* Chemists with Extended Hours p44.

Access: 2 automatic doors. Public lift and escalator on the left, staff lift available for double pushchairs. Wide clear aisles.

Ground: Baby food, toiletries, dispensing chemist.

1st: Baby toiletries, stationery and toys.
See Children's clothes p15, Maternity wear p12.

2nd: Coffee shop. *See* Eating Out p62. **Toilets.**

Feeding and changing room at rear of ground floor (no access for double pushchairs). Men welcome to use this room, but should ask first in case a mother is feeding. Bottle warmer, wipes, nappies etc usually available.

C & A
33 Princes St
556 4411
Mon-Wed 9-5.30; Thurs 9.30-8; Fri, Sat 9-6.

Access: Automatic doors. Good to all departments with lift situated near front door and escalators up and down.

2nd: see Children's clothes p16.

4th: see Maternity Wear p13.

7th: Staff **toilet** on request.

Debenhams
109-112 Princes St
225 1320
Mon-Wed 9.30-6; Thurs 9.30-8; Fri 9.30-7, Sat 9-6.

Access: Main access from Princes St with lifts to left of main entrance. Also escalators to all floors. Also access from Rose St where there are 2 glass lifts to Men's wear and Wedding departments.

Basement: Babywear, children's wear, including accessories. *See* Children's Clothes p16.

3

1st: Maternity Wear (Dorothy Perkins) see p13.

2nd: Ladies' wear including maternity/nursing bras.

4th: Restaurant. See Eating Out p65.

Toilets: on 4th floor opposite main lift. Toilet for the disabled is small, but has chair for feeding and small changing shelf.

Frasers
145 Princes St
225 2472
Mon, Wed, Fri 9-5.30; Tues 9.30-5.30; Thurs 9-7.30; Sat 9-6.

Access: Two entrances from Princes St to Ground floor. Lift at rear, escalators on right to all departments.

5th: Restaurant: See Eating Out p65.

Feeding and changing room tucked away in back left corner of ground floor.

Toilets on 5th floor.

Jenners
48 Princes St
225 2442
Mon, Wed, Fri, Sat 9-5.30; Tues 9.30-5.30; Thurs 9-7.30.

Upmarket store with large galleried well and many different levels. Because of its traditional design, this can be an awkward shop to get around in, especially with a pushchair, but it is worth persevering as it is a very attractive store with friendly staff. Best to ask for directions if you don't know your way about.

Access: Pushchair access is easiest from St David St or Rose St as both Princes St entrances have steps up. To get to the toilets on the 3rd floor, best enter by Rose St next to Travel

Agency and take the lift up. There are several lifts servicing different areas, all are small and often crowded.

Basement: Toys, children's books (lift behind perfume dept on Ground floor) see Toyshops p28, Bicycle shops, Birthdays and Celebrations p87, Children's Books p43.

Midway: Stationery, haberdashery see Make Your Own p22.

Midway/1st: Ladies' wear including lingerie.

Restaurants: Four to choose from. See Eating Out p67.

Toilets on **3rd** floor: Parent and baby rooms adjacent to ladies' toilet. Clean, comfortable and pleasant and not usually too busy. Nappy changing room and separate feeding room with sofa and chairs.

Also Junior Jenners, Rose St, opposite rear entrance to main store.

Baby and childrens' wear see p17, Nursery Equipment see p26.

John Lewis
St James' Centre
556 9121

Mon Closed; Tues, Wed, Fri 9-5.30; Thurs 9.30; Sat 9-6; Open 3 Mons prior to Christmas.

Large dept store providing a wide range of goods and services. Offers a price guarantee of being 'never knowingly undersold'. Delivers goods free throughout central Scotland, including Fife and the Borders.

Access: Two entrances within St James' Centre. Also entrance off Leith St; wide automatic revolving door into lower basement (opposite exit from Greenside Pl car park). Entrance into basement and Customer Collection Point from Little King St adjacent to St James' Centre car park. Movement within store is easy, with 3 roomy lifts (not to lower basement) to the right of main entrances, a glass lift to all floors to rear of store and 2 sets of escalators.

Lower Basement: Toys see p27, Outdoor Toys p31, Bicycle Shops p36.

Basement: Lighting, including night lights; Childrens' books see p40.

Ground: Selection of gloves and hats, fabrics and haberdashery see Make Your Own p22, Schoolwear p20, Birthdays and Celebrations p88.

1st: Maternity wear, see p13, Baby and Children's Wear see p17, Shoes see p24, Schoolwear see p20 and Nursery Equipment see p26.

2nd: Restaurant, see Eating Out p67.

Toilets on **2nd**.

Feeding and changing rooms on **2nd**: Mothers' Room, quite spacious but always busy. Fathers' room inside entrance to ladies' cloakroom on left.

Littlewoods
90/91 Princes St
225 1683
Mon, Tues, Wed 9.30-5.30; Thurs 9-7; Fri, Sat 9-6; Sun 12.30-5.

Access: From Princes St. Lift half-way along right side. Escalator up to 1st floor.

Basement: Food Hall, Restaurant see Eating Out p68.

Ground: Toilet for the disabled has access for pushchairs, a fold-down changing table and nappy vending machine.

1st: Baby and Children's wear see p17, school wear.

Marks and Spencer
53 Princes St ✔
225 2301
Mon, Tues 9.30-5.30;
Wed 9-5.30; Thurs 9-8; Fri 9-7; Sat 8.30-6
The Gyle Shopping Centre
317 1333
Mon, Tues, Wed 9.30-8; Thur 9.30-9; Fri 9-9; Sat 9-7; Sun 10-5.

Both stores have recorded messages of weekly store opening times on answerphone. Accept M & S chargecard only. Holders are invited to open evenings.

Princes St

Access: Easy access from Princes' St. Two entrances from Rose St. Left hand side with automatic door and level access. There are 5 levels, all connected by stairs, escalators and lifts. The lift from ground to lower ground is located at the near right from Princes St. There is a lift on the Rose St level to the right hand rear corner, which gives easy access from children's wear to other floors.

A collect-by-car service is available.

Rose St level: Baby and children's clothes see p17, school wear.

Basement: Foods including sweets suitable for party bags and ready-made novelty birthday cakes.

Feeding and changing room with separate **toilet** in Rose St level to right of checkouts.

The Gyle

Spacious store on one level with same selection as Princes St. Priority parent and child parking outside foodhall entrance.

See Shopping Centres and Markets p8.

John Menzies
107 Princes St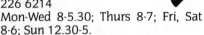
226 6214
Mon-Wed 8-5.30; Thurs 8-7; Fri, Sat 8-6; Sun 12.30-5.

Access: Good. Two lifts at back of store. Escalator to 1st floor on right; escalator to basement on left.

Basement: Toys *see* p29, music, videos, computers.

1st: Books *see* Children's Books p43. Restaurant *see* Eating Out p69.

Toilets on **1st:** Small changing shelf, nappy vending machine.

Mothercare
84a Princes St
226 6503
Mon-Sat 9-5.30; Thurs 9-8

Brightly decorated store with themed talking trees (safety and environment). Well-designed with child height handrails on stairs etc.

Access: Good to all floors. Escalator up at front right of shop. Lift at rear to all floors.

Some staff trained to help deaf parents and children. Catalogue available *see* Shopping from Home p53.

Basement: Maternity wear *see* p13, children's underwear, night-wear and footwear. Toys *see* p29. Seats and play area at rear.

Ground: Children's clothes from 1yr, *see* p17. Play area at rear with chairs, tables and toys.

1st: Babywear *see* Children's Clothes p14, Nursery Equipment *see* p26, toiletries and nappies.

Feeding and changing rooms at rear of **basement**: 'Mummy's Room' with complimentary wipes and nappies, chair for feeding. Parents' room with wipes etc, child and adult **toilet**. Mums are encouraged to use 'Mummy's room' to allow access to toilets for all.

Scotmid Co-op
158/160 Gt Junction St
555 1155
Mon-Sat 8.45-5.30
Access: Enter in Gt Junction St. Lift to 1st floor.
1st: Toys *see* p27, Nursery Equipment *see* p25.
No **toilet**.
Also at 52 Nicholson St
667 5888
Mon-Sat 8.45-5.30

Access: From Nicholson St. Lift at near left-hand side to all floors, also escalators.

1st: Toys *see* p27, Nursery equipment *see* p25.

3rd: Toilets: Ladies has chairs for feeding.

4th: Restaurant.

Toys 'R' Us
Kinnaird Park, Newcraighall Rd
657 4191
Mon-Sat 9-8; Thurs 9-9; Sun 10-6

Large toy warehouse with big selection, although generally no cheaper than town. Store directory guides to different areas and there is a pick-up point for bulky items and electrical toys. There is no play area and, as such a large array may prove tempting, parents may find it easier to shop without their offspring. **Toilets** on right-hand aisle.

See also Toyshops p30, Outdoor Toys p31, Bicycle Shops p36, Children's Clothes p19 and Shopping Centres and Markets p8.

6

Woolworth

142 Lothian Rd
229 4644
Mon-Sat 9-5.30
Also at 36 Raeburn Pl, 332 2613
St John's Rd, 334 6644
170 Constitution St, 654 3872

Access: Easy access from Lothian Rd. Store all on one level. Good selection of videos, tapes and stationery for children.

Baby and Children's wear *see* p19 and Toys *see* p31.

SHOPPING CENTRES AND MARKETS

Assembly Rooms

54 George St
220 4348

Lift to all floors.

Craft and collectors' fairs held about once a mth. Advertised in local press and windows. Christmas Charity Hypermarket held in December see Creches p50. Craft Fairs usually include baby and children's clothes (knitwear etc), wooden toys, patchwork. Fairs tend to get very busy especially at lunchtime which renders pushchairs and small children a liability. Children's shows held regularly during the school holidays eg puppet shows, children's theatre. **Toilets** at back left of ground floor down a few steps or at the right of the 1st floor where you can feed and change.

Cameron Toll Shopping Centre ✔

Lady Rd

Centre opening hrs: Mon-Wed & Sat 8-8, Thur & Fri 8-9, Sun 10-6. Hrs of individual shops vary but generally all open late on Thurs, and Sun afternoons.

Two large car parks serve both front and rear entrances. Can be very busy particularly on Fri and wkends. As there are no paved walkways in car park keep a tight grip on small children. Pedestrian access from Lady Rd to front entrance of centre but closely set bollards and a roll bar designed to prevent shoppers from taking trolleys out means large prams and pushchairs need careful manoeuvring. Self-opening doors, seats, public phones in a pleasant leafy mirrored mall. Petrol station and taxi rank. A variety of trolley designs to accommodate various ages of babies and small children. Many smaller shops do not allow trolleys inside.

A variety of shops including Adams Children's Wear *see* Baby and Children's Clothes p14, Boots *see* Chemists with Extended Hours p44, Forbuoys *see* Toyshops p28, Happit *see* Children's Clothes p16, K Shoes *see* Children's Shoes p24, Clark's *see* Children's Shoes p24, Mackay's *see* Baby and Children's Clothes p17, Hallmark (Thornton's chocolates at back *see* Annual Events, Easter p200) Dorothy Perkins *see* Maternity Wear p13, Safeway *see* Supermarkets p11 and Chemists with Extended Hours p45, Savacentre *see* Supermarkets p12, also while-you-wait shoe repairs, jewellers with Christening gifts, bank, building society — all on ground floor. The centre usually has lots of activities for Easter, Mother's Day etc eg puppet shows and entertainers.

Restaurant, The Terrace, 1st Floor, see Eating Out p78.

Toilets: on ground floor, small with awkward entrance. 1st floor (lift on left outside entrance to Savacentre), toilet for the disabled has special pull-down baby change unit suitable for small babies. Ladies' toilet has nappy change surface and seats for feeding. *See also* Supermarkets, Savacentre p12.

Gyle Shopping Centre
Gyle Avenue
South Gyle Broadway
539 9000

Centre opening hrs: Mon-Wed 8.30-8, Thur & Fri 8.30-9, Sun 9-6. Hrs vary for individual shops but generally all open late on Thurs.

Large colour-coded car park with Special Needs Parking close to all entrances which may be used by parents with young children. Petrol station and taxi rank. Central main entrance with additional entrances giving easy access to Safeway and Marks and Spencers. Pushchairs and child reins available to hire free (ID required) at Customer Service Desk in mall opposite main entrance. Outdoor play areas with climbing frames etc. Various entertainments and seasonal displays throughout the year, centred on the podium beside lift to upper level.

Self-opening doors, seats, public phones in a spacious well-planned centre with approx 60 shops on one level. A variety of trolley designs to accomodate various ages of small children. Lift and escalator to upper level where The Gyle Nursery provides an additional 'drop in' *creche* facility *see* Private Nurseries p115 and Creches while Shopping p50.

Shops include Safeway *see* Supermarkets p11, Marks and Spencer *see* Baby and Children's Clothes p17, Boots *see* Chemists with Extended Hours p44, Clarks *see* Children's Shoes p24 Disney Store *see* Toy Shops p27, Thorntons *see* Annual Events, Easter

p200, Mackays *see* Baby and Children's Clothes p17, Early Learning Centre *see* Toy Shops p28, Jigsaw World *see* Toy Shops p29, James Thin *see* Children's Books p41, Dorothy Perkins *see* Maternity Wear p13, John Menzies, banks, building society, travel agents, jewellers with Christening gifts, florist, etc.

Restaurants: Gyle Food Court on upper level *see* Eating Out p80.

Toilets: Ground floor beside main entrance and 1st floor by food court both include toilet for disabled. 1st floor also has separate Baby Change Room with screened area and chair for breast feeding.

Ingliston Market
Off A8 at Ingliston
Airport Rd
333 3801 (Spook Erection, market operators)
Sun 10-4

Open-air market of huge proportions with plenty of free parking space and good traffic marshalling. Variety of stalls including baby and children's clothing, denim jeans and cheap toys. Be wary of cheap toys, but there are bargains to be had. Tannoy system covers market. Enormous models (King Kong).

Toilets and feeding and changing room well signed. Clean and functional. Lost children's centre at First Aid Post.

Snacks. Snacks of all description, ice-cream, fish and chips, burgers, kebabs and curry from a variety of stalls and vans some with tables and chairs.

Kinnaird Park
Newcraighall
Access from A1
Quadrangle of around 20 outlets

around large car park, originally called **Craig Park**. Opening hrs of individual shops vary but most open late on Thurs and all day Sun.

Shops include Argos see Department Stores p2, Poundstretcher see Toyshops p30, Shoe City see Children's Shoes p24, Toys 'R' Us see Department Stores p6, Concepts, Scottish Power, Farmfoods, Olympus etc.

Also in the retail park are UCI, a 12 screen cinema see Places to Visit p189 and Megabowl a 10-pin bowling alley with unsupervised ball pool. Located to the right of UCI is a separate building housing Koko's Children's Leisure Centre see Activities for Children p151, Birthdays & Celebrations p84 and Castle Nursery see Pre-school Play and Education p108.

Restaurants: Chiquito, Deep Pan Pizza, McDonald's 'Drive Thru' and Concepts see Eating Out p73.

Toilets: Below Koko's. Ladies, gents and toilet for the disabled. No feeding or changing facilities.

Newkirkgate Shopping Centre
off Great Junction St, Leith

Opening hrs of individual shops vary. Closed Sun. Large car park.

Some shops around open square, others in covered mall. Includes Presto Supermarket, Woolworth see Department Stores p9, Boots (small), Woolwarehouse: good selection of wool and patterns. Various other shops.

Toilets: none in centre.

St James' Centre
Princes St/Leith St

Shop hours vary

Pedestrian access from the corner of Leith St, Princes St and St Andrews Sq Bus Station. Vehicular entrance to multi-storey car park from Leith St and Elder St (a small street off York Pl). If you enter from Princes St there is a lift to the St James' Food Court around the first bend on the left in the corner. A lift to Café St James is situated near the stairs up. Large shopping centre. On ground floor numerous shops including Adams see Baby and Children's Clothes p14, Boots see Chemists with Extended Hours p45, John Lewis see Department Stores p4, Mackays see Baby and Children's Clothes p17, John Menzies see Bookshops p43, Thornton's see Annual Events Easter p200, Presto Supermarket see Supermarkets p11, Happit, etc. Cash dispensers, seats and public phones. The shopping mall is well-patrolled by security guards and is clean and litter free.

Restaurants: Café St James, Crawford Country Kitchen, John Lewis and St James' Food Court see Eating Out p62.

Toilets: 1st floor.

Waverley Shopping Centre
Corner of Princes St and Waverley Bridge

Centre open 7 days/wk but opening hrs for individual shops vary and not all shops open on Sun.

The easiest entrance is from Princes St next to the Waverley Steps where there is a ramp which leads to the small busy lift which serves all floors. The Waverley Bridge entrance also has a ramp.

Busy upmarket centre on 3 levels (2 below ground) with lots to look at, pools, fountains, sculptures, kinetic figures and mirrors. Seasonal displays eg Chicks or Santa. Other impromptu entertainments sometimes occur. Edinburgh Tourist Office is on the roof, Princes St level.

Mainly specialist shops with only a few selling goods for children. The Wood Shop, The Owl and the Pussycat see Toy Shops p29, Streamers, see Birthdays and Celebrations p87, Bookworld see Children's Books p43, Jigsaw World see Toy Shops p29. One of the hand carts sells a huge selection of novelty buttons, hair ribbons and slides.

Restaurants: Waverley Food Court and Waverley Wharf see Eating Out p72.

Toilets: Two sets both on lowest level. 'Superloos' beside the Food Court, 10p. To the right of the superloos the toilet for the disabled and nappy changing room both free. The EDC toilets down a long flight of steps from Waverley Bridge are accessible through a set of doors marked Exit, to the left of Waverley Wharf, also has nappy changing room.

Wester Hailes Shopping Centre
Wester Hailes Rd

Centre open Mon-Sat 8.30-6 (8pm Thur & Fri). Opening hrs of individual shops vary, some close Wed pm.

Large car park.

Indoor shopping centre on 2 levels with travolator access between floors. Shops include Mackays see Baby and Children's Clothes p17, Presto Supermarket see Supermarkets p11, Lloyds (chemist), Iceland, Post Office and a variety of other food, gift, toys, hardware and clothes shops. Edinburgh District Council Local Housing Office also on site.

Toilets: none within centre.

Supermarkets

No one can ever say that doing the weekly shop with young children is easy, but hopefully this chapter will give you an idea of the most suitable place for you and your child to shop.

● **Hours** We have not listed stores opening hours as they are so varied. Most stores open Mon-Sat 9-7 or 8pm, Sun 12-5 and most are open on public and local holidays.

● **Car parks** All stores listed have car parks and many now have extra width 'parent and child' spaces, usually next to spaces for disabled drivers by the entrances to the stores.

● **Trolleys** We have listed the types of trolleys provided by the store. The safety instructions for each type of trolley should always be followed. These are often found on the bar or handle. Always use the reins and report any damaged or unusable trolleys. (Life is tough enough without the hassle of a trolley intent in describing circles in busy aisles) Do not forget that trolleys can be unwieldy when loaded with shopping and children, so be aware of your own physical limits!

As a general guide baby cradle types are suitable for babies up to 9kgs (20lbs) and toddlers types up to 3yrs. The other trolley types (baby, double baby, baby and toddler and double toddler) are less common, but the bigger the store the more are available. While all the stores said that **ALL** trolley types may be taken to the car park, in practice many stores do not allow the combination trolleys outside the store, especially at shopping centres! If the store owns the car park you may have more success. Rather than repack your shopping into another trolley why not ask for an escort to your car? Make the stores compete on service! If you take your pushchair you will have to provide your own bicycle chain. Always ask where to secure it.

● **Sweets** The day of sweet racks at the check-out is gradually dying out. We have indicated where the practice still continues.

● **Carry out service** All stores said that they offered such a service. Ask at the check-out if you need help.

● **Lost children** All stores said the had a lost child policy, but they varied greatly. The first rule is not to panic: contact a member of staff immediately you become aware of the disappearance. Describe the clothing and where you last saw the child. Think of anything that particularly attracted them on the way round the store. Try to carry some ID that identifies you as the carer of the child. A recent photograph of the child is always useful. Within shopping centres, stores always contact the centres' own security.

Asda
100 The Jewel
Duddingston Rd W
669 9151

Baby, double baby, baby and toddler, toddler and double toddler trolleys, also have kiddy trolleys.
See also Baby and Children's clothes p14, Toyshops p27.

Marks and Spencer
Trial of home delivery of foods at time of writing. See Department stores p5.

Presto
483 Calder Rd
Wester Hailes Shopping Centre
442 3721
St James Centre
556 1190

Small stores with toddler trolleys. Children may use staff toilets in an emergency. Sweets at check-outs. Escort for trolleys required at St James Centre. See Shopping Centres and Markets p9.

Kwiksave (formerly Shoprite)
Quite a few stores scattered around suburbs. Budget prices and few facilities.

Safeway
Cameron Toll Shopping Centre, Lady Rd
664 6190

Baby, toddler, double baby, double toddler and baby and toddler trolleys See also Shopping Centres and Markets p7.
38 Comely Bank S
332 4469
Baby, toddler and baby, double toddler and toddler trolleys.
Cramond Rd S
336 4234
Baby, toddler and baby and toddler trolleys.
Gyle Shopping Centre
317 1197
Large numbers of baby, double baby, baby and toddler, toddler and double toddler trolleys. Customer **toilets**, feeding and changing room to right of entrance within the centre. Post office within store. See Shopping Centres and Markets p8.
Bughtlin Market, Maybury Dve, East Craigs
339 2073
Baby, double baby, baby and toddler,

toddler and double toddler trolleys.

145 Morningside Rd
447 9955

Baby, baby and toddler, toddler and double toddler trolleys.

30 New Swanston, Hunters Tryst

Baby, double baby, toddler and double toddler trolleys.

4 Piersfield Ter
661 5661

Both these stores have baby, double baby, baby and toddler, toddler and double toddler trolleys. Coffee shop with children's play area allows breastfeeding. Customer **toilets** and nappy changing room in front of check-outs.

Sainsbury's
185 Craigleith Rd
332 0704

Large number of baby, double baby, baby and toddler, toddler, double toddler and disabled child trolleys. Customer **toilets** and feeding and changing room behind check-out area.

Savacentre
Cameron Toll Shopping Centre, Lady Rd
666 1144

Baby, baby and toddler, toddler and double toddler trolleys. Large store with clothes, toys, lighting and bakery offering personalised cakes. Changing room on right, off clothing sales area. *See also* Baby and Children's Clothes p18, Toys p30 and Shopping Centres and Markets p7.

Scotmid Co-op

Many stores throughout the city ranging from small local shops to larger stores. (*see* Phone Book for details).

Somerfield
114 Dalry Rd
337 6376

Baby and toddler trolleys, many with a calculator. Two sweet free check-outs.

Tesco
7 Broughton Rd
557 3203

Baby, double baby, baby and toddler, toddler and double toddler trolleys. Customer **toilets** and feeding and changing room to rear of check-outs also at 15 Drumbryden Rd, Wester Hailes
453 6822

94 Nicholson St
667 0404

Baby, double baby, baby and toddler and toddler trolleys. Feeding and changing facilities planned for summer '95.

MATERNITY WEAR

At long last there has been some improvement in the style of maternity wear on offer in Edinburgh's shops. Instead of 'white collared' tent dresses, it is now possible to find clothes that are more fashionable, comfortable and even flattering.

See also Make your Own p21, Shopping from Home p53, Hiring p57.

Boots the Chemist
101 Princes St only

1st: Maternity bras (but not a large selection of sizes) and other nursing accessories, including washable breast pads.

See Department Stores p3.

C & A

4th: Small range of dresses and separates.

See Department Stores p3.

Dorothy Perkins

Debenhams (*1st* floor), also Cameron Toll Shopping Centre and Gyle Shopping Centre.

Good range of co-ordinated separates for formal and casual wear. Selection of dresses also available. Look for the 'Anticipation' label.

Etam

82 Princes St
220 1452

Small selection of budget range dresses and separates under the label 'Mostly Mums'.

Frasers

2nd: Maternity and nursing bras.

See Department Stores p4.

Madam H Lazarska

123 Dalkeith Rd
667 4948

A real corsetiere! Specialises in made-to-measure bras in non-standard sizes.

John Lewis

Ground: Maternity tights, ✔ swimsuits and nursing bras.

1st: Casual co-ordinated separates and some more formal suits and dresses. Wide range of sizes in maternity and nursing bras. Helpful, trained staff.

See Department Stores p4.

Mothercare

Basement: Good selection of dresses — everyday and more glamorous,
matching separates, swimwear, nightwear, lingerie and hosiery. Trained fitters for maternity and nursing bras.

1st: Nursing accessories (breast pumps and bra pads) and a range of 'maternity' bodycare.

See Department Stores p6.

National Childbirth Trust

NCT (Maternity Sales) Ltd
Burnfield Ave
Glasgow G46 7TL 0141 633 5552
Contact Edinburgh Office 225 9191
Mon-Fri 9-12 noon

A catalogue is available showing swimsuits, nightwear and leisurewear all designed for maximum comfort during and after pregnancy. Mava bras specially designed by breastfeeding mothers and breastfeeding counsellors. Some have back lacing (ideal if you lose a lot of weight whilst feeding) and a hooked front opening. Others have zipped openings. High percentage of cotton. Sizes range from 32" to 46" in all cup sizes. Mava bras are recommended by midwives and are available to all whether NCT members or not. Phone Jill Cameron 556 2161 to arrange appointment for fitting. Also books, leaflets, breast pumps and natural cot mattresses.

See Health p259.

New and Junior Profile

An attractive shop catering for both the expectant mum and child. The maternity range offers mostly everyday wear, both casual and business wear, together with some outfits for special occasions. Nightwear, maternity and nursing bras, underwear, hosiery and swimwear are also available. A high percentage of natural fibres are used in the range where possible. Selection of

13

maternity wear available for hire. *See* Baby and Children's Clothes p17.

Pauline's of Morningside
422 Morningside Rd
447 9636
Mon-Fri 10-5.30; Sat 10-5

For those not wanting a trip into town, you may find a maternity or nursing bra here, also nightwear.

Accessories

The Body Shop
90a Princes St
220 6330
Mon-Sat 9-6; Thur 9-7

Also Waverley Market and Gyle Shopping Centre

'Mamatoto' is the Body Shop's range of mother and baby products, influenced by worldwide customs in body care. Using natural ingredients, the range includes products for massage and skin care.

BABY AND CHILDREN'S CLOTHES

Most department stores, some supermarkets and chemists stock baby and children's clothes, underwear and socks. Not all are listed here; we've mentioned only those with a good range, exciting stock, competitive prices or something special to offer. Apart from the problems of finding the right style, fabric and colour at the right price, there are two bugbears when shopping for children's clothes: the lack of any standard sizing system and seasonal availability.

The large department stores and major brand names all have different sizing systems. Most are based on an out-of-date British Standard, with manufacturers adding their own allowances for growth, comfort etc. The age range given to various sizes is only a guide and you are best to take along your child's measurements and a tape measure for accurate results. Most shops will refund if an item is unsuitable but you must keep receipts. Some of the smaller shops mentioned in this section will make to measure, at little or no extra charge for children with specific needs.

Small baby clothes (from about 3lbs) are available from Jenners *see* Department Stores p4 and also by post *see* Shopping from Home p53.

For children's ski wear *see* Outdoor & Ski Shops p36. For schoolwear *see* p19.

Adams Children's Wear
11-13 St James' Centre
556 0692
Mon-Wed 9-5.30; Thurs 9-7; Fri-Sat 9-5.30

Also at Cameron Toll Shopping Centre *see* Shopping Centres and Markets p7.

Babywear and girls up to 8 yrs downstairs. Boys 18 mths to 8 yrs upstairs (lift on left). Good value, attractive indoor and outdoor clothes and accessories. Underwear, sleepwear, casual clothes, school clothes and clothes for smarter occasions. Also shoes and boots. Some bedlinen and nursery equipment on 1st floor (see p25). Lego play area.

Asda
Mon-Fri 9-8; Sat 8.30-8; Sun 10-5

Attractive, reasonably priced baby and children's clothes and footwear. Bibs, padders, underwear, sleepwear, casual clothes, schoolwear and outdoorwear. Nappy changing facility in toilet for the disabled. Also toys and cafe.

See Supermarkets p11, *see also* Toy Shops p27.

Laura Ashley
126 Princes St
225 1218
Mon 9.30-5.30; Tues, Fri 9-5.30; Thurs 9-7; Sat 9-6

'Mother and Child Collection' range of co-ordinating upmarket clothes for mothers and girls (birth-12 yrs). Stylish romper suits for babies, traditional 'little girl' smocks and dresses.

The Baby Shop
75 Newington Rd
662 4706
Mon-Sat 9-5

Small shop specialising in special occasion dresses for 0-5 yrs. Also outdoor wear, underwear, padders etc. Use of staff toilet.

Baggins
12 Deanhaugh St
315 2011
Tues-Fri 10-5; Sat 10-5

Access awkward — down a flight of steps to a basement.
Good quality children's clothes in natural fibres, including 100% cotton. Hardwearing casual clothes (personalised on request), viyella dresses and tartan waistcoats. Will make to measure, ordered goods taking up to 3 wks. Toys to play with whilst you choose. *See* Shopping From Home p56.

United Colors of Benetton
61 George St
226 3006
Mon-Sat 9.30-5.30; Thurs 9.30-7
Gyle Shopping Centre
539 8782

Mon, Tues, Wed 9.30-7.30; Thur, Fri 9.30-8; Sat 9.30-6; Sun 10-5.

These are the only Edinburgh branches which keep children's wear. Casual, expensive Italian separates. Cords, jeans, shirts, leggings, T-shirts, knitwear, accessories all in bright colours. '012' sizes from birth to teens.

BhS
Princes St

Basement: Good range of everyday wear for babies and children at reasonable prices. Casual wear, outdoorwear, underwear, footwear and special occasion clothes. *See* Department Stores p3.

Boots the Chemist
Princes St

1st: Full range of baby and children's clothes up to 5 yrs. Hardwearing clothes, stylish in bold

The National Childbirth Trust

INFORMED CHOICE

"The National Childbirth Trust offers information and support in pregnancy, childbirth and early parenthood and aims to enable every parent to make informed choices."

and bright colours at 'high street prices'. Many in 100% cotton. Matching accessories. See Department Stores p3.

Burberrys and The Scotch House
39-41 Princes St
556 1252
Mon-Sat 9-5.30; Thurs 9-6

Situated on the first floor to the back of store. 'Scotch House' kilts, dresses, trews, and trousers in various tartans for 2-12 yrs. Large selection of knitwear, plain and fancy designs in lambswool, Shetland and Aran. Burberrys also have their own label children's clothes for 18 mths up; fashion knitwear and casualwear. Also selection of Toys in the famous Burberry check. See also Kilts p20.

C & A

2nd: Fairly large selection of attractive baby and children's wear to suit all occasions at good prices. Fitting room available. See Department Stores p3.

Clan House
9 South Clerk St
667 2486
117 Grove St
229 6857

Good selection of baby and children's wear, underwear and accessories, mainly at the lower end of the price range. The branch at Grove.St sells only schoolwear. See also Schoolwear p20.

Corstorphine Pram Centre

Selection of babywear 0-9mths. Also layettes and gift purchases. See Nursery Equipment p25.

Debenhams

Basement: low-priced fashionable, outfits for all occasions and ages.

New 'Bright Futures' brand. Trader jeanswear for toddlers, boys and girls. Sleepwear, underwear, casual wear, outdoorwear, schoolwear and padders. Will provide gift boxes for presents. Fitting rooms. See Department Stores p3.

The Disney Store

Selection of clothing for under 5s featuring Disney characters. T-shirts, sweatshirts and jogging suits. See Toy Shops p27.

Frasers

4th: Reached by lift at rear of shop, then 4 steps down to the department. Good selection of quality clothes 0-8 yrs (Sarah Louise, Absorba, Heskia, Gallipette). Partywear, school and leisure clothes. See Department Stores p4.

GAP
131 Princes St
220 4202
Mon-Sat 9-6; Thur 9-7; Sun 12-5

2nd: Ramp at entrance for pushchairs. Lift at rear of shop. Mostly fashionable, slightly upmarket daywear from 2-16 yrs. Range changes regularly. Nappy changing facility.

1st: Small selection of fashionable babywear 0-24mths.

Happit
Cameron Toll Shopping Centre
658 1257
25 Raeburn Pl
332 3212
16 St James' Centre
557 8856
Thurs, Fri 9-7.30
113 St Johns Rd
316 4137
47 Shandwick Pl
228 3186

All shops open Mon-Sat 9-5.30 unless otherwise indicated above. Good value for everyday wear children's clothes. Specialises in sweatshirts, jogging suits and knitwear. Also underwear, outdoor-wear and schoolwear. Stocks party dresses at Christmas time.

Irene's
28 Comiston Rd
452 8520
Mon-Sat 9.30-5.30

Small shop selling a huge variety of makes and quality clothes for 0-10 yrs. Exclusive designer wear from France and Germany. Nightwear, outdoor clothes, knitwear, hats, gloves and padders.

Jenners
3-15 Rose St

Extensive range of quality clothes 0-8 yrs. Premature baby clothes, beautiful christening gowns, padders. *See* Department Stores p4.

John Lewis
1st: Complete layette for baby can be bought here — from scratch mitts to christening robes. Lots of versatile clothes for toddlers and older children (some 100% cotton). Co-ordinating separates in bold, bright colours. Variety of makes and prices. *See* Department Stores p4.

Littlewoods
1st: Cheap baby and children's wear including underwear, bibs, nightwear, outdoorwear, leisurewear and schoolwear. See Department Stores p5.

Marks and Spencer
Rose St

Good quality baby and children's clothes, many in 100% cotton, for all occasions. Underwear, sleepwear, leisurewear, schoolwear, outdoor-wear and party clothes. Limited selection for under 6 mths. *See* Department Stores p5.

Mackays
Cameron Toll
664 8921
Mon-Sat 9-5.30; Thurs, Fri 9-7; Sun 11-5
15/17 St James' Centre
557 3819
Mon-Fri 9.30-5.30; Thurs 9.30-7; Sat 9-6
11 Westerhailes Centre
442 3122
Mon-Sat 9-5.15
Gyle Shopping Centre
538 8765
Mon-Fri 9-8; Sat 9-6; Sun 10-6

Good range of affordable baby and children's wear. Lots of co-ordinating outfits, sleepwear, leisure wear, outdoorwear, schoolwear, underwear, pram shoes and padders.

Mothercare
Ground: Wide range of clothes for all occasions for boys and girls 1-8 yrs. Partywear, schoolwear and everyday wear.

Basement: Children's basics, underwear etc for 1-8 yrs. Shoes.

1st: Baby fashion, basics and outdoor wear. Sleepwear, padders and pram shoes. Layettes, nappies, toiletries, feeding equipment. Transport; pushchairs etc. *See* Department Stores p6.

New and Junior Profile
88-92 Raeburn Pl
332 7928

Mon-Sat 9-5.30

Wide range of fashion children's wear 6 mth-6 yr. Includes 100% cotton hats, polonecks, tights and leggings in up to 15 colours. Nappy changing facility and use of toilet. *See also* Maternity Wear p13.

Next
141b Frederick St
225 2462
Mon-Sat 9-6; Thur 9-7
119-120 Princes St
225 6480
Mon-Sat 9-6; Thur 9-7
Gyle Shopping Centre
317 1511
Mon-Wed 9.30-7.30; Thur 9.30-8.30; Fri 9.30-8; Sat 9-6; Sun 10-5

NBG (Next Boys and Girls) clothes. Beginners from 0-24 mths and boys and girls from 2-8 yrs. Well-made, stylish and hard-wearing separates and casuals in strong colours. Underwear, footwear, outdoorwear and partywear, many in 100% cotton.

Nippers
137 Bruntsfield Pl
229 5056
Mon-Sat 9.30-6

Designer clothes at affordable prices for 0-6 yrs. Some styles can be made to measure: dungarees, play-suits, bomber jackets, jumpers in Shetland or acrylic.

Number Two
2 St Stephen Pl, Stockbridge
225 6257
Mon-Sat 10-5.30

Hand and frame-knitted adult and children's clothing in wool and cotton often in bright designs or with motifs. Durable babies' bootees in wool and suede, making them non-slip.

Pine and Old Lace
46 Victoria St
225 3287
Mon-Sat 10.30-5, closed Wed

Phone to check if making a special trip as this is a one-woman shop.

Stock usually includes antique Christening gowns.

Poundstretcher
Small range of inexpensive baby and childrens clothes.

See also Toy Shops p30.

Quality Mark Wholesale
56 Belford Rd
225 6861
Mon-Sat 9-5.30, Thurs 9-7, Sun 12-5

Large warehouse with a small selection of baby and children's clothes originally made for well-known chain stores now sold as cancelled contracts, end of lines and seconds, all at reduced prices. In order to purchase you must become an exclusive Privilege Card holder, by paying a fee of £5 (valid 1 yr, admits 2).

Raeburn Pram Centre
Selection of babywear 0-9mths. Layettes and gift purchases.

See Nursery Equipment p26.

Savacentre
Good range of everyday wear for babies and children at reasonable prices. Casual wear, outdoor wear, underwear, footwear, schoolwear and special occasion clothes.

See Supermarkets p12.

Seconds & Firsts
364 Morningside Rd
452 9588
102 Nicolson St
667 7448

Mon-Sat 9-5.30

Mixture of new clothes and chain store seconds for 0-12 yrs. Underwear, separates, outdoor wear, knitwear, bibs, padders.

The Shetland Connection
491 Lawnmarket
225 3525
Mon-Sat 10-5.30; Sun 11-5

Tiny little touristy shop at top of Royal Mile. Beautiful one-ply christening shawls in cobweb and lace, so fine they can be pulled through a wedding ring. Kilts from 2 yrs. Fair Isle berets, bonnets, mitts and sweaters. Sheepskin mitts and bootees. Aran and other cardigans, jumpers, hats, mitts and bootees with lambskin soles.

Sprogs, the Designer Children's Wear Sale Shop
45 William St
220 0320
Mon-Sat 10-5

European designer clothes for 0-10 yrs at 30-50% off normal shop prices. All clothes new and in perfect condition. Will refund difference if goods can be bought cheaper elsewhere.

Changing room and toys for playing.

Sunday Best
13 Colinton Rd
452 9321
Mon-Fri 10-5; Sat 10-5; Closed Wed.

Select baby and children's wear of high quality which is reflected in the price. Casual but smart designer-type outfits for the young upwardly mobile tot! Toys to play with.

Topsy Turvy
18 William St
225 2643
Mon-Sat 9.30-5.30

Exclusive boutique in fashionable William St selling upmarket baby and children's wear from birth-16 yrs. Toys to play with and chair for the weary or feeding baby.

Toddle In
130 Gorgie Rd
313 5521
Mon-Sat 9.30-5; Wed 9.30-1.30

Inexpensive children's clothes, competitively priced for 0-8 yrs. Some 100% cotton. Underwear, sleepwear, separates, party clothes, Christening gowns and bedding. Will stock to order. Changing room.

Toys 'R' Us

Range of inexpensive casual, night-wear, underwear and outdoorwear for 0-24 mths. *See* Department Stores p6.

What Everyone Wants
South Bridge

Ground and lower ground: No lifts or escalators in this discount store and pushchairs must be folded if taken upstairs. Underwear, bibs, sleepwear, outdoorwear, separates at knock-down prices. Also toiletries, bedding and nursery equipment. Occasionally has premature baby clothes. *See also* Toy Shops p30.

Woolworth

Value for money, co-ordinating casuals, nightwear, underwear, schoolwear, outdoorwear, hats and gloves, many in 100% cotton. The Ladybird collection for 0-8 yrs.

See Department stores p7, *see also* Toys p31.

SCHOOLWEAR

Shops and stores keep a selection of shorts, trousers, pinafores, skirts, shirts, blouses, socks in traditional school colours. Their stock is most extensive in Jul and Aug but most have a small stock tucked away somewhere throughout the yr.

In addition —

Aitken and Niven p2, Asda p11, BhS p3, Boots p3, C&A p3, Frasers p4, Happit p16, John Lewis p4, Littlewoods p15, Marks and Spencer p5, Mothercare p6, Savacentre p12, and Seconds and Firsts p18.

Aitken & Niven has leather school-bags, shoebags, plain socks, etc but not ballet shoes. Good stockist for private schools.

Clan House stocks blazers, in traditional colours and most Edinburgh school badges to sew on. Also stocks Edinburgh school ties and ballet shoes. Good stockist for private schools. *See* Children's Clothes p16.

John Lewis leather school-bags in luggage department and Cash's name tapes in Haberdashery — you pay for a postcard to fill in your details eg choose the colour and style. It is a good idea to add your postcode if there is room — lost items are often returned. Send it off and they should arrive in 2-3 wks.

Parent-teacher associations often sell track suits or sweatshirts for school funds which can form part of the school uniform. Contact your school secretary for details, she can also tell you which local shops sell the school tie and badge.

Many schools including private schools often operate a second-hand scheme and it's worth enquiring before buying new. Assistance with provision of clothing and footwear is available, eligibility is related to parental income. Parents who wish

to apply for assistance should complete an application form which is available from schools or the local Divisional Education Office, 40 Torphichen St 229 9166.

KILTS

We are including this short section on kilts as Edinburgh does seem to have a good choice when it comes to tartans and styles. Aitken and Niven p2, Burberry's and the Scotch House p16, Jenners p4, John Lewis p4 and Shetland Connection p19 all stock tartanwear and some accessories.

Proper kilt pleats should fold back behind the previous pleat giving them a wonderful swing but also making them very heavy as so much fabric is used — and very expensive. You will, however, have a family heirloom which will not only last your own children for many years but can be handed down the generations. A reasonable alternative is a 'half kilt', in which not all the pleats are full but it still swings well and looks good. Most shops sell kilted skirts off the peg. Small kilts can have straps or a bodice to hold them up and you can get jabot shirts with elastic around the waist to cover them up.

Shops which sell 'made-to-measure' kilts usually have books of tartan (you may need to choose a small pattern for a small kilt) and can help link your surname to a particular clan. They can also give your kilt a generous 'wrap around' and a good hem to let down. Some will change the wrap over side for different sexes.

You can really go overboard with accessories: jacket, shirt with jabot or bow tie, sporran, shoes, socks,

20

flashes. A kilt can look good with a Fair Isle, Aran or Shetland jumper, see Burberry's and the Scotch House p16 and The Shetland Connection p19 or just a plain white shirt and 'Pex' ribbed socks see Clan House p20. What is worn underneath is anybody's guess (except toddlers can't resist showing everybody!). If you only need the kilt for a special occasion a good alternative is to hire see Hiring p57.

Highland Laddie
6 Hutchison Ter
455 7505
Mon-Sat 10-5

Complete outfits sold. All accessories available; jacket and shirt, shoes, ties, sporran etc. See also Hiring p57.

Hugh MacPherson Ltd
17 W Maitland St
225 4008

Complete outfits made. Any size from a range of patterns. Also a selection of dresses, shorts and sweatshirts in tartan designs.

DANCEWEAR SHOPS

The shops listed below sell both children's and adult dancewear. Some department stores, see p2 also stock basic dance or keep-fit wear. It does pay to shop around. Some dance teachers also sell shoes and/or leotards etc. See Activities for Children p135 for information on children's dance classes.

Ballet School Supplies
161a Rose St
226 2833
Mon-Fri 9-5.30; Sat 9-5, closed Wed

Shoes for tap, Highland, ballet (satin and leather), jazz dance. Basic dancewear — leotards, catsuits, accessories etc.

Dancewear
182 Rose St
226 5457
Mon-Fri 9.30-5.15; Sat 9-5

Attractive shop selling shoes for ballet (satin and leather), tap, Highland, jazz, aerobics, country dancing and gymnastics as well as satin shoes suitable for bridesmaids. Also leotards, tights, catsuits, ballet skirts, cross-over cardigans, tutus, sequin trimming and stage make-up. Satin and silk shoes dyed.

MAKE YOUR OWN

Edinburgh has an excellent choice of wool and fabric shops and you always end up with an 'exclusive' outfit. We feel the ones listed below have something special to offer and you may not know about some of the more out-of-the-way ones. Of the department stores. **Liberty**, 47 George St, and **Laura Ashley**, 90 George St, often have good value remnants in natural fibres at sale times.

John Lewis and **Kings Fabrics** probably have the largest choice of pattern books and paper patterns. In these tomes you will find everything from maternity wear and smocked dresses to pyjamas, dressing gowns, easy to make skirts and shorts. 'Teen' dolls can have an extensive wardrobe made to match your own and you can also make a soft toy which is currently popular.
There are many wool shops scattered around the suburbs and most stock baby wools. Pingouin have children's knitting patterns in up-to-the-minute, colourful designs and usually have a toddler/baby

21

magazine. Patons have a wide range of knitting patterns for small babies starting at 14".

See also Shopping from Home p52.

The Cloth Shop
24 Craighall Rd
552 8818
Mon Closed; Tues-Sat 9.30-5; Thurs 9.30-8

Excellent 'market style' fabric shop. Rummage under bales of cottons, cords, towelling, silks, Viyella, wools, and you're sure to come out with a bargain. Friendly, helpful staff provide a basket of toys to occupy tinies. Will allow use of **toilet**.

The Cloth Shop Too!
122-126 Granton Rd
552 7425
Tues-Sat 9.30-5; Thurs 9.30-8

Lots of bargains in all kinds of soft furnishing fabrics, sheeting, coloured linings, stencil kits in children's designs. Some toys in a corner and helpful staff.

The Embroidery Shop
51 William St
225 8642
Mon-Fri 10-5; Sat 10-4

Embroidery supplies, birth sampler kits, lace and tapestry supplies. Specialist shop which also runs classes.

The Finishing Touch
17 St Patrick's Sq
667 0914
Mon-Sat 10-5.30

A huge range of buttons in all shapes, sizes and colours including mother-of-pearl, leather, bone and wood. Novelty greetings cards, gift wrapping paper, ribbons. Every imaginable utensil and ingredient for cake decorating. Lots of helpful hints and advice.

See also Birthdays and Celebrations p87 and Hiring p57.

Helios Fountain
Selection of craft materials, huge range of beads. Some wooden toys and children's books. *See* Eating Out p67.

Jenners
Basement: Good range of haberdashery, through knitting wools and patterns and needlework kits. Fabrics. Lots of ribbons and buttons. Exhibition of needlework and kits in the Spring.

See Department Stores p4.

John Lewis
Ground floor: Good choice of fabrics from basic and

cheap to exotic. Sheeting, quilted fabrics, braids, ribbons, buttons, motifs, lace, extensive haberdashery. Handicraft materials eg beads, felt, fur fabric, tapestry and embroidery yarns, craft and needlework kits including samplers. Dolls' house kits, knitting wools and patterns, sewing and knitting machines and craft books.

2nd: Soft furnishings. Delightful children's patterns, light proof curtain lining and blinds.

See Department Stores p4.

Kings Fabrics
43-45 Lothian Rd
229 5135
88 Newington Rd
667 7210
Mon-Sat 9-5-30; Thurs 9.30-7.30

Large selection of fabrics from cheap and cheerful cottons to silks. Also stocks a range of sheeting, fur fabric, felt, quilting, cords, wools and remnants sold by weight very cheaply. Lots of trimmings and motifs. Paper patterns (Vogue is kept in stock at Lothian Rd).

CHILDREN'S SHOES

Many mothers think that retailers put children's shoe departments in basements or on 1st floors, simply to irritate them and add to the hassle of a shoe-buying trip. In fact it is for safety — so that junior does not take a trip straight out of the door when asked to take a few steps to see if the shoes fit. Many shops have a ticketed queuing system — always take a ticket before you look around. Avoid Sats and school holidays if possible as they tend to be particularly busy.

The shops below with a * before

their name are listed in the Children's Foot Health Register whose aims are supported by the British Medical Association, and other health, chiropody and shoe associations. The CFHR lists shops which promise to: stock children's shoes in whole and half length sizes from infants size 3 to size 5+ for boys and girls; stock 4 width fittings; employ trained staff to measure both feet and carefully fit shoes at time of sale. The list is updated annually and is available from The Children's Foot Health Register, Bedford House, 69/79 Fulham High Street, London SW6 3JW, enclosing a 9" X 6" SAE. Some libraries keep a copy for reference. It also gives the full aims of the register, useful information on foot care and lists footwear retailers throughout Britain, who promise to abide by the register's aims.

Don't be shy where your child's feet are concerned. If you don't think a shoe fits, ask to have it checked by another fitter. Complain to management if you feel a shop's standards have dropped. Several shops which sell nursery equipment also sell soft shoes for babies and toddlers.

See also Nursery Equipment p25 and Baby and Children's Clothes p14.

The following shops sell 'good brand' names in width fittings:

*Aitken and Niven

Medium sized ground floor department. Start-rite shoes and slippers.

See Department Stores p2.

*Bayne and Duckett
382 Morningside Rd
452 8529

88 St John's Rd, Corstorphine
334 3685
Mon-Sat 9-5.30

Small shops, helpful staff. Clarks shoes and slippers. Staff toilets can be used in an emergency.

*Clarks
79 Princes St ✔
220 1261
Mon-Wed, Fri 9-5.30, Thurs 9-7.30, Sat 9-6, Sun 12-5.
Also at Unit 11, Cameron Toll ✔
Shopping Centre
664 9111
Also at Gyle Shopping Centre
317 1456

Children's department downstairs. Pushchairs can be left with staff on the ground floor. Good selection. Large stock of Clarks. Wall Lego, lifesize teddy, books. Car ride (profits from which go to charity).

Children may use staff toilet if accompanied by a parent and a member of staff.

Also has an 'odd shoe service': once your child's feet have been accurately measured you select a suitable shoe (most styles are available). This information is then sent to head office and the pair is sent to the shop in approx 3 wks. These shoes cost 25% more than the standard pair.

*K Shoes
Cameron Toll Shopping Centre, Lady Rd
658 1115
Mon-Wed, Fri, Sat 9-5.30; Thurs 9-7; Sun 10.30-5

Play table and toy box. Clarks and a small selection of Clark's Kidproof shoes, which seem to defy the hardest wear. Ticketed queuing system.

John Lewis
Busy department on 1st floor ✔
which offers a timed
appointment service during busy periods. Stocks Start-rite, Clarks and continental makes.

See Department Stores p4.

*Russell and Bromley
106 Princes St
225 7444
Mon, Wed, Fri 9-5.30; Tues 9.30-5.30; Thurs 9-7.30; Sat 9-6. Open public holidays.

An escalator takes you to this large 1st floor department — there is no guard at the top (in case of pile-up) so youngsters must be carefully watched. Stairs down. Pushchairs may be left with staff on ground floor. Always very busy but there is a ticketed queuing system. Distorting mirrors. Beware sharp edges on seats. Large selection of Start-rite and Clarks. Account holders get first choice of sale bargains. Children are generally not allowed to use the staff toilet and you are usually directed to the John Menzies cafe toilet next door.

Shoe City
48 Kinnaird Park, Newcraighall
657 4201
Mon-Fri 10-8; Sat 9-6; Sun 10-5

New selection of Hush Puppies for Children. Fitters fully qualified in unique 3D fitting system. Birthday brand shoes, also slippers and wellies. Chute, blackboard and abacus in play area.

*Shoos
8 Teviot Pl ✔
220 4626
Mon-Sat 9-5.30
Start-rite main stockist with a comprehensive range of shoes and

24

boots in up to 6 width fittings, starting from baby size 2. Also slippers, wellies, sandals, canvas shoes and leather trainers in width fittings. Continental boots in leather and Gore-tex. Fully trained staff with a member of the Society of Shoefitters usually present. All on ground level with toilet facilities.

Start-rite, odd shoe service *see* Shopping from Home p54.

NURSERY EQUIPMENT including REPAIRS

Many shops in Edinburgh sell well-known brand-name equipment (listed below). If you decide to buy secondhand or an uncommon (usually foreign) make, you must satisfy yourself as to its safety. Secondhand equipment can be in very good condition but may not conform to current safety standards.

After sales service should be an important consideration when making your choice of equipment, ask about servicing and repairs before you buy. Most of the outlets that we have listed will do both to the brands they sell, and most will consider lending you a temporary replacement if the repair will take some time. It is a good idea to retain your receipt for a long time as this is usually required as proof of purchase before repairs will be undertaken. Talk to friends before you buy — you only discover the pros and cons of equipment once you have lived with it for a while.

Shops usually keep one demonstration pram in stock and order your style and colour. This can take from 6 to 20 wks. No shop will make you buy a pram if you suddenly don't need it (if you discover you're having twins for instance) and most will store it until you need it. All other equipment is usually held in stock. *Which?* magazine often has reports on nursery equipment and it is worth checking back numbers in the library, even if it's just to see what to look out for.

See also Hiring p57.

Adams Children's Wear

Small selection of MacLaren pushchairs and other equipment. A receipt is required for repairs under guarantee.

See Baby and Children's Wear p14.

Argos

Moderate selection of equipment. One yr guarantee on pushchairs. Superstore in Kinnaird Park has a much larger selection displayed in newly-established nursery department.

See Department Stores p2.

Scotmid Co-op

Good selection of Britax, Silver Cross and MacLaren pushchairs and prams. Also small range of highchairs and cots and accessories. Free delivery service.

See Department Stores p6.

The Corstorphine Pram Centre
115-117 St John's Rd
334 6216
Mon-Sat 9-5.30, Sun 12-4

Wide selection of prams, pushchairs, cots, playpens, backpacks, car seats and other equipment required for baby. Also a selection of layette and babywear (to 9 mths). A repair service is available for prams and pushchairs purchased from the shop.

The Foam Centre
176 Causewayside
667 1247
Mon-Sat 9.30-5.30. Later at Christmas

Different foams cut to any size and shape. Can be made to fit cots, Moses baskets (also in stock), bumpers, booster seats, etc. 'Beans' to top up or make your own bags. Visiting children usually receive a balloon. Maternity wedges, lumbar rolls, brightly coloured cubes also supplied.

Jenners

A selection of pushchairs, cots, highchairs and prams from Continenta and Mamas and Papas available from Junior Jenners. A range of nursery accessories and bedding also available.

See Department Stores p4.

John Lewis

Good selection of equipment including pushchairs, prams, highchairs and cots. British and Continental makes. Larger items of furniture also available.

See Department Stores p4.

Mothercare

Large selection of baby equipment and accessories, including safety equipment, from the essential to the frivolous. Own and many other major brand names. Offer a full repair service and replacements on all equipment purchased from the Edinburgh store. Staff are very helpful.

See Department Stores p6.

Nappy Days
Nappy laundry service.
See also Shopping from Home, p55.

National Childbirth Trust
Contact Office 225 9191 ext 237
Mon-Fri 9-12 noon.

Supply a catalogue from which you can order some items of baby wear and equipment, also leaflets on many aspects of pregnancy, birth, breastfeeding and early parenthood. Phone office for details of all services.

See Health Care Facilities p259.

Raeburn Pram Centre
48 Raeburn Pl
332 8214
Mon-Sat 9-5.30

Good selection of prams, pushchairs, cots, mattresses (including safety mattresses with ventilation), as well as Snugli baby carriers, baby clothes, toys and all other equipment needed for a baby. A repair service is available for prams and pushchairs purchased from the shop.

Royal Blind Asylum Shop
1 Bruntsfield Pl
229 1294

A selection of Moses baskets, children's chairs and wicker chests. May make stands for Moses baskets to order.

Shapes Furniture Ltd
33 West Mill Rd
441 7963

Reproduction, traditional design high chairs. Understandably, they prefer children to be kept well under control.

Graham Tiso
115-123 Rose St
225 9486
Mon-Sat 9.30-5.30; Thurs 9.30-7

Karrimor and Wild Rover baby carriers. Will help to fit and may offer refund if uncomfortable. Toddler size backpacks. Very helpful staff. *See also* Outdoor and Ski-shops p37.

Toys 'R' Us

Wide range of pushchairs, cots and highchairs by MacLaren, Cindico, Britax and Mamas & Papas. One yr guarantee on items, but must retain the receipt. Car and home safety equipment also stocked.

See Department Stores p6.

TOY SHOPS, SPECIAL GIFTS AND DOLL REPAIR

Make sure you satisfy yourself as to the safety of toys particularly if you are buying from unorthodox sources. When buying for playgroups etc it is worth asking whether discounts are available. Many shops and department stores expand their range and extend their opening hrs before Christmas. Also refer to the specialist party shops in Birthdays and Celebrations p87.

Argos

A wide selection of popular toys, competitively priced. Superstore has most products. *See* Department Stores p2.

Arkadia

Edinburgh Zoo, Murrayfield
334 9171
Mon-Sat 9-5; Sun 9.30-5

Run by the zoo, but with a separate entrance so you do not have to go into the zoo. A real treasure trove full of animal and bird related toys, games, books, clothes, and gifts including pocket-money toys. *See* also Places to Visit p182.

Asda

Selection of big name toys including Duplo, Lego, stationery etc. *See* Supermarkets p11.

BhS

Small selection within children's clothes department, including baby and pre-school toys. *See* Department Stores p3.

Scotmid Co-op

Toys on 1st floor, mostly big names, only in Great Junction St branch. *See* Department Stores p6.

Digger

35 West Nicolson St
668 1802
Mon-Sat 10-6

Small shop up 3 steps. A treasure trove of handmade and traditional wooden toys. Dolls' house furniture, wooden framed mirrors, bookends, clocks decorated with teddies, stocking fillers and party goods. Small selection of children's knitwear.

The Disney Store

18 Princes St
557 2772
Mon-Wed, Fri 9.30-5; Thurs 9.30-7; Sat 9.30-5.30
Gyle Shopping Centre
339 4944
Mon-Wed 9.30-7.30; Thurs-Fri 9.30-8; Sat 9.30-6; Sun 10-6

Colourful stores which sell everything in the Disney theme. Friendly cast. Both stores have lively laser screen video entertainment for children. The Princes Street store is on two levels with the children's clothing section on the lower floor. *See* Baby and Childrens Clothes p16.

27

Early Learning Centre

67-83 Shandwick Pl
228 3244
Mon-Sat 9-5.30; Sun in Dec
Unit 11, Gyle Shopping Centre
538 7172
Mon-Wed 9-7.30; Thu-Fri 9-8; Sat 9-6;
Sun 10-5
61 St. James Centre
558 1330
Mon-Sat 9-5.30; Sun 12-4

Toys that are educational, safe and robust, catering particularly for younger children. Laid out in the shop under sections, eg First Years, Pretend Play, books, construction, finding out, sound and music, etc. Each store has a large play area including a Brio train set. St James' Centre store is the largest and carries an extended range. **Toilet** available at Shandwick Place store specifically for children (accompanied by a member of staff), **toilet** for the disabled and well-equipped **mother and baby room** at St James' Centre store. See also Shopping from Home p54 and Outdoor Toys p31.

Forbuoys

Cameron Toll Shopping Centre
664 8623
Mon-Fri 8-7.45; Sat 8-7; Sun 10-5

Large newsagents with about a third of the shop selling toys and books, including pocket-money toys.

Geraldine's of Edinburgh and Dolls' Hospital

35a Dundas St
556 4295
Mon-Fri 9-5; Sat 9-1

Antique and reproduction dolls and dolls accessories for sale in this basement shop. Porcelain dolls and teddies are made here. It is also an 'Emergency Ward 10' for dolls and teddies, and any type of doll or soft toy can snuggle up in bed in the 'admission ward' while waiting for a facelift, new hair, limbs, eyes, ears, or a growl!

Harburn Hobbies Ltd

67 Elm Row, Leith Walk
556 3233
Mon-Sat 9.30-6;

Specialises in model railways (Hornby, Lima etc) and Scalextric car racing. Large range of Thomas the Tank Engine and friends by Ertl and Hornby. Die cast metal cars, Britains, Sylvanian family, dolls' house furniture etc.

Jenners

Excellent, enormous and competitively priced toy department in the basement, with everything from cheap party toys to expensive dolls, rocking horses, train sets and small bikes. Galt toys

The Mulberry Bush

Children's toys & books. Stained glass.
Rugs. Pottery. Basketry. Cards.
General Crafts supplies & Books.
77 Morningside Road, Edinburgh
447 5145
Garvald Centre Craft Shop
Mon to Sat 9.30-12.30 and 1.30-5 pm

available and there is also a lovely book section. Special events held periodically including puppet shows, face paints, Lego competitions and large displays. *See* Department Stores p4.

Jigsaw World
Unit 39, Gyle Shopping Centre
538 7720
Mon-Wed 9:30-7:30, Thu-Fri 9:30-8; Sat 9-6; Sun 10-5

Selection of puzzles inc Michael Stanfield, Orchard Toys, Jumbo, Falcons suitable from 1 year upwards

Jolly Giant Superstore
Peffermill Industrial Estate
667 7344
Mon, Thurs 9-8; Tues, Wed, Fri, Sat 9-5-30; Sun 10-5

Warehouse with large selection of big name toys Galt, Fisher Price etc. Bikes, dolls' prams, play houses and pocket-money toys but generally no cheaper than town prices. Car park. **Toilets**. *See also* Outdoor Toys p31.

John Lewis
Lower Basement: (Direct access from Leith St) Wide selection ranging from big name, constructional toys, soft toys and games to pocket money toys. Expands at Christmas. *See* Department Stores p4, Outdoor Toys p31 and Bicycle Shops p36.

John Menzies
Basement: Large toy department with most big names ✔ in stock. Wide price range with good selection of pocket money toys. Many toys are television related and also divided into Girls' Toys and Boys' Toys. Children's stationery, drawing and painting materials on ground floor. *See* Department Stores p6.

JR's Toys & Cycles
46 Silverknowes Rd.
312 6046
Mon-Fri 9-6; Sat 9-5; Sun 10-4

Small, friendly shop with selection of toys, puzzles and games, inc pocket money toys. Easy parking.

Mothercare
Toy department includes own brand toys — from small bikes, trikes and sit and ride cars to books, pencil cases and rattles. *See* Department Stores p6.

Mr Macawz
10 Roseneath St
228 3327
Mon-Sat 11-6; Sundays Nov/Dec.
18 St Peter's Pl
229 1826
Mon-Sat 12-6; Sundays Nov/Dec

Small gift shops with a nature theme. Extensive range of cuddly toys, puzzles, cards, badges, brightly coloured mobiles, ceramics etc. Shop has a low price policy.

The Mulberry Bush
77 Morningside Rd
447 5145
Mon-Sat 9.30-5; Wed 9.30-3.45

Garvald Centre's craft shop. Beautifully-made wooden toys — rocking horses, puppet theatres, dolls' prams, houses and furniture. Also musical instruments (wooden drums, xylophones, lyre), handcraft materials and books. Order dolls' houses by early Oct for Christmas.

The Owl and the Pussycat
Waverley Market, Lowest Level
557 4420
Mon-Sat 9-6; Thurs 9-7; Sun 11-5
22 Deanhaugh Street, Stockbridge
343 6893

Mon-Sat 10-6; Sun 12-5

Wide selection of teddies and other soft toys, as well as badges, cards, miniature figures and handmade German nursery accessories.

Polly-Wolly Doodle
43 Raeburn Pl
317 2928
Tue-Sat 9.30-5.30

Good selection of pre-school jigsaws, wooden mobiles for babies. Easy access for all pushchairs. Small play table.

Poundstretcher
42 Shandwick Pl
226 7610
10 West Harbour Rd
552 0213
Mon-Fri 10-5; Sat 9-5.30; Sun 12-4.30
4/6 Brunswick Pl
557 0693
100/106 South Bridge
225 8540
Kinnaird Park, Newcraighall Rd
657 4244
Mon-Tue 10-6; Wed-Fri 10-8; Sat 9-6; Sun 10-5

Selection of inexpensive toys, including some educational toys, and stationery, including small bikes. See also Bicycle shops p36.

Royal Mile Miniatures
154 Canongate
557 2293
Mon-Sat 10.45-4.30

Collectors' shop selling beautifully made, handcrafted dolls' houses and miniatures, dolls' house kits and fittings. Also stock a cheaper range of dolls' houseware, more suitable for young children.

Savacentre

Small selection of toys, including Duplo, Lego and own brand stationery, expands at Christmas. See Supermarkets p12.

Studio One
10-14 Stafford St
226 5812
Mon-Fri 9.30-6; Thur 9.30-6.30; Sat 9.30-5.30; Sun in Nov and Dec

Down very steep steps to basement shop full of pocket-money toys, stocking fillers, novelties, Christmas decorations, wooden toys etc.

Toys Galore
193 Morningside Rd
447 1006
Mon-Sat 9-5.30, 9-5 Jan to Mar; Sun in Dec

Good choice of toys for all ages with some to try out while you look.

Includes Galt, Brio, Playskool, Tomy, etc 10% discount to playgroups.

Active Playmobil display in shop. Difficult to manoeuvre pushchairs, but they can be left supervised at front of shop.

Toys 'R' Us ✔

Large ranges of pre-school toys, soft toys, dolls, games, Lego, Playmobil and pocket money toys. A store directory guides to the different areas and there is a pick-up point for bulky items and electrical toys. There is no play area and, as such a large array of toys may prove tempting, parents may find it easier to shop without their offspring. **Toilets**. See also Department Stores p6.

What Everyone Wants
Variable selection of inexpensive toys, including a range of bikes. See Baby and Children's Clothes p19.

Wind Things
11 Cowgatehead
220 6336
Mon-Sat 10-5.30; Sun in Dec & Festival 12-5

Selection of small kites, various balloons inc modelling balloons, face paints, puzzles, kaleidoscopes, bubble making equipment, spinning tops, small sailing boats etc.

Woolworth
Large selection of big-name toys, Lego, Duplo, etc, cassettes, videos, stationery. Wide range of pocket-money toys. See also Department Stores p7.

Wrap
17 Stafford St
220 2328
Mon-Fri 10-6; Sat 9.30-5.30; Sun 12-5 in Nov-Dec

Selection of toys within interesting gift shop. Small Galt selection. Friendly staff.

OUTDOOR TOYS

For bikes and sit-and-ride toys. See Bicycle Shops.

Sand for sandpits is often available at builders' yards (such as John & James Lawrence, 72/74 Eyre Pl, Canonmills), but make sure you buy washed or silver sand as orange sand stains clothes. Washed sand is sometimes sold in bags in the spring and summer, by shops selling sandpits.

Early Learning Centre
Climbing frames, slides, swings, sandpits, sand, trampolines. See also Toy Shops p28.

Jolly Giant Superstore
Slides, swings, climbing frames, bikes. See also Toy Shops p29 and Bicycle Shops p35.

John Lewis
Extensive range of climbing ✔ frames, swings, slides, bikes and other outdoor toys. Choose from 'top activity sports' brochure, delivered to your home. Occasionally some samples on display, particularly in summer months. See Department Stores p4.

Montrose
See Shopping from Home p54.

Outdoors
30 Dalry Rd, Haymarket
337 6360
Mon-Sat 9-5.30

Climbing frames, swings, slides, trampolines, sports gear. Deliver free within city boundary.

Toys 'R' Us
Climbing frames, slides, ✔ swings, sandpits and Wendy houses with samples on display. See Department Stores p6.

BICYCLE SHOPS

Introduction

Where to buy? The best place to buy a child's bike is in a specialist bike shop. Bikes purchased elsewhere often come flat-packed and dangerous mistakes can be made in assembling them. Most specialist shops are staffed by knowledgeable people who can give advice and fix a bike on the premises rather than sending them away.

Which bike? Try to buy the best bike you can afford, and a well-known make. Look for the Reynolds R531 sticker on the frame for adult bikes. Cheap bikes have nylon bushes rather than steel bearings, which do not last very long and can often not be repaired. A more expensive bike which is maintained will last longer and survive more than one child.

After Sales Service Bike shops should ask you to bring your bike back about 4 wks after purchase so that the brakes and cables can be tightened and bearings checked.

Which Size? Measure the inside leg of your child before shopping for a bike. When sitting on the saddle, the ball of the foot should rest comfortably on the ground. Specialist bike shops will ensure you have the correct size.

Guarantee Most manufacturers offer at least 1 yr guarantee on parts and up to 5 yrs on frames. However tyres, inner tubes, cables and any other parts that wear out, are not included in the guarantee. Sit-and-ride toys sometimes have no guarantee, but your rights are covered under the 1979 Sale of Goods Act.

Child seats There is a wide range available and you get what you pay for. The more expensive seats — Hamex, Kaddy, Rex, Kiddy Ryder all have high backs to protect the child's neck and strong over-the-shoulder harnesses to keep a child firmly in place. Other features to look for are: footwells, plastic cover for rear wheel spokes and for springs on saddle which can pinch tiny fingers, chest pads, a padded bar in front of the child and strong metal fitments. Child seats can be purchased that will fit both on the front of the bike

by the handle bars and at the rear of the bike. You can get an extra saddle attached to the crossbar in the centre of the bike and have your child in between your arms.

Fitting a child seat can be tricky. Most bike shops will fit a child seat free or a nominal charge if you have purchased it at their store. It is well worth having them fit it, unless you are very handy. Do not lose any of the nuts and bolts as some are unique and irreplacable.

The addition of a child and seat will affect the handling and stability of your bike, as well as placing greater strain on it. One important factor is the weight ratio between the pedaller and the passenger — the child must not weigh more than $\frac{1}{4}$ of the weight of the adult. The style of the bike is also important, heavier built bikes are able to take the extra weight better than light frame bikes.

Trailers Rather than a child seat attached to your bike that affects your stability you can pull a child or 2 along behind you. The advantages of a trailer are safety for both you and the child, you can ferry 2 children and extra luggage and if your child is more than $\frac{1}{4}$ your weight you can still cycle with them. The child is securely strapped to an aluminium frame resembling the cage of a car covered in canvas, protecting them from both the weather and accidents. Most trailers are imported from the USA or Europe and are expensive. You will find them at specialised bike shops or through cycle magazines either second-hand or mail order. Resale value is very good.

Helmets A variety of makes are available. Most are made of expanded polystyrene, some may also be covered with a hard polycarbonate shell. It is important to take your child to the shop to have them properly fitted so they do not wobble. Helmets come with padding which the staff will fit in the correct position.

Look out for Australian or American standards on helmets. ANSI or Snell standards, they are much higher than British standards.

Helmets are all 'first impact' so after a serious bash, in an accident or in play, they are damaged and should be replaced. Try and buy a brightly coloured helmet to attract attention.

Reflective Bands You and your child must be visible when cycling. Always wear brightly coloured clothing, even in daylight, with highly reflective bands on arms and legs. You can buy rolls of stick-on or sew-on

reflective material quite cheaply from many of the shops.

ACT Member This indicates membership of the Association of Cycle Traders, to which you can complain if the shop does not give satisfaction.

For information about cycling in Edinburgh *see* Travel and Transport p233.

Specialist Bicycle Shops

Jocky Allan Cycles
115 Leith Walk
554 6698
Mon-Sat 9.30-5.30

Children's bikes and helmets from 3 yrs up. Child seats, spares and safety accessories. Small functional shop. Christmas Club. Will repair any make of bike, but you must book it in; admissions taken Sat 4.30-5.30. Will

also accept emergency repairs. Charge around £2 to fit child seat.

Blazing Saddles
'Great Bikes No Bull'
25-27 Iona St
555 5333
Mon-Sat 9-5.30; Thurs 9-7

Children's bikes new and second-hand. Full range of safety accessories including child seats and helmets. Christmas Club. After sales service and full repair service.

See Recycling p35, see also Hiring p57.

City Cycles
30 Rodney St
557 2801
Mon-Sat 9-5.30; Sun 12-4

Specialists in children's cycle helmets, child seats, cycle clothing, spares and safety accessories. Comprehensive range of quality bicycles from 4 yrs up at competitive prices. Free after sales safety check on all new cycles and fast repair service on any make of cycle. Massive range of car roof and boot racks in stock to transport bikes for all the family.

Cycles Williamson
60 Hamilton Pl
225 3286
Tues-Sat 10-6; Sun 12-5; Mon closed all day.

Bikes to cater for all ages from 2-adult. Large selection of children's bikes including all safety accessories, child seats, helmets and clothing.

Child trailers and cycle tandems also available enabling everyone in the family to cycle together.

Free after sale service with every new bike, in-store open plan workshop with full service facility. Will fit child seats.

Edinburgh Bicycle
5-9 Alvanley Ter, Whitehouse Loan
228 1368
Tues-Sun 10-6; Thurs late night

Large selection of approved children's helmets. Child seats from America, that can be detached or permanently fixed to your cycle. Children are welcome and there are toys to keep them amused while you shop. Free customer newsletters and mail order catalogue available.

Sandy Gilchrist
1 Cadzow Pl
652 1760
Mon, Tues, Fri, Sat 9-5.30; Thurs 9-7

Children's trikes and bikes — Giant, Peugeot and Townsend. Wide selection on view. Several types of child seats both high back and low back. Children's helmets, spares and safety accessories. ACT member. Christmas Club. Repairs done on any make of bike, 24 hr turn around when possible. Free estimates. Charge approx £7 to fit child seats.

Halfords Superstore
Seafield Rd
554 9294
11 Straiton Mains
448 2282
Mon-Fri 8-8; Sat 8-6; Sun 9-5

Good selection of children's sit-and-ride toys, trikes, pedal cars and bikes — Apollo and Raleigh. Child seats, spare parts and accessories. Christmas club. Free after sales service. Usually only repair bikes bought here, but may occasionally do small outside repairs. Major repairs in-store. Free fitting of child seat if bike bought at Halfords.

MacDonald Cycles
26 Morrison St
229 8473
Mon-Sat 9-5.30

Good selection of children's trikes and bikes — all Raleigh. Cycle parts (amongst others), child seats, children's helmets, children's cycle capes, spare parts and safety accessories. Christmas club. ACT member.

Free after sales service. Will repair any bike, if parts available. Usually 24 hr turn around, sometimes quicker for own customers. Estimates £2. Will fit child seat Free if both bike and child seat are bought here, otherwise around £8.

New Bike Shop
13-14 Lochrin Pl
228 6363/6633 (repair)
Mon, Wed-Sat 10-5.30; Sun, Tues closed all day. Extended opening Summer and Christmas.

Cycle parts, child seats, children's helmets and some children's bikes aged 3 and up — Peugeot, Giant, Ridgeback, etc. Six mths guarantee on secondhand bikes, excl wear and tear. Free after sales service. Bike repair shop at no.13 will repair any make of bike, including children's bikes. 24 hr turn around; as fast as possible — miracles take longer. Free estimates. Free advice on cycle matters, local cycle routes, etc.

See also Central Cycle Hire in Hiring p57.

Thomas Piper
23 South Clerk St
667 7777
Mon, Tues, Thurs, Fri 9.30-5.30. Closed 1-2; Wed 9.30-1; Sat 9.30-5, closed 1-2.

Children's scooters, trikes and bikes — all Raleigh. Child seats, children's helmets, spares and safety accessories. ACT member. Christmas Club.

Will repair Raleigh bikes only, 48 hr turn around. Free estimates. Charge around £7 to fit child seat.

Recycling
31-33 Iona St
553 1130
Mon-Sat 9-5.30

Reconditioned bikes for sale. Toddlers to adults. Guaranteed for 3 mths.

Also offer hire before you buy service both adult and children. If you decide to purchase the hire charge is deducted.

See Hiring p57.

Other Shops

Argos
Good selection of children's sit-and-ride toys, trikes, go carts and scooters. 1 yr guarantee on all.

See Department Stores p2.

Co-op (Scotmid)
Good selection of sit-and-ride toys, scooters, trikes and bikes (Vivi). Repairs are sent to local cycle shop, may only take a few days.

See Department Stores p6.

Jenners
Reasonable range of children's sit-and-ride toys, trikes and Raleigh bikes. Bikes returned to Raleigh for repair.

See Department Stores p4.

Jolly Giant Superstore
Reasonable range of children's sit-and-ride toys, trikes and bikes up to age 10 — Sharma, Vivi, Village

35

Cycles, Townsend. Six mths guarantee on Townsend, but shop effectively operates a 1 yr guarantee if you keep receipt.

Repairs are done in-house. They send away to manufacturer for larger parts as required.

See Toy Shops p29.

John Lewis

Reasonable selection of children's sit-and-ride toys, trikes and Raleigh bikes in Toy Dept (lower basement). Repairs are sent away — can take 2-3 wks.

See Department Stores p4.

Mothercare

Very small range of children's sit-and-ride toys.

See Department Stores p6.

Poundstretcher

A few sit-and-ride toys and two sizes of Triang bikes.

See Toy Shops p30.

Toys 'R' Us

A range of sit-and-ride toys, trikes and bikes.

See Department Stores p6.

OUTDOOR AND SKI SHOPS

For those parents wishing to take their children outdoors in Britain, the weather always causes problems. Keeping the small members of the family warm and dry is essential to enjoying any outing. There has been an explosion of outdoor shops in Edinburgh in the past few years and most of these now have some clothing and equipment for under 5s. Babycarriers (or backpacks) allow you to go off the beaten track with your child safely away from mud, wet grass, sheep droppings and all the other delights a young child can find in the countryside. They are equally useful in town. They allow you to negotiate busy streets with the child safe from the usual problems associated with pushchairs such as people tripping over the pushchair, getting through doors and riding on escalators.

The big drawback is your poor back! Make sure when you purchase a babycarrier that you 'try it before you buy it'. Also think about your use of the carrier. If you intend to go out into the countryside you want a carrier that is rugged as well as comfortable.

As with most things you get what you pay for. If money is no object and you are a dedicated hillwalker look at the Macpac carriers, but you should also check out the others first; they may meet your needs more cheaply.

Blues
1 Wemyss Pl
225 8369
Tues, Wed, Fri 10-6; Thurs 10-7; Sat 9.30-5.30

Jackets, suits, salopettes, goggles and sunglasses from 2+ yrs, also helmets, poles, hats, mitts, etc. Junior skis from 80 cm.

C & A

Selection of jackets, salopettes, goggles, hats and mittens for 3+ yrs (2nd floor) from end of Sept.

See Department Stores p3.

Elliott Sports Ski Shop
14-15 Bruntsfield Pl
229 2402
Mon-Fri 9.30-6; Sat 9-5.

Stock a few clothes for children 2+

yrs jackets, suits, salopettes on ground floor. In basement, skis, helmets, goggles, poles for 2 + yrs, boots from children's 12 up. Have ski-ing videos to keep your child amused while shopping.
See also Hiring p59.

Millets
12 Frederick St
220 1551
Mon-Sat 9-5.30, Thur 9-6.30

Stock the Karrimor Papoose Standard babycarrier, a good selection of Reynard (own brand) waterproofs suitable for 3yrs upward. Also bodywarmers, fleeces, socks and boots from size 8. Hats, mitts, reflective strips etc. Access good and friendly staff will help with pushchairs to 1st floor sales area if asked. Staff toilet available.

Nevisport
81 Shandwick Pl
229 1197
Mon-Sat 9-5.30; Thurs 9-7.

Stock babycarriers from Karrimor and Vango, suitable for babies from 6 mths. Also carry a range of waterproof clothing from toddler upwards, fleeces and lightweight boots. For skiers there is a small range of clothes and equipment for children. Skis from 70 cm up, boots from size 16' (monopoint sizing). Access good, ask to have doors opened for tandem pushchairs and help to basement sales area. Staff toilet available.

New Heights
134 Lothian Rd
229 2233
Mon-Sat 9-5.30, open Sun in Dec phone for times

Have two babycarriers from Macpac-Koala and Possum. They may have

to order these at times. Also carry waterproofs for 2 yrs upwards. Fleeces, mitts and lightweight boots. Good access. Staff toilet.

One Step Ahead
177 Morningside Rd
447 0999
Mon-Fri 9.30-6; Sat 9-5.30

Stocks the Vaude, Calange and Jack Wolfskin babycarriers. Waterproofs from Bryncinr are suitable from 6mths upwards. Also stock fleeces, thermal underwear. Access good. Staff toilet available.
also at
51a George St
226 6045
Mon-Fri 9.30-6; Thur 10-7; Sat 9-5.30.

Same ranges as above. Access is down steps from pavement, watch for steps inside door.

Sports Warehouse
24-26 Coburg St
553 6003
Mon-Sat 9-5.30; Sun 11-4

This sports and outdoor supplier have the Karrimor Papoose Super and Standard babycarriers. Pentland cagoules and trousers, suitable 3yrs upwards. Also carry boots from size 12 up, junior sleeping bags. Also stock swimming aids. Reasonable access. Staff toilet.

Graham Tiso
115/123 Rose St
225 9486
Mon-Sat 9.30-5.30; Thurs 9.30-7

Store on 3 floors has Vango and Wild Rover (own brand) babycarriers, suitable from 6 mth to 4 yrs. Also waterproof cape/hood for carriers. Several ranges of waterproofs including Trespass, Wild Rover and Chuck Roast, suitable for 6 mths upwards. Selection of insulated clothing and fleeces. Stock both leather boots from size 10 and lightweight boots from size 9. Ski goggles, hats etc for 4+ yrs. Staff toilet available.

See Nursery Equipment p26.
also at
13 Wellington Pl
Leith
554 0804
Hours as above

Same ranges as above. This branch also stock secondhand childrens boots. Easier to park nearby. Access to 1st floor sales area by narrow staircase, need to attract attention of warehouse staff for help with pushchairs.

BUYING CHILDREN'S BOOKS

Edinburgh is well served with bookshops stocking a good range of children's books. Conditions are not always ideal, but on the whole booksellers try to accommodate children. Most shops have some sort of distraction for young toddlers, boxes of toys, tables and chairs, crayons and books are often provided. The better shops have staff who are well trained and specialise in children's books and give invaluable advice and recommendations. If you cannot find the book you require, most bookshops will be happy to order for you.

Despite television and videos, books are still very popular with under 5s. Books can be introduced at the baby stage and by 9 mths most babies will be happy to sit on your knee to look at a book, for a few seconds at least. The bedtime story for a toddler is an ideal way to wind down after a hectic day, and to spend 10 mins talking with the child. Books

introduce children to words and language they would never hear in normal conversation, and greatly increase language development. They can also help to introduce children to concepts, ideas and situations out of their normal everyday life, so helping to stimulate their imagination. There is a wonderful choice of books for this age group, superbly illustrated in many different styles, entertaining for child and parent alike.

We list here the best stocked and most helpful bookshops. Children's books are also sold in supermarkets, most department stores, most toy shops, some stationers and by mail order *See* Shopping from Home p55. New books may seem expensive but compare well with the price of toys and videos, and offer excellent value for money. Ladybird titles, for example, are widely available and are excellent quality for the same price as some cheaper toys. Savacentre, at Cameron Toll, stock an excellent range of children's books, at incredibly low prices, produced exclusively for them by one of the best children's publishers. Give book tokens as presents and ask for them for your child's birthday and Christmas; from 3+ yrs children will enjoy choosing a book for themselves. Look out also for charity shops, church book sales, secondhand and jumble sales, and library sales which can sometimes provide '10 for the price of one'. Library tickets are available to children from birth *see* Libraries p126 and regular library visits help to expand the choice of books available to your child. Some toy libraries also lend books and cassettes *see* Toy Libraries p132.

Edinburgh Book Festival *see* Annual Events p203 is a biennial festival which has some storytelling and author sessions suitable for 3 + yrs as well as a good and well-displayed selection of children's books. **Creche** see p50.

The Edinburgh Children's Book Group is a registered charity aiming to bring children, parents and books together. They will hold book evenings in your home, arrange book centred events, read to children in hospitals. Newsletter for members, also evening meetings with guest speakers, eg publishers, artists, editors. Contact Marion Donohoe — 229 2997.

Balerno Children's Book Group run a Tape Library which is housed in Glowworm Bookshop see Bookshops below. Annual Family Membership costs £3 and entitles you to borrow story cassette tapes — well over 150 to choose from. Contact Joan Tervit 449 3652.

Some books with an Edinburgh theme which appeal to young children are:

The Tale of Greyfriar's Bobby by Lavinia Derwent, Puffin, 1985, £3.25. A simply written but long version of the tale of the faithful dog.

Maisie Comes to Morningside, Maisie's Festival Adventure etc by Aileen Patterson, The Amaising Publishing House £3.95 approx. Detailed illustrations of identifiable places in Edinburgh; Maisie is a kilted kitten who visits her granny in the city. There are many books in the 'Maisie' series, most of which are set locally.

Edinburgh: A Capital Story by Frances and Gordon Jarvie, Chambers, £4.99. Packed with illustrations and information on the history of our city.

A Child's Garden of Verse by Robert Louis Stevenson. Penguin £2.99. A classic. 'The Lamplighter' lit the lamp outside RLS's home in Heriot Row, and it's still there, although it's electric now.

Bookshops

Bauermeisters Booksellers
19 George IV Bridge
226 5561
Mon-Fri 9-6; Sat 9-5.30

General and academic bookshop with small children's section on the ground floor next to the stairs to the basement.

Books and cassette sets (including Scottish stories) in the children's department with other cassettes in the paperback shop/record department a few doors along. Also stock some videos. The shop is divided up into separate shops almost adjacent to each other so you may have to go to other departments to finish your shopping for stationery and gift wrapping etc. Will allow the use of staff **toilet** for children.

Campbell and Stillwell
74 South Bridge
226 7177
Mon-Thur 9.30-7; Fri,Sat 9.30-5.30; Sun 1-5

Easily accessed store carries only publishers' remainders, thus have a selection of books from 99p. Chunky baby books and selection of picture books. Children's section by wide entrance with all books at child height. Browsing encouraged with chairs available.

G.T. Books
44-45 South Bridge
556 8032
Mon-Fri 10-6; Sat 10-5

Stocks Ladybird books and a variety of remainders. Also secondhand children's books. Reasonable access. Staff **toilet** available.

Glowworm
7 Main St, Balerno
449 4644
Mon-Sat 9-5; closed 12.30-1.30 except Sat

Children's and adults' books, stationery, cassettes, gifts. Children's play area. Discount for schools and playgroups. Staff **toilet** available.

John Lewis
Book dept in basement with good access by lift. Stock a wide range of board, picture and story books. Also have musical/noise books. Any book which is in print can be ordered, 'many arriving within 24 hrs'.
See Department Stores p4.

STOCKBRIDGE BOOKSHOP
26 North West Circus Place

BOOKS FOR LEARNING & FUN
Tel: (031) 225 5355

Stockbridge Bookshop
26 NW Circus Pl
225 5355
Mon-Fri 9-8; Sat 9-6; Sun 12.30-5

Bright, colourful children's section up 2 steps at back of shop, marked by a rainbow above the entrance. Good selection of paperbacks, boardbooks, bargain books, cassettes, and some hardbacks. FREE coffee available for parents (out of reach of children) along with table and chairs for browsing.

Birthday cards and wrapping paper. Friendly staff will allow use of their **toilet** and would find space for breastfeeding. Newly opened well-stocked school showroom in basement has large selection of non-fiction titles — please ask staff. Can produce computerised booklists on any specific topics requested.

James Thin
53-59 South Bridge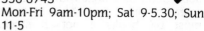
556 6743
Mon-Fri 9am-10pm; Sat 9-5.30; Sun 11-5

General and academic bookshop with a stationery department. There is a large, bright children's section downstairs (long flight of steps, no lift), with little table and chairs, toys and books to read. Large reference section for children of all ages. Range of Galt toys. Children's tapes (including Edinburgh stories eg 'Maisie'), also more tapes in Music Department.

Also at:
57 George St
225 4495
Mon-Fri 9am-10pm; Sat 9-5.30; Sun 11-5

Excellent children's department with

a large selection of books, up short stairs at the back (left) of the ground floor. Good play area with plenty of room for pushchairs. Able to order most UK books if not in stock. **Toilets** and Mother and Baby facilities are situated upstairs beside the Coffee House.

Coffee House *see* Eating Out p71.

Also at:
Gyle Shopping Centre
539 7757
Mon,Wed 9-8; Tues 9.30-8; Thur, Fri 9-9pm; Sat 9-6.30; Sun 10-5.30.

Well-stocked children's section on ground floor. Good access.

See Shopping Centres p8.

Waterstone's Bookshop
83 George St
225 3436
Mon-Sat 9.30am-10pm; Sun 11-6

A large, high quality bookshop on 2 floors and a mezzanine with a vast range of books for both adults and children. Its emphasis is on 'fun for all the family' with events and long opening hours. The shop is packed with books but has been made more pushchair friendly. The children's department is on the ground floor. Brightly decorated with unusual kites. Huge selection of titles, can be a bit daunting with many books stacked edge on, upon shelves that are out of reach. Excellent Baby Room and public **toilet** adjacent to the children's section. Baby room (for feeding and changing) has complimentary wipes and cream. Friendly staff always willing to answer questions.

Also at:
13/14 Princes St (East end)
556 3034
Mon, Wed-Fri 9.30-9; Tues 10.30-9; Sat 9.30-7.30; Sun 10.30-7

Well-designed children's section at back of ground floor. Bold colour scheme, lowered ceiling, shelves that children can reach, and seating. The books are classified in age groups. Excellent selection of hardback and paperback books. Regular activities for children — ask to be put on the children's mailing list. Happy to donate posters and publicity material to teachers. Staff **toilet** is available for emergencies; it is in the basement so need to be escorted by member of staff. There is a lift which can be used for prams and pushchairs, but again ask for assistance.

Also at:
128 Princes St (West end)
226 2666
Mon-Thurs 9-9; Fri-Sat 9-7; Sun 11-6

Lift to children's department in basement to the rear of shop. Good range of books, cushions to sit on. **Toilet** for the disabled near the children's department and a baby room for feeding and changing at front of basement up a few steps.

Wesley Owen Books & Music
117-119 George St
225 2229
Mon-Sat 9-5.30; Tues 9.30-5.30

The children's bookshop is next door to the main bookshop. It has a wide range of attractively displayed books including religious books. The shop also has cards, stationery, videos, CDs and cassettes, posters, jigsaws and a few gifts. Friendly staff will allow the use of their **toilet**.

West and Wilde Bookshop
25 Dundas St
556 0079
Tues-Sat 10-7; Sun 12-5

Small bookshop with specialisation in gay books. Children's books about gay parents. HIV/AIDS, gay picture books, child abuse, etc. Also adult books on child abuse, HIV/AIDS, sex education, coming out, etc. Staff **toilet** may be used in emergencies.

The following shops also stock a selection of children's books.

Bargain Books, 100A Princes St — some very cheap picture and activity books.

Bookworld, 63 Princes St and Waverley Mkt — popular children's paperbacks and very low-priced picture and story books, some as low as 30p-50p, great for party prizes and stocking fillers.

Early Learning Centre — good selection, though limited range see Toy Shops p28.

Jenners — good selection of popular authors and publishers. Children's books in the basement, next to the toy department see Department Stores p4.

Kay's Bookshop, 390 Morningside Rd — small friendly shop with selection of Ladybirds, Puffins, etc. Also at: 213 St John's Rd.

John Menzies — good selection of all children's books see Department Stores p6.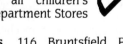

Read Books, 116 Bruntsfield Pl, Bruntsfield and 27b Raeburn Pl, Stockbridge — selection of paperbacks for children; friendly staff will order books for you.

Royal Museum of Scotland Shop — excellent selection of children's reference books, special emphasis on natural history and activity books.

SECONDHAND GOODS

Charity shops throughout the city eg Oxfam, Barnardo's, Family Care, Cancer Research, Shelter, St Columba's Hospice, ECSS, are worth keeping an eye on for children's clothes. See under 'Charitable and Benevolent Organisations', in the Yellow Pages for addresses of their shops. Most are voluntarily staffed so opening hrs tend to be short with lunch time closing.

Other suggestions: Evening News, Edinburgh Herald and Post, The Capital, The List see Sources of Information p205. Also Jumble Sales, YWCA Toy Fairs and other local festivals and fairs throughout the yr see Annual Events p200. Notices in newsagents, supermarkets, playgroups etc. You could also put up a 'wanted' notice.

See also Bicycle Shops for second hand bikes p35.

Bairnecessities
297 Easter Rd
553 2116
Tues-Sat 10-5

New and used clothing and toys. Good access for prams, children's toy box, toilet available.

Dress Sense
44 Hanover St (Top Floor)
220 1298/220 1400
Tues-Sat 10.30-4.30

Good quality up-to-date clothes for 3-8 yrs plus large selection of ladies quality clothes, all sizes. 3rd floor, no lift.

Hand-in-Hand
3 NW Circus Pl, Stockbridge
226 3598
Tues-Sat 10-5.30

Antique christening gowns, Shetland lace shawls and some children's clothes, as well as clothes and textiles.

Jolly Babies
Nearly New Shop
238 Leith Walk
555 0039
Mon-Sat 10-5
Modern brand names. Baby clothes, prams, pushchairs, high chairs, Moses baskets, cots and toys at reasonable prices.

Lullaby
193 Gorgie Rd
313 2355
Mon-Sat 9.30-5
Secondhand and new clothes for children, birth-8 yrs. Nursery equipment. Purchase items in very good condition for approximately 50% of their selling price.
See also Hiring p58.

National Childbirth Trust
225 9191
Mon-Fri 9.30-11.30
Fund-raising events often have a secondhand clothes stall. Check press for details.
See Health Care Facilities p259.

Next Best
Secondhand toys by party plan.
See Shopping from Home p56.

Nurseryland
260 Dalry Rd
313 3370
Mon-Fri 10-5; Sat 10-4.30
Secondhand clothes; new and secondhand equipment. All equipment has been serviced and carries up to 3 mths guarantee.

St Fillan's 'Nearly New' Children's Clothes Shop
St Fillan's Church Hall,
8 Buckstone Dr
Open 1st Mon pm 7-9 and 1st Tues am 9.30-12 of each mth during term time.
Good quality reasonably priced clothes for babies-teens including school, dance, organisation and sports wear. Contact Heather Emerson 664 3035.

Song of Sixpence
26 E Barnton Ave
336 5939
Tues 2-4; Fri 9.30-12 noon or by appointment
Children's clothes agency for 0-10 yrs. Good quality eg M&S, Laura Ashley, Absorba, Heskia, Osh Kosh. Own label designer clothing also available.
See Shopping from Home p56.

CHEMISTS WITH EXTENDED HOURS

The Lothian Health Board Primary Care Division, Northern General Hospital, Ferry Rd, 557 1000, keep a list of chemists and operate a rota to provide pharmaceutical services outside normal shop hrs. There is also an Emergency Prescription Dispensing Service. This operates through local police stations so that if you have a prescription that has been marked 'Urgent' by your doctor you should call at, or phone your local police station who will advise you how to contact a chemist participating in the scheme.

Open Sunday

Boots the Chemists
48 Shandwick Pl
225 6757
10-5pm;
Cameron Toll Centre
6 Lady Rd
666 1111
12 noon-4.30

Heron Pharmacy
22 Hillhouse Rd
332 3602
10.30 am-12.30 pm

E. Moss
Asda Superstore
The Jewel
Portobello
669 3550
10-5pm

Safeway Pharmacy
1 Bughtlin Mkt
Maybury Dr
East Craigs
339 1188
10 am-2 pm;
Cameron Toll Centre
6 Lady Rd
664 6852
10 am-1pm;

Comely Bank Rd
332 5573
10 am-2 pm

Open after 6 pm

Allan Ltd., G W
102 Ferry Rd
554 1394
Mon, Tues, Thurs, Fri 7 pm

Boots the Chemists
Cameron Toll Centre
6 Lady Rd
666 1111
Thurs, Fri 8 pm;

Gyle Shopping Centre
Mon,Tue Wed,7pm; Thur 8.30pm; Fri
7.30pm; Sat 6.30pm
101-103 Princes St
225 8331
Thurs 7 pm
See also Department Stores p3;
5-7 St James Centre
556 1062
Thurs 7 pm;
48 Shandwick Pl
225 6757
Mon-Sat 9 pm.

Craiglogan Pharmacy
98 Craigentinny Rd
661 2523
Mon-Fri 7 pm

Mohammed Iqbal
79 Nicholson St
667 4032
Mon-Fri 7pm

Lindsay & Gilmour
11 Elm Row
556 4316
Mon-Fri 6.30 pm

Morningside Pharmacy
207-209 Morningside Rd
447 6188
Mon-Fri 8 pm

Millar Pharmacy
153 Morningside Rd
447 2041
Mon-Fri 6.30pm

Moss, E
Asda Superstore
100 The Jewel
669 3550
Wed, Thurs, Fri, Sat 8 pm

Safeway Pharmacy
1 Bughtlin Mkt
Maybury Dr
East Craigs
339 1188
Mon-Fri 8 pm
Cameron Toll Centre
6 Lady Rd
664 6852
Mon-Fri 8 pm
Sat 6 pm;
38 Comely Bank Rd
332 5573
Mon-Fri 8 pm

Open Public Holidays (phone first to check).

Safeway Pharmacy
Cameron Toll Centre
6 Lady Rd
664 6852
9 am-1 pm;
38 Comely Bank Rd
332 5573
10 am-2 pm

Hairdressers

Having a haircut can be a traumatic experience for a small child. Some children love it, enjoying the attention, while others need a little more persuasion. If you already use a hairdresser regularly, it is worth asking if they would cut your child's hair, and how much they would charge. But remember, what suits you may not necessarily be the best for your child. You need to find someone who feels relaxed with children and has a calm approach to them. Many hairdressers have special seats so that children can sit at the right height, and have books and toys to help keep them amused while they are waiting. A few even have videos on show, which is one way of getting children to keep their heads still. If your child is shy, it is worth asking if he/she can sit on your knee, or hold your hand while his/her hair is being cut.

Timing of the haircut can be critical, both for your child and the hairdresser. Choose a time when your child is usually in good form, perhaps early morning or after a nap. If you can also arrange it for a quiet period for the hairdresser then there is likely to be a calmer atmosphere as well as having less time to wait around. If it is your child's first visit to a salon, it may be helpful to make the appointment in person, giving your child the chance to see where he/she is going, and what it will be like.

If you are looking for a new hairdresser for your whole family, why not have a haircut first yourself, and use the time to chat to the stylist and find out how keen he/she is to cut your child's hair, or if one of the stylists in the salon specialises in children's cuts. Some salons offer reduced rates for children when a parent has a haircut too. Check out local salons, there may be no need to trail across town with your toddler.

Another option, if you find it difficult to get out, or if your child is intimidated by the surroundings of a salon, would be to have a hairdresser come to your home. We have mentioned only one home hairdresser below, but there are several to choose from in the Yellow Pages see also The Capital and The Herald and Post in Sources of Information p205. All allow use of their toilet and have limited space for pushchairs. You may find haircuts at home a more practical solution for your family, and an exciting afternoon for your small children.

There are dozens of hairdressers in Edinburgh, and listed below are only a few which come recommended by people associated with the production of this book. All allow use of their toilet and have limited space for pushchairs. While they all

welcome small children, they are by no means the only salons in the city who will be happy to cut your child's hair. Ask around friends, toddler groups and playgroups for recommendations. If ever your child is distressed at the hairdressers, don't be afraid to just give up and try again another day. We all have our off days.

When looking for suitable hairdressers, we highlighted the following facilities as important:

Children welcome
Any age limits
Cost/discounts
Use of toilets
Children's seats
Toys, books, videos
Space for pushchairs.

Ruth Ball
18 Comely Bank Ave
315 2110
Mon, Tues, Fri 8.45-6.00; Wed 8.45-1.30; Thurs 8.45-7.00; Sat 8.45-3.00

Welcome children from babies up, approx £4. Appointments not always necessary. Special seats and children's books available.

Sheana Dowie
Cuts in your own home
Day and evenings
539 9858

Children from £3.50, men from £8 and ladies from £12.50. Discounts for complete families. Also does perms and colours. Please phone for appointment.

The Edge
94 Marchmont Rd
447 2222
Mon-Wed 9-6; Thurs, Fri 9-7; Sat 9-5

Welcome children of all ages, £3.50 for under 5s. Appointment recommended. Special seats and children's books available.

Greig Firth Hairdressing
2 Bruntsfield Ave
229 1324
also at
101 Colinton Rd
444 1244
Mon, Tues,Wed, Fri 9-5; Thurs 10-7; Sat 9-5

Children from 1 yr very welcome. Cost £7. Appointment not always necessary early in the week. Children's books.

Jon Francis
24 Rodney St
556 2009
Mon-Sat 9-6

Children welcome, when parent is also having a haircut. Child £3-4, adult £11.50. Appointments for children on Tuesdays and Wednesdays.

Hairizons
6-7 Teviot Pl
225 6627
also at
5 Commercial St
554 9499
Tues-Fri 9-6; Sat 9-4

Welcomes children of all ages, from £3. Appointment not always necessary in mornings. Special seats and children's books and toy box available.

Klownz
1 North West Circus Pl   ✔
226 4565
Salon actively encourages parents to bring their young children with them providing toy box, colouring books, pens, as well as juice, to keep them amused while their parents are being attended to. For children's cuts, the first 'few' cuts are free as long as a parent is having a cut too, thereafter children's cuts at £3-5 with adult cuts starting at £18. Good access for pushchairs.

Raymond
11 Comiston Rd
447 3177
79 Saughton Rd N
334 7509
20 Brandon Ter
556 7186
Sat-Thur 8.45-6, Fri 8.45-7

Welcome children of all ages. Offers first cut free for children. Appointments only necessary Fri/Sat. Morningside salon has videos; all salons have toys and books. Children's gowns and special seats. Tues and Thur open until 6.30 for model training offering reduced prices at Morningside branch. Appointments essential.

Special Effects
210a Newhaven Rd
552 2899
Tues, Wed, Thurs 9-6; Fri 9-6.30; Sat 8.30-3.00

Welcome children of all ages, up to 2 yrs £3.60; preschool £4.90; children £6.15. Prefer no children on Sat. Appointments not always necessary. Special seats, toy box, and children's books avaliable.

Gordon Wilson Hairdressing
9-13 Salisbury Pl
667 2692
Mon-Sat 8.45-6; Thurs 8.45-7.30

Welcomes children of all ages, from £4.75. First cut free if adult is having a haircut. Appointment not always necessary. Videos, toy box and books to entertain children. Special seats available.

Recording the Event

Whether it's videoing the birth, putting an announcement in the paper or having a family portrait taken for posterity most families find 'recording the event' comes into their lives with the arrival of a baby.

A birth announcement can be placed in The Scotsman or Evening News *see* Sources of Information p205. Unlike Death Notices no proof is required to place your announcement and they can be made in person at The Scotsman Offices or by phone with a credit card. Payment is required at the time of order.

See Hiring p59 for video camera hire.

Department stores such as Debenhams and Frasers and shopping centres like Cameron Toll or The Gyle Centre often have visiting companies who specialise in photographing young children. Look out in the Herald and Post for details of these companies.

The Herald and Post and The Capital often have details of firms who are willing to video or photograph your party or christening. The following companies specialise in working with under 5s.

Bell Photography
447 9827

Family portraits taken in your home. Christenings and special occasions. Special rates for nurseries, playgroups etc.

Contact Walter Bell Bsc LRPS

Colorfoto Ltd
229 7556

Specialises in nurseries, playgroups, toddler groups etc. Sessions can be arranged for the whole family. Emphasis is on children being happy and relaxed. Bookings require groups of 20 + .

Dimple Photos
Kippielaw, Haddington
0620 842441

Specialises in newborn babies in hospital and children under 3 but will also cover playgroups on request.

Fiona Good ABIPP
17 Eildon St
556 3558

Fully equiped studio at her home. Patient, calm approach to young children and family groups.

David Johnston
31 Bridgeside Ave
Whitburn
West Lothian
01501 742710

Children's portraits, babies, christenings, family groups, etc. 'At home' or studio service available.

Danny Kaye
554 7163

Child studies a speciality, also does playgroups, toddler groups, nurseries, etc. At home service only as he has no studio as such.

Raymond Lintern
667 7224

Well-known Edinburgh photographer who specialises in playgroups, nurseries and toddler groups. Has lots of patience.

49

Peter McKenzie ABIPP, ARPS
Jenners Ltd
Princes St
260 2293 (Direct dial line)
Personal service in studio portraiture by appointment only. Very good with young children and will visit your home to take lovely informal/formal family group studies.

CRECHES WHILE SHOPPING

Edinburgh has, at last, an all year round **creche** at The Gyle Shopping Centre. In addition there are sometimes 'one-off' creche facilities provided for particular annual events, dependent on availability of funds and an appropriate venue. These include the Edinburgh Book Festival, Edinburgh International Festival and Festival Fringe. See Annual Events p203.

The Gyle Nursery
Gyle Avenue
South Gyle Broadway
539 7099
Opening hrs: Mon-Wed 8-6, Thur&Fri 8-7, Sat 9-6, Sun 10-4.

Located within the Gyle Shopping Centre on the 1st floor (access by lift and escalator). 'Drop-in' nursery offering 1 hr full-time placement. Fully registered with professionally qualified staff. Two large playrooms cater from ages 12 wks-2 yrs and 3-8 yrs. Good selection of toys and activities inc outside visits when suitable.

Any child staying over 2 hrs provided with snack and drink. At 4pm every day, children's tea available FREE, provided it is requested when booking in your child. Can be busy at wkends and school holidays. No advance booking

possible unless Membership taken out (£5 annually) which includes special offers and newsletter.

Ages 12wks-2yrs £2.50/1hr. Ages 2-8yrs £2/1hr. Hourly rate reduces for longer periods.

Charities Hypermarket

Many charities benefit from the Arts & Crafts sold at this annual event which takes place at the Assembly Rooms in Dec. The Women's Royal Voluntary Service run the **creche** (0-5 yrs) and donations are gratefully accepted. Dates are well publicised or phone the WRVS, 556 4284 for details.

Christmas Shoppers' Creches

Organised by Edinburgh District Council Women's Committee, the actual venue(s) change yearly but it is well advertised beforehand. It is a 'drop-in' creche and operates for 3-4 wks leading up to Christmas. Children can be left for up to 2hrs. Cost varies with location (free-£1.50). Facility may be withdrawn or curtailed due to lack of funds.

It's also worth keeping an eye out at your local shopping centre, many of whom are now seeing the benefit of providing a **creche** during the run-up to Christmas.

Toilet Stops

Public toilets are maintained by Edinburgh District Council. Some are below street level and may have a flight of steps — they are however generally very clean and staff most helpful.

Toilets shown with a ★ are shown on the map on page vi-vii with [symbol $\boxed{\text{T}}$], shops with nappy change facilities are also highlighted on the city centre map.

The following toilets have a **baby room**:

Waverley Market Shopping Centre
Open 10am-10pm, down a long flight of steps from Waverley Bridge or during the Shopping Centre's open hours on the lowest level (to the left of Café Noir Restaurant in Main food court).

Bath St: Portobello 10-10

Canonmills: 10-8

High St: South Queensferry 10-10

Taylor Gdns: Leith 10-10

West End: Princes St Gdns 10-10

No gent's toilets have provision for changing or feeding babies.

The following toilets are open 7days/wk all year:

10-10
Ardmillan Terr, Gorgie; Bath St, Portobello; Haymarket; High St, South Queensferry; Hunter Sq; London Rd; *Mound; Taylor Gdns; Leith; Tollcross; *West End.

10-8
Bruntsfield; Canaan Lane, Morningside; Canongate; Canonmills; *Castlehill; Castle Ter Car Park; Hamilton Pl, Stockbridge; *Middle Meadow Walk; Nicolson Sq; St James Centre.

10-6
Colinton Rd, Colinton; Cramond; Currie; Fairmilehead; Granton Sq, Granton; Hawes Pier, South Queensferry; Hope Park; Joppa; Juniper Green; Liberton Gdns, Liberton; Silverknowes; St John's Rd, Corstorphine; Westerhailes.

Seasonal Opening May-Sept 10-10
Pipe St, Portobello; *Ross Bandstand, Princes St Gdns; Pittville/Bellfield, Portobello.

Any comments about the Public Conveniences and their facilities — or lack of same — should be sent to: Director of Cleansing, 18/20 King's Stables Rd, Edinburgh EH1 2JZ.

Shopping from Home

How often have you thought 'there must be an easier way to shop!' whilst struggling through crowds with a pushchair, fractious children and bulging bags. Shopping with small children is NOT easy. Mail order firms have responded to this by producing catalogues filled with good quality goods which can be studied at your leisure. Listed below are some of the more popular and smaller mail order firms. Phone or send a stamped addressed envelope (sae) for a catalogue. Points to note when ordering through the post:

1) Check your information is up-to-date;
2) Read the advertisement carefully, including the small print;
3) Most firms require payment with the order (never send cash), keep a note of amount/cheque details;
4) Set a time limit for delivery (eg 28 days) and add 'Time is the essence of the contract';
5) Keep a copy of the advertisement, your order and date sent;
6) Always include your home address with any correspondence.

Citizens' Advice Bureaux, *see* Welfare p246, can assist should any problems arise.

CHILDREN'S BOOKS

Discounted books to club members. You must buy a min number of books in your first yr's membership. Postage charged.

Books for Children
PO Box 70, Cirencester, Glos GL7 7ZA
0793 420000

Monthly catalogue, book of the month sent automatically, hardbacks.

Children's Book of the Month Club
Guild House, Farnsby St, Swindon, Wilts SN99 9XX
0793 512666

Monthly catalogue, book of the month sent automatically, hardbacks and paperbacks.

My Adventure Books
PO Box 6, Bristol BS99 1FP

Hardback books with personalised stories (friends' names included).

The Red House Children's Book Club
Witney, Oxon OX8 5YF
0993 771144/774171

Monthly catalogue, no automatic selection, hardbacks and paperbacks. *See also* Party-Plan p56.

CLOTHES

Clothkits
PO Box 2500, Lewes, East Sussex BN7 3ZB
081-679 6200

Original, brightly coloured clothes 0-12 yrs and ladies. Mainly readymade but a few kits for children's clothes.

Cotton-On Ltd.
Monmouth Pl
Bath, BA1 2NP
0225 461155

Good quality, 100% cotton clothes; underclothes, tracksuits, sleepwear with mittens for babies and children, also some adult clothes.

First Needs
Kay & Co Ltd, Worcester WR1 1BR
0905 27141

Maternity and baby clothes, nursery equipment from a well-known mail order firm.

Mothercare Home Shopping
PO Box 145, Watford WD2 5SH
0923 210210

Order from the Mothercare catalogue: maternity wear, clothes 0-8 yrs and equipment. *See* Shopping p6.

Next Directory
FREEPOST 1, Leicester LE5 5DZ
0345 100500

Large catalogue, with brightly coloured babies', children's and fashionable adults' clothes. Also shoes and accessories. Charge for catalogue refunded with 1st order. See Shopping p18.

Children's Clothes

Baby Care by Dollycare
13 Elmtree Rd, Cosby, Leics
0533 773013

Clothes made especially for small babies from 1+ lbs. Reasonably priced, available locally at Jenners. *See* Department stores p4 and Nursery Equipment (NCT) p26.

Blooming Kids
Blooming Marvellous Ltd, PO Box 12F, Chessington, Surrey KT9 2LS
081 391 4822

Colourful children's clothes 0-6 yrs. Mix'n'match range, reasonably priced.

Freemans (Adams)
0800 900200

Colourful, reasonably-priced children's clothes as sold in Adams shops. *See* Shopping p14.

Kids' Stuff
10 Hensmans Hill, Bristol BS8 4PE
0117 970 6095

Send sae or phone for mail order catalogue. Comfortable cotton track-suits, T-shirts, leggings, nightwear and more!

Maternity Clothes

Blooming Marvellous
PO Box 12F, Chessington, Surrey KT9 2LS
081 391 4822

Colourful, cheerful clothes: T-shirts, leggings, shorts, dresses, night-dresses, swimsuits.

NCT Trading Ltd
Burnfield Ave, Glasgow G46 7TL
041 633 5552

MAVA bras, nightdresses and swimsuits. Also books, leaflets, breast shields and pumps, cards and gifts. All profits covenanted to the NCT. See Health Care Facilities p256.

New Conceptions
081 688 3312

Sweatshirts and smart dresses, sizes 8-22.

FOOD

Nature's Best
Health Products Ltd, 1 Lamberts Rd, FREEPOST, PO Box 1, Tunbridge Wells TN2 3EQ
0892 534143

Vitamins and dietary supplements.

Nature's Gate
83 Clerk St, Newington
668 2067

Specializes in vegetarian, vegan and macrobiotic wholefood. Usually same day service.

Real Foods Ltd
37 Broughton St, Edinburgh 557 1911 and 8 Brougham St. 228 1651

Natural and organic foods, all foods suitable for vegetarians. Mail order service available.

SHOES

Start-rite Shoes Ltd
Customer Services Officer, Crome Rd, Norwich NR3 4RD 0603 423841

Handmade shoe service for child with large difference in shoe size, costs about 25% less than the price of 2 pairs. See also Shopping, Clarks p24.

TOYS

Montrose (UK) Ltd
Tennant House, London Rd, Macclesfield, Cheshire SK11 OLW
0625 511511

Outdoor play equipment including sand and water play, at reasonable prices. Distributors of well-known brand names.

Early Learning Centre
Mail Order Dept,
South Marston, Swindon, Wilts SN3 4TJ
0793 832832

Order from catalogue by post or phone, carriage charge. Wide range of educational toys, also outdoor play equipment. See Toy Shops p28.

Frog Hollow
01672 64222

Personalised toys and gifts.

Stockingfillas
Euroway Business Park,
Swindon SN5 8SN
0793 480330

Large selection of stocking fillers with something for all ages. Party catalogue with tableware etc available to Party Club members.

The Red House Party Post
Witney, Oxford OX8 5YF
0993 779959

A good selection of tableware, stocking fillers and presents. *See also* Party-Plan p56 and Children's Books p52.

Tridias
124 Walcot St, Bath BA1 4BG
0225 469455

Wide range of toys; cheap party presents to good quality expensive dolls' houses and rocking horses.

MISCELLANEOUS

Cash's Name Tapes
J & J Cash Ltd, FREEPOST CV2176,
Coventry CV4 9BR
0203 466466

Woven name tapes, very useful when child starts at nursery etc. *See also* Shopping, John Lewis p4 and Aitken & Niven p2.

Celebration Books
PO Box 14, Hindhead, Surrey GU26 6EJ
0428 656175

Baby keepsakes and personalised christening stationery.

Cosmetics To Go
Poole, Dorset BH15 1BR
0800 373366

'Cruelty-free' toiletries for babies including shampoos, soaps, lotions and bombinos (bubble baths).

Croft Mill
Lowther Lane, Foulridge, Colne, Lancs BB8 7NG
0282 869625

Fabric by post, including sweat-shirting, corduroy and cottons. Very reasonable prices.

Heinz Baby Club
Cherry Tree Rd, Watford WD2 5SH
0923 221717

Nursery equipment, toys, and clothes for babies. Discount for members but membership is not necessary to order goods.

Lefties
PO Box 52, South DO, Manchester M20 8PJ
061 445 0159

Equipment and teaching aids for left-handers.

Nappy Days
FREEPOST EH 2855
Edinburgh EH8 0LN
659 6460

A nappy laundry service providing a cost effective environmentally friendly alternative. Free demonstration on request. Also a same day quilt laundry service with pick-up and delivery.

PARTY-PLAN

If you want to see before you buy, but avoid the shops, then party-plan buying could be for you. Agents bring samples to your home or group, and give you a % of their sales. There are several firms that sell through party-plan in Edinburgh.

Baggins
315 2011

Babies' to adults' clothes, mainly made of sweatshirting. See Shopping p15.

Child's Play
Joan Mackenzie, Area Agent
453 5793
Head Office
0800 373328

Educational and fun books, games and puzzles, from 0-12 yrs. Also available in some book shops

Dorling Kindersley Family Library
Joyce Forrester, Independent Distributor
447 8918

Choose from over 1,000 quality Dorling Kindersley books, CD roms, games and videos.

Next Best
664 5351

Secondhand toys. Hostess receives 10% of takings. See Secondhand p44.

The Red House Children's Book Club
Mrs Gillian Stewart, Area Organiser
319 2300

Selection of books available to view. Membership of club required to order books.
See Children's Books p55.

Song of Sixpence
Judy Sutherland 336 5939

Good quality secondhand clothes. Will visit homes or playgroups etc. See Shopping p44.

Swedish Rainwear
Ann Douglas
337 2899

Range of totally waterproof children's rainwear-overtrousers, all-in-one suits etc in bright colours and attractive styles. Phone for appointment.

Tryst Crafts
Lesley Protheroe
445 5789

Handmade cards for any occasion, can be personalised.

Usborne Books
Irene Sommerville, Area Agent
440 2885

Good selection of educational and storybooks. Also available in bookshops.

Hiring

Please phone in advance to make sure that what you require is available and, particularly when the business is run from home, that someone will be available to see you.

BICYCLES

Central Cycle Hire
13 Lochrin Pl
228 6333
Mon-Sat 10-5.30 all yr
Sun 10-5 Jun-Aug only

Adult bikes for hire from £8/day or £35/wk. Child bike seats £2/day or £5/wk. If you hire a bike and child seat for a wk, seat comes **FREE**. Children's helmets also for hire. From 5 yrs your child can experience the joys of cycling on a bike trailer (similar to a tandem but child has independent pedalling) £5/day.

Recycling
31-33 Iona St
553 1130
Mon-Sat 9-5.30

Adult bikes from £5/day or £25/wk. Deposit required. Also hire of children's bikes. Uplift and return can be arranged outwith shop hours. *See* Bicycle Shops p35.

CAKE TINS

The Finishing Touch
Refundable deposit, £1/night. Over 40 novelty tins to hire, plus numbers, letters, squares, hexagons etc. Good instructions.

See Shopping p22 and Birthdays and Celebrations p87.

Studio One
71 Morningside Rd,
447 0452
Mon-Sat 9.30-6

£5 deposit, £1.50/night. Letters, numbers, hearts, squares.

CLOTHES

Butterflies
29 Grassmarket
225 2476
Mon,Tue,Fri,Sat 10-5; Wed 10-1,Thur 10-7

Evening appointments by arrangement

Hire or purchase of maternity evening wear. Children welcome in shop, toilet available.

Davison Menswear
Dress Hire Shop
31-33 Bruntsfield Pl
229 0266
Mon-Fri 10-5; Sat 9-5

Hire of Highland outfits, morning suits (with tails) and top hats from age 2-adult.

Highland Laddie
Hire of complete Highland outfits including shoes, from £26. Toddler to adult sizes available. *See* Kilts p21.

McCalls of the Royal Mile
11 High St
557 3979
Mon-Sat 9-5.30;Thur 9-7.30;Sun 12-4

Hire of Highland dress for children. Kilts, jackets, accessories. From waist 16 in and chest 18 in. Toybox available.

EQUIPMENT
see also Travel and Transport p237 for car seat hire

Baby Equipment Hire
45 Glendevon Pl
337 7016
Fife Agent: 01383 (Dunfermline) 720711

Run from the proprietor's own home and can supply all baby needs, from car seats, backpacks and alarms to cots, travel cots and lightweight pushchairs. All equipment regularly checked, cleaned and serviced. Hire from one day to 3 mths. Delivery available.

Member of the Baby Equipment Hirers Assoc.

Buckstone Baby Hire
22 Buckstone Circle
445 2825

Travel cots (holdall type), lightweight pushchairs, car seats, cots, folding highchairs, door bouncers, backpacks and alarms. Run from the proprietor's own home. All equipment cleaned and checked between hires and regularly serviced and renewed. Member of Baby Equipment Hirers Assoc.

Lullaby
193 Gorgie Rd
313 2355
Mon-Sat 9.30-5

A wide variety of baby equipment available. For details please telephone.

National Childbirth Trust
Edinburgh Office
225 9191
Mon-Fri 9-12

Hire of Egnell breast pumps. Contact the office for your local agent.

See also Health Care Facilities p259.

INFLATABLES

Recent press reports have highlighted dangers relating to 'bouncy castles'. If you are hiring an inflatable please read, or listen carefully to, the instructions you are given by the hire company to ensure you avoid any unnecessary accidents.

If you are having a gala and plan to charge a fee for the use of the inflatable, there is an invaluable set of safety instructions published by The Health and Safety Exec. and do not forget your Public Liability Insurance!

A & D Hire & DIY Garden Centre
9 Featherhall Ave
334 2348 or 539 7477
Mon-Thur 8.30-8; Fri 8.30-5.30; Sat 9-5.30; Sun 10-5.

Small bouncy castles for home

indoor or outdoor use available £35/day. Large inflatable suitable for fêtes, galas also for hire.

Bennets Hire Centre
9 Meadowplace Rd
334 4545

Bouncy castles in various sizes. One ideal for young children (10' x 10') suitable for garden or indoor use, fully enclosed. Full delivery and set up service.

Monkey Business
167 Morrison St
228 6636
Mon-Sat 10-6

Clown mini-bouncer for hire, suitable for indoor or outdoor use. Full size bouncers also available. Sell a large range of balloons and hire out an automatic balloon pump.
See also Birthdays and Celebrations p87.

SKIS

Elliott Sports Ski Shop
14/15 Bruntsfield Pl
229 2402
Mon-Fri 9.30-6; Sat 9-5

Skis from 1 metre, boots from children's size 8, poles. All-in cost for skis, boots and poles approx £6/day, £22.50/wk. Phone first to check availability.
See also Ski Shops p36.

TOYS

See Toy Libraries p132.

VIDEO CAMERAS

Radio Rentals Ltd
29 Castle St
226 2929
(8 other shops in the city)

Hire a video camera to record birthday/Xmas/family celebrations. Current costs are from £12.99/day to £179.99/3 mths plus insurance — cheaper if you become a Video Camera Club Member at £5/yr. Leaflet available from all RR shops.

MISCELLANEOUS

Nappy Days - Laundry Services
See Shopping from Home p55.

Eating Out

Eating out with young children can and should be an enjoyable experience for both the parents and the children. The attitude towards children on the continent is more relaxed and tolerant, where children are welcomed at all times, and catered for.

Is there some unspoken condition to parenthood in this country that one has to shed any desire to eat outside of the home until one's children are school age and beyond?

A recent drive to make Edinburgh a more child friendly city has resulted in more entries in this section than ever before, and we look forward to seeing this trend continue.

We surveyed over 200 hotels,

restaurants, pubs and coffee shops by questionnaire and have added personal experience where possible. We have included all premises which have a high chair and other facilities, or who show a willingness to cater for parents and young children.

Pubs have a small section to themselves p82. Information is given throughout the chapter on whether establishments are licensed to serve alcohol.

Hours under the address are the hours during which your family will be made welcome, this may not necessarily be the opening hours of the establishment.

60

£ This symbol represents the approximate price of an adult main course. £ — under £3, ££ — £3-5, £££ — over £5.

High Chair Clip-on seats, booster seats — with the number of each. Remember reins!

Tables suitable for clip-ons This has been mentioned, if provision of the above may not be adequate, or for those who prefer to use their own seat.

Breastfeeding permitted This applies only to the eating area. If there is a private facility it is mentioned in the text — try to be discreet as other guests can be easily embarrassed.

Bottles heated This also applies to baby food. If you are using your own food and drink it is courteous to ask permission.

Nappy change surface What constitutes a 'good changing surface' to an experienced Mum and that of a manager with no children is very different. A shelf with a rim is so easy to install and does not take up much space, and is much more pleasant than crawling around on the floor of a public toilet. We hope more proprietors will consider providing one. (M&F) indicates where the feeding and changing facilities are available to both parents.

Family room Scottish Law does not permit pub landlords to allow children into a 'bar'. This is an area where alcohol is served. Many get around this by providing a 'family room'. This is often the function dining room which is not used during the day; it rarely has any

facilities for families and most don't feel very welcoming. However, look out for pubs with Children's Certificates, as these comply with strict rules and conditions required of a child friendly family pub.

Garden Most pub gardens are very busy in good weather. Mum and Dad can relax and the children can run about. However, if it does rain, unless there is a family room, you cannot go inside. *See also* Pubs p82.

No Smoking Area This means just what it says, and thankfully many restaurants do now provide one. Some have gone one step further and prohibit smoking throughout the entire eating area, these state simply 'No Smoking'.

Licensed Generally restaurants can only serve alcohol with food — *See* Pubs p82 if you wish a drink on its own.

Parties Hosted Contact management for details. *See also* Birthdays and Celebrations p84.

Some places cannot allow prams or pushchairs. If there is a covered area nearby we have said so, but remember your pram is your responsibility — invest in a bicycle chain for only a few pounds and this should deter most thieves.

Toilet Access should be reasonable. We have said if there are stairs or other hazards on the way.

Try to keep your child under control, for their safety as well as staff and other guests' peace of mind. The more pleasant experiences proprietors have with young children, the more they will provide the appropriate facilities.

If you are choosing a meal for a special occasion you are always best to book first mentioning that you will have children under 5 (and that you found the restaurant listed in this book), also checking the facilities that you need (some premises have had high chairs stolen between editions!). Generally hotels are best for Sunday lunch. A few have entertainment and run promotions where under 5s can eat free — check the local papers for details of current offers. All Italian restaurants make children welcome and Latin upbringing does not restrict this to lunchtime.

The establishments have been split into 5 areas: Centre (C) where the restaurants have been numbered to correspond to the locations indicated on the map pvi and vii, and North (N), South (S), East (E) and West (W). Suburban locations have the area included in the address, and you can refer these to the map on p176.

We hope we have covered everything to help you choose the most suitable venue for your meal.

Please let us know of any other places where you and your children have enjoyed a meal and any good or bad experiences in those included here — comments please to the address at the front of the book.

EATING OUT IN CENTRAL EDINBURGH

(1) **Bewleys**
4 S Charlotte St
220 1969
Mon-Sat 7.30-7; Sun 9.30-6
££, High chairs (8), breastfeeding permitted, bottles heated, nappy change room, no smoking area, licensed, seats 240.

Coffee/teashop at street level. Fixed menu with dish of the day, light snacks and vegetarian dishes; children's portions available. Push-chairs and prams allowed inside. Nappy changing (M&F) and toilets not on ground floor.

(3) **BhS Patio Restaurant**
64 Princes St
226 2621
Mon-Wed 9-5.30; Thurs 9-8; Fri 9-6; Sat 9-5.45; Sun 12.30-4.45.
££, High chairs (8), breastfeeding permitted, bottles heated, nappy change surface, no smoking area, licensed, seats 200.

Large spacious self-service restaurant. Level access from Rose Street entrance but up from main store escalator to centre of eating area — beware! Extensive choice from snacks to lunches; children's menu available for under 12s. Each high chair comes with a disposable bib, very handy if you find you have forgotten yours. Toilets and a feeding and nappy changing room up a floor (3 flights of stairs).

See also Shopping p3.

(2) **Boots Coffee Shop**
101-103 Princes St
225 8331
Mon-Sat 9-5
££, High chairs (3), breastfeeding permitted, bottles heated, nappy changing room, no smoking.

Self-service coffee shop serving light snacks. On 2nd floor, access by lift or stairs. Children's menu. Toilets on 2nd floor, nappy changing room on ground floor.

See also Shopping p3.

(5) **Burger King**
118 Princes St/Castle St
220 1644
Mon-Thurs 8am-11pm; Fri,
Sat 8am-12.30am; Sun 10am-
10.30pm
£, High chairs (8), tables suitable for clip-ons, breastfeeding permitted, bottles heated, nappy change surface, no smoking area, parties hosted, seats 250.

10-15 Princes St, East End
557 4575
Mon-Thurs 8-11.30; Fri, Sat 8-12.30;
Sun 10-11.30.
£, High chairs (6), tables suitable for clip-ons, breastfeeding permitted, bottles heated, nappy change surface, no smoking area, parties hosted.

Fast food counter service restaurants, both on 2 floors (great views of the castle from no. 118). Hostesses available to help parents and children. There is often a promotional gift offered with chilren's meals. Toilets and nappy changing room on the ground floor at no.118 and on the first floor at no. 10.

(50) **Cafe St James**
St James' Centre (upper level)
557 2631
Mon-Sat 9-6
££, High chairs (2), bottles heated, nappy change surface, no smoking area, licensed, seats 200.

Spacious bar/restaurant on the upper level of the centre, with a terrace area overlooking the shopping mall. Access by lift or stairs. Children are welcomed in the coffee bar and a side section of the self-service restaurant. Varied menu including Mexican, Chinese and vegetarian dishes, children's portions available. Toilets on same level, a

chair will be provided in the ladies' room for breastfeeding, on request.
See also Shopping p9.

(56) **Cafe Rioz**
Waverley Market (lower level)
558 1138
Mon-Sun 9-6
££, High chairs (1), booster seats (2), breastfeeding permitted, bottles heated, no smoking area, licensed, seats 150.

Situated beside the Food Court (access by lift and escalators), this cafe serves a range of light snacks and meals. Children's dishes highlighted on the menu. Pleasant atmosphere and staff. Changing facilities available in nearby baby room/toilet for the disabled.
See also Shopping p9.

(6) **Caledonian Hotel**
Princes St, W End
225 2433
Mon-Sun 12 noon-2.30 pm, 6.30 pm-10.30 pm
£££, High chairs (3), bottles heated, nappy changing surface, courtyard garden, no smoking area, licensed, seats 160.

The Carriage restaurant is a spacious informal restaurant serving hot and cold meals. A buffet is available on Sun. Children's menu provided. There is a chair in the powder room for breastfeeding.

(8) **Circles Coffee House**
324 Lawnmarket
225 9505
Mon-Sun 10-6
££, breastfeeding permitted, bottles heated, tables suitable for clip-ons, licensed, seats 60.

Self-service restaurant near the Castle. Home-baking, salads. Children's portions available.

(9) **City Art Centre**
7 Market St
220 3359
Mon-Sat 8.30-5 (winter); Mon-Sat 8.30-6, Sun 12.30-5 (summer)
££ High chairs (2), breastfeeding permitted,bottles heated, no smoking, nappy change surface, licensed, seats 72.

Self-service café bar/bistro, prt of the Art Centre. Serves light snacks & vegetarian dishes. Children's portions, baby food available. Welcoming to all ages of children, occasional exhibitions aimed at young children as well as adults to encourage social mixing.

(10) **City Cafe**
19 Blair St
220 0125
Mon-Sun 11-8
££, High chairs (1), tables suitable for clip-ons, breastfeeding permitted, bottles heated, nappy change surface (M&F), licensed, seats 100.

Friendly café bar serving varied light snacks and meals, children's portions available. Toy box offers entertainment to tots. Toilet for disabled on ground floor, more toilets in basement. Access to cafe up small flight of steps.

(11) **Cornerstone Cafe**
St John's Church, Lothian Rd (corner with Princes St)
229 0212
Mon-Fri 9.30-4, Sat 9.30-5 later in Aug
£, clip-ons (3), breastfeeding permitted, bottles heated, nappy change surface, no smoking, seats 70.

Basement restaurant under church, serving vegetarian and vegan wholefoods, coffee, choice of herbal and Indian teas, and home-baking.

Access by steps or ramp from Princes St. The restaurant has a quiet seating area outside. Toilets up steps.

(7) **Crannog Seafood Restaurant**
14 S St Andrews St
557 5589
Mon-Sat 12-2.30; 6-10pm.
£££, High chair (1), breastfeeding permitted, bottles heated, tables suitable for clip ons, nappy change surface (M&F), pushchairs allowed, no smoking area, licensed, seat 60 floor.

Self-service café/bar on ground floor serving light snacks, children's portions available. Restaurant in basement serving Scottish seafood from own boat and smokehouse. Fixed dish of the day, vegetarian dishes. Toilets in basement.

(12) **Crawfords Country Kitchen**
90 Princes St
225 4469
Mon-Sat 8-6.30; Thurs 8-7.30; Sun 11-5,
££, High chairs (2), 2 tables suitable for clip-ons, breastfeeding permitted, bottles heated, no smoking area, licensed, seats 110.

A few steps down and along a corridor into large self-service restaurant. Varied menu, children's menu, home-cooking as well as fast food.

(50) **Crawfords Country Kitchen**
St James Centre
556 3098
Mon-Sat 8-5.15
££, High chairs (3), tables suitable for clip-ons, breastfeeding permitted, bottles heated, no smoking area, seats 100.

Self-service 'country kitchen' restaurant with very easy access. Nappy change facilities in the Ladies,

but dads may use the office on request.
See also Shopping p9.

(13) **Debenhams**
Freebody's Restaurant (4th floor)
Mon-Wed 9-5; Thurs 9-7.30; Fri, Sat 9-5.30.
£, *High chairs (5), breastfeeding permitted, bottles heated, nappy change surface, no smoking, seats 96.*

Large self-service restaurant with excellent views of Castle. Varied menu including hot food, salads and baking. Children's menu, baby food available. Toilets and Mother's rooms nearby. *See also* Shopping p3.

(14) **Délifrance**
7/8 Queensferry St
220 0474
Mon-Fri 8-6, Sat 8-6, Sun 10-5,winter; Mon-Sat 8-8pm, Sun 8-6 summer & Dec
££, *High chairs (3), breastfeeding permitted, bottles heated, no smoking area, seats 60.*

French style products prepared and baked on the premises, light snacks and vegetarian dishes, waitress service. Novelty carton containing French bread pizza, pastries and juice for children. Carry-out food, delivery within the city. Toilets on first floor, toilet for the disabled on ground floor. Pushchairs allowed, folded is preferred.

(15) **Fat Sams**
The Old Meat Market
Fountainbridge
228 3111
Mon-Sun 12 noon-late.
£££, *High chairs (7), tables suitable for clip-ons, breastfeeding permitted, bottles heated, nappy change surface, licensed, seats 250.*

Friendly waiter service American-style restaurant with a lively atmosphere. Large automated puppets hang from the ceiling, huge tanks with fish, including piranha, plus a phantom piano. Emphasis is 'Italo-american' dishes, vegetarian dishes and children's menu. Live jazz Tues-Thurs evenings. Booking advisable, ask for high chairs if required.

(16) **The Filling Station**
235 High St
226 2488
Mon-Sun 12-mnight
££, *High chairs (3), tables suitable for clip-ons, breastfeeding permitted, bottles heated, nappy change surface, licensed, seats 120.*

Children welcome in the eating area of this bar/restaurant. Car theme throughout, fun atmosphere, TV and video provide entertainment for both parents and children. American, Mexican and Italian food, children's portions. Changing area adjacent to toilet for the disabled. A chair can be provided for feeding in ladies room.

(17) **Frasers**
145 Princes St
Mon, Wed, Fri, Sat 9-5.30; Tues 9.30-5.30; Thurs 9-7.30
££, *High chairs (2), bottles heated, nappy change surface, no smoking area, seats 150.*

5th floor self-service restaurant with easy access from lifts. Spacious eating area, children's menu. Toilets nearby. Mother and Baby room on ground floor, (ask for directions as it is not signposted.) *See also* Shopping p4.

(19) **Garfunkels**
31 Frederick St
225 4579
Mon-Sun 12-11.30 (open from 10 for tea/coffee)

£££, *High chairs (12), tables suitable for clip-ons, breastfeeding permitted, nappy change surface, bottles heated, no smoking area, licensed, parties hosted.*

Comfortable, waitress-service restaurant serving a wide range of food including a children's menu. All children receive a bag containing 'goodies'. Toilets in basement.

(20) **Gennaro**
64 Grassmarket
226 3706
Mon-Sun 12-mnight
££, *Clip-on seats (2), breastfeeding permitted, bottles heated, licensed, seats 60.*

Traditional Italian restaurant, where families are always welcome. Varied menu with children's portions available. No prams, pushchairs folded. If not too busy, waiters like to entertain children, allowing parents to enjoy their meal in peace. Carry-out food available.

(21) **George Hotel**
19-21 George St, E end
225 1251
Mon-Sun 12-3, 6.30-10.
£££, *High chairs, bottles heated, nappy change surface, no smoking area, licensed, seats 160.*

Large spacious hotel 'welcomes children in all areas of the hotel'. The Carvers Table restaurant would make a delightful treat for a special occasion. Children enjoy seeing the roasts being sliced especially for them. The 'Bedrock Menu' children's menu has quizzes and pictures of each dish. Ladies' rest room in the back lounge suitable for feeding.

(22) **Granary**
42-45 Queensferry St
220 0550

Mon-Fri 7.30-8pm; Sat 7.30-6; Sun 9.30-8
£££, High chairs (2), tables suitable for clip-ons, bottles heated, nappy change surface (M&F), licensed, seats 93.

Cafe bar offering a range of European dishes. Children's portions available.

(24) Helios Fountain
7 Grassmarket
229 7884
Mon-Sat 10-6, Aug 10-8; Sun 11-5, Aug 11-6 .
££, High chair (1), breastfeeding permitted, bottles heated, nappy change surface, no smoking, seats 35.

Friendly self-service, wholefood, vegetarian and vegan restaurant using mainly organically grown produce, half portions available. Stools for seating may be tricky for toddlers or feeding, but benches at wall are fine. Basket of toys to help keep children amused. The cafe is found behind a shop selling books, toys and craft materials.

(25) Hendersons
94 Hanover St
225 2131
Mon-Sat 8-10.30; Sun 9-9 in Festival
££, High chairs (4), tables suitable for clip-ons, breastfeeding permitted, bottles heated, nappy change surface (M&F), no smoking area, licensed, seats 180.

Basement buffet restaurant serving broad range of vegetarian and vegan food. Half portions served and lovely snacks for finger foods. Quiet alcoves make pushchair access tricky, but good for breastfeeders. Carry-out service available.

(26) Jenners ✔
Rose St restaurant (1st floor)
Mon, Wed, Fri 9.30-5; Tues 10-5; Thurs 9.30-7; Sat 9-5.
£, High chairs (2), tables suitable for clip-ons; breastfeeding permitted, bottles heated, nappy change surface (M&F), no smoking area, licensed, seats 138.

There are 4 restaurants in Jenners, Rose St being the most suitable for children. Large self-service restaurant, children's portions served. Prams and unfolded push-chairs allowed. Toilets and changing facilities 3rd floor.

The Precinct Restaurant (Rose St, across from main shop)

The Precinct Restaurant also has a children's menu and adjacent toilets, and is just upstairs from Junior Jenners.

See Department Stores p4.

(50) John Lewis ✔
The Place to Eat (St James' Centre)
556 9121
Tues, Wed, Thurs 9.30-5.15; Thurs 9.45-7.15; Sat 9.30-5.45
££, Highchairs (6), bottles and food heated, breastfeeding permitted, feeding and changing facilities available (M&F), no smoking, licensed, seats 206.

A large self-service restaurant in John Lewis (2nd floor) with pleasant views from the large windows. Easy access by lifts. Vegetarian dishes available as well as children's portions. Several different fast-food outlets to choose from. Plenty of room for prams and pushchairs.

See Department Stores p4.

(27) The Kennilworth
152-154 Rose St
225 8100

££, *Breastfeeding permitted, bottles heated as well as baby food, family room, licensed.*

Pub in the pedestrian part of Rose St. The family room is reached most easily from the rear in Rose St Lane, it is on the right just inside the doors. Traditional Scottish pub fare, children's menu available. No nappy change facility and no high chairs.

See Pubs p82.

(28) Lazio Restaurant
95 Lothian Rd
229 7788
Mon-Sun 12-late
££, *Clip-ons (1), breastfeeding permitted, bottles heated, licensed, seats 60.*

Families welcomed at this restaurant, as is typical of all Italian establishments. Varied menu, children's portions available.

(29) Littlewoods
Mon-Fri 9-5; Sat 9-5.30
£, *High chairs (5), tables suitable for clip-ons, bottles heated, nappy change surface, no smoking area, seats 400.*

Spacious and popular, self-service basement restaurant. 'Traditional food' as well as having a small selection of jarred baby foods and juices available. Lift access. Toilets and changing facilities ground floor.

See Shopping p5.

(30) Lorenzo's
5 Johnston Ter
226 2426
Mon-Sun 12-11
£££, *Clip-on seats (2), breastfeeding permitted, bottles heated, licensed, seats 80.*

Italian restaurant where children are welcomed. Children's portions, crayons and colouring books avail-able. Children may help prepare their pizza when the restaurant is not too busy. Carry-out service provided. Easier access via rear of the building to avoid a flight of stairs.

(31) Lower Aisle Restaurant
St Giles Cathedral, Parliament Sq, High St
225 5147
Mon-Fri 10-4.30; Sun 10-2; Sat 10-4.30 in Festival
£, *High chairs (1), tables suitable for clip-ons, breastfeeding permitted, bottles heated, no smoking area, seats 65.*

Spacious self-service restaurant. Soup, rolls, light snacks. Fraternised by the legal profession. It often gets very busy, especially after services and with tourists visiting the Cathedral. Friendly staff. Toilets in basement.

See also Places to Visit p182.

(32) McDonalds Restaurant
137 Princes St
226 3872
Mon-Sun 8 am-mnight
£, *High chairs (10), clip-on seats (10), booster seats (10), tables suitable for clip-ons (2), breastfeeding permitted, bottles heated, nappy change surface (M&F), family area, no smoking area, parties hosted, seats 160.*

Spacious fast food restaurant over 3 floors. Burgers, milk shakes, etc. Children's area with small yellow tables with toadstool seats at rear of first floor. Toilets nearby have child height sinks and driers (no more toddlers with wet armpits!) there is a 'McDonalds Changing Station' in the entrance foyer of the toilet for the disabled on the right of the ground floor.

See also Birthdays and Celebrations p85.

(33) The Malt Shovel
11/15 Cockburn St
225 6843
Mon-Sat 12-8; Sun 12.30-2.15 pm
£, Tables suitable for clip-ons, breastfeeding permitted, bottles heated, nappy change surface (small), seats 100.

Children welcomed in the food bar area of this pub. Self-service food, children's portions available in most dishes. Prams and pushchairs allowed depending on how busy. **Toilets** down 4 steps.

(34) Mamma's American Pizza Co ✔
30 Grassmarket
225 6464
Sun-Thurs 11-late; Fri, Sat 11-mnight
££, clip-ons (1), booster seat (1), breastfeeding permitted, bottles heated, licensed, seats 60.

Fun, unpretentious restaurant serving various North American starters and pizzas. 'We don't discriminate against children, they are people too!' Children can choose any of the freshly made toppings for their pizza (and the baby can chew the crusts!). Pizzas to take away. Drawing pad provided for children while they wait. No nappy changing facilities.

(35) John Menzies ✔
Princes St
Mon-Sat 9-5.30; Thurs 9-6.30
£, High chairs (4), breastfeeding permitted, bottles heated, nappy change surface, no smoking area.

Spacious self-service café on 1st floor, access by lifts at rear of the store. A range of light snacks and children's dishes available. Toilets nearby.
See Shopping p6.

(36) The Netherbow
See Places to Visit p187.

(37) The Pancake Place
35 Shandwick Pl
228 6322
Mon-Sat 7.45 am-8 pm, Sun 11-7
£, High chairs (2), clip-ons (4), breastfeeding permitted, bottles heated, nappy change surface, no smoking area, licensed, seats 100.

130 High St
225 1972
Mon-Fri 8-5; Sat 10-6; Sun 10.30-6
£, High chairs (3), tables suitable for clip-ons, breastfeeding permitted, bottles heated, nappy change surface, licensed, seats 100.

Waitress service, children's menu available. As the name suggests, specialists in pancakes, savoury (meat and non-meat), sweet fillings, baking. Families warmly welcomed.

(18) Piazza Open Air Café
W Princes St Gardens
See Parks and Playgrounds p211.

(39) Pizza Hut
36 Hanover St
226 3652
Mon-Thurs, Sun 11.30-11.30; Fri, Sat 11.30-mnight
££, High chairs (5), booster seats (1), breastfeeding permitted, bottles heated, no smoking area, licensed, parties hosted, seats 120.

113-117 Lothian Rd
228 2920
Sun-Thurs 11-mnight; Fri, Sat 12-mnight
££, High chairs (4), booster seats (2), breastfeeding permitted, bottles heated, nappy change surface (M&F), no smoking area, licensed, parties hosted, seats 90.

46 North Bridge
226 3038

Mon-Sun 12-11.30; Sat 12-mnight
££, *High chairs (4), booster seats (2), breastfeeding permitted, bottles heated, nappy change surface, no smoking area, licensed, parties hosted, seats 99.*

All restaurants have a children's menu which has suggestions from the adult menu. Salad bar. Some have rusks available. Crayons are provided to colour in their placemat which is then entered into a competition within the branch and winner sent off to compete with other branches for a larger competition. All have ground floor seating accommodation. Carry-out food available. *See* Birthdays and Celebrations p86.

(42) **Pizzaland**
15 Castle St
225 2801
Mon-Sat 9.30-11pm; Sun 12-10.
££, *High chairs (3), booster seats (1), tables suitable for clip-ons, breastfeeding permitted, bottles heated, nappy change surface, no smoking area, licensed, parties hosted, seats 96.*

5a Frederick St
225 8187
Mon-Sat 9.30-11pm; Sun 12-10.
££, *High chairs (1), tables suitable for clip-ons, breastfeeding permitted, bottles heated, no smoking area, licensed, parties hosted, seats 72.*

7/9 Hanover St
225 4808
Mon-Sat 9.30-11pm; Sun 12-11; Food Mon-Sat 11-11 prior to this time drinks and Danish pastries only.
££, *High chairs (7), tables suitable for clip-ons, breastfeeding permitted, bottles heated, no smoking area, licensed, parties hosted, seats 126.*

56 North Bridge (on corner of High St)

225 2044
Mon-Sat 9.30-11; Sun 12-10. Later in Festival
££, *High chairs (2), breastfeeding permitted, bottles heated, no smoking area, licensed, parties hosted, seats 90.*

All Pizzalands have a children's menu, pizza, baked potatoes, etc. Large varied help-yourself salad bar, and a range of vegetarian dishes available. Staff often hand out crayons (to colour in menu) or hats. Most have 2 floor eating areas and the toilets are always up or downstairs.

(46) **Place Pigalle**
44 Candlemaker Row
220 2580
Mon, Wed 8.30-5.30; Thurs, Fri 8.30-10; Sat 10-10; Sun 10-5.30
££, *Breastfeeding permitted, table suitable for clip-ons, bottles and food heated, no smoking, licensed, seats 50.*

Charming little bistro in the old part of Edinburgh. The staff are friendly and helpful and will even assist you by opening doors. Prams and pushchairs permitted, but as there is limited space preferably folded. There is a small box of toys to entertain the children. Vegetarian dishes available as well as dishes of the day and light snacks. Toilets (ladies) on the ground floor (no nappy changing facilities). More room upstairs. Waitress service.

(47) **Round Table Restaurant**
31 Jeffrey St
557 3032
Mon-Sat 10-5.30; dinner Tues-Sat 6.30-10.
£, *High chairs (1), breastfeeding permitted, bottles heated, no smoking area, licensed, seats 40.*

Small friendly restaurant specialising

in international dishes, serves open sandwiches and slices of gateaux at lunchtime, half portions available.

(48) Royal Museum of Scotland ✔
Museum Cafe
Mon-Sat 10-4.30; Sun 12-4.30
£, *High chairs, Breastfeeding permitted, bottles and baby food heated, no smoking area, parties hosted.*

Pleasant airy and spacious self-service cafe selling light snacks and home-baking. Small toilet.
See Places to Visit p178.

St Andrew Square Bus Station Cafe
See Travel and Transport p238.

St James' Centre
See Cafe St James p63, Crawford's Country Kitchen p64, John Lewis Restaurant p67, and St James' Food Court p71.

(50) St James' Food Court
St James' Centre (upper level)
558 3756
Mon-Sat 8.30-5.15; Thurs 8.30-7.15
£, *Highchairs (15), breastfeeding permitted, bottles heated, nappy change surface (M&F), no smoking area, seats 400.*

A spacious and light food court overlooking shopping thoroughfare. 4 counter-service fast food outlets sharing a common eating area, and 2 waitress service areas. A variety of meals available from light snacks and coffee, to Chinese or American meals, or fish and chips. Children's portions served. Carry out food available.

Occasionally have special offers on meals and look out for children's entertainment, especially on public hols or wkends. Santa's Grotto at Christmas.

Easy access from ground level by escalator or lift (corner by Dolcis).

Toilets and nappy changing room on same level.

(51) Scandic Crown Hotel
80 High St, The Royal Mile
557 9797
Open for lunch and dinner each day.
££, *High chairs available, tables suitable for clip-ons, breastfeeding permitted, bottles heated, nappy change surface, no smoking area, licensed, seats 90.*

Situated right on the Royal Mile, why not try something a little different, an authentic Scandinavian Smorgasbord in the Carrubbers Restaurant. Children's menu and vegetarian choices available. Ladies' cloakroom can be used for feeding and changing. Access to the Carrubbers level by lift of stairs (one floor down from reception). On-site car parking available.

(52) James Thin Bookshop Café
57 George St
Mon 8-5; Tues-Fri 9.30-9; Sat 8-5; Sun 11.15-4.30
££, *High chairs (2), breastfeeding permitted, bottles heated, nappy change surface, no smoking area, seats 120.*

Self-service café on 1st floor, offering a varied menu, accommodating most tastes. Child portions available. Tables in corners and balcony, quite private for feeding mothers. Toilets and changing room near to restaurant. Willing and helpful staff.
See also Shopping p41.

(53) Traverse Theatre
10 Cambridge St
228 1404

Mon-Sat 10.30-8; Sun 12-5
££, *High chairs, breastfeeding, bottles heated, nappy change surface, no smoking area, licensed, seats 56.*

A spacious and open café and bar with friendly and welcoming staff. The waitress service café serves a wide range of vegetarian dishes and homebaking supplied by Henderson's; children's portions are available. Lift to café bar and theatres, newspapers and board games.

There's a good wine list and American and continental beers are available at the bar. The atmosphere is very relaxed; there's plenty of space for toddlers to run around; it's centrally located. An ideal place for parents with young children to enjoy a drink, a coffee and something to eat.

(54) **Trusthouse Forte Coffee Shop**
Top Shop (5th floor)
30 Princes St
557 4578
Mon-Sat 9.30-5
££, *High chairs (2), clip-on seats (3), breastfeeding permitted (at the back please), bottles heated, no smoking area, seats 130.*

Fairly easy access through racks of clothes to lift and up to buffet style restaurant. Children's menu available and promotions often run which include free meals and drinks for under 12s. The office may be used for nappy changing on request.

(55) **Verandah Restaurant**
17 Dalry Rd, Haymarket
337 5828
Mon-Sun 12-2, 5.30-7
£££, *High chair, tables suitable for clip-ons, breastfeeding permitted, bottles heated, licensed, seats 72.*

A friendly Indian restaurant with a very high culinary standard. Children's portions served, and crayons and colouring books provided to keep little ones amused.

(56) **Waverley Foodcourt**
Located on the Lower Level, Waverley Shopping Centre, Princes Street.
Mon-Sat 8.30-6.30; Thurs 8.30-7.30; Sun 11.00-5.00. Open longer hours during the Festival and Christmas.
£, *high chairs (5), breastfeeding permitted, bottles heated, nappy change surface (M&F), no smoking area.*

The newly refurbished foodcourt is a very exciting place for children. Pools, fountains and sculptures all keep youngsters amused. Situated on the lower floor, access via escalators or a small glass lift and there can be a bit of a wait for the lift are nine self-service fast food outlets. They share a large common eating area. Many do half portions and children's specials. You are sure to find something your child will enjoy. Baby changing unit situated next to the superloo toilets.

See also Shopping p9.

(56) **Waverley Market**
See above for Cafe Rioz, Waverley Food Court and Waverley Wharf.

(57) **Waverley Station**
See Travel and Transport p240.

(56) **Waverley Wharf**
Waverley Centre (lowest level)
558 1991
Mon-Sun 9 am-1 am
£££, *High chairs (3), breastfeeding permitted, bottles heated, nappy change surface (M&F), no smoking area, licensed, seats 235.*

Children warmly welcomed into the restaurant area of this wharf theme bar/restaurant. Dark and intriguing, there's lots to see and do, with videos, TV and hand-held video games to entertain.

Varied menu including vegetarian and vegan dishes. Very reasonable children's menu.

Toilets and baby changing room nearby.

See also Shopping p9.

EATING OUT IN EAST EDINBURGH

Chiquito
6 Kinnaird Park, Newcraighall
657 4444
Mon-Sat 12-11; Sun 12.30-10.30
£, High chairs (7), booster seats (5), breastfeeding permitted, excellent nappy change surface, licensed.

Bright and airy Mexican restaurant. Exciting children's menu which doubles up as colouring page (crayons provided for each child).

See also Shopping p8.

Deep Pan Pizza Co
Kinnaird Park, Newcraighall
669 0839
Sun-Thur 11.30-11; Fri, Sat 11.30-mnight
£, High chairs (3), breastfeeding permitted, nappy change surface.

Large pizza restaurant at same handy location as Chiquito. Varied menu with excellent salad bar, children's menu, good sized portions.

See also Shopping p8.

Lady Nairne Hotel
228 Willowbrae Rd
661 3396
Bar Mon-Sun 12-10; Restaurant Mon-Sat 12-2.30, 5-10.30; Sun 12-10.30

£££, High chairs (2), breastfeeding permitted, bottles heated, no smoking area, nappy changing facilities, children's license, parties hosted, seats 110.

Steak House restaurant within hotel. Colouring books and crayons to keep youngsters amused. Chairs in ladies suitable for feeding. Children's menu (to 8 yrs), Junior diner's menu (to 14 yrs).

McDonald's
Kinnaird Park, Newcraighall
657 5363
Mon-Sun 8-11pm
£, High chairs (6), booster seats (6), tables suitable for clip-ons, breastfeeding permitted, bottles heated, nappy changing facilities (M&F), parties hosted, seats 100.

Spacious fast-food restaurant with drive-through window service. McVideo machine showing cartoons. Children's menu. *See also* shopping p8.

Refreshment Room
Portobello Swimming Centre
Bellfield St
657 2210
Mon-Fri 9-7.30; Sat 9-3.30; Sun 9-3.30.
£, High chair (2), breastfeeding permitted, use of the refreshment room alone is permitted.

Refreshment room run by women's co-operative, home-cooking, vegetarian, kids' corner, toys/books.

See also Activities for Children p147.

EATING OUT IN NORTH EDINBURGH

Giuliano's on the Shore
1 Commercial St, Leith
554 5272
Mon-Fri 12-2, 6-10.30; Sat 12-11; Sun 12-10.30

£££, High chairs (8), tables suitable for clip-ons, breastfeeding permitted, bottles heated, nappy changing room, licensed, parties hosted, seats 120. Carry-out food available.

Children are the mainstay of this lively Italian restaurant. Children's menu and can cater for any diet. Children can make their own pizzas. Toys and books available. Access good. Toilets on ground floor. Space for prams and pushchairs.

Hilton National Hotel
69 Belford Rd
332 2545
Restaurant: Mon-Sun 6.30-10
The Granary (food): Mon-Sun 12-2, 6-9
£££ (Restaurant), ££ (Granary), High chairs (3), tables suitable for clip-ons, breastfeeding permitted, bottles heated, nappy change surface (M&F), no smoking area, licensed.

A la carte, self-service and pub food are all served in different areas of this large hotel. Keep a close eye on junior as there is an open fire, indoor and outdoor water features with goldfish, and the Water of Leith nearby. A conjuror is available at Sun lunch, and there are always books and crayons to hand.

See Walks and Country Places, (Water of Leith) p230.

The Peacock Inn
Lindsay Rd
552 8707
Mon-Fri 11-2.30, 4.30-11; Sat, Sun 11-11. Food served Mon-Fri 11-2.30, 4.30-11. Sat, Sun 11-11.
££, High chairs (6), breastfeeding permitted, bottles heated, feeder beakers, licensed.

Large table service family room in this 'inn' on the Forth. Extensive bar menu including soup, salads, fish, steak. Children's menu.

Pierre Victoire
5 Dock Pl
555 6178
Mon-Sat 12-3, 6-8; Sun 12-3.
££, High chairs (2), breastfeeding permitted, children's portions, bottles heated, nappy change surfaces (M&F), licensed, parties hosted, seats 90.

Economical, quality French food is served in this friendly restaurant. Eating area and toilets on the ground floor. Space for pushchairs and prams.

Ping On
28 Deanhaugh St
332 3621
Mon-Sat 12-2; 5.30-mnight; Sun 5-mnight
£££, High chairs (3), breastfeeding permitted, bottles heated, nappy change surface, licensed, seats 97.

Friendly Chinese restaurant with children's portions available. Parties hosted at wkends.

Rachael's Tearoom
Royal Botanical Garden
See Walks and Country Places p228.

Scottish National Gallery of Modern Art
Café
Mon-Sat 10.30-4.30; Sun 2-4.30 (Lunch 12-2.30)
£, clip-on seat (1), breastfeeding permitted, bottles heated, feeder beakers, no smoking area, licensed.

Access by lift to self-service café in basement. Delicious home-cooked soups, hot meals, salads and cakes. Vegetarian meals.

See Places to Visit p175.

The Tattler
23 Commercial St
554 9999

Mon-Fri 10.30-2, 6-10; Sat 10.30-10; Sun 11.30-10
££-£££, High chairs (2), tables suitable for clip-ons, breastfeeding permitted, bottles heated, nappy change facilities, licensed, seats 100.
A traditional style bar and restaurant, the emphasis heavily on food. The comfortable surroundings enable parents to enjoy themselves while being made welcome with their children. Varied menu with children's portions served.

The Telford Arms
78 Telford Rd
332 4647
Mon-Sun 11-4.30
££, High chairs (2), tables suitable for clip-ons, breastfeeding permitted, bottles heated, nappy change surface (M&F), no smoking area, licensed, seats 70.
Families are warmly welcomed in the lounge area of this bar. There is a fixed but varied menu, and a children's menu, with waitress service. Toys and crayons available to entertain young children.

Theatre Workshop
Hamilton Pl
225 7942
Mon-Sat 10-5. Later during Festival.
£, High chair (1), breastfeeding permitted, bottles heated, no smoking in main cafe area, licensed, seats 40.
Unpretentious, self-service cafe. Varied menu including vegetarian. Room for pushchairs.

EATING OUT IN SOUTH EDINBURGH

Braid Hills Hotel
Buckstone Bistro
134 Braid Rd
447 8888

Mon - Sat 11.00- 9.00
££ High chairs (3), breastfeeding permitted, bottles and baby food heated, nappy change surface (F), no smoking area, licensed, seats 70.
Families welcome in bistro serving varied menu. Children's menu available.

A wide choice in lovely surroundings without being costly. Waitress service. No prams.

Brattisani
85/87 Newington Rd,
667 5808
Mon-Sun 9.30am-12mnight (teas and coffees), 11.30am-11pm (meals)
£, High chair (1), breastfeeding permitted, bottles heated, seats 40.
A fish and chip shop fronts this friendly restaurant and this is reflected in the menu. Waitress service. Children's portions served

The Bruntsfield Hotel
(The Potting Shed Restaurant)
69 Bruntsfield Pl
229 1393
Mon-Sat 12-2, 6-10; Sun 12.30-2, 6-10
£££, High chairs (2), tables suitable for clip-ons, breastfeeding permitted, bottles heated, nappy change surface, no smoking area, licensed, seats 70.
Waitress-service brasserie in conservatory of large hotel serving a wide range of good food. Listed in Egon Ronay and Peaudouce guides. Children's menu. Room available for feeding.

Conservatory Coffee Shop
Klondyke Garden Centre
Frogston Rd E
666 2471
Mon-Fri 10-5; Sat 9.30-5; Sun 10-5
£, High chairs (2), breastfeeding

permitted, bottles heated, no smoking area, seats 80.

Self-service restaurant situated within garden centre. Friendly, relaxed atmosphere. Children's portions served. Outdoor play area. Live fish, birds and animals in garden centre pet shop will appeal to children.

De Niro's Ristorante
140 Nicolson St
662 4185
Mon-Sat 12-2.30, 5.30-11.30; Sun 5-11.30
££, High chairs (2), clip-on seats (1), breastfeeding permitted, bottles heated, no smoking area, licensed, seats 70.

Families welcomed in Italian restaurant. Books and lollipops available and children can help to make their own pizza. 'We will make them feel like grown-ups'.

The Engine Shed Cafe
Garvald Community Enterprises
19 St Leonard's Lane
662 0040
Mon- Thu 10.30-3.30; Fri 10.30-2.30; The cafe is now open at weekends. Sat 10.30- 4.00; Sun 11.00- 4.00 (Check opening hrs during holiday periods)
£, High chairs (6), tables suitable for clip-ons, breastfeeding permitted, bottles heated, nappy change surface (M&F), no smoking, seats 50.

Run by Garvald Community Enterprises, the Engine Shed houses a bakery, as well as bright, cheerful vegetarian cafe on the 1st floor, accessed by lift or stairs. Reasonably-priced menu changes daily and children's portions are available. All the food is made on the premises. Carry-out service, delivery within the City and outside catering available.

Children made very welcome. Relaxed atmosphere and friendly staff. Toilet for the disabled on the ground floor and toilets adjacent to cafe. Moveable nappy changing unit suitable for use in Ladies or Gents.

See also Toy Libraries p132, Health Care Facilities p?and Shopping p29.

The Infilling Coffee Shop
94/96 Marchmont Cres
447 6477
Mon- Sat 10.30- 4.30.
££ High chairs (2), breastfeeding permitted, bottles and baby foods heated. No smoking. Seats 32

Families welcomed in this light and airy coffee shop. Light snacks and meals served. Fixed menu with dish of the day, vegetarian food and children's portions available. Waitress service. Carry-out service. Children's corner with a small table, 2 chairs, books, crayons and Lego.

Ample space for prams and pushchairs.

Friendly and caring staff serve you in a peaceful atmosphere.

The Iona Hotel
17 Strathearn Pl
447 5050
Mon-Sat 12-2, 6.30-9; Sun 12-2, 6.30-8.30
££, High chairs (2), breastfeeding permitted, bottles heated, nappy change surface, garden, licensed, seats 100.

Good value bar food served in family lounge. Restaurant also welcomes children. Children's portions available. Parents can enjoy their meals with relative freedom for the children. Listed in the AA, RAC and Michelin guides. Ladies toilet with nappy change surface upstairs. Gents downstairs, no nappy facilities.

Little Chef
46 Dreghorn Link, City By-pass
441 3497
Mon-Sun 7am-10pm
££, High chairs (3), tables suitable for clip-ons, breastfeeding permitted, bottles heated, nappy change surface in toilet for disabled, no smoking area, licensed, seats 108.
Good choice of menu. Friendly, efficient service and free lollipops for children when they leave. Free baby foods served on a specially designed baby dish. Prams and pushchairs to be left at entrance.
Coffe shop area for quick snacks and service.

The Merlin
168-172 Morningside Rd
447 4329
Sun - Thur 10am- 12mnight; Fri,Sat 10am- 1am
££, High chairs (4), tables suitable for clip-ons, breastfeeding permitted, bottles heated, nappy change surface (M&F), licensed, seats 60.
Spacious bar/bistro open from 10am for coffees and patisserie. Wide variety of snacks, hot meals, popular vegetarian counter and salad bar available until 6pm. Evening menu served 6pm - 9.30pm Friendly staff, waitress service. Children's menu and 'Kiddies Cocktails' available all day. Easy access (ramp at front of building), car park to rear. Toilets for the disabled.

Mr Boni's
4-8 Lochrin Buildings, Gilmore Place
229 5319
Mon-Fri 10.30-10.30; Sat 10.30am-11.30pm; Sun 12.30-9.30, (counter service only for final + hr daily).
££, High chairs (2), booster cushion (1), breastfeeding permitted, bottles heated, nappy change surface, no smoking area, licensed, parties hosted, seats 60.
Ice cream parlour which also sells burgers etc. Monumental ice cream sweets will have toddlers' eyes huge with wonder. Shop at front sells take-away sizes. Toilets downstairs. *See also* Birthdays and Celebrations p85 & p88.

The Old Bordeaux Coachhouse
47 Old Burdiehouse Rd
664 1734
Mon-Sun 12-10
££, High chairs (4), tables suitable for clip-ons, breastfeeding permitted, bottles heated, nappy change surface, no smoking area, licensed, seats 95.
Children welcome in restaurant serving French food. Children's portions available. Meals available all day in relaxed atmosphere. Crayons and colouring books available.

The Open Door
420 Morningside Rd
447 9757
Tues-Fri 10-4.30
£, tables suitable for clip-ons, breastfeeding permitted, bottles heated, no smoking, seats 18.
Small Christian Community Centre providing a place for people to meet and staffed by volunteers. Self-service cafe selling drinks and light snacks. Centre provides a good neighbour and befriending service. Separate areas for feeding and changing. No prams. Pushchairs allowed, space permitting. See also Pre-School Play and Education p95.

The Queens Hall
Clerk St
668 3456
Mon-Sat 10-5; Festival 12.30-5

££, *High chairs (2), breastfeeding permitted, bottles heated, nappy change surface in toilet for disabled, no smoking area, licensed, seats 120.*

Children welcome in this spacious self-service restaurant on 2 levels. Soup, baked potatoes, quiche, salads, etc. Children's portions available. Children's events planned in the long term programme of this international concert hall. *See* Places to Visit p188.

The Riccarton Arms Hotel
198 Lanark Rd W, Currie
449 2230
Mon-Sat 12-3, 7-10; Sun 12.30-2, 7-10
££, *High chairs (2), tables suitable for clip-ons, breastfeeding permitted, bottles heated, licensed, seats 70.*

Small hotel with varied menu. Children welcome in restaurant. Food ordered at bar during day, waitress service at night. No prams.

Seeds Cafe
53 W Nicolson St
667 8673/8729
Sun-Thur 10-9; Fri,Sat 10-10 (10-mdnight during Festival)
£, *High chairs (1), tables suitable for clip-ons, breastfeeding permitted, bottles heated, nappy change surface (F), no smoking, seats 47.*

Small self-service vegetarian cafe also serving vegan food. Children's portions available. No prams. Pushchairs allowed, space permitting.

Sherry's
372 Morningside Rd
447 9217
Mon-Sat 9-6.30
£, *High chairs (2), Breastfeeding permitted, bottles heated, feeder beakers, no smoking area, licensed, seats 44.*

Very pleasant, friendly self-service coffee shop. Home-baking and cooking, salads. High teas with set price menu and reductions for children. Pushchairs allowed but prams must be left outside (large window near tables for easy viewing). **Toilets** downstairs.

The Sycomore Tree (Coffee House/Bookshop)
The Eric Liddell Centre
15 Morningside Rd, Holy Corner
452 9171
Mon-Sat 10-4
£, *High chairs (2), tables suitable for clip-ons, breastfeeding permitted, bottles heated, nappy change surface (M&F), no smoking area, seats 40.*

Self-service cafe run jointly by the 3 churches and staffed mainly by volunteers. Home-made cakes, scones and rolls served all day. Hot meals, salads and vegetarian dishes served from noon. Children's portions available. Friendly staff welcome young and old alike.

The Terrace
Cameron Toll Shopping Centre, Lady Rd, Newington
Mon-Wed 8-6; Thurs-Fri 8-8; Sat 8-7; Sun 10-5
£, *High chairs (4), breastfeeding permitted, bottles heated, nappy change surface in Ladies and toilet for disabled, no smoking area, parties hosted.*

Large spacious eating area on 1st floor shared by several self-service units, burgers/pizza etc. One side overlooks shopping mall. Easy access by small lift tucked away behind the stairs left of Savacentre.

See also Shopping p7.

EATING OUT IN WEST EDINBURGH

Barnton Hotel
Queensferry Rd, Barnton Roundabout
339 1144
Mon-Sun 10.30-10.30
££, High chairs (3), tables suitable for clip-ons, bottles heated, licensed, parties hosted, seats 80.

BB's restaurant has families in mind. A variety of dishes to appeal to most tastes and children's menu. Toys, books and crayons. Chair suitable for feeding in the cloakroom.

The Bridge Inn
The Edinburgh Canal Centre, Ratho
333 1320/1251
Mon-Sat 12 noon-8; Sun 12.30-8
££, High chairs (4), clip-on seats (5), tables suitable for clip-ons, breastfeeding permitted, bottles heated, nappy change surface, family area, play area and patio, licensed, parties hosted, seats 120 (including 2 Canal Boats).

Egon Ronay's Family Pub of the Year '94. Very friendly and welcoming atmosphere with something for all the family. Good and varied menu including large children's menu. Barge-shaped adventure play area outside. Resident family of ducks live beside the canal. Rosie and Jim Canal Safety Campaign promoters.

See also Birthdays and Celebrations p86, Places to Visit p185 and Walks and Country Places p229.

Burger King
Gyle Shopping Centre
317 1561
Mon-Wed, Sat 9-7; Thur, Fri 9-8; Sun 10-5.30
£, High chairs (8), tables suitable for clip-ons, breastfeeding permitted, no smoking, counter service, children's menu and portions, carry-out available.

Offers fast food in clean, child-friendly environment. Excellent soft play area on ground floor, next to eating area. FREE kids club membership. Willing staff help to take food to table (essential if eating downstairs beside soft play).

See also Shopping p8.

Commodore Hotel
Marine Dr, Cramond Foreshore
336 1700
Mon-Sun 12 noon-2; 6.30-9.30
££, High chairs (4), breastfeeding permitted, bottles heated, feeder beakers, family room, garden, parties hosted.

Table service in this refurbished, friendly hotel overlooking the sea. New, extensive children's menu featuring Tony the Tiger.

Cramond Brig
Cramond Brig, Queensferry Rd
339 4350
Mon-Sat 12-10; Sun 12-9.30
££, High chairs (12), booster seats (20), breastfeeding permitted, bottles heated, nappy changing room (M&F), waitress service, licensed, parties hosted, seats 180.

Family orientated dining 'concept', children are encouraged to bring their parents! Children's menu. Eating areas on 3 levels with stairs between them. Excellent indoor and outdoor play areas. TV and video, colouring posters and pens. Space for prams and pushchairs. *See also* Walks and Country Places p222.

The Ellersly House Hotel
Ellersly Rd,
337 6888
Food Mon-Sun 12 noon-2.30; 6-10

£££, High chairs (3), bottles heated, garden with swing, licensed.

This friendly hotel has an attractive menu with children's fun pack provided.

Gyle Shopping Centre — Food Court
539 9000
Mon-Wed, Sat 9-7; Thur, Fri 9-8; Sun 10-5.30
££, High chairs (8), breastfeeding permitted, bottles heated, baby-changing room (M&F), self-service, seats 400.

The Food Court offers a wide range of foods. The Bistro is licensed with waitress service, serving Italian cuisine. Excellent facilities for children in the Centre, see shopping p8.

Hawes Inn
New Halls Rd, S Queensferry
331 1990
Mon-Sun 12 noon-10
££ in bar, £££ in restaurant, high chairs (4), tables suitable for clip-ons, breastfeeding permitted, bottles heated, nappy change surface, family room, no smoking, parties hosted.

This delightful Inn, made famous by Robert Louis Stevenson in Kidnapped, is set under the Forth Rail Bridge right on the edge of the River Forth. Garden with chute, swings and monkey bars and inside books and toys.

See also Out of Town Trips p194.

Holiday Inn Garden Court
Queensferry Rd, Blackhall
332 2442
Food Mon-Sat 12-5.
£££, High chairs (4), tables suitable for clip-ons, bottles heated, feeding and changing room, family area,

garden, no smoking area, licensed, seats 90.

A very inventive children's menu provides plenty of choice. There is a play area for use on Sun lunch times with chute, tunnel, etc. Jazz music in the afternoon.

Lauriston Farm Restaurant
Lauriston Farm Rd,
312 7071
Mon-Sat 12 noon-10; Sun 12.30-10.
££, high chairs and booster seats, breastfeeding permitted, bottles heated, changing area (M & F), no smoking. Birthday parties catered for.

Open and spacious restaurant providing both indoor and outdoor play areas and some toys. The menu for parents is varied and for the children, Charlie Chalk menu plus hats etc. Baby foods are available. The restaurant is very close to both the sea shore at Cramond and Lauriston Castle. Regular children's entertainer — phone for details.

See also Places to Visit p181.

McDonald's
Builyeon Rd, S Queensferry
331 5981
Mon-Sun 8-11pm
£, High chairs (6), booster seats (6), tables suitable for clip-ons, breastfeeding permitted, bottles heated, nappy changing facilities (M&F), parties hosted, seats 50.

Spacious fast-food restaurant with drive-through window service. Children's menu. Giveaways — balloons, flags, pens, etc.

Mr Marios
103/5 Dalry Rd
337 6711
Open 7 days (booking recommended)

£££, High chairs (2), tables suitable for clip-ons, breastfeeding permitted, bottles heated, changing room suitable for both parents, licensed, seats 30.

Very friendly restaurant welcomes children and provides excellent food, relaxed atmosphere with fish tanks.

Norton Tavern

Norton House Hotel, Ingliston (opp showground)

333 1275

Mon-Sat 12 noon-2.30, 5.30-9.30; Sun 12 noon-9.30.

££, High chairs (4), tables suitable for clip-ons, breatfeeding permitted, bottles heated, large outside play area, licensed, seats 50.

This restaurant is an attractively converted stable block, the play area is large and grassy with swings, chute, seesaw etc on a bark surface. Tables outside next to play area. Children's portions or children's menu available. Booking recommended.

Post House Hotel

Corstorphine Rd

334 0390

Mon-Sun (food) 10.30-10.30

£££, High chairs (6), bottles heated, nappy change surface, licensed, seats 80.

Next to Edinburgh Zoo this large hotel has a magician at Sunday lunchtime plus at all times a lego table in the lounge. The 'Marvin the Moose' menu is cheerful and varied.

Ratho Park Hotel

101 Dalmahoy Rd

Kirknewton

333 1242

Mon-Sat 11-11; Sun 12-11

££, High chairs (6), tables suitable for clip-ons, breastfeeding permitted,

bottles heated, nappy change area (M & F). Family area and outdoor play area, licensed, parties hosted, seats 120.

Joint winner of ERDC Child Friendly Initiative this restaurant offers a relaxed atmosphere. Large play area with bark surface overlooked by restaurant with section specifically for under 5s. Charlie Chalk's menu together with hats, balloons and badges will encourage everybody to eat. New indoor building with Fun Factory. Bouncy castle outside.

The Westbury Hotel

92/98 St John's Rd,

316 4466

Mon-Sun 9-6

££, High chairs (2), bottles heated, licensed, parties hosted, seats 100.

Children welcome in restaurant or conservatory area of this friendly hotel. Waitress service for light snacks or meals. Children's menu. Good atmosphere.

See also Birthdays and Celebrations p87.

PUBS

Adults do not naturally lose the habit of enjoying a drink after the birth of a child — a fact which may surprise some breweries. Some do make 'a bit of an effort' and provide a family room. When asked in our questionnaire what they provided for families the most inspiring answers were 'comfy seats away from the bar' — enough said.

The new Children's Certificate available to landlords should improve this state of affairs. At least it will not be against the law to allow children into pubs with this certificate.

Below is a list of pubs and hotels which allow children. Generally, gardens are only open in good weather and children may only be welcome in family rooms at lunchtime so if you are making a special trip, phone first. Please satisfy yourself as to whether the atmosphere (and language) is suitable for your child. Remember it is not the landlord's fault if your 'al fresco' pint is ruined because it rains and he cannot allow you indoors.

Central Edinburgh

Eglinton Hotel
Eglinton Cres 337 2641
Dining area — for meals only. High chairs available.

The Green Tree
182-184 Cowgate 225 1294
Beer garden only.

The Kennilworth
See Eating Out p67.

The Malt Shovel
See Eating Out p69.

North Edinburgh

The Peacock Inn
See Eating Out p74.

Raeburn House Hotel
112 Raeburn Pl 332 2348
Family room and garden. High chairs available.

Telford Arms
See Eating Out p75.

West Edinburgh

The Bridge Inn
See Eating Out p79.

Ellersley House Hotel
See Eating Out p79.

Hawes Inn Hotel
See Eating Out p80.

Holiday Inn Garden Court
See Eating Out p80.

Lauriston Farm
See Eating Out p80.

Old Inn
Main St
336 2437.
Bar meals available. Garden with tables and conservatory next to bar.

Norton Tavern
See Eating Out p81.

Ratho Park Hotel
See Eating Out p81.

South Edinburgh

Iona Hotel
See Eating Out p76.

The Merlin
See Eating Out p77.

The Old Bordeaux
See Eating Out p77.

Peartree House
36 W Nicolson St,
667 7533
Garden: 11-8.30.

Birthdays & Celebrations

THE VENUE

Several venues specialise in organising parties and the 'Eating Out' section on p? identifies those restaurants willing to host parties. Contact the management for details of numbers, food and facilities. Many church halls, public halls, community centres and sports clubs will hire out their premises for an afternoon; it's always worth asking in your area. These sports centres will hire out a suitable venue:

Ainslie Park Leisure Centre
551 2400

Parties last 2 hrs — 1 hr swimming or in the games hall and 1 hr eating, choice of 2 menus, £3.50/child.

See Activities for Children p144, Activities for Parents p166.

Gracemount Leisure Centre
658 1940

Parties last 2 hrs — 1 hr in hall playing games, football or on bouncy castle and 1 hr eating. Min 10 children, £3.60/head.

See Activities for Parents p169, Activities for Children p139.

Jack Kane Centre
669 0404

Birthday party facilities available for all ages (you bring the food). For under 5s there is a bouncy birthday cake in a room with soft mats on floors and walls. Large carpeted room for birthday tea. Payment is for facility hire only, not per child. Party room has a lovely mural from the Jungle Book story on walls.

See Activities for Parents p169.

McLeod Street Sports Centre
337 3252

Available Fri 4-6, other times by arrangement, £4.50/head with £15 deposit. You supply the cake, they do the rest. One hr in the hall, ½hr eating and watching cartoons (if you want), then ½hr in the hall. Children are supervised.

See Activities for Parents p170.

The following have something special to offer — see the relevant section for full addresses and phone numbers. Phone management for full details. Remember Sat afternoons tend to be very busy — youngsters can be quite frightened if it is too crowded especially in the more energetic venues and you may have to book a long time in advance.

Bonnyrigg Leisure Centre
663 7579

Hall and Soft Play room can be hired for parties, £11.90 (£13 at peak times). You bring the food but you can use their kitchen facilities for storage.

See Activities for Children p145.

Craiglockhart Sports Centre
443 0101/02

Provides room set with tables and chairs for self catered parties. A bouncy castle (set up in a squash court) can be hired on an hrly basis, and toys can be provided in the activity room. Availability is limited to wkends only.

See Activities for Children p139, Activities for Parents p167.

Edinburgh Zoo
334 9179 or catering 334 5001 A J Blair ✓

Parties are held in the Members' house and the price includes admission to Zoo. For under fives the tea consists of sandwich finger rolls, chipolata sausages and crisps, with a fruity drink followed by ice cream and jelly and costs £3.50/child. Entrance fees for adult helpers (in the ratio of one adult per two children under 5) are waived. Parties are normally held Mon-Sat in the afternoon with times arranged according to the season. A television and video with various cartoons can be provided for a donation of £5. Parties for over 5s also catered for at £6/child.Parking is available at or near the Members' house.

See Places to Visit p182.

Fort Fun (Portobello Fun Fair)
669 3548

Birthday Parties catered for £3.75/head. Party food, balloons, hats, streamers, decorated table, etc. provided. Parental supervision required and bring your own cake. One hr in play area and 1 hr eating.

See Activities for Children p147.

Garfunkels
225 4579 ✓

Children's menu and goodie bag.

See Eating Out p65.

Gorgie City Farm
337 4202 ✓

The party includes a special visit to the farm and the chance to meet Jemima and all her friends. Three different priced menus to choose from for the birthday tea. The party ends with ½hr of games and music with a party bag to take home. Min 10 children and max 25 can enjoy tea in Jemima's pantry. There is also parking on the farm.

See Places to Visit p184 and Activities for Parents 156.

Koko's
669 0082 ✓

Indoor adventure playground. Parties last 2 hrs — 1½hrs play, ½hr in party room for food and games. Package includes invitations, visit from Koko the Clown, prizes for games, present from Koko plus photo taken with him and party bags including hats and blowers. £5.00/child (min. 10). Mum and Dad can have a cup of tea in the café too.

See Activities for Children p151.

Leith Waterworld
555 6000 ✓

Party bookings available from 12 noon-10 Mon-Fri and 9-5 Sat/Sun. Birthday package includes invitations, 1 hr in pool and 1 hr in function room, party hats, balloons, present for birthday child and party food. Choice of 2 menus. Special diet needs can be catered for. Bring your own cake. Min 6 children, £3.60/head. Leaflet available with booking form, 10 days notice required with 10% non-returnable deposit. Although life guards are on duty, parental supervision is required at all times.

See Activities for Children p146.

Leo's (Forecourt Leisure)
555 4533

Birthday parties catered for in the video theatre — a nice bright airy room with low tables and chairs (10-25 guests). Choice of menus, £5.25/child for snacks; £6.75/child for burgers, milk shakes etc. Dietary needs can be catered for. Bring your own cake or speak to the catering manager for their suggestions. Parties last 2hrs. Play for 1hr and eat and watch videos for the other hr. Children get a party box.

See Activities for Children p151.

Little Marco's
228 2141

All parties include invitations/ acceptance cards, 'Happy Box' containing juice, crisps, sweets, etc, take home 'Happy Bag' containing novelties and sweets and a balloon. The birthday child receives a badge, a special song and a photograph taken with 'Little Marco' to take home. Fixed price. Parties last 2hrs, 1½hrs play ½h for food and games. Recommend midweek parties for under 5s. A hostess is always available to help and a special Marco bear cake can be provided or you can arrange to bring your own. Parties are hosted at special tables next to play area. A 'party plus' is also available but is probably more suitable for over 5s. Birthday leaflet available.

See Activities for Children p152, Activities for Parents p170.

Lo-gy Ltd
440 4495

Birthday parties are held on Sat from 11.30-1.30, 2-4 and 4.30-6.30. First hr is spent in main hall playing under supervision on trampolines — some of which are set into the ground for safety — and large foam holes used for gymnastics, etc. Next ½hr is spent eating and watching cartoons — bring your own food — under parental supervision and then last ½hr is spent playing traditional party games under supervision. Prizes must be provided. £30 for 20 children (min charge) plus £1/extra child up to a max of 30 children.

See also Activities for Children p140.

Meadowbank Sports Centre
661 5351

Soft play area — private parties and playgroups etc can book this room for 1 hr. The café upstairs can reserve tables and there are 3 party menus to choose from. Best to avoid lunchtimes in the cafe if possible.

See Activities for Children p152, Activities for Parents p171.

Mr Boni's
229 5319

Fixed price party menu, hat, balloon and Mr Boni's badge. For the birthday child a FREE personalised ice cream cake with his/her name and favourite cartoon character. Punch and Judy, video, cartoons can be arranged at extra cost. Leaflet available.

See also Eating Out p77.

McDonalds
226 3872

Parties for 8 or more children on Sun afternoon. Hats, balloons and a gift for the birthday child all provided, you just pay for the food. A hostess will play games, etc.

See Eating Out p68.

Netherbow Theatre
556 9579 Kirsten Cook

Bright airy gallery available for parties, also outside courtyard depending on weather. Flexible menu from sandwiches, juice, etc. to a proper tea of burgers, chips, ice cream, juice, etc. It's up to you how much you spend. Birthday cakes can be provided as are balloons, hats and party bags. Parental supervision required. Resident puppeteer usually available but if not, magicians can be provided. Very helpful staff who go out of their way to ensure a good time is had by all.

See Places to Visit p187, Activities for Children p135, Annual Events p201.

Pizza Hut

Birthday package includes invitations, party items, playmat with picture to colour in, slices of pizza, drink, etc., birthday cake and party games £3.50/child. Min 6 children with parental supervision. Hostess to greet children and show them to specially decorated table. Party lasts for 1 ´ hrs. Sundays only. Start times Lothian Rd 11am (before restaurant is open), North Bridge between 12 and 3. Leaflet available.

See Eating Out p69.

Portobello Pool Refreshment Room

Friendly staff will decorate the café and have 2 flexible menus to suit your child's needs. There will be a sign above the table saying 'Happy

Birthday . . .' and each child receives a balloon.

See Activities for Children p147, Activities for Parents p172.

The Pride of Belhaven Cruising Barge

A highly unusual and exciting venue for a party. Everything from hats and balloons to cakes and entertainment can be supplied. Children are not allowed on the deck whilst the barge is moving so parents can enjoy the party. £5.00/head.

See Eating Out p79.

Richards Pizzerama
669 4795

No effort is spared to make your child's party one to remember. The restaurant will be opened earlier if there is a large party to allow the children to 'run riot' (their words not ours.) Everything is supplied from hats to cake. Parents need only tell the waitress that there is a birthday child in the restaurant and they will receive a free cake with a sparkler in it. Mickey Mouse sometimes appears to hand out goodies.

Royal Commonwealth Pool

After normal swimming session, birthday teas are available in the Cafeteria area. Two party menus £2.50 and £3.00. Leaflet available.

See Activities for Children p148.

Trefoil Holiday & Adventure Centre for the Handicapped
Gogarbank
339 3148

Soft play area and/or swimming pool available for hire on an hrly basis at £8.00 each/hr. Maximum of 15 children. Facilities are let to raise funds for the Centre and are not available during Jul/Aug. Priority is given to their disabled visitors. Birthday tea can be provided or you can bring your own food, tea and coffe making facilities available. Contact the centre manager.

The Westbury Hotel
316 4466

Provides function room, music and staff to help, food, balloons and hats. Menus at £4.75 and £5.00/head.

See Eating Out p81.

Wester Hailes Education Centre
A 'Birthday Tea' supplied for your swimming party.

See also Activities for Children p150, Activities for Parents p173.

Windygoul Farm
Open 7 days with good separate play rooms inside and secure outdoor adventure playground with supervision. Menu £4.00/head. Bring your own cake.

See Out of Town Trips p191.

CHILDREN'S PARTIES AT HOME
There's a lot to remember if you decide to hold your child's party at home. We hope the following pages will help. Useful books with lots of useful ideas are available in libraries.

This may serve as a checklist:

Banners	Balloons
Bangs	Cakes & Tins
Candles & Holders	Cups
Fancy Dress	Hats
Indoor Fireworks	Invitations
Masks	Mats
Plates	Prizes
Serviettes	Straws
Streamers	Stocking Fillers
Swag Bags	Tablecloths
anything else	

A wide range of these items is available at the following shops.

The Finishing Touch
A wonderful shop, especially for cake decorating — but with lots of other party paraphernalia.

See Make Your Own p22 and Hiring p57.

Monkey Business
167 Morrison St
228 6636.
Mon-Sat 10-6

A huge selection of hats, masks, wigs, jokes (although many are geared towards a more adult market). Fireworks are stocked all yr round. Some fancy dress to buy but none unfortunately small enough to hire. 300 adult costumes to hire, bouncing castles, automatic helium balloon pump hire.

See also Hiring p59.

Streamers
Unit 16 Waverley Shopping Centre
557 4637
Mon-Sat 9-6, Thur 9-7, Sun 11-5

Super selection of balloons, party paper plates, cups, etc, invitations, helium balloons with legs and arms (free helium refill) which can be personalised. Good selection of 'party bag' gifts.

See also Shopping p9.

Also recommended when planning your party are the following:

Jenners
Good selection of hats, masks and other dressing up requirements also lots of small gifts.

See Shopping p4.

87

John Lewis

Large choice of tablecloths, serviettes, cups, plates — all in paper. Also good selection of small gifts and stationery stocking fillers.

See Shopping p4.

Toys Galore

Selection of party goods and lots of stocking filler toys.

See Shopping p30.

Toys 'R' Us

Party bag gifts, cups, plates, etc. on various themes.

See Shopping p30.

Many of the firms mentioned in Shopping from Home p52 stock party goods.

CATERING AND CAKES

Most parents provide their own food for 'home hosted' parties and there are books in the library to inspire you. There are always plenty of names in the Herald and Post and The Capital, see Sources of Information p205, which claim to do 'all types of catering'. We found however that many did not in fact do under 5s parties and many did not understand the needs of young children at a party. The following has been tried and tested.

Julie's

667 8907

Cakes, sandwiches, sausages etc. Most diets can be catered for.

Cakes

Cakes are usually the centrepiece of any party and again libraries often have books with easy to follow recipes and ideas and a number of shops in Edinburgh hire out cake tins and instructions, see Hiring p57. However if you don't feel ambitious enough to tackle one, Edinburgh seems to be teeming with people who are. A look through The Capital or the Herald and Post will produce a number of possible 'novelty cake' makers. Local bakers and confectioners often supply cakes. Playgroups and toddler groups usually produce a mum willing to tackle your child's choice of cake. The following firms have something special to offer:

Mr Boni's

Award winning ice cream cakes in a variety of designs. Numbers, hearts, trains and a 'house' to serve up to 20. Placed in the U.K. Championships. Remember to leave room in the freezer. Leaflet available. Parties hosted, see p85.

See Eating Out p77.

The Cake and Chocolate Shop

12 Bruntsfield Pl
228 4350
Mon-Fri 9-5.30, Sat 9.30-5

Will make cakes to any design (the only limit is your imagination) and there are lots of books of photographs to give you ideas.

Celebration Cakes

117 Bruntsfield Pl
229 4006
Mon-Sat 10-5; Wed 10-2

Cakes from £6.80. Will make cakes in most popular designs.

Marks and Spencer

See Shopping p5.

Savacentre

See Shopping p12.

ENTERTAINMENT

Many of the entertainers we contacted felt that their acts weren't suitable for under 5s and stressed that there was nothing worse than granny giving a running commentary to tots. It is most important when looking for an act to tell them the age span of the children and whether you have seen them before as many have several routines. The ones below have been recommended and enjoyed by young children.

Abracadabra
54 Princes St, Hawick
01450 373945 Bill Stewart

Punch and Judy puppet show with or without magic. Lots of audience participation and can adjust show to suit age or venue. Some shows include balloon sculptures others have an educational theme e.g. Road Safety, Respect for others, etc. Available for all events — outdoors or indoors. Leaflet available and prices on application.

Buena Vista Entertainments
442 4445

An agency which can supply all entertainment needs: clowns, magicians, face painters, costumed characters and disco parties.

Cartoon Hire
118 Braid Rd
447 5059

Over 50 films to choose from Disney, Star Wars, etc. Tommy brings along a projector and large screen.

Jimmy Craig
11 Barry Rd, Kircaldy
01592 261706

This experienced fun magician provides prize-winning fun-filled magical entertainment for children.

He specialises in shows suitable for children of playgroup age and up.

Gordon's Magic and Punch and Judy Show
7 Royal Park Ter
657 3204

Entertainment for birthday parties and special occasions includes 40 mins of good fun, balloon animals, real live rabbit which allows 'hands on'! Colourful puppet show and lots of audience participation. Leaflet available with instructions on making a magic wand.

Scott Lovat
102 Provost Milne Grove, South Queensferry
331 5387

Many varied shows including magic, puppets and balloon sculpture. For older children Scott will even run the whole party, including games and a junior disco. Some shows include an excellent theme of 'Say No to Strangers'. Birthday party shows are structured around the birthday child but all shows feature maximum audience participation. Children get a picture to colour at the end of the show and when handed in at future shows receive a 'balloon sculpture' as does the child chosen to help with the magic.

Magic Bob
Main St, Gordon
01573 410363

This popular magician performs a variety of colourful, cheerful shows which children and adults love. Lots of good humour and audience participation with souvenirs for all partygoers. Traditional yet innovative.

Jack Martin
21 Bruntsfield Gardens
229 4147

Jack and his wife Jill have been entertaining children for 30 years. With three grown sons and two baby grand-daughters, their insight into what children enjoy is second to none. Show includes magic and life sized puppets.

Mr Boom
Lindsayland's Cottage, Biggar
01899 20471

. . . and he comes from the moon! An entertaining one-man band now mainly available for galas and children's concerts rather than birthday parties. Ideal for youngsters. Help bang the big bass drum. Audience participation is part of the show. Mr Boom writes his own songs but also includes nursery rhymes, favourite hits and Scottish children's folk songs. Book early.

Peter Pepper
01585 636634 Ian Simpson

A colourful magic show which is filled with laughter, fun, lots of tricks and plenty of audience participation and will run the whole party if required. Will also entertain playgroups and schools using magic to increase children's awareness of road safety. Distance no object.

Rainbow Magic
224 Mansefield, East Calder
01506 880139

A lady magician with lots of tricks to entertain youngsters. Her show features a loveable puppet called 'Honey Bear' who gets up to all sorts of antics.

Stardust Mobile Children's Disco
26 East Clapperfield, Liberton
455 7466

Children's music and party games for 2-12 yrs approx. Ideal for birthdays, Xmas parties, etc.

George Thomson
01333 424341

A magical surprise show which may include two white rabbits, 'The vanishing elephant', 'The acrobatic monkey', 'Mr. Sam Willoughby, the wizard' and a 'special appearance' of Mickey Mouse.

Pre-School Play and Education

Pre-school children are offered a number of opportunities to meet others in the same age range. From birth, there are groups where parents can meet informally while children play with a larger range of toys and equipment than most homes can provide.

Progression is normally:
Up to age 1 — Parent and Baby group.
Age 1-2½ — Parent and Toddler group.
Age 2½-5 — Playgroup, Home Playgroup, Private Nursery, Lothian Regional Council Nursery or Independent Nursery.

Information about all these groups is listed below. Those looking for full or part day care for their children should look under the Private Nurseries section p107 and also under the section Childcare p120, which covers nannies and childminders. Details of multi-lingual groups and groups for children with special needs may be obtained from the Scottish Pre-School Play Association and the Social Work Department (addresses below).

The Scottish Amateur Gymnastics Coaching Award for Pre-School Gymnastics and Movement can be taken by playgroup leaders and nursery workers. Some playgroups may participate in this activity. See Activities for Children p138.

Should you be unable to find a suitable group from the lists below, information may also be obtained from the following sources:

1. The National Childbirth Trust. See Health Care Facilities p257.
2. Your Health Visitor and Health Centre/Doctor's noticeboard.
3. Lothian Regional Council, Department of Social Work, Community Care, Registration and Inspection Service, Claremont House, 128-130 E Claremont St, 556 6787. Records of registered playgroups, home playgroups and private nurseries, as well as lists of registered childminders.
4. The Scottish Pre-School Play Association. See Local Play Organisations p119.
5. Noticeboards in libraries, newsagents, supermarkets, toy shops and church halls (many groups meet in church halls — you do not need to be a member of the church to attend).

We have compiled our lists from questionnaires sent to groups registered with the Social Work

Department, those sent to groups listed in the last edition of Edinburgh For Under Fives and information supplied by the authors and members of the National Childbirth Trust.

Contact numbers have been given where possible, but contacts change frequently. All groups which care for children under 8 for more than 2 hrs without a parent or guardian in attendance are inspected and registered by the Social Work Department. This will not apply to baby and toddler groups so it is advisable to check personally for atmosphere and safety standards. In particular, check if large outdoor equipment like a climbing frame, is on a safe surface such as wood chip, rubber matting or grass.

Groups are listed by area in alphabetical order.

PARENT AND BABY GROUPS

These groups cater for parents and babies and are generally held in health centres or in someone's home. Your Health Visitor or clinic and the National Childbirth Trust, 225 9191, Mon-Fri 9-12 will put you in touch with other parents in your area.

PARENT AND TODDLER GROUPS

These groups are generally set up by local parents and, as adults usually stay with the children, they are places where you can meet other adults and babies and toddlers for a few hrs once or twice a wk, normally during school terms. Most children are taken by their mothers but fathers, grandparents, nannies, child-minders, etc, are also welcome. Sometimes pre-walking babies meet in a separate room and some groups have specific days for under ones or first babies.

Facilities and standards vary, but most places have a selection of toys and puzzles, books, crayons and some larger pieces of equipment (eg slides, climbing frames, play cookers). Prices range from nothing to approximately £5/term, with a small charge for tea, coffee and juice. There is often a rota for providing snacks and making coffee, and parents usually help to set up and tidy away the toys. Where we know that outdoor play is available, this has been mentioned. There is a Gaelic Toddlers see Tollcross p97 and see Tollcross p97 and Dalry p94 for details of groups specifically for minders and their charges.

BALERNO

Balerno Parish Church Hall, Deanpark Ave/Mon, Thurs 10-11.30/Contact Fiona McKerron 451 5779.

BLACKHALL

St Columba's Parish Church, Hillhouse Rd/Tues 9.30-11.30, 1.30-3.30/For am contact Mrs Robertson 539 2878, for pm Mrs Miller 315 2300.

BRUNTSFIELD

Barclay Bruntsfield Church Hall, Barclay Pl/Tues 10-11.30/Contact Katherine Ellis 228 4136.

CANONMILLS
Logie Green Hall, Logie Green Rd/Tues 10.30-12/Contact Andrea Morris 663 9562.

CARRICK KNOWE
Carrick Knowe Church, Saughton Rd N/Thurs, Fri 10-11.30; Thurs 1-2.30/ Contact Linda Cooper 334 8109.

CLERMISTON
Parkgrove Parent & Toddler Group, The Munro Centre, Parkgrove St/Thurs 10-11.30/Contact Joyce Samson 539 1912.
St Andrew's Church, Clerwood Cres/Tues, Thurs 10-11.30/Contact venue.
St Kentigern's Church, 24 Parkgrove Ave/Tues 10-11.30/Contact Mrs Douglas 336 1827.

COLINTON
Colinton Toddler Group, St Cuthbert's Church Hall, Westgarth Ave/Mon 9.30-11.30; Tues 2-4/Contact venue.
Stableroom Toddler Group, Colinton Mains Parish Church Hall, Spylaw Bank Rd/Thurs 9.30-11.30, 1-3/Contact Stableroom Playgroup 441 4475.

COMISTON/BUCKSTONE
St Fillan's Church, Buckstone Dr/Thurs 2.30-4.30/Contact Fiona Simon 445 3074.

CORSTORPHINE
Belgrave Mother & Toddler Group, Belgrave Halls, 34 Belgrave Rd/Tues 10-11.30/Contact Ann Howard 336 3540.
Craigsbank Church, Craigsbank/Mon 10-11.30/Contact Kirsten Duncanson 339 3871.
Fox Covert Toddler Group, Fox Covert School, Clerwood Ter/Tues 1.30-3/ Contact Anne Thomas 334 7459.
Gylemuir Primary School, Wester Broom Pl/Tues, Thurs 10-11.30; Thurs 1.30-3/Contact Sandra White 334 4144.
Jack and Jill Club, St Anne's Church Hall, Kaimes Rd/Wed 9.30-11.30/Contact Anne Morrison 334 2191.
St Ninian's Church Hall, St Ninian's Rd/Tues 10-11.30/Contact Morag Buist 334 4079.
St Thomas's Church, 79 Glasgow Rd/Tues 10-11.30/Contact Ruth McLeish 334 0812.

CRAIGLOCKHART
Craiglockhart Church Hall, Craiglockhart Dr N/Mon 10-11.45/Contact Venue.

CRAIGMOUNT
Craigmount School, Craigs Rd/Tues, Fri 10-11.30; Wed 1.45-3.15/Wed 1st time mums only/Contact Val Blair 334 0626.

CRAMOND

Cramond Kirk Hall, Cramond Glebe Rd W/Tues 10-11.30/Contact venue.

CURRIE

Gibson Craig Hall, Lanark Rd/Wed 2-4; Fri 10-11.30/Contact venue.

DALRY/GORGIE

Gorgie Memorial Hall, Gorgie Rd/Minders group Tues 9.30-11.30/Parents group Thurs 9.30-11.30/Contact Wendy Duffy 337 9098.
St Bride's Centre, Orwell Ter/Fri 9.30-11.30/Contact venue 346 1405. *See* Activities for Parents p172.

DAVIDSON'S MAINS

Davidson's Mains Parish Church, Quality St/Thurs 10-11.30/Contact venue.
Holy Cross Church, Quality St/Mon 9.30-11.30/Contact venue.
St Margaret's Church Hall, Main St/Tues 10-12/Contact Church Office.

DUDDINGSTON

Duddingston Kirk, Old Church Lane/Wed 10-11.30/Contact Ann White 669 2115.

EAST CRAIGS

East Craigs Church Centre, Bughtlin Market/Thurs 10-11.30/Contact Avril Murray 539 0574.

EASTER ROAD

Calton Centre, 121 Montgomery St/Tues, Thurs 10-12/Contact venue 661 9121. *See* Activities for Parents p166.
Leith St Andrews, 410 Easter Rd/Tues, Thurs 9.30-11.30/Contact Lesley Burgen at venue.

FAIRMILEHEAD

Fairmilehead Parish Church, Frogston Rd W/Mon, Tues, Thur, Fri 10-11.30; Tues,Wed 2.30-4/Contact Julia Melton 445 2500.

GILMERTON

Gilmerton Community Centre/Thurs 10-11.30/Contact venue 664 2335. *See also* Activities for Parents p156.

JOPPA

Brunstane Community Centre, Magdalene Dr/Thur 9.30-12/Contact Caroline Lemond 669 8760.
St Philip's Church, Brunstane Rd N/Fri 10-11.15/Contact venue 669 3641.

JUNIPER GREEN

Juniper Green Community Education Centre, Village Hall, 2 Juniper Park Rd/ Mon 2-3.30/Contact venue 453 4427.

KIRKLISTON

Kirkliston Community Education Centre, Queensferry Rd/Tues 10-11.30/ Contact venue 333 4214.

LEITH

Bonnington Primary School, Bonnington Rd/Mon, Wed 9.15-11.15/Contact venue.
Forth Community Wing, North Fort St/Tues 10-12/Contact venue 553 1074.
Leith Community Centre, New Kirkgate/Mon, Tues, Thur 10-12.15; Mother and Baby Mon 2-3.30/Contact venue 554 4750. *See also* Activities for Parents p156.
St Paul's Church, Lorne St/Mon 1.30-3.15/Contact Marilyn Tait 554 1842.

LIBERTON

Liberton Kirk, Kirk Gate/Mon, Thur, Fri 9.30-11.30/Contact Jackie Tait 664 4205.

LOCHEND

Lochend YWCA, Restalrig Rd S/Mon, Wed, Fri 10-12/Contact Heather Blacklaw 554 4716.
St Margaret's Church Hall, Restalrig Rd S/Tues 9.30-11.30/Contact venue.

MARCHMONT

Marchmont St Giles Parish Church, Kilgraston Rd/Thurs 10-12/Contact Jessica McCraw 667 4514.
St Catherine Argyle Church, 61 Grange Rd/Tues 10-12/Contact Linda Sivewright 228 1803.

MORNINGSIDE

Cluny Parish Church, Cluny Church Centre, Cluny Dr/Mon, Thurs 10-11.30/ Contact Church Office 447 6745.
Greenbank Church, Braidburn Ter/Wed, Thurs 10-11.45/Contact Church 447 9969.
Morningside Baptist Church, Morningside Rd/Mon 9.30-11.30; Tues 9.30-11.30; Thurs 9.30-11.30/Contact venue 447 9787.
The Old Schoolhouse, 140 Morningside Rd/Thurs 9.45-11.30/Contact Adele Thomson 445 5726.
The Open Door, 420 Morningside Rd/Fri 2-3.30/1st Babies only/Contact venue 447 9757. *See also* Eating Out p77.

MURRAYFIELD

Murrayfield Parish Church, Ormidale Ter/Mon, Tues, Thurs, Fri 10-11.30/Mon under 1; Tues 1-2 yrs; Thur, Fri 2-3 yrs/Contact venue.

NEWINGTON

Stewart House, Craigmillar Park Church/Fri 10.30-12/Contact Philip Hunsley 667 3858.

Duncan Street Baptist Church, Duncan St/Tues, Thur 10.15-12/Contact Clair Turner 662 4892.
Lower Hall, Mayfield Church, Mayfield Rd/Tues, Thurs 9.45-11.30/Contact Alison McRoberts 667 0220.
Reid Memorial Church Hall, 182 West Saville Ter/Wed, Thurs 10-11.30/Contact Yvonne Collins 667 8777/ Wed under 2 yrs, Thurs over 2 yrs.
St Peter's 0-5s, St Peter's Episcopal Church, Lutton Pl/Mon, Thurs 9.45-11.30/Contact Lorri Williams 667 3376.

NIDDRIE

Greengables Parent & Toddler Group, Greengables, 8A Niddrie House Gdns/ Wed 9.30-12, 1.30-3/Contact Kate Frame 669 9084. *See also* Toy Libraries p133.

OLD TOWN

St Anne's Community Centre, 6 South Gray's Close/Tues, Thurs 10-12/Contact venue 557 0469.

OXGANGS

Pentland Community Education Centre, Oxgangs Brae/Wed 2-3.30/Contact venue 445 2871.

PILTON

Prentice Centre, 1 Granton Mains Ave/Fri 10-3/Contact venue 552 0485.

PORTOBELLO

Portobello Old Parish Church, Bellfield St/Tues 9.15-11.15/Contact Marion Buchanan 669 5312.

RATHO

Ratho Community Centre, 1 School Wynd/Tues, Thurs 10-12/Contact Lawrence Arscott 333 1055.

SLATEFORD

St Michael's Church, 1 Slateford Rd/Wed 10-11.30/Contact venue.

SOUTH QUEENSFERRY

South Queensferry Community Centre, Kirkliston Rd/Wed 9.30-11.30/Contact venue 331 2113.

STOCKBRIDGE/COMELY BANK

Comely Bank Toddlers, St Stephen's Comely Bank Church, East Fettes Ave/ Thurs 9.30-11.30/Contact Mrs Cormack 332 5485.
Dean Tots, Dean Parish Church Hall, Dean Path/Tues-Thurs 9.30-12/Contact venue.

International Toddlers, St Stephen's Church, St Stephen's St/Fri 9.30-11.30/ Contact Elisabeth Duncan 332 6449.
St Ninian's Church Hall, Comely Bank Rd/Tues 10-11.30, 2-3.30/Contact venue.
St Stephen's Church, St Stephen's St/Mon 9.30-11.30/Contact May McDougall 552 2023
Stockbridge Health Centre, 1 India Place/Tues 10-11.30, 2-4/Contact Barbara Ross or Lesley Horn 225 9191.

TOLLCROSS

Gaelic Toddlers, Tollcross Community Ed. Centre, Fountainbridge/Wed 9.30-11.30/Contact venue 229 8448
Minders & Tots, Tollcross Community Ed. Centre, Fountainbridge/Fri 9.30-12.30/See also Childcare p120 and Activities for Parents p157.
Mother & Toddlers, Tollcross Community Ed. Centre, Fountainbridge/Tues, Thur 9.30-1/Contact venue 229 8448.

TRINITY

The Acorn Club, Inverleith Church, Ferry Rd/Thurs 9.45-11.15/Contact Susan Barr 552 0111.
Trinity Toddler Group, Craighall Gdns/Mon-Fri 10-12, Tues-Thur 2-4/Wed am 2¨ group and baby group/Contact Jane Sutherland 467 3642 or Anne Davidson 554 1891.

PLAYGROUPS AND HOME PLAYGROUPS

These should be registered with the Social Work Department see p91, who can provide lists of registered groups. Please remember that an entry is not necessarily a recommendation. Safety standards should be checked personally.

Most playgroups operate during school terms only, some groups have even shorter terms. The age range is usually 2½ (or 3) to 5. Many groups run on a part day basis, 2 or 3 sessions per week but most are 5 days. Some require children to be potty trained.

There is often a waiting list for playgroups and it is advisable to put your child's name down as soon as possible, usually on their 2nd birthday.

Community Playgroups receive a grant each year from the Social Work Department, to cover wages, rent, insurance and fees.

Term fees vary from group to group, and many groups have fundraising events, at which parents are expected to participate. Groups are usually run by a committee of parents elected each year and parents help regularly on a rota basis. Some groups charge extra if parents are unable to undertake rota duty, but childminders, nannies, etc. can take their place.

There is a French Playgroup (*see* Bruntsfield p99).

Home Playgroups are small groups of between 6 and 20 children usually run in a Playleader's home. Costs are normally higher than private playgroups, and can be compared with private nurseries. There is not normally a parental rota, although parents may be asked to help out on occasion. Most groups run for the school term, although some have a summer scheme during the long holidays.

Private Playgroups do not receive a Social Work Department grant, so fees are usually higher than community playgroups. Some are run by a parents' committee, some ask for a rota of parent helpers.

There is a 'Montessori Nursery School' see Murrayfield p104.

Groups are listed by area in alphabetical order.

BALERNO

Compass Playgroup, Dean Park Community Wing, 31 Marchbank Gdns/2 groups of 20 places/Mon-Thurs 9.30-12 Mon, Thurs, Fri 1-3/Age 2½-5/75p per session/Duty rota/ Contact 449 4530.

Dean Park Playgroup, Community Centre, Main St/25 places/Mon-Fri 9.15-12/Age 2½-5/Contact Flora Skelly 449 5573.

BARNTON

St Margaret's Kindergarten, 47a Barnton Park View/16 places/Mon-Fri 8.45-12.15/Age 3-5/No duty rota/Outdoor play/Contact Mrs Newbigging 339 2971.

BROUGHTON

Drummond Nursery, Drummond Community High School, Cochran Ter/20 places/Mon-Fri 9.15-11.45/Contact Mrs Ireland 556 8291. See also Toy Libraries p132.

BLACKHALL

Blackhall Playgroup, St Columba's Church, Hillhouse Rd/20 places/Wed, Thurs 9.30-12 Mon, Tues 1-3.30/Age 3-5/50p per day/Duty rota/Contact Mrs Stewart 336 2845.

The Pre-Nursery Playgroup, 210 Craigcrook Rd/12 places/Mon,Tue,Thurs,Fri 9.30-12.15/Age 2-3/£7.50 per session/outdoor play/Contact Mrs Coad 336 4155

BROOMHALL

Broomhall Playgroup, Scout Hall, Broomhall Ave/48 places/Mon-Fri 9.30-11 and 1-3/Age 2½-5/£20 per month/Duty rota/Outdoor play,summer only/ Contact Mrs Stewart 539 5409.

BROOMHOUSE

Broomhouse Playgroup, St David's Church Hall, Broomhouse Cres/16 places/ Mon-Fri 9.15-11.45/£2.50 per wk/Outdoor play/Contact Lorraine Williamson 539 3946 or Susanne Riley 477 0538

Broomhouse Centre Playgroup, 79/89 Broomhouse Cr/Mon-Fri 1-3/Age 2½-5/£2.50 per week/Outdoor play/Contact Margaret Craigens 445 7731.

BRUNTSFIELD

Barclay Church Playgroup, Barclay Bruntsfield Church, Barclay Pl/21 places/ Mon-Fri 9-11.50/Contact Jennie Morris 229 4533.

Bruntsfield Playgroup, Bruntsfield Primary School, Montpelier/22 places/Mon-Fri 9-11.45/Age 3-5/50p per day/Duty rota/Outdoor play/Contact Sonja Peterson 229 9837 or venue 228 1526.

La Petite Ecole, Bruntsfield Primary School, Montpelier/36 places/Tues 4-5.20pm/Age 3-11/£20 per term/Children must be bilingual with French/ Contact Madeleine Rogers 228 6328.

BURDIEHOUSE

Burdiehouse Playgroup, Burdiehouse Church Hall, Gracemount Dr/25 places/ Mon-Fri 9-11.45/Age 2½-5/Contact venue 664 6994.

CHURCHILL

Holy Corner Community Playgroup, Christ Church Morningside, 4 Morningside Rd/24 places/Mon, Tues, Thurs, Fri 9.15-11.45/Age 3-5/£4.25 per wk/Duty rota/Outdoor play/Contact venue.

CLERMISTON

Clermiston Playgroup, Child Health Centre, Rannoch Ter/20 places/Mon-Fri 9.15-11.45/£1.20 per wk/Rota or charge/Outdoor play/Contact Mrs S. Dick, 5 Primrose Ter.

Parkgrove Playgroup, The Munro Centre, Parkgrove St/20 places/Mon, Wed, Fri 9.15-11.30/Age 2½-5/50p per session/Contact venue.

COLINTON

Colinton Nursery, St Cuthbert's Episcopal Hall, Westgarth Ave/Tues-Fri 9-12; Wed, Fri 12.45-2.45/Outdoor play/Contact Mrs Williamson 441 4190.

Cranley Nursery, Paties Football Pavilion, Katesmill Rd/21 places/Mon-Fri 9-12.30/Age 2½-5/Contact Mrs Philpot 447 7227.

Stableroom Playgroup, Colinton Parish Church, Spylaw Bank Rd/16 places/ Mon, Wed, Fri 9.15-11.15; Mon, Wed 12.30-2.30/£2.40 per session/Duty rota/ Outdoor play/Contact venue 441 4475.

COLINTON MAINS

Colinton Mains Playgroup, Colinton Mains Community Centre, Firhill Loan/16 places/Mon-Fri 9.15-11.45/Age 2½-5/50p per day/Outdoor play/Contact venue 441 6597.

COMISTON/BUCKSTONE

Braid Mount Kindergarten (Home Playgroup), 15 Braid Mount/8 places/Mon-Fri 9-12/No duty rota/Outdoor play/Contact Mrs Hunter 447 5951.

St Fillan's Playgroup, St Fillan's Church, Buckstone Dr/29 places/Mon, Tues, Thurs, Fri 9.15-11.45/Age 2½-5/£1.75 per session/Contact Mrs MacKenzie 445 4018.

CORSTORPHINE

Belgrave Playgroup, Belgrave Halls, 34 Belgrave Rd/24 places/Mon, Wed, Thurs, Fri 9.30-12/Outdoor play/Contact Mrs Hunt 334 6416.

Craigsbank Playgroup, Craigsbank Church Hall, Craigsbank/24 places/Tue-Fri 9.15-11.45/Age 2½-5/Contact Mrs Greig 539 1652.

East Craigs Playgroup, East Craigs Church Centre, Bughtlin Mkt/24 places/ Mon-Fri 9.15-11.45/Age 2½-5/Contact Mrs Greig 539 1652.

Forrestine's Playgroup, St Augustine's High School, Broomhouse Rd/24 places/Mon-Fri 9.15-11.45/Age 2½-5/£1 per day/Contact venue 334 6801.

Fox Covert Playgroup, Fox Covert Primary School, Clerwood Tce/40 places/ Mon-Fri 9.15-11.45/Age 3-5/£1.75 per day/Outdoor play/Duty rota/Contact Anne Bunyon 334 6586.

New Corstorphine Village Playgroup, Old Parish Church Hall, Corstorphine High St/24 places/Mon-Fri 9.15-11.45/Age 2½-5/£1.90 per day/Contact venue 334 1258.

Playgroup, Craigmount Community Wing, Craigs Rd/24 places/Mon, Thurs, Fri 9.30-11.50/Outdoor play/Contact 339 1884.

St Thomas's Playgroup, St Thomas's Clubhouse, Glasgow Rd/24 places/Mon-Fri 9.30-12/£1.50 per day/Outdoor play/Contact Mrs Anderson 339 6578.

CRAIGENTINNY

Craigentinny/Lochend Social Centre Playgroup, Loaning Rd/16 place/Mon-Fri 9.10-11.30/Age 3-5/50p per session/Contact venue.

Christiemillar Nursery, 58 Christiemillar Ave/11 places/Mon-Fri 9-12/Age 2½-5/£3 per day/Outdoor play/Contact Linda McKinney 657 5381.

CRAIGLOCKHART

Craiglockhart Playgroup, Craiglockhart Church, Craiglockhart Dr N/25 places/ Wed-Fri 9.15-11.45/Age 2½-5/Duty rota/Outdoor play/Contact Gill Hayden 444 0787.

CRAIGMILLAR

Craigmillar Playgroup, Craigmillar Boys Club, 76 Craigmillar Castle Ave/Mon-Fri 8.45-12/Contact venue 661 4064.

CRAMOND

Cramond Playgroup, Cramond Church Hall, Cramond Glebe Rd/40 places/ Mon-Fri 9-12/Age 2½-5/Contact Caroline Duncan 539 0954.

CURRIE

Currie Community Playgroup, Gibson Craig Hall, 144 Lanark Rd W/20 places/ Mon, Wed, Thur 9.30-11.30/50p per day + 50p voluntary contribution/ Outdoor play/Contact venue.

Currie Playgroup, Currie Baptist Church Hall, Kirkbrae/16 places/Mon-Fri 9.30-11.40/Age 2 Û-5/60p per session/Contact venue.

Jubilee Playgroup, Youth Club, Lanark Rd W/12 places/Mon-Fri 9.30-11.45/ Age 2½-5/Outdoor play/Contact Joan Ballie 538 5347.

Riccarton Playgroup, Riccarton School, 59 Curriehilll Rd/16 places/Mon-Fri 9-11.30/Outdoor play/Contact venue 449 7494.

DALRY

Nari Kallyan Shangho, 200 Dalry Rd/10 places/Mon,Fri 10-1.30; Tue,Wed 12.30-3.30/age 3-5/Contact 346 7493.

St Martin's Playgroup, St Martin's Church, Muireston Cres/24 places/Mon-Fri 9.15-11.30/Age 2½-5/Contact Mrs Stewart 337 9714 (9.15-11.30).

DAVIDSON'S MAINS

Panda Playgroup, Davidson's Mains Parish Church Hall, Quality St/16 places/Tues-Fri 9.15-11.45/Contact Mrs Humphries 336 1347.

Reindeer Playgroup, Holy Cross Church Hall, Quality St/24 places/Tues-Fri 9.15-12/Age 3-5/Contact venue.

FAIRMILEHEAD

Pentland Playgroup, Frogston Rd E/24 places/Mon-Fri 9.15-12.15/Age 2½-5/Contact venue 445 1963.

GOLDENACRE

Edzell Nursery Class, St James's Church Hall, Inverleith Row/Age 3/12 places/Mon,Wed,Fri 9-11.45/Age 4/12 places/Mon-Fri 9-11.45/Outdoor play/Contact venue 551 2179.

St Serf's Playgroup, St Serf's Church Hall, Clark Rd/30 places/Mon-Fri 9.15-11.45/£28-50 per term approx/Outdoor play/Contact Mrs Bonnington 552 4010.

GORGIE

The Ark Playgroup, 431 Gorgie Rd/21 places/Mon-Wed 9.30-11.30/Age 2½-5/£1.50 per session/Duty Rota/Contact venue 346 2875.

GRANGE

Grange Kindergarten (Home Playgroup), 5 St Thomas's Rd/8 places/Mon, Tues, Thurs, Fri 9.30-12/Age 3-5/£130 per term (3 10 wk terms/yr)/Outdoor play/Contact Mrs Sinclair 667 4250.

GRANTON

Granton Toddlers Playgroup, Granton Parish Church, Boswell Parkway/24 places/Mon-Fri 9.30-11.30/Age 2½-5/Contact venue 552 8624.

The Funtime Nursery, St Margaret Mary's Church Hall, Boswell Parkway/20 places/Mon-Fri 9.30-11.30/Age 2½-5/£3 per wk/Duty rota/Outdoor play/Contact Frances Wallace 552 8299.

GYLE

Gylemuir Playgroup, Gylemuir School, Wester Broom Pl/24 places/ Mon, Wed, Fri 9-12, 12.45-2.45/£3 fee per week/Contact Mrs Scott 334 6689.

INCH

New Life Nursery, 70 Dinmont Dve/20 places/Mon-Fri 9.30-12, Mon-Thur 1.15-3.15/Age 2½-5/Fee depends on income, 75p per session for unemployed or low wage/Outdoor play/Contact Christine McPake 666 1826.

JOPPA

Joppa Playgroup, 27 Hope Lane/15 places/Mon-Fri 9-12/£5 per day/Outdoor play/Contact Mrs Crichton 669 5208

JUNIPER GREEN

Juniper Green Nursery Playgroup, Community Education Centre, Village Hall, 2 Juniper Park Rd/30 places/Mon-Fri 9.15-12/Age 2½-5/Outdoor play/Contact Mrs Buchanan 453 4427.

KIRKLISTON

Kirkliston Playgroup, The Pavilion, Allison Park/Mon-Fri 9.30-11.30; Mon-Thur 12.30-2.30/Age 2½-5/£1.25 per session/Contact venue 333 5456.

Kirkstyle Playgroup, Thomas Chalmers Church Centre, The Square/24 places/ Tues-Fri 9.30-12/Age 2½-5/£4 per day/Outdoor play/Contact Mrs Goodall 333 3724 or venue 333 4088.

LEITH

Dalmeny Street Playgroup, Lorne Primary School, Lorne St/18 places/Mon-Fri 9-12/Age 3-5/60p per session/Duty rota/Outdoor play/Contact Mrs Sommerville 669 1891.

Leith/St Andrew's Playgroup, Leith/St Andrew's Church, Easter Rd/24 places/Mon-Fri 9-11.30/Age 2½-5/Contact venue.

New Kirkgate Nursery, Room 5, Leith Community Centre, Kirkgate/15 places/ Mon-Fri 9.15-11.45/Age 2½-5/£1.50 per day/Contact Jacky Perry 554 4750.

LEITH WALK

Brunswick Playgroup, Leith Walk Primary School, Brunswick Rd/20 places/ Mon-Fri 9.15-11.45/Age 2½-5/£2.50 per week, £1.25 for single parents/ Outdoor play/Duty rota/Contact Mrs Sheffield 556 3810.

LIBERTON

Liberton Northfield Playgroup, Liberton Northfield Church, Gilmerton Rd/24 places/Mon, Tues, Thur, Fri 9.15-11.45/Age 2½-5/Duty rota/Outdoor play/ Contact Jane Montgomery 467 6090.

LONGSTONE

Longstone Playgroup, Longstone School Annexe, Redhall Grove/16 places/ Mon-Fri 9-11.30/Age 3-5/£2.50 per week/Duty rota/Contact venue.

Redhall Playgroup, 113 Redhall Dr/16 places/Mon-Fri 9-11.30/Age 2½-5/ £2.50 per wk/Duty rota/Contact venue 538 7339.

MARCHMONT

Marchmont St Giles Playgroup, Marchmont St Giles Church Hall, Kilgraston Rd/24 places/Tues-Thurs 9.30-12/Age 2½-5/£2.25 per session/Duty rota/ Outdoor play/Contact Catherine Buchanan 449 5378.

MAYFIELD

Mayfield Playgroup, Mayfield Church House, 18 W Mayfield/24 places/Mon 9.30-11.45; Tues, Thur, Fri 9-11.45/Age 2½-5/£7.25 per wk/Duty rota/Outdoor play/Contact Mrs Hay 667 6193.

Playtime Nursery, Reid Memorial Church, 182 W Savile Ter/26 places/Mon-Fri 9.30-12 /Age 2-5/Nappies allowed/£4.40 per session/No duty rota/Outdoor play/Contact Mrs Morris 455 7466.

Playtime Trainers, Reid Memorial Church,182 W Saville Ter/16 places/Mon, Fri 9.30-12/Age 2½+/£4.50 per session/Music,movement,dance and drama/ Contact Mrs Morris 455 7466.

MOREDUN

Moredun Playgroup, Moredun Primary School, Moredunvale Pl/16 places/ Mon-Fri 9.15-11.45/Age 3-5/Contact venue 664 2384.

MORNINGSIDE

Cluny Church Playgroup, Cluny Church Centre, Cluny Dr/24 places/Mon-Fri 9-12/Contact Mrs Adams 447 6745.

Greenbank Playgroup, Greenbank Church Hall, Braidburn Ter/30 places/Mon-Fri 9-11.45/Outdoor play/Contact Mrs Myddleton 447 3847.

Mrs Coutts (Home Playgroup), 17 Cluny Ave/8 places/Mon, Tues, Thurs, Fri 9-12/Age 3-5/£100 per term/Contact Mrs Coutts 447 5639.

Mrs Simpson (Home Playgroup), 118 Braid Rd/13 places/Mon, Tues, Thurs, Fri 9.45-11.45/Age 2½-5/Outdoor play/ Contact Mrs Simpson 447 5059.

Nile Grove Community Playgroup, Braid Church Hall, Nile Gr/24 places/Mon-Fri 9.15-11.45/Outdoor play/Contact Enrolment Secy 447 1129.

MUIRHOUSE

Craigroyston Community Centre Playgroup, Community Centre, 1a Pennywell Rd/16 places/Mon-Fri 9.15-11.15/Age 2½-5/£2.50 per wk/Contact Mrs Docherty 332 7360. *See also* Activities for Parents p156.

Inchmickery Playgroup, Inchmickery Court, Muirhouse Gr/16 places each session/Mon-Fri 9-11.30; 1-3.30/Age 2½-5/Contact Mrs Knight 312 7948.

St Paul's Playgroup, St Paul's Church, 4 Muirhouse Ave/Mon-Fri 9-11.30; 11.45-2.15/Age 2½-5/£2.50 per wk/Outdoor play/Contact Mrs Falconer 332 3320.

MURRAYFIELD

Little Acorns Montessori Nursery School, Good Shepherd Church Hall, Murrayfield Ave/20 places/Mon-Fri 8.45-12.30/Age 3-5/Outdoor play/Contact Miss Anderson 346 8921.

MUSSELBURGH

First Steps, 37 Galt Ave/9 places 1-2½ yrs/15 places 2½-4 yrs/Mon-Fri 9-11.45, Mon, Wed, Thur 1-3.15/Age 1-4/15p per session/Duty rota/Outdoor play/Contact Carol Meaney 665 0848.

NEW TOWN

Doune Terrace Playgroup (Home Playgroup), 8 Doune Ter/20 places/Mon-Fri 8.45-4/age 2½-5/£420 per term am or pm/Outdoor play/Contact Margaret Coupe 226 2722.
St Mary's Playgroup, St Mary's Primary School, E. London St/20 places/Mon-Fri 9-11.45/Age 2½-5/£1 per session/Duty rota/Outdoor play/Contact Heather Rankin 657 4468.

NEWBRIDGE

Norwood Playgroup, Community Wing, Station Rd, Ratho Station/22 places/Tues-Fri 9.30-11.45/Age 2½-5/Contact venue 333 1021.

NEWINGTON

Duncan Street Playgroup, Baptist Church Hall, Duncan St/16 places/Mon-Thurs 9.30-11.50; Fri 9.30-11.45/Age 2½-5/£5.50 per wk/Outdoor play/Contact Lorraine Adam 667 8097.

NIDDRIE

McGovern House Playroom, McGovern House Community Centre, 52 Niddrie House Park,/10 places/Mon-Fri 10-12, 2-4/Age 1½-5/30p per session/Outdoor play/Contact Andrea McKirdy 657 4546
Niddrie Playgroup, 65 Niddrie Mains Ter/14 places/Mon-Fri 9-12, 12.15-3.15/Age 2½-5/Contact Alison Jappy 661 5897.
St Martin's Pre-school Playgroup, St Martin's Church, Magdalene Dr/24 places/Mon-Fri 9.30-11.30/Age 2½-5/50p per session/Contact Mrs Sneath 669 6158 or Mrs Rush at venue.

OLD TOWN

Youth Training Creche, Canongate Youth Project, Infirmary St/Mon, Wed 10-12/Age 2-4/£1 per session/Contact Shona Montgomery 556 9389.

OXGANGS

Comiston Playgroup, Pentland Community Education Centre, Oxgangs Brae/Mon-Fri 9-11.20/Duty rota/Outdoor play/Contact Eileen Dickinson 441 6958 or venue.

St John's Playgroup, St John's Church Hall, Oxgangs Rd N/24 places/Mon-Fri 9.15-11.45/Age 2½-5/50p per session/Duty rota/Outdoor play/Contact Mrs Brown 445 3754.

PILRIG

McDonald Rd Nursery, 51McDonald Rd/8 places/Mon-Fri 8.30-12.30/Age 2½-5/£2.25 per hr, £9 per am/Outdoor play/Contact Eileen Smillie 557 3082.

PILTON

Royston/Wardieburn Playgroup, Community Centre, Pilton Dr N/24 places/Mon-Fri 9.20-11.30/Outdoor play/Contact venue 552 5700.

West Pilton Playgroup, The Prentice Centre, 1 Granton Mains Ave/12 places/Mon-Thur 9-12,Fri 9-11/Age 2½-5/£1 per week/Outdoor play/Duty rota/Contact Mrs Thompson 552 0485.

POLWARTH

Harrison Playgroup, Phoenix Youth Club, Harrison Gdns/28 places/Mon-Fri 9.30-11.30/Age 3-5/50p per session/Outdoor play/Contact venue 337 2171.

North Merchiston Playgroup, 48 Watson Cres/20 places/Mon-Fri 9.30-11.45/10 places/Mon-Fri 1-3/£5 per wk/Contact 538 2937.

PORTOBELLO

Portobello Toddlers, Beach Lane/24 places/Mon-Fri 9.15-11.45/Age 3-5/Contact venue 669 6849.

St James's Playgroup, Parish Church Hall, Rosefield Pl/Mon, Tues, Thurs, Fri 9-11.40/£3.50 per week/Outdoor play/Contact Mrs Peden 669 6277

RESTALRIG

Restalrig Playgroup, St Margaret's Church Hall, Restalrig Village/20 places/Mon-Fri 9.20-11.30/Age 2½-5/Duty rota/Contact venue.

SAUGHTON

Balgreen Playgroup, Balgreen Bowling Club, Paney Walk, Balgreen Rd/16 places/Mon-Fri 9-11.30/£1.50 per day/Outdoor play/Contact Gwen Scott or Pat Hughes 313 5097.

SIGHTHILL

Calder Playgroup, Sighthill Primary School, 1 Calder Park/15 places/Mon-Fri 9.30-11.30/£1.75 per wk/Contact venue.

Sighthill Tall Flats Playgroup, Sighthill Community Centre, Sighthill Wynd/30 places/Mon-Fri 9.15-11.45/£1.50 per wk/Duta rota/Outdoor play/Contact Mrs Lorimer at venue 453 6078.

SOUTH QUEENSFERRY

Rosebery Playgroup, Rosebery Hall, High St/32 places/Mon-Fri 9.15-11.45/Age 3-5/£2.50 per session/Contact Mrs Bain 331 1558.

South Queensferry Community Centre Playgroup, Community Education Centre, Kirkliston Rd/40 places/Mon-Fri 9.15-11.30; Tues, Thur 1.15-3.30/Age 3-5/No duty rota/Contact Playleaders at venue 331 2113.

Tom Thumb Playgroup, YMCA Hall, 3 The Vennel/15 places/Mon-Fri 9.30-11.30; Mon, Thur 12.15-2.15/Contact venue 319 1530.

SOUTHSIDE

Department of Psychology Nursery, University of Edinburgh, 7 George Sq/25 places/Mon-Fri 9-12/Age 3-5/£2 per wk/Outdoor play/Contact Mrs Slade 650 3440/3448.

STOCKBRIDGE/COMELY BANK

International Playgroup, St Stephen's Church, St Stephen's St/24 places/Tue, Wed, Thurs 9.15-11.45/Age 3-5/£25 per term approx/Duty rota/ Contact Angela Lamb 558 1854.

Stockbridge Playgroup, Youth Wing, Broughton High School, Carrington Rd/25 places/Mon-Fri 9.10-11.25/Outdoor play/Contact Mrs Burden 332 6316.

VIEWFORTH

Viewforth Playgroup, Viewforth Church, 104 Gilmore Pl/24 places/Mon-Fri 9.30-12/Age 2½-5/Contact Myra Jameson 229 7659.

WARDIE

Wardie Playgroup, Wardie Resident Hall, 125 Granton Rd/Mon-Fri 9-11.45/Age 3-5/£40 per mth/Contact Mrs Dunlop at venue 552 2446.

WEST END

Manor Playgroup, 4 Manor Pl/12 places/Mon, Tues, Wed, Fri 9.30-11.30/Age 2½-5/£3 per morning/Contact Mrs Platfoot 220 1466 or Mrs Duff 337 7765.

Wester Coates Nursery, 13 Wester Coates Ter/16 places/Mon-Fri 8.50-12.10/ Age 2½-5/£8 per am/No duty rota/Outdoor play/Contact Mrs Hawkins 346 7398.

WESTER HAILES

Hailes Playgroup, Hailesland Primary School, Hailesland Pl/24 places/Age 2´-5/Mon-Fri 9.30-11.45/£2 per week/Outdoor play/Contact Mrs Flockhart 442 3891.

WILLOWBRAE

Northfield Playgroup, Northfield Community Centre, Northfield Rd/32 am places, Age 3; 40 pm places, Age 4/Mon-Fri 9.15-11.45, 12.30-3/50p per session/Duty rota/Outdoor play/Contact Mrs Cook 661 5723.

Willowbrae Play Centre, The Clinic, Willowbrae House, 86 Willowbrae Rd/30 am places, 24 pm places/Mon-Fri 9.15-11.45; Mon, Wed, Fri 12.45-3.15/Age 3-5/70p per session/Contact Mrs Robertson 661 3360.

PRIVATE NURSERIES

All private nurseries should be registered with the Social Work Department, who can provide a list of registered groups (556 6787). Lists are updated regularly by them, and it is worth phoning them if you cannot find a suitable nursery in the required area. Please remember that an entry is not necessarily a recommendation. Facilities, type of care, and safety standards should be checked personally. Most private nurseries are open 5 days a week with extended hours to help working parents. Some nurseries operate an after school club to collect childen and look after them until the parents return from work. Check with the individual nurseries to see if they offer this service. Nurseries indicated with a † accept children under the age of 2. Places for the under 2s can be hard to find so try to register with the nursery as soon as possible, even before the baby is born. Scottish Independent Nurseries Association (SINA) was set up in 1991 to provide support and information for members nurseries. It aims to introduce a Code of Conduct to ensure high standards of care, safety and play are met by its members. For information about the Working Mothers Association *See* Childcare p120. Nurseries are listed by area: Central, where the nurseries have been numbered to correspond to the locations indicated on the map pvi-vii, and East, South and West, alphabetically within area. Where a range of prices is given, the higher price usually refers to under 2s where the ratio of staff to children is high.

Central

†**The Birrell Collection,** 17 Walker Street/25 places/Mon-Fri 8.15-6/2-5 yrs/ £85.50 per wk/Outdoor play/Contact Karen Flight 225 8031.

Early Days Nursery, 36 Palmerston Pl/36 places/Mon-Fri 8-6/0-5yrs/£16-20 pd/Outdoor play/Contact Lorraine Ewing 226 4491

N2†EDC Workplace Nursery, Level 3, City Chambers, High St/29 places/Mon-Thur 8-6/Fri 8-5/3 mths-5 yrs/Costs on request/Contact Linda O'Neill 529 4335

N1†Elim Nursery Centre, 29 Candlemaker Row/40 places/Mon-Fri 8.30-5.30/ 3 mths-5 yrs/£69-83 per wk/Special rates for one parent families/Contact Mrs Veitch 225 3633.

N3†Royal Infirmary of Edinburgh NHS Trust Day Nursery, 3 Lauriston Park/ 29 places/Mon-Fri 8-5.30/6 mths-5 yrs/£70-£80 per wk/£1.56-£1.78 per hr/Outdoor play/Contact Kareen Dallas 229 4795.

N4†Royal Mile Nursery, Stamp Office Close, 215 High St/20 places/Mon-Fri 8.15-5.45/3mo-5 yrs/£75-90 per wk/Outdoor play/Contact Alison Laurie 226 6574.

Welcome Nursery, 2A Nelson St/12 places/Mon-Fri 8-6, Sat Sun on request/ 2yrs up/Mon-Fri £2.20 ph, Sat&Sun £5.50 ph minimum 2 hours/Special needs children welcome/Outdoor play/Contact Lee Long 557 5770

†**Westside Nursery,** 29 Grove St/20 places/Mon-Fri 8-6/3mths-5 yrs/£10 ps/ £80 per wk/Outdoor Play/Contact Moira Anderson 229 9089

East

†**Brighton Nursery,** 17 West Brighton Cres/18 places/Mon-Fri/18 mths-5 yrs/£16.50 pd/£82.50 per wk /Outdoor play/ Contact Jenny Allison 669 1185.

†**The Castle Nursery,** Kinnaird Park, Newcraighall Rd/58 places/Mon-Fri 7.45-6.00/0-5 yrs/£85 per wk/£11 ps (am), £10 ps (pm)/Outdoor play/Special needs children welcome/Contact 669 9200.

†**East Craigs Nursery,** 78 Craigs Rd/15 places/Mon-Fri 8-6/From birth/Cost on application/Not open to the public/Scottish Office Employees only/Outdoor play/Contact Mrs Marilyn Morris 244 8986.

Mannafields Christian Nursery School, 170 Easter Rd/15 places/Mon-Fri 10-12.30/3-5yrs/approx £15 per wk/Outdoor play/All welcome/Contact Josee Scott 556 5050.

Mr Squirrels Nursery, 27 Cargil Ter/15 places/Mon-Fri 8.15-5.30/2-5 yrs/ £90 per wk/Outdoor play/Contact Mrs B Campbell 552 0499.

The Pelican Nursery, 227 North High St, Musselburgh/20 places/Mon-Fri 8-6/2-5 yrs/£75 per wk/£15 pd/Outdoor play/Contact Mr K Fowler 652 2576 alternatively Liz or Wendy on 653 6882 day.

†**Rooftop Kindergarten,** 11 Lochend Rd/16 places/Mon-Fri 8.15-5.45/0-5 yrs/ £80-90 per wk (lunch extra)/After school club/£35 per wk/Outdoor play/ Contact 553 1250.

†**Seabeach Nursery**, 27 Straiton Pl, Portobello/25 places/Mon-Fri 8-6/0-5 yrs/ £16pd £80 per wk/Outdoor play/Contact Jeanne Macmillan 657 3249

North

†**Bellevue House Nursery**, 2a Bellevue Cres/25 places/Mon-Fri 7.30-6.15/ 3 mths-5 yrs/£90-95 per wk/£18-19 pd/Outdoor play/Contact Mrs May Morrison 556 7085.

†**Claremont Nursery**, 18 East Claremont St/36 places/Mon-Fri 6 mths-5 yrs/ £85-97.50 per wk/Outdoor play/Contact Mrs Gallacher 556 5382.

†**Edinburgh Nursery Creche**, 13 East London St/18 places/Mon-Fri 8-5.45/ 3mths-2 yrs/£18.25 pd/£10 per half-session/Outdoor play/Contact Karen Fairlamb 557 9014.

†**Edinburgh Nursery**, 3 Beaverhall Rd/31 places/Mon-Fri 8-5.45/1-3 yrs/£17-18.25pd/£9-10per half day/Outdoor play/Contact Karen Fairlamb 556 9252

Edinburgh Nursery School, 129 Broughton Rd/20 places/Mon-Fri 8-5.45/2-5 yrs £17 pd/Outdoor play/Contact Karen Fairlamb 557 5675.

†**Edinburgh Nursery Creche II**, 71a Broughton St/8 places/Mon-Fri 8-5.45/ 3mths-2 yrs/£18.25 pd/£10 per half day/Outdoor play/Contact Karen Fairlamb 556 3373.

†**New Town Nursery**, Dean Ter/55 places/Mon-Fri 8.15- 5.45/3mths-5yrs/ £77.50-90 per wk/Outdoor play/Contact Yvonne McLellan 332 5920.

†**Summerside Kindergarden,** 1 Summerside St/14 places/Mon-Fri 8-6/0-5 yrs/£90 per wk/£18 pd/Outdoor play/Contact Mrs Carol-Anne McLeod 554 6560.

South

†**Astley Grange Nurseries,** 133 Grange Loan, 20 places/Mon-Fri 8-6/Baby Creche/3mths-14mths//£9.75 ps/Tweenie Nursery/27 places/14mths-3yrs/ £8.50-9.75 ps/Toddler Nursery/2-5yrs/£8.50 ps/Outdoor play/Contact Sue Martin or Sue Rankin 668 2773

†**The Birrell Collection,** 7 Blantyre Ter/27 places/Mon-Fri 8.15-6/3 mths-5 yrs/ £85.50 per wk/Outdoor play/Contact Morag Skinner 447 9797.

†**The Birrell Collection,** Princess Margaret Rose Hospital, Frogston Rd W/34 places/Mon-Fri 7.30-6/3 mths-5 yrs/£92.25 per wk/Outdoor play/Contact Nancy Cockburn 445 4450.

†**Braid Hills Nursery,** 38 Craiglockhart Ave/29 places/Mon-Fri 8-6/3mths-5 yrs/£15 pd/£75 per wk/Outdoor play/Contact Miss A Black 444 0880.

†**Buckstone Nursery,** 226 Braid Rd/25 places/Mon-Fri 8-6/3 mths-8 yrs/£70-80/Outdoor play/After School Club/Contact Alison Bruce 445 2227.

†**The College Nursery School,** 23 Hope Ter/20 places/Mon-Fri 8-6/3 mths-5 yrs/Outdoor play/Contact 447 7688.

†**Craiglockhart Nursery,** Napier University, Craiglockhart Campus, 219 Colinton Rd/30 places/Mon-Fri 8.30-5.30/15 mths-5 yrs/From £65 per wk/Students at Napier may apply for financial assistance/Nursery also open to public/ School holiday places available/Outdoor play/Contact Mrs Marilyn Morris 455 4281.

†**First Class Nurseries,** 50 Kirk Brae/36 places/Mon-Fri 8-6/3mths-5 yrs/£80-98 per wk/£15 pd/Outdoor play/After School club/Contact Mrs Gail White 664 3031.

†**Florence House Nursery,** 46 Bruntsfield Pl/Mon-Fri 8-6/3mths- 5yrs/£9-10 ps/Outdoor play/Contact Nancie Kelly 229 1970

†**Florence House Nursery II,** 82 Newbattle Ter/Mon-Fri 8-6/3mths-5yrs/£8.50-£9.50 ps/Contact Nancie Kelly 229 1970

†**Kath's Kindergarten,** 27 Angle Park Ter/20 places/Mon-Fri 8-5.30/3 mths-5 yrs/£75-85 per wk/Outdoor play/Contact Kath Stewart 337 7793.

†**Maisie's Creche,** 21a Millerfield Pl/36 places/Mon-Fri 7-5.30/6mths-3 yrs/ £3.00 ph/Min stay 3 hrs/Priority to children of LHB employees/Outdoor play/Contact Rosie Oliver 668 4249.

†**Mayfield Baby Creche,** 28 Kilmaurs Rd/9 places/Mon-Fri 8-6/3mths-1yr/£90 per wk/Outdoor play/Contact Samantha Jameson 667 1832

†**Mayfield Nursery,** 119 Mayfield Rd/57 places/Mon-Fri 8-6/12 mths-5 yrs/ £85-90 per wk/Outdoor play/After School Club/Contact Miss V Hunter 667 3908.

†**Meadows Nursery,** 11 Meadow Pl/27 places/Mon-Fri 8.15-5.45/3 mths-5 yrs/£65-£75 per wk/£2 ph/Outdoor play/Contact 229 5316.

Morningside Day Nursery, 64 Morningside Dr/40 places/Mon-Fri 8.15-5.45/ 2-5 yrs/£100 per wk/Outdoor play/After School Care/Contact Mrs Miller 447 4778.

†**Papoose Nursery,** 65 Nile Grove/24 places/Mon-Fri 8.15-5.45/3 mths-5 yrs/ £17-18.50 pd/£85-92.50 per wk/Outdoor play/Contact Rosemary Flannigan 447 6580.

Pippin Nursery, 20 Valleyfield St/10 places/Mon-Fri 9-5/2 1/2-5 yrs/£7.50 £80 per wk/Contact Mrs.M.J Whitelock 229 0498

†**St Denis and Cranley School,** Ettrick Road/28 places/Mon-Fri 8.15-5.30/ 6mths-5yrs/£90-110 per wk/Outdoor play/Contact 229 1500

†**Tipperlin Nursery,** Royal Edinburgh Hospital, Morningside Pl/60 places/0-5yrs/7-6/£85 per wk/Discount and priority for employees of Edinburgh Healthcare Trust/Outdoor Play/Contact Marilyn Morris 445 7466

†**Totos Nursery,** 11A Bruntsfield Cres/24 places/Mon-Fri 8-6/3mths-5yrs/ ú19.44 pd £405 per mth/Outdoor play/Contact Ann-Marie Davidson 447 0413

†**University Day Nursery,** 79/81 Dalkeith Rd/48 places/8.45-5, 15 mins extra am and pm by arrangement/6 wks-5 yrs/£90-110 per wk/Preference given to students or employees of Edinburgh University/Students pay pro rata depending on income and available subsidy/Outdoor play/Contact Mrs N Clouston 667 9584.

†**Young Edinburgh Kindergarten,** 34 Upper Gilmore Pl/20 places/Mon-Fri 8-6/3 mths-5 yrs/£85-95 per wk/Outdoor play/Contact Mrs Kristine Henderson 229 9055.

West

†**Balgreen Private Day Care,** 11 Balgreen Ave/21 places/Mon-Fri 8-6/0-5 yrs/ £15 pd/Outdoor play/Contact Miss Leigh Gordon or Mrs Vivienne Watt 337 4619.

†**Barnton Nursery,** 534 Queensferry Rd/60 places/Mon-Fri 8-6/3 mths-5 yrs/ £75-90 per wk/£17-19 pd/After School Club/Contact Alison Bruce 339 6340.

†**The Birrell Collection,** Queen Margaret College, Clerwood Ter/29 places/Mon-Fri 8.15-6/3 mths-5 yrs/£85.50 per wk/Outdoor play/Contact Rowena Sword 317 7713.

Crewe Road Nursery, Fet-Lor Youth Centre, 122 Crewe Rd/20 places/Mon-Fri 8.15-5.45/2-5 yrs/£60 per wk/£7 per half session/Outdoor play/Contact Lorraine Suggit 332 8392.

†**Croilegan Nursery,** 40 Corstophine Hill Gdns/13 places/Mon-Fri 8-5.45/0-5yrs/£92.70 per wk £386.25 per mth/Outdoor play/Contact Christine Sinclair 334 2960

†**The Gyle Nursery,** Gyle Shopping Centre/39 places/Mon-Fri 8-6, Sat 9-5, Sun 10-5/3mths-6yrs/£2.50 ph £18.25pd/A 'drop-in' nursery 1hr min, full-time places also available/Outdoor play/Contact Karen Fairlamb 539 7099. See Shopping p?.

†**Heriot Watt University Nursery,** Riccarton Campus/40 places/Mon-Fri 8-5.30/From birth/From £70 per wk/Nursery also open to public and for conference users/Outdoor play/Contact Mrs Marilyn Morris 451 5236.

Juniper Green Private Nursery, 8 Woodhall Drive/30 places/Mon-Fri 8-6/2-5yrs/£8.50ps, £80 per wk/Outdoor play/Contact Moira Hallyburton/ 458 3003

†**Playhouse Nursery,** 20 Old Kirk Rd/15 places/Mon-Fri 8-5.45/3mths-5 yrs/ £11.50 per session, £95 per wk/Contact Karen Brown 334 5859.

Ratho Children's Nursery, 20 Baird Rd, Ratho/14 places/Mon-Fri 8-6/2-8yrs/ £15 pd £60 per wk/Outdoor play/Contact Donna Morgan 335 3848

†**Red Apple Nursery School,** 11 Ardmillan Ter/30 places/Mon-Fri 8.15-5.45/3 mths-5 yrs/From £8 ps/Outdoor play/Also at Bankton Sq, Muirston, Livingston/Contact Diane Peden 337 5940 or 0506 462200.

†**Wester Hailes Child Care Project,** 26a Hailesland Pk/49 places/Mon-Fri 8.30-6/0-5 yrs/£3.50 per wk/Outdoor play/Urban Aid funded project providing care for single families within the Wester Hailes area/Contact Audrey Millar 453 1819.

Westland Kindergarten, 19 Hillview Rd/10 places/Mon-Fri 8-6/2-5 yrs/£8 ps/Contact Mrs A W Hanlin 334 5758.

NURSERY SCHOOLS AND NURSERY CLASSES IN SCHOOLS

These are run by the Lothian Regional Council Department for children aged 3-5 years. Lothian performs well above national standards by guaranteeing a place for all 4 year-olds (and about 50% of 3 year-olds), although available places may not be in the nearest school. Classes are normally operated on a part-day basis (either am or pm) 5 days a week during school terms but some full-time places may be available. Parents are encouraged to participate in all activities but there is no duty rota. There may be a long waiting list for your school of choice and you should put your child's name down as soon as possible after his or her 2nd birthday. At some schools you may be more likely to get a place if you request an afternoon session — check with the Head Teacher when you fill in the application form. Below is a list of Nursery Schools and Primary Schools with Nursery Provision in Edinburgh. Your child need not be going to attend the Primary School to which the Nursery School is attached. Special needs children are integrated in all nursery classes. There is a Gaelic nursery class at Tollcross Primary. There are also 'Under 5 centres' based in secondary schools which allow parents to attend academic or recreational classes. Copies of the complete list containing all the schools below and all others in the Lothian area may be obtained from Lothian Regional Council, Education Department, 40 Torphichen St EH3 8JT (479 2175).

NURSERY SCHOOLS

Balgreen School, 175 Balgreen Rd EH11 3AT/337 1454
Calderglen School, Wester Hailes Rd EH11 4NG/453 5754
Cameron House, Cameron House Ave EH16 5LF/667 5117
Children's House, Wauchope Ter EH16 4NU/661 1401
Cowgate, 144 Cowgate EH1 1RP/225 7251
Grassmarket, 11/15 The Vennel EH1 2HU/229 6540
Greengables, 8a Niddrie House Gdns EH16 4UR/669 9083/Offers full-time places 8pm-6pm
High School Yards, High School Yards EH1 1LZ/556 6536
Hope Cottage, Cowan's Close, East Crosscauseway EH8 9HF/667 5795
Levenhall, Moir Pl, Musselburgh EH21 8JD/665 7599
Liberton, Mount Vernon Rd EH16 6JQ/664 3155
Lochrin, West Tollcross EH3 9QN/229 7743
Princess Elizabeth, Clearburn Cres EH16 5ER/667 0946
St Leonard's, North Richmond St EH8 9SY/667 4674
Stanwell, Junction Pl EH6 5JA/554 1309
The Spinney Lane, 13a The Spinney EH17 7LD/664 9102
Tynecastle, McLeod St EH11 2NJ/337 5461
Westfield Court, Westfield Court EH11 2RJ/337 4914

NURSERY CLASSES IN PRIMARY SCHOOLS

Abbeyhill, Abbey St EH7 5SJ/661 3054
Bonaly, Bonaly Grove EH13 0QD/441 7211
Bonnington, Bonnington Rd EH6 5NQ/554 1370
Broomhouse, Saughton Rd EH11 3RQ/443 3783
Broughton, Broughton Rd EH7 4LD/556 7028
Brunstane, Magdalene Dr EH15 3BE/669 4498

Buckstone, Buckstone La East EH10 6UY/445 4545
Burdiehouse, Burdiehouse Cres EH17 8EX/664 2351
Campie, 3 Stoneyhill Farm Rd, Musselburgh EH21 6QS/665 2045
Carrick Knowe, Lampacre Rd EH12 7HU/334 4505
Colinton, Redford Pl EH13 0AL/441 1946
Clermiston, Parkgrove Pl EH4 7NP/336 3361
Clovenstone, 54 Clovenstone Park EH14 3EY/453 4242
Corstorphine, Corstorphine High St EH12 7SY/334 3865
Craigentinny, Loganlea Dr EH7 6LR/661 2749
Craigmillar, Harewood Rd EH16 4NT/661 3481
Craigmuir, West Pilton Park EH4 4ET/332 6666
Cramond, Cramond Cres EH4 6PG/312 6450
Curriehill, 210 Lanark Rd W EH14 5NN/449 3359
Dalry, Dalry Rd EH11 2JB/337 6086
Drumbrae, Ardshiel Ave EH4 7HP/339 5071
Duddingston, Duddingston Rd EH15 1SW/669 5092
Dumbryden, Dumbryden Gdns EH14 2NZ/453 5686
East Craigs, 79 Craigmount Brae EH12 8XF/339 7115
Fernieside, Moredun Park Rd EH17 7HL/664 2154
Ferryhill, Groathill Rd N EH4 2SQ/332 4244
Flora Stevenson, Comely Bank EH4 1BG/332 1604
Fort, North Fort St EH6 4HF/554 7101
Gracemount, Lasswade Rd EH16 6UA/664 2331
Granton, Boswall Parkway EH5 2DA/552 3987
Gylemuir, Wester Broom Pl EH12 7RT/334 7138
Hailesland, Hailesland Pl EH14 2SL/442 3894
Hermitage Park, Hermitage Park EH6 8HD/554 2952
Holy Cross RC, Craighall Rd EH6 4RE/552 1972
Hunter's Tryst, Oxgangs Green EH13 9JE/445 1510
Inchview, West Pilton Ave EH4 4BX/332 8186
James Gillespie's, Whitehouse Loan EH9 1AT/447 1014
Juniper Green, 20 Baberton Mains Wynd EH14 3EE/442 2121
Leith, St Andrew's Pl EH6 7EG/554 4844
Leith Walk, Brunswick Rd EH7 5NG/556 3873
Liberton, 229 Gilmerton Rd EH16 5UD/664 2337
Lismore, Bingham Ave EH15 3HZ/669 4588
London Street, East London St EH7 4BW/556 4008
Longstone, Redhall Grove EH14 2DU/443 4743
Loretto RC, 20 Newbigging, Musselburgh EH21 7AH/665 2572
Muirhouse, Muirhouse Pl W EH4 4PX/332 2793
Murrayburn, Sighthill Loan EH11 4NP/453 5339
Musselburgh Burgh, Kilwinning St, Musselburgh EH21 7EE/665 3407
Newcraighall, Whitehill St, Newcraighall, Musselburgh EH21 8QZ/669 3598
Niddrie, Niddrie Mains Rd EH15 3HG/669 1658
Orwell, Orwell Pl EH11 2AD/337 6181
Oxgangs, Colinton Mains Dr EH12 9AE/441 3649
Peffermill, Craigmillar Castle Av EH16 4DH/661 3456
Pirniehall, West Pilton Cres EH4 4HP/332 5256
Prestonfield, Peffermill Rd EH16 5LJ/667 1336

Roseburn, Roseburn St EH12 5PL/337 6096
Royal Mile, Canongate EH8 8BZ/556 3347
Royston, Boswall Parkway EH5 2JH/552 4534
St David's RC, West Pilton Pl EH4 4DF/332 3500
St Francis's RC, Niddrie Mains Rd EH16 4DS/661 3053
St John's RC, Hamilton Ter EH15 1NB/669 1363
St John Vianney RC, Ivanhoe Cres EH16 6AU/664 1742
St Joseph's RC, Broomhouse Cres EH11 3TD/443 4591
St Mark's RC, 63 Firhill Cres EH13 9EE/441 2948
St Mary's RC, Links Gdns EH6 7JG/554 7291
St Ninian's RC, Restalrig Rd South EH7 6JA/661 3431
St Peter's RC, 25 Falcon Gdns EH10 4AP/447 5742
Sighthill, 1 Calder Park EH11 4NF/453 2464
Silverknowes, Muirhouse Gdns EH4 4SX/336 1508
Stenhouse, Stevenson Dr EH11 3HL/443 1255
Stockbridge, Hamilton Pl EH3 5BA/332 6109
Tollcross, Fountainbridge EH3 9QG/229 7828
Towerbank, Figgate Bank EH15 1HX/669 1551
Westburn, 55 Sighthill Rd EH11 4PB/442 2997
Whitecraig, 44a Whitecraig Cres, Whitecraig, Musselburgh EH21 8NG\665 3278

INDEPENDENT SCHOOLS

Some of the independent schools in Edinburgh have nursery departments. These are listed below, with fees for 1994/95. Most offer the choice of a morning, afternoon or whole day placement. The minimum age of entry is 3 yrs. The Scottish Independent Schools Information Service at 11 Castle St EH2 3AH (220 2106) will send you a free booklet containing basic information about all the Independent Schools in Scotland.

Cargilfield School, 37 Barnton Ave W EH4 6HU/336 2207/£450-£590 per term/Co-educational.

Clifton Hall School, Newbridge, EH28 8LQ/ 333 1359/ £400-£880 per term/ Coeducational.

The Compass School, West Rd, Haddington EH41 3RD/Haddington 2642/ £525-880 per term/Co-educational nursery from 4yrs.

Edinburgh Academy Preparatory School, 10 Arboretum Rd EH3 5PL/552 3690/£272-684 per term/Co-educational nursery.

George Heriot's School, Lauriston Pl EH2 9EQ/229 7263/£285-435 per term/ Co-educational.

George Watson's College, Colinton Rd EH10 5EG/447 7931/£294-442 per term/Co-educational.

The Mary Erskine and Stewart's Melville Junior School, Queensferry Rd EH4 3EZ/332 0888/£548 per term/Co-educational.

Rudolf Steiner, 60 Spylaw Rd EH10 5BR/337 3410/£410 per term/co-educational. The kindergarten is an integral part of the school and the central aim of the education is to develop and unite in a harmonious way the child's thoughts, feelings and actions.

St Denis and Cranley School, 3 Ettrick Rd EH10 5BJ/229 1500/£400-760 per term/Co-educational nursery.

St George's School, The Lodge, Lansdowne House, Coltbridge Ter EH12 6AB/ 337 2885/£430-725 per term/Co-educational nursery.

St Margaret's School, East Suffolk Rd EH16 5PJ/668 1986/£643 per term/Co-educational nursery.

LOOKING FORWARD TO STARTING SCHOOL

There is only one entry date for primary school in Scotland, and that is in August. A child whose 5th birthday falls between 1st March and 28th February the following year may start school in August. Some children will be entering school 6 months after their 5th birthday, while others will be starting school 6 months before their 5th birthday. For the younger children it is not compulsory to start in August. If you want advice about the best starting date for your child, get in touch with your local school or the Divisional Education Officer (address below) — this also applies if you have just arrived from England or Wales, where the admission ages differ.

To enrol your child at the school in your catchment area, telephone the Head Teacher and arrange an appointment. This can be done any time during the 12 months prior to your child's admission to school.

If you wish to send your child to a school which is outside your catchment area, your request will be considered provided there is a place available. You must apply for a place at a non-district school between November and February for the following August. A pink form for this purpose may be obtained from the Assistant Director of Education (Property and Support Services — Administration), Lothian Region Education Department, 40 Tor-

phichen St, EH3 8JT (229 9166). You must also inform the Head Teacher of your catchment school that you have applied to a school outwith that area.

A list of all primary schools may be obtained from the Divisional Education Officer (Edinburgh Division), Lothian Region Education Department, address as above. A prospectus for the school should be available from the Head Teacher.

For details of school uniform stockists *see* Schoolwear p19.

SPECIAL SCHOOLS

If you feel that your child may benefit from attending a special school, for whatever reason, contact the Special Education Services, address as above.

LOCAL PLAY ORGANISATIONS

Scottish Pre-School Play Association
15 Smith's Place, Leith
553 2185
Mon-Fri 10-3 (school term only)

Provides information and gives guidance regarding parent and toddler groups and playgroups, including how to set them up. Resource centre, providing related publications and creative play material e.g. paint, clay, paper etc. in bulk at reduced cost to members and non-members.

Creches can be provided for conferences and annual meetings which take place at the Association.

National Centre for Play
Moray House College of Education
Cramond Rd N
312 6001
Jon Busby- Centre Manager

The NCP is a SCOTVEC approved centre and also a resource facility for information, training and research on childcare, children, play and playwork. Set up in 1982 as the Play Resource Unit, the NCP caters for everybody with an interest in the subject, from parents and playworkers to local authorities and voluntary sector organisations, offering a wide range of services to both subscribers and non-subscribers.

Information on play related topics ranging from health and safety,

equal opportunities and anti-bullying to childcare legislation and fund raising.

See Adult Classes and Training p163.

Mobile Projects Association
(Scotland)
12 Picardy Pl
556 7580

A charity which exists to provide support, information, advice and training to those involved in establishing, developing and running mobile community resources. It also aims to promote the concept of mobility.

MPAS has a particular interest in mobile provision for under 5s and many of its members run playbuses and mobile creches.

Various publications on mobile provision for under 5s, including a directory of Scottish mobile projects.

Childcare

If you return to work or to studies, are ill, or for some other reason are unable to look after your child, you will have to make arrangements for someone else to do so. If circumstances are particularly difficult, Lothian Regional Council Social Work Department may be able to assist — contact your local Children's Centre or District Social Work Centre *see* Welfare p247. There are many private nurseries which provide full or part day care. *See* Pre-School Play and Education, Private Nurseries p107. Alternatively you may take your child to be looked after by a childminder in her own home. The search for, and selection of, someone else to care for your child can be extremely stressful and

the arrangement you settle for may not be what you would have wished. Children's needs do change however, and forced changes in childcare arrangements, while unwelcome for their disruption at the time, can also bring with them new opportunities. Remember too, childcare expenses are not tax deductible. This section provides some guidance on how to go about finding someone to care for your children; it should also be of interest to anyone considering looking after children other than their own.

A group which may help minimise the stresses of the working parent is

Parents at Work (Formerly, Working Mothers Association)
77 Holloway Rd, London
0171 700 5772/2

The group provides an informal support network for working parents and mums-to-be who are interested in combining career and family. Contact national organisation for details of local group.

See Parent and Toddler Groups Dalry p94 and Tollcross p97 for details of minders groups.

CHILDMINDERS

Childminders care for children in their own homes. By law, they must be registered with the Social Work Department Community Care Registration and Inspection Service if they care for a child under 8, to whom they are not closely related, for more than 2 hours a day for reward. Registration involves health, police, fire and home safety checks and is reviewed annually. Childminders are approved to care for a maximum of 5 children under 8, of whom no more than 3 are under 5. These figures include the childminder's own children. In practice, many childminders are not registered and this could mean prosecution for both childminder and parent under the new Children's Act. If you are in any doubt, ask to see a registration certificate.

How to Find a Childminder

A list of all registered childminders is available from the Community Care Registration and Inspection Service. Health Visitors may also have copies of this list, and may know local childminders or have a knowledge of a vacancy list organised by childminders in their area. Other working parents are also worth approaching since they may have been through this themselves and know of a childminder who might be suitable.

How Much Will it Cost?

The Scottish Childminding Association recommends a minimum rate which increases each autumn. Rates in Edinburgh are currently £1.50/hr minimum. The average rate is £2/hr but charges may be much higher. Childminders are responsible for their own Tax and National Insurance payments and should have their own Public Liability and Accident Insurance cover. The latter has, in the past, been provided by Lothian Regional Council, at no cost to the childminder. This continues to be the case at the time of going to press but it is possible that the practice will be discontinued. You should check that your childminder carries appropriate insurance cover.

Choosing a Childminder

You will need to decide the area in which you wish your child to be cared for before phoning the Registration and Inspection Service. You may wish to find a childminder close to your home so that your child can visit local toddler groups and carry friendships through playgroup to school. You may on the other hand prefer your childminder to reside near to your place of work.

Working from the list for your chosen area you will need to phone round to find out who has vacancies and arrange to go to see them. You will need to know the times you will be dropping off and collecting your child (remember to add 5-10 mins at each end so that the handover is not hurried and you have time to discuss the day's events). You may also wish to ask at this stage about the childminder's own children and any others they mind. Be prepared to find few childminders with vacancies. During the visit to your potential childminder discuss the details of the contract eg cost; min and max hours and flexibility of these; whether the child will need taken to and collected from playgroup (the childminder should be paid during playgroup hours); what is included in the cost (food, nappies and outings etc may or may not be); what holidays the childminder takes and whether you will have to pay a holiday retainer; any particular exclusions (eg not school holidays). Public holidays may need to be paid for in full.

Try to find out what style of care is being offered eg activities, other responsibilities of the childminder which might impinge on the care offered to the child, diet, approach to discipline. There may be other things important to you which you will want to ask about (eg smoking, sexism, racism, use of TV). Discussion and negotiations early on can help to make things easier for both you and your childminder. Try to be clear about expectations on both sides and remember to treat your childminder as you would yourself wish to be treated. Most employees would be appalled at the thought of no holiday pay, no sick pay, sudden unexpected overtime. Most childminders will form a written contract with the parent using forms supplied by Lothian Childcarers Association.

Selecting a Suitable Childminder; A Parent's Guide to Childminding is a useful booklet to read. It is issued by the Scottish Childminding Association and can be obtained from their Administration office or from the Lothian Child Carers' Association, (see 'Organisations involved in Childcare' p123), at a cost of £2 + 50p p&p.

In the end, you will probably choose the person with whom you feel most comfortable. It is worth following your feelings about whom your child will be most 'at home' with, and a good childminder will usually ask you a lot of the above questions.

CHILDCARE IN IN YOUR OWN HOME

You may consider it preferable to employ someone to look after your child/ren in your own home. 'Nannies' may 'live in' or 'live out'. The choice between these options will depend on the nature of your childcare needs, your available accommodation, how you feel about sharing your living space and also on your financial resources. Nannies are not required to be registered in the same way that childminders are, the onus will therefore be on you to vet applicants' suitability. If you wish to employ a nanny the following suggestions may help you to find the right person.

Local contacts or friends may be able to suggest and recommend someone. Newspaper advertising usually elicits many responses and a one-day advert should be sufficient. The majority of such adverts appear in The Scotsman and Evening News on Fridays and need to be with the publishers at least two days earlier. It is worth thinking beforehand about the sort of person you are looking for and to specify your requirements with regard to eg training, experience, age. This can reduce the responses to a more manageable number. If you seek an NNEB trained person (nursery nurse) and wish to employ someone newly qualified, contact the local Colleges of Further Education which offer this training

(Esk Valley College 663 1951, Stevenson College 453 6161, West Lothian College, Bathgate 634300). Alternatively you may wish to approach a local agency for help in finding a suitable nanny (see Professional Help with Childcare and Babysitting, p124.

Conditions of Service

You should decide beforehand what you are offering in terms of hours, holidays, extra duties (eg babysitting, housework, making meals, taking child to playgroup, classes, etc). In the case of live-in help you should also decide what restrictions, if any, you wish to place upon the use of your home. Rates of pay vary widely both for live-in and live-out care. At present full time live-out care costs £125-150/wk net, or £3.50-4/hr part time. Live-in care costs £100-125/wk net but don't forget to take account of all additional costs. When deciding what you will pay take into account training, experience, number of children, extra duties and range of responsibilities. Remember too the additional cost to you of N.I. contributions and Income Tax payments. These can amount to ⅓ more than the person's take-home pay.

Interviews

Prepare your list of questions in advance. Selecting the right person will be based on your intuition as well as what you know about the person. Be sure to obtain references from previous employers wherever possible.

Contract

It is important to have mutual expectations clear at the outset. A written contract stating all the agreed conditions of service, is very helpful in preventing problems later on, or at least making them easier to sort out.

CHILDREN'S CENTRES AND DAY CARE

Children's Centres

Lothian Regional Council Social Work Department run 19 Children's Centres to help care for young children who, for social or health reasons, would benefit from this care. The service is free and may be offered Mon-Fri 8-6. For further information contact Lothian Regional Council Department of Social Work. See Welfare p247.

Day Care

This may be offered as an alternative to Children's Centres. Day carers are assessed by the Social Work Department to care for children in the carer's own home. This service is free. Application for places is through a Children's Centre (or through the District Social Work Centre in Lothians outlying areas) and, as with the Centre applications, this offers a service to parents who have social, financial or health problems.

ORGANISATIONS INVOLVED WITH CHILDCARE

Lothian Child Carers' Association
15 Smith's Pl
553 7289
Mon, Wed and Fri 9-1 (Answerphone at other times)

Information and help with any

aspect of childminding or daycaring. Also informal meetings and coffee mornings for childcarers and the children they are looking after. Organises training for childminders.

Scottish Childminding Association

Room 7
Stirling Business Centre
Wellgreen
Stirling FK8 2DZ
01786 445377
Advice line 01786 449063

A Scottish organisation which promotes good quality childcare within a home environment. It provides support, advice and information to all who are interested in childminding.

One Parent Families Scotland (Formerly Scottish Council for Single Parents)

See Welfare p247.

Local Authority Social Work Departments

See p247.

PROFESSIONAL HELP WITH CHILDCARE AND BABYSITTING

The following will provide help in the home:

Applecart Nannies

661 5665 Carole-Ann

A friendly, personal and sympathetic agency which specialises solely in the recruitment and placement of quality childcare staff. They provide qualified and/or experienced nannies, mothers' helps and baby-sitters, and all types of emergency cover.

Babybusters

538 4271 Susan

NNEBs and nannies available for evening and weekend baby sittites, any age, any area.

Helping Hands

45 Barclay Place
228 1382

Home helps, trained nannies and mothers' helps. Min 3 hrs/session.

Edinburgh Creche Co-op.

11a Forth St
558 3319

A mobile creche service who will set up and run a professional creche on your premises. Co-op members are trained in first aid and can provide everything from baby care, painting, music, trampolining, to special games for older children. Works closely with the Social Work Department and meets Lothian Regional Council guidelines on creche safety. Anything from conferences to a group of parents needing a break can be catered for.

Edinburgh Sitters

13 Gayfield Square
557 3121

Provide a sitter service for lone parent families and carers of children and adults with disabilities.

This service is for those who have no other regular or reliable sitters, and the sitters provided are either volunteers or one of the project workers. Sitters do not undertake nursing or domestic tasks. Due to the high demand, there may be a waiting list and volunteers are always required.

Emergency Mums
313 2316 Veronica Wilson
01505 873168 Fiona Scott

A team of experienced people who will give instant care in the home, enabling parents to attend to their own career responsibilities without disruption. 'Mums' are personally interviewed and vetted very carefully. Aim to have relief help in the home within an hour of an emergency phone call. Can also be used to cover your absence during jury duty.

Night Nannies
467 6363 Fiona

Small group of NNEB qualified or experienced ladies, all over 21. Available for babysitting any evening, occasional daytime. Very reasonable rates.

The Nanny Service
313 2316 Veronica Wilson
01505 873168 Fiona Sott

This nanny agency, formed in Edinburgh 5 years ago by a mother of 4, now has an agency in Glasgow, run by a mother of 3! They offer comprehensive guidance on childcare options, including help with practicalities of employing a nanny (full or part-time), nanny shares, interview questions, contract advice etc. Constant liaison between offices ensures maximum availability of quality temporary staff, especially help or 'another pair of hands'. They also run nanny training courses for parents-to-be. Nanny-link scheme.

Peter Pan Nannies
557 5311

Placement of nannies, mothers' helps and au pairs.

BABYSITTING CIRCLES

These are groups of parents who get together to provide a babysitting service on a 'token' rather than payment basis. You are given a number of tokens and a list of local babysitters (often within walking distance). Tokens are normally for ˝hr or 1 hr each, and you are issued with up to 20 depending on your circle. You can call on babysitters as long as you have enough tokens to pay them, and more tokens can be earned when you go out to babysit for someone else. Double tokens after midnight is the norm! Some circles also operate overnight and daytime services. To find out about circles in your area ask neighbours, local parents, your Health Visitor, local NCT or look on notice boards. All these circles are organised on a purely informal basis and it is up to you to decide if you are happy with the way the circle is run. Many circles will arrange to meet informally, with the children, at regular intervals, so the children know the people they are being left with.

Babysitting
You can, if you wish, employ a neighbouring teenager to babysit for you but bear in mind that she or he should be 16 or over. Current rates are about £2-2.50/hr, double after midnight.

Libraries

"MOM, ARE WE GOING TO THE LIBRARY <u>AGAIN</u>?"

There is a complete list of public libraries with addresses and telephone numbers in the phone book, listed under Edinburgh on the pages devoted to the City of Edinburgh District Council, subsection Recreation Department. Piershill Library will be opening in Spring 1995, and there are plans to upgrade Kirkliston Library in the near future.

Opening hours can vary locally as some of the smaller libraries are only open part-time. Generally, most libraries are open Mon-Fri 9-8.30; Sat 9-1.

To obtain books for children of any age, complete an application form at your local library where you will be issued with a computer card for each child. The card entitles the child to borrow up to 6 books, including books on tape, from any library. The parent is responsible for their children's borrowed books and for handing them back in good condition and on time, although there are no fines on overdue books issued on a child's card. Children may reserve books free of charge.

Categories. In all libraries, children's books are arranged by subject interest and reading level. Shelves are clearly marked and there is a leaflet available explaining the system.

Activities. For information about activities such as storytelling sessions, author visits and craft events look out for leaflets and posters in the library. During the school holidays special events are organised. In 1994 the theme was pirates: 'Treasure Trail — Read your Way To Gold' which required children to read a number of books over the holiday period, write book reports and draw pictures. A card was stamped for every book they read, and as well as getting an edible prize of chocolate coins, their name was entered on the library role of honour.

A guide to school holiday activities for children, which are organised by the Council's Recreation Department, can be obtained from the Recreation Marketing Unit, 17 Waterloo Pl, 529 7905.

Information. The Library public notice boards can be a great source of useful information both of local and more general interest, and are well worth keeping an eye on.

Libraries maintain a diary of forthcoming local events, as well as lists and books of local information.. Many of the libraries now have a 'Capital Information Point', an inter-active multi-media public information system, providing details on all aspects of the council's services such as recreation and education, and other community information. This service is also available at other District Council sites, such as the City Chambers and the Common-wealth Pool, *see* Sources of Information p205. In the libraries listed below, CIP indicates that this service is available.

Look out for **Library Arena** the Libraries' bi-monthly What's On Guide to events, displays and talks which are organised by the Library Service. For further information on general policy and library services for children, contact the Youth

Services Team, Edinburgh Central Library, George IV Bridge, 225 5584.

Kinderbox. All libraries, including mobile libraries, have boxes with a stock of board books and other books for babies and toddlers. Stock includes up-to-date children's fiction and a wide range of information books; poetry, arts and crafts etc. 'Noisy' and 'feely' books are being introduced and pop-up and interactive books are available to borrow and for reference.

Books dealing with 'problem areas' — topics such as the death of a parent or a grandparent, going into hospital, starting playgroup etc are available for children to borrow and there are also 'Parent's Collections' available at Central, Corstorphine, Craigmillar, Leith and Morningside. These books are for parents to borrow to help children with areas of concern, such as starting school, the arrival of a new baby and the 'problem areas' mentioned above.

Drawing facilities with tables, chairs, paper and crayons and a reference stock of magazines including comics such as The Beano, Garfield, Fireman Sam etc. are available in all libraries.

Toys for children to play with are available in all libraries which have enough space. Board games are also available in nearly all libraries. Some libraries have Sega computer games machines and games to play in the library. Some libraries also have **Personal Computers** (PCs), with printers, which can be booked for a period. In the libraries listed below, PC indicates this service. Collections of **large print books** for children are available in all libraries, and within the 5 mobile libraries.

The Libraries' **Audio Service** boasts the largest collection of compact discs in the UK and a vast selection of tapes. The record collections are being gradually phased out. Children can take out membership of the Audio Service for music on CDs and cassette tapes for a nominal annual subscription of £3 (£6 for adults). Up to 2 audio items can be borrowed at any one time. The Audio Service is currently available in the Central Music Library, Oxgangs, Blackhall, Leith, Currie, Craigmillar, Muirhouse, South Queensferry, Portobello, Morningside and Newington libraries.

Children's books on tape are currently available in the following libraries:—

Central Children's, Blackhall, Currie, Corstorphine, Sighthill, Leith, Muirhouse, McDonald Road, Morningside, Oxgangs, Newington, Craigmillar, Fountainbridge, Gilmerton and Moredun. This is a FREE service and up to 6 tapes can be borrowed on the child's library ticket.

Access and toilets. Standards of access vary a great deal, mostly because of the limitations of the buildings. The new purpose-built libraries usually have excellent all-round facilities. All but five of the 23 libraries have wheelchair access, but not all libraries have toilets for the disabled, and a few do not have any public toilet facilities at all. The library staff will allow use of staff toilets if possible.

Nappy changing facilities. Many of the libraries have nappy change units and these are listed in the entries below.

Children's Ethnic Picture Book Collections are available in Bengali, Chinese, Gujarati, Hindi, Punjabi, Urdu and Gaelic languages. Comprehensive collections in 6 languages can be found at Leith,

McDonald Road, Fountainbridge and Central Children's libraries. Libraries which stock smaller collections are Newington, Sighthill, Stockbridge, Morningside, Blackhall, Portobello, Craigmillar and Oxgangs.

There is also a circulating collection of picture books in French.

For further information contact the Ethnic Services Librarian, McDonald Road Library, 529 5636

The Youth Services Team offer advice on aids for children with disabilities and/or special needs. Picture books with sign language, Braille picture books, tactile games, CCTV magnifiers, sub-titled videos and large print books are only a few of the services offered. Big Books can also be found at Blackhall, Leith, McDonald Road, Newington, Oxgangs and Central Children's Libraries. **Large print books** are available in all libraries. Special open days featuring and promoting aspects of the service to children with disabilities are occasionally held. For full details of the services available, contact the Youth Services Team, 225 5584.

The following libraries offer special facilities for young children:

Balgreen Library
173 Balgreen Rd
529 5585

Ramp access to this small library. There are toys available in the bright children's area. Board games are also available. Wide range of children's books. Coin-operated photocopier. CIP.

Blackhall Library
56 Hillhouse Rd
529 5595

Ramp access and car park. The children's section is roomy and attractive with a large stock including sub-titled videos, some for children, available in the adult's section. There are regular story telling sessions, check with staff for dates. Community Room available. Coin-operated photocopier. CIP. PC. **Toilets** for the disabled. Nappy change unit.

Craigmillar Library
7 Niddrie Marischal Gdns
529 5597

External wall mural based on a 'library book' theme featuring designs by local children. Ramp access. The children's area is attractively decorated with posters, and the artistic creations of local children. There is a good selection of children's books, books on tape, toys, audio cassettes and games. Coin-operated photocopier. Sega. CIP. **Toilet** (key at the desk). Nappy change unit.

Edinburgh Central Library
George IV Bridge
225 5584

Comprehensive public reference and information services, major collections of local history material, a large stock of adult fiction and non-fiction and the largest local collection of books about children eg parenting, play, education, problems etc. Boxes of children's books are available in the Fiction and Non-fiction departments, and these may be borrowed as normal.

Extensive Music and Fine Art collections. A Kurzweil reading machine for the blind and a good selection of reading and audio aids for people with disabilities are available. Contact the Domiciliary Section, 225 5584 ext 232.

Toilets in basement. If the toilets are not open, a notice is posted at the top of the stairs. **Creche**, run by the Edinburgh Creche Co-operative, available to library users on Tues, Thurs 10-12. It is intended for the under 5s but older children are also welcome. It is situated upstairs in the Board Room. Access by lift with some stairs to negotiate.

Central Children's Library
George IV Bridge

Next door to the Central Library. Level access. Small compact library which is attractively decorated and laid out to appeal to young children.

Fountainbridge Library
137 Dundee St
529 5616

The entrance in Murdoch Terrace has ramp access. Large selection of children's books, toys, games (ask at the counter). Community Room available. Coin-operated photocopier. Sega. CIP. PC. **Toilets** for the disabled (key at the desk). Nappy change unit

Gilmerton Library
64 Gilmerton Dykes St
529 5628

Ramp access and car park. Small but bright library with a pleasant children's area with toys and books on tape. Games are available at the desk. Coin-operated photocopier. CIP. PC. **Toilets** for the disabled (key at the desk). Nappy change unit.

Mobile Library Service

The Librarian-in-Charge is based at Oxgangs Library, 529 5683. The Mobile Library Service visits more than 70 locations in the Edinburgh area ranging from small villages such as Dalmeny, to large urban locations such as Wester Hailes. Other stops include Lochend, Inch, Craigentinny, Juniper Green, Buckstone, Cramond, Clermiston, Prestonfield, Liberton and Gracemount. A wide variety of books are available, including a varied and ever-changing selection of children's books.

Moredun Library
92 Moredun Park Rd
529 5652

Ramp access. Small friendly library with bright children's area. Lots of board games available. Coin-operated photocopier. Sega. CIP. **Toilets** for the disabled (key at the desk). Nappy change unit. *See* Toy Libraries p133.

McDonald Road Library
2 McDonald Rd, off Leith Walk
529 5636

Ramp access. Largest local collection of ethnic and dual language books and many children's large print books. Wide range of ethnic music audio cassettes. Coin-operated photocopier. PC. CIP. Large hall (Nelson Hall) for hire.

Muirhouse Library
15 Pennywell Court
529 5528

Level access. This spacious and attractive library has an external wall mural designed and painted by a local artist and children. Children's area is roomy and brightly decorated with posters and drawings. Games available at the desk. Video and audio cassettes. Small community room for hire. Coin-operated photocopier. Sega. PC. CIP. **Toilets** for the disabled (key at the desk).

Newington Library
17-21 Fountainhall Rd
529 5536

The library won an award for its access for people with disabilities. Spacious and attractively decorated with children's drawings, friezes and 'artistic creations'. Large collection of children's books on tapes, games and tactile games for children with disabilities. Large collection of audio cassettes. Story-telling sessions and activities for children often organised, see the notice board for details. Car park. Coin-operated photocopier. CIP. **Toilets** for the disabled. Nappy change unit.

Oxgangs Library
343 Oxgangs Rd N
529 5549

Modern library with excellent facilities and level access. Automatic doors at the entrance and manual internal doors, which are usually kept closed. Be aware of children escaping as they could get out into the car park. Carpeted community room with kitchen facilities available. Coin-operated photocopier. PC. Sega. CIP. **Toilet** for the disabled. Nappy change unit.

Portobello Library
14 Rosefield Ave
529 5558

Bright library with ramp access and two disabled parking spaces immediately outside. The children's area is small, but pleasantly decorated and has some toys.

Games available at the desk. Coin-operated photocopier. CIP. **Toilet** and nappy change on request. These facilities are upstairs, and require a member of staff to unlock the door. *See* Toy Libraries p133.

Sighthill Library
6 Sighthill Wynd
529 5569

Exceptionally spacious library with level access. Foyer, where prams and pushchairs can be left, is decorated with a mural designed by local children. Good stock of children's books, supplemented by books on tapes, comics, toys, games. Community room available. Coin-operated photocopier. Sega. CIP. **Toilets** for the disabled (key at the desk). Nappy change unit. *See* Toy Libraries p133.

South Queensferry Library
9 Shore Rd
529 55765

Level access. Bright children's area with toys. Coin-operated photocopier. CIP.

Stockbridge Library
Hamilton Place
529 5665

Access by three steps but there are plans for level access in the future. Bright children's area with toys and comfortable seats for adults. Community hall available. Coin-operated photocopier. CIP. **Toilet** on request. Nappy change unit.

Toy Libraries

As their name suggests, toy libraries are centres for lending toys to under 5s and to children with special needs. They are all drop-in centres and guidance can be given on toys best suited to your child.

There is usually an initial registration fee, and toys can be borrowed for a nominal charge (20p-25p) for two or three weeks.

The Women's Royal Voluntary Service, 44 Albany St, 556 4284, run most of the toy libraries in Edinburgh and these (marked with a ★), and two others are listed below.

The Toy Library Co-ordinator, Rosemary Mutch, can be contacted at the W.R.V.S. office, number as above. Opening times are mainly during school terms but please ring the office to check as they may occasionally change.

Drummond Toy Library
Drummond Community High School
Cochran Ter
556 2651
Mon, Tues 10-11
Organiser: Helen Finney

Garvald Community Enterprises Ltd
The Engine Shed
19 St Leonard's Lane
662 0040
Tues 1-3
Organiser: Marion McDonald
See also Eating Out p76 and Shopping p29.

★ **Greengables Toy Library**
Greengables Nursery School
8A Niddrie House Gdns
669 9083
Wed 9.30-11.30 1.30-3
Organiser: Jeannette Scholes
See also Private Nurseries p96.

★ **Kirkliston Toy Library**
Kirkliston Community Centre
Queensferry Rd, Kirkliston
333 4214
Tues 10.30-12
Organiser: Jan Close

★ **Leith Toy Library**
Leith Community Centre
New Kirkgate
554 4750
Wed 9.30-11
Organiser: Margaret Wilson

★ **Moredun Toy Library**
Moredun Community Library
Moredunpark Rd
529 5652
Thurs 11-12.30
Organiser: Elaine Appleby
See also Libraries p130.

★ **Oxgangs Toy Library**
Pentland Community Centre
Oxgangs Brae
445 2871
Thurs 9.45-11.45
Organiser: Susan Sheavills
See also Toddler Groups p96 and
Activities for Parents p171.

★ **Pilton Toy Library**
Craigroyston High School — Under
Fives Unit
Pennywell Rd
332 7801
Wed 10-11.30
Organiser: Grace Anderson

★ **Portobello Toy Library**
Portobello Community Library
(upstairs)
Rosefield Ave
529 5558
Wed 9.15-11
Organiser: Denise Morrison

★ **Prestonfield Toy Library**
Cameron House Community Centre
Cameron House Ave 667 3762
Mon 9-2
Organiser: Jessica McCraw

★ **Sighthill Toy Library**
Sighthill Library
6 Sighthill Wynd
529 5569
Thurs 9.45-11.15
Organiser: Susan Young

★ **South Queensferry Toy Library**
South Queensferry Youth and
Community Centre
South Queensferry Primary School
(in 'the Hut')
Kirkliston Rd
331 2113
Fri 9.30-11.30
Organiser: June Gaw

★ **Springwell House Toy Library**
Springwell House Child Health Clinic
Ardmillan Ter
337 6235
Fri 9.30-11.15
Organiser: Teresa Carr

★ **St Bernard's Toy Library**
Resource Centre
St Bernard's Education Centre
Dean Park St
332 2710
Thurs 1.45-3.45
Organiser: Helen Dickinson

This toy library is open to local
parents and professionals working
with children, e.g. toddler groups,
playgroups, nurseries etc.

These groups pay a membership fee
and can borrow toys for longer
period.

★ **Special Needs Toy Library**
St Bernard's Resource Centre
Dean Park St
332 2710

Thurs 1.45-3.45
Organiser: Doreen Dinwoodie
There is a large selection of toys and equipment available for any child with special needs. The library is open to parents, professionals and therapists throughout the city.

The W.R.V.S. hope to re-open the toy library in the Wester Hailes area early in 1995. Please contact Rosemary Mutch at the W.R.V.S. office for details.

The following toy libraries are run by the Midlothian branch of the W.R.V.S. Their Toy Library Co-ordinator is Ruth Aird (phone 01968 673901)

Bonnyrigg Toy Library
Old Library
Lothian St
Mon 9.30-11.30
Organiser: Jan Forbes

Dalkeith Toy Library
Woodburn Community Centre
6 Woodburn Rd
663 9280

Wed 9.30-11
Organiser: Maggie Donaldson

Loanhead Toy Library
Child Health Centre
17 George Ter
440 0590
Fri 9-11.30
Organiser :Irene Hogg

Mayfield Toy Library
Mayfield Community Centre
10 Mayfield Pl
663 2219
Thur 10-11.30
Organiser: Kathryn Blain

Newtongrange Toy Library
Newtongrange Leisure Centre
5 Main St
Fri 10-11.30
Organiser:Gillian Eunson

Penicuik Toy Library
Ladywood Leisure Centre
14A Yarrow Court
Penicuik 678473
Wed 9.30-11.15
Organiser: Barbara Jessop

Activities for Children

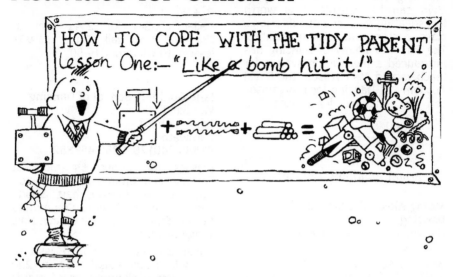

For Playgroups, Toddler Groups and Nurseries, *see* Pre-School Play and Education p91.

ART

There are very few art classes offered to under 5s in Edinburgh outside a nursery environment. However, the following do offer classes for younger children.

The Fruit Market Gallery
225 2383
Sarah Knox, Activities Co-ordinator

Activities for under 5s inspired by exhibitions, run on an occasional basis. Ground floor cafe, lifts to the upper gallery. *See* Places to Visit p175.

The Netherbow
556 9579
Some workshops, eg puppet-making, suitable for under 5s. *See* Places to

Visit p187, Birthdays and Celebrations p86.

DANCE

Classes for younger children (ie 2 + - 4 + yrs) usually teach music and movement. This may include nursery rhymes and simple dancing (hopping, skipping, toe-pointing, mime and moving in time to music). Socialising (learning to wait your turn etc) is a key element in all dancing classes. A fair number of boys attend these early classes. Footwear is sometimes light shoes, available from Mothercare and local shoe shops, more often ballet shoes. *See* Shopping p21 for stockists. There are many local dance classes, some of which are listed here, others may be found through friends' recommendations, adverts in local libraries, community centres, shop windows and local daily and free newspapers.

Choosing the right class for your child can be difficult, it is worth investigating teacher's qualifications, class content and studio facilities. The Royal Academy of Dancing has introduced a registration system for teachers and Ms J Wilson, the Royal Academy of Dancing local organiser, can be contacted for advice 228 4129.

Dance Teachers Registered with the Royal Academy of Dancing

Morag Alexander School of Dancing
Dalrymple Loan, Musselburgh
01875 853027

Ballet classes for 3+ yrs, Fri 2.45-3.30. Classes at the studio in Musselburgh, also in Dalkeith, Longniddry, North Berwick, Haddington. All children can have a 3 wk trial period.

Buckstone Dance Club
Buckstone Primary School,
Buckstone Loan
Deirdre Tait
445 4734

Ballet for 4yrs or preschool year. Tap and modern. B.T.D.A. from P1. £1.20/class for children at Buckstone Primary School or living in Buckstone area.

Central Scotland Ballet School
Mrs Jacqueline Clark
0324 716425

Basic ballet and movement to music for 2½+ yrs. Sat classes at Echline Primary School, South Queensferry £1.75/class, pay for 10 wk term. Teachers exams in ballet. Also ISTD registered.

Cramond School of Ballet
Elizabeth Wilkinson
312 6360

Ballet classes for 2½+ yrs at Cramond Kirk hall, Thurs. £1.95/lesson, 10 wk term £19.50.

Jane Goulding School of Dancing
Waulkmill
Edinburgh Rd
Carnwath
01555 840170/0850 458852

Classes for under 5s Mon at Fairmilehead Church Hall, Frogston Rd; Wed at Craiglockhart Sports Centre;Thurs at Balerno Community Centre; Fri at Greenbank Church Hall, Braidburn Ter.

Ballet 3+ yrs £27.50/10 lessons. 1st wk 'Taster Class', pay at 2nd class. Dress: all pupils wear leotards and ballet shoes.

Tracy Hawkes
667 1327

Simple ballet, mime, movement to music from 2½ yrs; ballet, tap and modern jazz for older children. £2.50/class (reductions for advance termly payments). Mon 3.15 (2½-3½ yrs), 4pm (4-6 yrs), Sat 9.15 (3-4 yrs) at Dance For All Studios, 9b Grange Road; Thurs 3.15 (2½-3 yrs), 4pm (4-6 yrs) at St James' Church, Goldenacre. Dress: comfortable, easy-to-move-in clothes plus ballet shoes.

Lothian Dance Academy
Miss M Phillips
669 9073

Pre-school dance 3½ yrs — ballet based music and movement, singing, clapping, jumping, skipping, galloping, miming and tap. Aim to stimulate imagination, develop co-ordination, balance, rhythm, social and sharing skills through fun-based dance. Classes at Portobello Pool, Gracemount Leisure Centre, Greenside and Newington. £20-25/ 10 wk term. Trial lesson £5. Enquiries to office only, not on day.

Manor Ballet School
Mrs Noel Platfoot (Dir)
220 1466

Music and movement (2½-4 yrs), ballet (4½+ yrs). ¾hr classes £3/ class. Studios 4 Manor Pl, West End. Also classes at Marchmont St Giles Church, Kilgraston Rd; Old Parish Church, High St, Corstorphine; St Serf's Church, Goldenacre. Dress: youngest pupils wear normal clothes plus ballet shoes, which the school sells at a reasonable price. Children start to wear leotards at 3½ yrs. The school employs several teachers who are all RAD and ISTD registered. *Creche*. *Cafe* downstairs..

The Theatre School of Dance and Drama
106 St Stephen St
226 5533

Nursery, ballet for $3^{1}/_{2}$+. £2.40 for $^{3}/_{4}$hr classes payable termly. Teachers prefer leotard and ballet socks for ballet class. Limited range of dancewear at a reasonable price stocked. *Cafe* on Sat.

Dance Teachers Registered With Other Organisations

Pamela Allam AISTD, BTDA
(01259) 742973

Music and movement and the beginnings of ballet for $2^{1}/_{2}$-$4^{1}/_{2}$yrs. Older children do ballet and modern jazz dance. Mon, St Cuthbert's Church Hall, Westgarth Ave, Colinton; Thurs, St Columba's Church, Queensferry Rd. Classes last $^{3}/_{4}$hr, 3 x 10 wk terms. Youngest pupils wear normal clothes + ballet shoes. Start to wear leotards etc at $4^{1}/_{2}$ yrs. All classes accompanied by an expert pianist. Fully qualified staff. Registered teacher recognised by The Council for Dance Education and Training.

Dance Base
Assembly Rooms, 54 George St
225 5525 Cindy Sughne, General Manager

Dance for under 5s, weekly classes based on creative movement with emphasis on enjoyment, held in the studio. Teachers can travel when required, to run creative movement sessions for groups, either regularly or as one-offs.

Edinburgh Dance Centre
Westfield Studios, Westfield Ave
337 0748

Ballet and tap classes for $2^{1}/_{2}$+ yrs. Highland and modern dance for $4^{1}/_{2}$+ yrs. For $2^{1}/_{2}$+ yrs, ballet and tap are combined to include basic steps which help co-ordination and use of space. Most classes are weekly (incl summer holidays with 3 wk holiday allowance). Sat programme available, paid weekly. Lessons £1.30-2.50 paid for 8 wk term. Teachers registered by BBO and UKAPTD. Cafe with drinks and snacks.

Mhairi Hogg School of Dancing
Mhairi Hogg MBATD
Pentland Community Centre
445 2072

Tap classes for 3-5yrs on Sat am. Dress is easy to move in clothes plus tap/soft shoes. Enrolment by phone.

GYMNASTICS

Gymnastic classes are increasingly popular and fortunately also increasingly available in Edinburgh. When choosing a class, convenience is usually the prime consideration. However, it is worth also checking on the teacher's qualifications for teaching pre-school children, the facilities available and on their insurance cover in the event of an accident.

All British Amateur Gymnastics Association coaches (BAGA) will charge a set amount to all children who attend their classes. This is paid to the Association for insurance purposes. This sum will be paid irrespective of the cost of the course. Anyone working with young children, ie nursery groups, playgroups etc, might be interested in taking the Scottish Amateur Gymnastics Coaching Award for pre-school gymnastics and movement. For information, copy of syllabus and general advice on gymnastics classes, phone Gordon Kerr, Scottish Coaching Organiser, Scottish Gymnastics Association 01324 612308 or 01387-55505.

See also Pre-School Play and Education p91.

Ainslie Park Leisure Centre
551 2400

'GYMTEDS' programme for under 5s. Run on block course. Details from Centre.

See Swimming p144 and Activities for Parents p166.

Craiglockhart Sports Centre
443-0101/2

SAGA 'GYMTEDS' programme for Under 5s. Under 3s (accompanied by adult) Mon 9.30-10.15, 1.15-2, 3-5 yrs Mon 10.30-11.15, 2.15-3, Wed 1.15-2, 4-5 yrs Wed 2.15-3. Course run on 6 week block, £10.80. Priority given to children already on programme. There is a Gymnastic Link Transistion Programme to allow children to progress from 'GYMTEDS' to 5+ yrs gymnastics Wed 3.30-4.30.

Creche Tues, Wed, Thurs to fit in with Centre programme, £1.15. FREE to LAC/SLAC card holders.

Pre-booking essential. *See* Birthdays & Celebrations p84, Activities for Parents p167.

Gracemount Leisure Centre
658 1940

Mini gymnastics available for 3-5 yrs Mon, Wed 1-2 and 2-3 £1.15/class, block of 4 wks. Possible waiting list. Creche Mon, Wed, & Fri 10-12.

See Activities for Parents for creche details p169, Birthday Parties and Celebrations p83.

Gym Monkeys
Meadowbank Sports Centre
661 5351

Gym Monkeys for under 5s Mon 1.30-2.30, Tues 9.30-10.30, 10.30-11.30, 2.00-3.00, Thurs.9.30-10.30, 10.30-11.30, Sat 10-11.30, 11.30-12.30.

See Activities for Parents p171, Playcentres p152 and Birthday Parties and Celebrations p85.

Gymsters
St Augustine's High School, Broomhouse Rd
538-2331 Vivien Gourlay

The Kestrel Gymnastics Group run classes for all ages of children and work to the SAGA 'GYMTEDS' programme. Sat Parents and Toddlers. 9.45-10.15. £1.75 /class; 3 yrs 10.30-11.15, 4yrs 11.30-12.15 (both classes £2/class). Physical movement in a play situation, both on floor and on apparatus: rolling, jumping, climbing, action songs and games, walking along beams etc. Coaches are BAGA and SAGA (Scottish Amateur Gymnastic Association) qualified to teach pre-school gymnastics and movement. The Group is registered with each association, parents are asked to pay an annual affiliation/insurance fee to SAGA and BAGA (£3.60 95/96).

Jack Kane Sports Centre
669 0404

Pre-school gymnastics Tues 10-10.45 (under 3s); 11-11.45 (3-5 yrs); 1.00-1.45 (under 3s), 1.50-2.30.(3-5 yrs) £9 per six week session. Details from Centre.

See also Activities for Parents p169,

Birthday Parties and Celebrations p83.

Lo-Gy Centre
Polton Road
Loanhead
440 4495

Pre-school gymnastics with movement learning programme and trampolining classes. During school terms, classes are available on wkday mornings and afternoons for parents and toddlers, pre-school gymnastics (16 mths-3 yrs), pre-school classes (3-5 yrs) and recreational trampolining (under 5s). Basic introduction to human movement using gymnastics and/or trampolining to teach balance, co-ordination, climbing, jumping and landing, tumbling, swinging etc. £13.50-£15/8 wk block (pay before 2nd lesson). Check summer holiday programme for Jungle Gym play-schemes wkday mornings. Coaches are STA/BAGA qualified and assistants will be training for qualifications.

See Birthday Parties and Celebrations p170.

Musselburgh Sports Centre
653 6367

Gymnastic classes Wed 3.15-4, Fri 1.30-2.15 (18 mths-3 yrs, parents must stay); Wed 4-4.45, Fri 2.30-3.15 (3-5 yrs). £12/class booked in advance. Waiting list. Teacher is BAGA approved coach. **Creche** 75p. Details from Centre.

See Activities for Parents p171.

'Kindergym'
Pentland Community Centre
445-2871

45 min class accompanied by parent. Booking in blocks of 4 wks.

£1/session. Thurs 9.30-10.15 (Under 3s), 10.15-11 (3-5yrs), 11.15-12 (Under 3s), 12.15-1 (3-5yrs), 1.15-2. (Under 3s).

Ratho Community Centre Gym Club
School Wynd, Ratho
333 1055 Lawrence Arscott

Gym Club for pre-school children Fri 2.45-3.30 £1/child. Classes involve gymnastics in a play situation with action games, floor exercises and use of equipment e.g. benches, chute, mini-trampoline, horse etc. Teacher is BAGA approved coach.

Tumbletots
445 1464 Karan Dewar

Vennel Hall, S. Queensferry, Mon; Cluny Church Centre, Cluny Dr, Morningside, Tues/Fri; Murrayfield Parish Church, Wed; Queen Margaret Hall, Linlithgow, Thur.

Specially designed programme (for 1 + yrs) of gymnastic activities to help develop co-ordination, balance, climbing skills and agility. All with appropriate equipment. Supervision is by specially trained staff. Parents stay with under 3s. Membership and insurance £11.45/yr (includes T-shirt, comic, Right Start magazine 6 issues/yr and insurance cover). $^{3}/_{4}$ hr sessions/£2.80, paid in advance, as 10 wk block, after 1 or 2 trial sessions.

Wester Hailes Education Centre
Parent and toddler gymnastic group, Sat 12-1. Details from Centre.

See Swimming p150 and Activities for Parents p157.

MUSIC

Most of the music classes mentioned below teach listening skills and moving in time to music. Under 5s generally are not physically able to specialise in a particular instrument — their hands are not big enough, they don't have the lung power etc. The exception to this is the violin which can be successfully reduced in size without sacrificing its normal tone.

It is advisable to book in advance for all classes.

Nina Craighead
5 Willowbrae Ave
661 4641

Music for fun, finger rhymes, action songs, dancing games, percussion playing. Run by former primary school teacher in her home. Tues, Wed 10.45-11.30; Tues, Wed, Thurs 1.45-2.30. £2/class.

Mini Minstrels
18 Bonaly Cres
441 3750 Hazel Stewart

Music sessions for 3-5yrs. Songs, percussion movement, games and stories.

3yrs, various classes on Tue. £1.50/30min class

4-5yrs, various classes on Thur. £2/45min class

Payable termly in advance.

St Mary's Music School
Old Coates House, Manor Pl
538 7766

Mrs Richardson Mon-Fri 9.30-3.30. Classes (4+ yrs) of 40 mins, Sat 9.45-1. £2.60/class. Includes musical games, singing, listening and using percussion instruments. There is generally a waiting list.

Marjorie Turkington
667 8930

Mon 2.40-3.10 (3++ yrs) at Mayfield Church, West Mayfield. Music and movement class with percussion and introduction to rhythm and SOLFA. Children are encouraged to listen and to move in time to music. £23/10 wk term. Pre-school class is the beginning of a course that continues into Primary 1 and Primary 2 (Primary 2 includes an introduction to recorder playing).

Piano

Mary Spencer
14 Cramond Bank
336 4642

Ms Spencer is a graduate teacher of the European Suzuki Association. The Suzuki Method uses the 'mother-tongue' approach to learning, so the child listens to tunes on tape before starting lessons. The parents, who do not have to be able to play music, are taught by the trained Suzuki teacher how to teach their children. Group lessons and individual lessons, observed by other pupils and parents.

For further information on the Suzuki Method and list of registered teachers contact The British Suzuki Institute, 4D The High St, Wheathampstead, Herts HL4 8AA (0158283) 2424.

Violin

Julia Fowler
2 Birch Court, Barnton
339 7463

Classes (3-4 yrs) offering rhythm training, simple percussion and singing leading on to lessons, taught with a version of the Suzuki method, though Ms Fowler is not registered with the Suzuki Institute. Stress is laid on learning to listen as children learn to play by ear. Parental involvement is essential.

Tuition in groups of up to 6. £2.50-£4.50/+ hr lesson according to size of group. Small brothers and sisters welcome, toys and large garden, weather permitting!

READING

Magic Readers
7 Park Ave
669 2834 Nicola Morgan

Early reading fun for preschool/early school age children. Max 8/group. Qualified and experienced teacher working on pre-reading skills. Several groups in Edinburgh area.

£3/hr/wk.

SKATING

Murrayfield Ice Rink
Riversdale Cres
337 6933

Sessions daily from 2.30. Best times for under 5s and their families are Beginners Sessions Mon, Fri 5-7. Group tuition Wed 5-7 and Sun 10-11.30 or family skating Thurs 7-9 and Sat 10-12. Groups can be taken wkday mornings by prior arrangement with resident instructor. From £1.40 admission at Beginners Session to £2 at Group Tuition Sessions plus 50p for skate hire. Skates available from children's size 5.

Shop sells all manner of skates and accessories.

Cafe open most sessions serving hot drinks, hot snacks, toasties etc. Hot drinks and snacks from machines at other times.

SWIMMING

Most babies love moving in water once the initial fear of being uncovered has gone. Swimming is an excellent way of exercising the body and more and more parents are introducing their children to the pleasures of water early in life. Safety is obviously a motivating factor.

Opinions vary as to when to start your child off (some professionals recommend that the baby should have completed the initial vaccination programme), but whenever you start, here are a few things to remember.

1) Have a healthy respect for the dangers of water. Always stay near to your child when in or near water.

2) Allow at least 1 hr after a feed before entering the water.

3) Respect your child's wishes. Do not force youngsters into the water if they dislike it. Wait and try again in a week or so.

4) Babies get chilled easily. Take them out at the first signs of cold.

What to Wear Most local parents dress babies in miniature bathing suits although towelling pants are equally suitable. Nappies are far too cumbersome when wet.

Buoyancy Aids Small arm bands are available. The type with 2 or more air chambers and non-returnable valves are the safest. The triangular type with a flat section next to the body will stop your child wobbling too much. Available from swimming pools, Early Learning Centre *see*

Shopping p28, sports shops etc. Also available is the 'Floaties' range of buoyancy aids which include arm bands, a body vest and an inflatable ring seat, ideal for young babies and available in two sizes. Available from Mothercare *see* Shopping p6, Jenners Toy Dept *see* Shopping p4 and Sports Shops. Remember that arm bands and inflatable rings are not life-savers.

Early Classes are intended to develop your child's confidence and pleasure in the water. They teach some of the basic skills, leading towards learning to swim, and show parents how they can help their children.

As regards a proper stroke, experts say that it is better to let under 5s develop their own way of swimming, through playing regularly in water. Perfecting a stroke can come later. In fact, the longer you leave it, the quicker they learn. The Amateur Swimming Association offers the following useful publications by mail order:

'Babes in the Water' — £1.15 include P&P

'Water Activities for Parents and Babies' — £6.69 include P&P

*'Teach Your Child to Swim' (Usborne Pubs) — £5.65 include P&P

Send your order and remittance to Swimming Times Publications, Harold Fern House, Derby Square, Loughborough LE11 0AL (01509 230431).

* Copies of this book are available through the EDC library service.

Swimming in the Sea Edinburgh beaches from Cramond to Mussel-burgh are generally reasonably clean, but are unlikely to be consistently clear of sewage debris until about 1996. Most do not meet current EEC standards on the required quality of bathing water. All water is sampled by the Forth River Purification Board but EEC designated beaches are tested more frequently than non-designated during the year.

The beaches that are EEC designated along the coastline are Cramond, Gullane, Yellowcraigs, Milsey Bay (east of the harbour at North Berwick) and Belhaven, Dunbar. Belhaven beach will be one of the cleanest along the coastline with the recent introduction of a new sewage treatment scheme. The area from Fisherrow to Port Seton is badly contaminated and is likely to remain so until 1995.

Beaches which are most suitable for toddlers, as they have toilets, are Gullane and Seacliffe. Gullane has toilets (FREE) which are open during the summer months from Apr-Sept. Seacliffe Beach (non-EEC) is one of the cleanest beaches on the Lothian coast *see* Out-of-Town Trips p191.

Family Swimming During the summer holidays, Wester Hailes runs family sessions. During the yr Trinity Academy, Currie High, the Royal High, Queensferry High, Dr Bell's Primary, Portobello High, James Gillespie's and Gracemount High all offer evening swimming sessions to families as part of the Community Education programme, 229 9166 for up-to-date informa-tion. Moray House College, Cramond Campus pool can be booked by playgroups etc at wkends for family sessions.

Many of the large city hotels have private leisure clubs with swimming pools. Membership of these clubs is usually expensive. See the Yellow Pages for listings of these clubs.

Pools Guide

General Notes (Please read these first)

The pools in this section are all local authority run. For details of the EDC Leisure Access Scheme (LAC) which gives reduced admission rates to cardholders (LAC/SLAC holders), see Activities for Parents p166.

1) The water temperature ranges from 80-84° F.

2) All pools have showers and hairdriers. Most hairdriers take 10p coins.

3) In general the admission charge entitles you to unlimited swimming time. However, when pools are busy eg during school holidays, they may run sessions of limited duration, usually 40 mins.

4) The pools all sell armbands, shampoo sachets, soap, combs and goggles.

5) All pools without cafeterias have hot and cold drinks machines and sweet/snack machines.

6) Spectators are allowed into all EDC pools, cost 55p (FREE to LAC/SLAC holders).

7) During school holidays and at wkends, most of the pools have fun play-sessions with toys, inflatables etc.

8) Children under 8 must always be accompanied by an adult at all EDC pools.

9) At EDC pools, lessons are VERY popular and must be booked in advance. Booking procedures are currently being reviewed, so enquire at your local swim centre for details.

10) For details of the school holiday activities and play-sessions, contact the Recreation Marketing Unit, 529 7905 for a current seasonal leaflet.

Ainslie Park Leisure Centre

92 Pilton Dr

551 2400 ✔

Mon-Fri 10-10; Sat, Sun 10-6

Adults £1.55; LAC holder £1.20; SLAC holder and U18s 75p; Under 5s FREE

Car Parking: FREE

A modern leisure centre offering a large pool (25m x 8 lanes) a shallow teaching pool, sunbeds, steamroom, sauna, spa pool, flume and splash pool. A sports hall, fitness room, a function room, bar, cafeteria, audio visual library and *creche* facility. *See Activities for Parents p166.*

There is an extensive range of activities and coaching sessions. Due to lack of space in the changing area, pushchairs are discouraged. However, a limited number of pushchair lockers available.

Changing area: Mixed, with 3 large family cubicles. Coin-operated

lockers (10p non-returnable). Wall-mounted hairdriers, playpens and high chairs are available.

Learner pool starts with a gentle water-filled slope leading into a shallow pool which is very suitable for introducing small babies and toddlers to the water. At one end is a jet pressurised water system which older toddlers and children enjoy. Entrance to the spectator area overlooking the pool is through the cafeteria area.

Parent and Child sessions are held Tues, Thurs 10-10.30 and Sun 10-10.25 and aim to familiarise the baby/toddler with the environment of water. No booking necessary.

Classes: Blocks of swimming lessons for 3-5s. (Lessons are very popular and must be booked in advance.) Programme available from Centre.

Cafeteria
Mon-Fri 10-5.30; Sat, Sun 9.30-4.00
3 High chairs, bottles and food heated, breastfeeding permitted, seats 36
Self-service cafeteria overlooking the pool. Snacks and hot food at a reasonable cost. Parties hosted in a separate room. **Toilet** facilities available nearby.

See also Activities for Parents p166, Birthday Parties and Celebrations p83 and Gymnastics p139.

Bonnyrigg Leisure Centre
King George V Park
Park Rd
Bonnyrigg
663 7579
7 days/wk. Pool available Fri, Sat, Sun 7-10pm for private bookings.
Adults £21.60/hr, £16.20/hr for juniors and concessions
Peak times: Adults £1.40, 80p for children and concessions

Off-Peak times: Adults £1, 55p for children and concessions.
Car Parking: FREE

The Centre was re-opened in 1992 having been refurbished and extended. Facilities include 2 pools (1 deep pool and 1 'lagoon pool') with features such as water cannons, water geysers, slides and jacuzzi. No spectating area. Swimming sessions usually last 1hr 20 mins. Other facilities include a multi-purpose games hall, fitness suite, sauna suite, sunbed, tennis courts and soft play area. Programme available from Centre. **Creche** facilities weekday mornings to suit the Centre programme.

Changing Areas are mixed family changing rooms, coin-operated lockers (20p refundable), 2 baby changing tables and **toilet** facilities.

There are no cafeteria facilities but a hot/cold drinks and sweet/snack machine is available in a lounge area with tables and chairs.

See Birthday Parties and Celebrations p83.

Dalry Swim Centre
Caledonian Cres, Nr Haymarket
313 3964
Mon-Fri 8-9am, 11-3, 5-7.40; Sat 12-3.40; Sun 9-3.40. Other times also — contact the Centre
Adults £1.15; LAC holder 90p; SLAC holder and U18s 65p; Under 5s FREE
Car Parking: On-street parking available but it is in a busy and often congested area. Disabled spaces.

Victorian swimming pool with changing cubicles and coin-return lockers upstairs. Baby changing facilities and playpens on poolside. Ample space for parking pushchairs. Help available from very obliging staff. **Creche** available at certain times — phone for details. Purpose-built facilities for people with disabilities with changing, shower and toilet facilities.

'Parent and Child' sessions Tues, 9.40-10.20. This session is supervised by friendly, qualified coaching staff from whom advice and assistance is available. No booking necessary.

Classes: Blocks of 8 x 25 min swimming lessons (lessons must be booked in advance) are available for children 3-5 yrs on Mon, Wed, Fri afternoons, and Sat mornings £8.80. Programme available from Centre. Staff fully trained to service the special needs of under 5s and their parents.

Dunbar 'Splash' Leisure Pool

See Out of Town Trips p191.

Glenogle Swim Centre

Glenogle Rd, Stockbridge
343 6376
Mon-Fri 8-9 am, 11-3 and 5-7.40; Sat 10-3.40; Sun 9-3.40. Other times also — contact the Centre
Adults £1.15; LAC holder 90p; SLAC holder and U18s 65p; Under 5s FREE
Car Parking: On-street parking.

Victorian swimming pool with changing cubicles around the pool. Ample space for parking pushchairs. Stairs up to reception and pool but help available on request (push bell) from very obliging staff. Baby changing facilities and play-pens on poolside. **Creche** available at certain times — phone for details.

'Parent and Child' sessions on Mon, Wed 9.40-10.20, supervised by friendly, qualified staff from whom advice and assistance is available. No booking necessary.

Classes: Blocks of 8 x 25 min swimming lessons are available for children 3-5 yrs on Tues, Thurs, Fri afternoons and Sat mornings (Lessons must be booked in advance). Programme available from Centre.

See Activities for Parents p168.

Infirmary St Swim Centre

Infirmary St, off Sth Bridge
557 3973
Mon 8-6.40; Tues 8-3; Wed 9-7.40; Thurs 8-6.40; Fri 8-10 am; Sat 9-3.40; Sun closed
Adults £1.15; LAC holder 90p; SLAC holder and U18s 65p; Under 5s FREE
Car Parking: On-street meter parking in a busy area.

Victorian swimming pool with changing cubicles around the pool. Pool is upstairs but help available on request from very obliging staff. Baby changing facilities and playpens on poolside.

Programme available from Centre.
See Activities for Parents p169.

Leith Waterworld

Easter Rd, Leith
555 6000
Mon-Fri 9am-10pm (9.30pm finish); Sat, Sun 9-5. Available for private hire Sat, Sun 5.30-9.
Adults £2.15; LAC holder £1.75; SLAC holder and U18s £1.35; Under 5s FREE
Car parking: FREE car park
Leith Waterworld is EDC's show-piece 'state-of-the-art' family leisure pool. Water features incl waves, geysers, water cannons, bubble beds, spa, 80m and 60m water chutes with a river run for inflatable rides. Main pool slopes from the 'beach' to 1.7m at the deepest part of the pool. A wave machine operates twice every hr for 10 mins in this area.

A community programme is in operation every wkday morning from 9-12 noon. See Activities for Parents p170.

Classes: Blocks of 8 x 25 min swimming lessons (must be booked in advance) available for children 3-5 yrs on some wkday afternoons.

Creche See Activities for Parents p170.

Programme and information leaflets available from Centre.

Changing Area has wide level access to all public areas. Coin-operated lockers (50p returnable) with 10 pushchair lockers. Communal changing area with family cubicles and a special designated baby changing area with sinks and changing tables in the cubicles. Nappy changing unit and playpens also in this area. Hairdriers available in toilet and changing areas (20p). There is also a special changing cubicle for people with disabilities with self-contained showering and toilet facilities. **Toilets** for bathers and also in cafeteria area.

Cafeteria

Mon-Fri 10-9; Sat, Sun 10-4
High chairs, bottles and food heated, breastfeeding permitted, seating approx 50, nappy changing facilities, children's parties hosted.

Known as the 'Surf Shack Cafe'. Serves a good range of meals and snacks throughout the day at reasonable prices. Bar facilities Mon-Fri 12-2, 6-10. Cafeteria **toilets** (M & F) have nappy changing units.

See also Activities for Parents p170, Birthday Parties and Celebrations p84.

Moray House College
Cramond Rd N
312 6056

Classes: 'Parents and Babies' (3mths-21/2 yrs) and 'Parents and Toddlers' (21/2-5yrs) sessions held during school yr. Book in advance for a course of 10 x 30 min lessons. Programme available on request.

Modern and almost entirely on 1 level. No playpens in the changing area but you can take pushchairs in. There are sockets so you can use your own hairdrier — none are provided. Coin-operated lockers (20p). No parking on college premises during term-time 8.30-5.

Self-service student dining room available to users of the college facilities, Mon-Fri, 10-4. Meals and snacks at very reasonable prices. However, the facilities for children in the dining room are very limited and no high chairs are available.

See Annual Events p201 for school holiday activities, Activities for Parents p171 for adult classes with creche, Pre-School Play and Education p120 and Adult Classes and Training Courses p163.

Portobello Swim Centre
Bellfield St
(entrance on Promenade)
669 4077
Mon-Fri 8-7.40; Sat, Sun 9-3.40.
Sessions in operation if Centre is busy
Adults £1.15; LAC holder 95p; SLAC holder and U18s 65p; Under 5s FREE
Car Parking: FREE on-street.

Victorian swimming pool. Facilities include a 25yd pool, small teaching/ activities pool, sunbeds, fitness centre with exercise and weights machines, Turkish baths (closed until refurbishment), aerotone (an old-fashioned type of jacuzzi) and cafeteria. The small pool has been imaginatively retiled and decorated on a nautical theme and is used for lessons, birthday parties, ante/postnatal and aquafit classes. The Centre will be closed for refurbishment some time late 1995 possibly to coincide with the re-opening of Leith Victoria Baths in mid-August 1995.

Classes: Parent and Baby and Parent and Child sessions supervised by an instructor. Blocks of 8 x 25min swimming lessons (must be booked in advance) for children 3-5 yrs on Tues, Thurs, Fri. Programme available from Centre.

Changing areas: Men on the ground floor and women upstairs. Both have playpen and changing table. Coin-operated lockers (50p returnable). Wheelchairs can be brought in by special request via a side entrance. There is a bar with padlocks for prams and pushchairs.

Refreshment Room
657 2210
Mon-Fri 9-7.30; Sat, Sun 9-3.30
High chair (2), tables suitable for clip-on seats, breastfeeding permitted, bottles heated, nappy change surface, no smoking area, parties hosted, seating 40

Small self-service cafeteria run by a co-operative of local mums who know the needs of parents with young children and try to cater for them. Wholesome snacks and light meals, soups, salads, pizza, home-baking etc. A child's menu and childsize portions are available. Children's 3 course tea-time menu is available from 4.30-7, Mon-Fri. Vegetarian choices always on the menu. Wide range of drinks including herbal teas. Children's activities corner with toys and

books. Prams and pushchairs allowed although access to the cafeteria is up one flight of stairs. **Toilets** nearby.

See also Activities for Parents p172, Birthday Parties and Celebrations p86.

Royal Commonwealth Pool
Dalkeith Rd, Newington
667 7211
Summer: Mon-Fri (except Wed) 9-9; Wed 10-9, Sat, Sun 8-7
Winter: Mon-Fri (except Wed) 9-9; Wed 10-9, Sat, Sun 10-4

Flume Complex: contact Pool for opening hrs as they vary throughout yr.

Swim only Core £1.55; LAC holder £1.20; SLAC holder and under 18s 75p; Under 5s FREE

Swim & Flume Core £2; LAC holder £1.65; SLAC holder and under 18s £1.05

Car parking: Limited; the overflow car park can also be crowded at off-peak times, so it is advisable to leave plenty of time for parking before lessons.

Built for the 1970 Commonwealth Games. Facilities include a large competition sized 50m pool, shallow teaching pool, diving pool, fitness centre equipped with exercise and weights machines, sunbeds, separate male and female saunas, large cafeteria and creche see Activities for Parents p172. For reasons of hygiene, pushchairs must be left in foyer. Padlocks and chains are provided — keys can be obtained from cashier's desk.

Flumes: 4 water slides. Admission to the flume complex is £1.20 and offers unlimited rides. Tickets are only valid on day of purchase. Children must be 8yrs+ to use flumes and able to swim.

Changing Areas are down a steep flight of stairs. Women's changing room has high chairs (you can take these into your cubicle) and play-pens, nappy bins and a nappy change table. Hand hairdriers are available as well as wall-mounted driers. Coin-operated lockers — 50p returnable. Dads can have high chairs transferred to their area on request. There is a table for dressing babies in the men's changing room. Pushchairs are available downstairs for sleeping babies.

The **teaching pool** is usually occupied by young children, and many parents change their babies' clothes on the wide shelf surrounding the pool, so they stay uncovered for the minimum time. The teaching pool temperature is 85-86°F, and even higher when babies' classes are scheduled (It is reported however that these temperatures are not always met). Playpen and chairs on poolside.

Classes for under 5s are available during term time and must be booked and paid for in advance. Pre-school classes for 3-5yrs are held at 2.15, 2.45 and 3.15 on wkdays. Classes for over 5s are run during term time, Sat mornings and the summer holidays. Cost £9.20 for a course of 8 x 25 min lessons for children.

Parent and Baby sessions held every wkday am. Under 1s at 10 am and under 2s at 10.30 am. Parents and babies are introduced to early water skills under the supervision of an instructor.

Parent and Child sessions at 1.15 each day for under 5s with teaching staff available to offer assistance if required.

Toilets available upstairs and down.

See also Activities for Parents p172,

Birthday Parties and Celebrations p86 and Gymnastics p139.

Cafeteria
Mon-Fri 9-9 (main meals served 11.30-6.30); Sat, Sun 10.30-3.30
High chairs (6), breastfeeding permitted, bottles heated, no smoking area, parties hosted, seating 200.

Bright, spacious self-service cafeteria selling snacks and hot food at reasonable cost. Children's portions. After 6.30pm, pies, sausage rolls, chips etc available. **Toilets** nearby.

Warrender Swim Centre
Thirlestane Rd, Marchmont
447 0052
7 days/wk. Opening hrs vary from day to day. Programme available from Centre or telephone in advance to check opening times
Adults £1.15; LAC holder 90p; SLAC holder and U18s 65p; Under 5s FREE
Car parking: FREE on-street.

Bright airy Victorian swimming pool with changing cubicles around the pool. Coin-operated lockers (10p returnable). Playpen and 2 baby changing tables beside the pool. Also wide bench suitable for changing babies & toddlers. Prams/pushchairs may be left in the foyer.

Creche: Mon, Tues, Thurs 9-1; Wed 8.45-1; Fri 9-12 £1.10. FREE to LAC/SLAC holders.

Fun play-session on Sat 1-2 with mats, toys and inflatables.

Parent and Child session on Wed 9.45-10.30. No booking necessary.

Classes: Blocks of 8 swimming lessons (must be booked in advance) available for babies & children £9.20. Programme available from Centre.

Antenatal swimming session Wed 10.30-11.15.

See also Activities for Parents p173.

Wester Hailes Swimming Pool

Wester Hailes Education Centre
5 Murrayburn Dr
442 4217
Mon, Tues, Thurs, Fri 9.30-8.10; Wed 9.30-5.10 (Ladies night 5.10-7.10); Sat 10.30-3.30; Sun 9.30-3.30. These times are session times. Last admission time is 20 minutes later.

Adults £1.10, Children 3-16 yrs £0.50 (10p key deposit refunded as you leave)

In the summer, there is an early am quiet swimming session mostly for adults and young children from 8.50-9.30. Hr long sessions starting at 10 to, 10 past, and 30 mins past the hr. The colour of your band indicates the session you belong to. When the light goes on behind your colour on the indicator board, you must leave the water.

Modern pool operated by Lothian Region. Amenities include a large pool, children's pool, a diving pool with 2 boards. The children's pool is graded in depth so small children can touch the bottom at one end. There are large plastic animals in and around the pool, also a frog house with slide into the water. Under 4s must be supervised on the slide. There is a wide shelf next to the children's pool for dressing a baby.

Changing Areas: The women's area has playpens. These are taken to the poolside or into the men's area on request. The ladies' changing room has a family changing area with facilities for nappy changing. Men's changing area has nappy changing table. Lockers lock automatically on closure, so beware of locking the key inside. The women's area has a large mirrored area with power points, so you can use your own

150

hairdrier. Pushchairs can be taken into the changing area and will be locked away by the attendants.

Classes: Swimming lessons (must be booked in advance) (30 mins) for children. Details on request.

Creche available 20p/session.

Cafeteria

Mon-Fri 9-9; Sat, Sun 10-4

High chairs (2), breastfeeding permitted, bottles heated, parties hosted, seating 200.

Self-service cafeteria, overlooking pool, offering an inexpensive range of snacks and meals. Wholefood and vegetarian meals are available on wkdays. The staffroom may be used on request for breastfeeding. Prams and pushchairs allowed inside. Take-aways available. **Toilets** by cafeteria.

See also Activities for Parents for adult activities with creche p157, Birthday Parties and Celebrations p87 and Gymnastics p140.

The following High Schools also run classes for small children:

Balerno High School

449 2834

Parent and toddler swimming classes and lessons for pre-school children 4-5 yrs on various wkdays. Places (10 x 30 min sessions) must be booked in advance.

Public swimming (inc family sessions) day, evening and wkends and school holidays. Under 5s FREE.

Creche Mon-Fri 9-1, 40p/session, is well equipped in a purpose-built area with qualified creche workers.

See also Activities for Parents p155.

Drummond Community High School
Cochran Ter
556 2651
Parent and Toddlers' swimming session Fri 9.10-10.30.
See also Activities for Parents p156.

PLAY CENTRES

Balerno High School
5 Bridge Rd, Balerno
Contact David Hillson 449 5833
Daytime gymnastics and swimming for pre-school children. Also music for fun for under 5s. Classes run for 10 wks, day and time vary each term, places bookable. **Creche** available, 40p. Phone for details.

Clambers Royal Commonwealth Pool
667 7211

Three levels of slides, tubes and lots of safe surfaces to clamber over. Parents must remain in the surrounding area (the cafe) or may accompany the child. Suitable for children with special needs. Ages 3-10 (8-10 only allowed after 6.30), max height 1.45m. Mon-Fri 10am-8pm, Sat & Sun 10am-5pm. *See* Activities for Children p150 and Celebrations p86.

Koko's
Children's Leisure Centre, Kinnaird Park, Newcraighall Rd
669 0082

Membership £30/yr. Admission price for 1 + hr play sessions: 10-2 £2.50/child; 2-7 £3.50/child; Sat/Sun 10-7 £3.50/child. Group prices (10 or more children) 10-2 £1.50; 2-7 £2/child Mon-Fri, bookable in advance. Last entry is 5.30. Children's indoor activity play centre with soft play areas, bouncy castles, climbing nets, rocking play toys, wobbly walkways, tube chutes, adventure maze and aerial runways. Reasonably supervised by mainly youngsters, under 3s may find it a bit daunting at first, but there is a play area for babies and toddlers by the cafeteria. No bookings (apart from groups), just turn up, however there is a maximum of 150 children so it may be worth phoning during peak times ie Sat/Sun, public holidays/school holidays. Nobody over the age of 10 or 55 ins/1.4m allowed to use equipment. There is no wheelchair/push-chair access to the entrance except up a flight of 20 + steps. **Toilets** Boys and girls both with nappy change surface. Downstairs is a communal baby room shared with the rest of the centre, but this would mean leaving older children. Snack Bar High chairs, breastfeeding permitted, bottles heated, parties hosted, seating 50 Children's fast food menu at reasonable prices, filled baked potatoes, hamburgers and chips, pizzas, crisps, fizzy drinks and squash. Birthday parties hosted in a very attractive room off snack bar area (max 35). Gift vouchers available — £4 and £3 — for 1 play session and a helium balloon on leaving (either morning or afternoon session). *See also* Birthdays and Celebrations p84.

Leo's (Forecourt Leisure)
555 4533
Open 7 days/wk from 9-8. Sessions last for 1 + hrs. Costs — Off peak (Mon-Fri 9-4) under 2s £1.80 Over 2s £2.60. Peak hrs (Mon-Fri 4-8, Sat/Sun all day). Under 2s £2.60, Over 2s £3.50. Bright airy room with

large ball pool with tunnel chute and Leo the Lion who loves to eat blue balls and says 'yum yum'. Also ghost house, rope walks, maze, aerial glides, pendulum swings, roller squeezes and soft play area with separate ball pool and chute for under 2s. Good supervision at all times but under 2s require parental supervision. Best to avoid peak hrs with little ones. Entertainment sometimes available in video theatre/ party room. Phone for details. *See also* Activities for Parents p168 and Birthdays and Celebrations p85.

Little Marco's
Marco's Leisure Centre
51-95 Grove St, Haymarket
228 2141

Contact Louise Cardwell Mon-Fri 9.30-7, Sat, Sun 9.30-8 Member's children £2 for 1+hrs, non-members children £3.50. Playgroup or other outing £2/child for 2 hrs play. Playgroup leaders must stay. Children's indoor adventure playground with lots of large play apparatus — bouncy castle, slides, tunnels to crawl through, soft play area, large ball pool — as well as slot rides and roller derby. Under 3s can find the centre daunting at first. Suitable for children 31-55 ins tall — under this size at parents' risk. With under 4s pick a quiet time as over 5s can be overpowering. If children 3 yrs and under, parents must stay. If older, parents are encouraged to use downstairs lounge or other Marco's facilities especially during peak periods (Sat/Sun pm and school holidays) when parents of older children are not allowed to stay. Wheelchair and pushchair access is available via lift. Parties hosted in special part next to play area in Little Marco's. **Toilets** are nearby and Ladies has nappy change surface.
Lounge (ground floor)
£, *Tables suitable for clip-on seats, breastfeeding permitted, bottles heated, licensed.*
Counter service bar/cafe with large comfy seating area. Food served includes burgers, quiche, salads, soups, etc. Vegetarian dish available, also children's menu. Space for pushchairs. **Toilets** nearby.

Little Marco's Cafe
£, *High chair, breastfeeding permitted, nappy change surface.*
Fast-food area serving pastries, tea, capuccino, etc. *See also* Activities for Parents p170, Birthdays and Celebrations p85.

Meadowbank Sports Centre
139 London Rd
661 5351

Soft play equipment especially suitable for under 5s and special needs groups. Open every day 9am-8pm. Open for casual use Tues, Thurs 9.30 and 10.30, Wed, Fri 10.30, Sat, Sun 10.30 and 12.30 Mon, Tues, Thurs 1.30 and 2.30 £1/child for 1 hrs play. The whole room can be hired at other times for £8/hr. You should provide your own supervision. Bookings can be taken up to 4 wks in advance. Equipment includes giant building blocks, ball pool, cylinders, a slide and maze, all made of plastic covered foam. Children have fun while developing movement skills. *Cafe*. *See also* Activities for Parents p171 and Birthdays and Celebrations p85.

Portobello Fun Fair
Portobello Promenade (Edinburgh end)
Outdoor fun fair with roundabouts,

dodgems, sideshows, space invaders, ghost train, bouncy castle. Also indoor games room and 'Fort Fun' for younger children.

Fort Fun is open 10-9 from Easter to Sept 7 days/wk and 10-5 Mon-Fri and 10-7 Sat/Sun for the rest of the year. Enclosed play area consists of ball swamp, rope walks, soft bouncy chute, tunnels and lots of soft play type toys. **Toilets** Communal area upstairs with separate facilities in downstairs video games room. Changing area available.

Cafeteria
£, High chairs, breastfeeding permitted, bottles heated, Children's menu available — fish fingers, burgers, etc.

Good views of the beach (on a nice day). Access is by a flight of approx 20 stairs either through outdoor funfair and games room (noisy and smoky) or by separate entrance from Promenade. Pushchairs can be stored upstairs.

See Birthdays and Celebrations p84.

Activities for Parents

We could write a whole book on this subject alone! Clearly we do not have enough space here to include everything, so we have selected those activities which provide creche facilities. As a result we cover mostly daytime classes. However a wide variety of evening classes is provided in Edinburgh by many institutions. *See* Sources of Information on Adult Classes and Training Courses p160. The increase in recent years of the provision of creche facilities to accompany a wide range of activities has been very welcome. The best creches allow you plenty of time to settle your child, before you go off to your class, thus allowing you both to enjoy your experience. If a particular venue sets such strict time-limits on the use of the creche that this is impossible, then we recommend that you point out the value to all concerned of allowing this extra time, especially to themselves, in having happy customers and unhassled creche workers. The widening of Open Learning provision in Lothian is another boon for parents who wish to study, but cannot cope with a formal class situation due to childcare or other commitments. There are courses to enhance future job training prospects, as well as courses purely for interest. Changes to days, times and venues are always taking place, so please check on a particular activity in advance for details of times, cost and enrolment. Equally this list does not claim to be complete, so it would be worthwhile approaching your local school, community centre or further education college to ask what they have to offer. Community centres are also very pleased to receive requests for activities and creches, and do their best to respond where there is sufficient demand. Most centres like their users to pay a nominal membership fee.

CENTRES OFFERING A VARIETY OF ACTIVITIES

See also Women's Groups and Parents' Centres p158. Rather than listing every class available at the time of writing we have used broad descriptions to indicate the range of courses available at individual venues. *Active* eg swimming, yoga, keep-fit, aerobics, dancing, sports etc. *Arts and Crafts* eg art, patchwork, embroidery, pottery, knitting, needlework, photography, woodwork etc. *Alternative Therapies* eg reflexology, aromatherapy, relaxation. *Languages* eg foreign languages. *Computing* including word processing. *Miscellaneous* to cover all others. The classes available often vary from published information and it is best to contact the venue for information. *See also* Sources of Information on Adult Classes and Training p160.

Balerno High School
449 2834 David Hillson

The Community Education Department runs many day-time classes during term time. Active, crafts, computing, languages, music etc. *Creche* for most classes 40p/session. Activities and classes also available evenings, wkends and during school holidays. *See* Activities for Children p150.

Burdiehouse and Southhouse Community Centre
Burdiehouse St
664 2210

Women's groups; Southhouse Women's Action Group (SWAG) Fri 10-12

Cameron House Community Centre
Cameron House Ave
667 3762

Daytime classes with *creche*. Art, old time dancing, Spanish, dressmaking. Phone for information. *See also* Toy Libraries p133.

Carrickvale Community Education Office
Stenhouse St W
443 6971

Daytime classes with FREE *creche*. Art and crafts, languages, computing, miscellaneous. Phone for information.

Centre for Continuing Education
See Adult Classes and Training Courses p162.

Clovenstone Community Education Centre
54 Clovenstone Pk
453 4561

Variety of social and educational activities catering for local residents of all ages. FREE *creche* mainly for women's activities. Programme on request.

Craigmount Community Centre
Craigmount High School, Craigs Rd
339 1884/827

FREE *creche* (under 5s) usually staffed by 2 people (one a qualified nursery nurse). Wide range of activities including arts and crafts, active, alternative therapies and miscellaneous. Women's discussion

155

group. Also Sat 9-1, class for Japanese children (3+ yrs) in their own language and culture, and an English class for their parents, with **creche** (0-3 yrs). See Ishihara Hiroshi at the class.

Craigroyston Community Centre
1a Pennywell Rd
332 7360 Linda Weeks

Various classes with creche run throughout yr. Details from Centre. See also Pre-School Play and Education p103.

Craigroyston Community High School
Pennywell Rd
332 7801 Chris McCormick

Under 5s Centre where people may come to play and learn with their children. Adult day and evening classes, with social base in community lounge. Phone for information.

Drummond Community High School
Cochran Ter
556 2651 ext 258 Jane Meagher

Wide variety of day classes with **creche** (0-5 yrs) 8.30-12.15, 1-4.30. Well supervised and extremely popular creche. Arts and crafts, activities, languages, computing, etc. Vocational courses (Highers, SCOTVEC). See also Toy Libraries p132.

Fort Community Wing
N Forth St
553 1074 Nancy Richards,
Kenny Pringle (9.30-1)

Wide variety of activities with creche (0-5 yrs). Arts and crafts, activities. Women's discussion groups Fri mornings. Toddler group Tues 10-12. Playscheme runs through Jul. See

also Pre-School Play and Education p95.

Gilmerton Community Centre
4 Drum St
664 2335

Women's interest group Wed 10-11.30. Oasis Mon, Thurs, Fri 10-12, Wed 1-3, a support group for women who feel lonely and are finding it hard to cope. Meet others in same situation and women who have come through it. FREE **creche** (0-5 yrs), with 2 experienced staff. Playgroup Mon-Fri 9.30-11.30, applications from centre. See also Pre-School Play and Education p94.

Gorgie City Farm
Low cost daytime and evening classes in arts and crafts. **Creche** with qualified supervision Wed mornings. See Birthdays and celebrations p84. See Places to Visit p184.

Inch Community Centre
225 Gilmerton Rd
664 4710 John Travers

Keep-fit class with FREE **creche** Thurs 2-3, £1/class.

Leith Community Centre
New Kirkgate
554 4750 Anne McCulloch

Activities with **creche** (0-5 yrs, 2 staff on duty) are; English a a foreign language Mon-Thurs1-3, yoga Thur 1-2.30. Cafeteria serving hot snacks etc. See Pre-school play and Education p95.

Leith Community Education Resource Centre
4 Duncan Pl
554 1509 (9.30-1.30) Colin Ventors

A variety of active and arts and crafts classes with **creche**. Centre policy includes positive discrimination in favour of women with children. Tue am, Discussions on Womens health related issues. Mother + Toddler Tue, Thur 9.30-11.30 (note: both exclusive to women).

Roundabout Centre (YWCA)
See Women's Groups and Parents' Centres p159.

St Bride's Community Centre ✓
See Sport and Leisure p172.

St Thomas of Aquins RC High School
12 Chalmers St
229 8734

'Twilight classes' with **creche** (5.30-7). Details from Castlebrae Community Education Office, 661 7463. See Sport and Leisure p173.

South Bridge Resource Centre
Infirmary St
556 2944 Pat Brechin, Fiona Mercer

Daytime classes with **creche** in dressmaking and pottery and some others. Phone for details.

South Queensferry Community Centre
Kirkliston Rd, South Queensferry
331 2113 Noreen Farrell

Womens badminton, Tue 9.30-11.30. Aromatherapy and reflexology, Tue 10-11.30.

South Side Community Centre
117 Nicolson St
667 0484

Classes with FREE **creche** (0-5 yrs). Yoga Wed 10-11.30. Aerobics Tue 6-7. Well woman group, Wed 10-12.

Cafeteria
Mon-Fri 10-1

£, High chair, breastfeeding permitted, bottles heated

Self-service cafe serving snacks and plain wholesome lunches — fixed menu with dish of the day. Meals served 11.30-1. Children's portions; usually a vegetarian dish.

Stevenson College of Further Education
See Adult Classes and Training Courses p164.

Edinburgh's Telford College
See Adult Classes and Training Courses p165.

Tollcross Community Education Centre
Tollcross Primary School
229 8448 Drew Easton

General day and evening leisure activities. FREE **creche** for some daytime Adult Education classes. Gaelic playgroup Wed 9.30-11.30 (all welcome). Toddler group Tue, Thur 9.30-1 See also Pre-School Play and Education p97 & p118.

Wester Hailes Education Centre
442 4217

Modern community school providing opportunities for all ages to study or play. Amenities include library, art, drama and music studios, technical workshops, swimming pools, games hall, gymnasium, racquet sport courts, and cafeteria. Variety of classes including active, typing, computing, languages, SCE subjects etc; adults may be integrated with older school pupils. Recreational classes are adults only. **Creche** (0-5 yrs) during school hrs for children of adults on courses, 10p/teaching period. Early registration for creche advisable. See Activities for Children p150 for information on swimming and cafeteria.

WOMEN'S GROUPS AND PARENT'S CENTRES

The first women's support groups to appear in Edinburgh started after the Scottish Women's Health Fair in 1983. Women get together informally to share their experiences and ideas on health and on coping with life in general. Each group is open to women of all ages, and you don't have to be ill to go along. Most groups have pre-arranged programmes of discussion and activities with topics suggested by group members eg PMT, AIDS, make-up, welfare rights, parenting etc. All welcome new faces and some offer woman-to-woman support with problems.

'The Women's Directory' published by Edinburgh District Council is an excellent source of information, contact the Women's Unit, 529 4445.

The aim of Parent's Centres is to provide somewhere local to meet other parents and somewhere to turn with problems.

For groups for Single Parents *see* Welfare p247.

For Problem Solving *see* Health Care Facilities p262.

Clovenstone Community Education Centre
See Centres Offering a Variety of Activities p155.

Contact Point Drop-in Centre
67 York Pl
557 3239 556 Bernie Mooney
Open to adults Fri 10-4 (women only); Sun 11-4. Practical advice on benefits, housing etc; counselling and a chance to make friends and relax. Coffee and tea.

Craigmount Community Centre
See Centres Offering a Variety of Activities p155.

Craigroyston Community Centre
See Centres Offering a Variety of Activities p156.

Drummond Community High School
See Centres Offering a Variety of Activities p156.

Fort Community Wing
See Centres Offering a Variety of Activities p156.

Gilmerton Community Centre
See Centres Offering a Variety of Activities p156.

Lasswade High School Centre
663 8170/7171 David Hand

Various discussion and health groups in the area. New members welcome. Rosewell Women's Group Tues 9.30-11.30, with **creche**; Hawthornden Health Group Wed 9.30-11.30, with **creche**. See Sports and Leisure p170.

Leith Community Education Resource Centre
See Centres Offering a Variety of Activities p156.

Lothian Racial Equality Council
14 Forth St
556 0441 Saroj Lal

Aim to work towards: the elimination of racial discrimination, racial equality and equal opportunities for all, and to promote good race relations. Phone for details.

Muirhouse Under Twelves and Parents' Centre
Silverknowes Primary School
Muirhouse Gdns
312 6677 Celia Goodings/Viv Carmichael

Informal social centre offering support, help and friendship to parents. Programme of activities includes drop ins and outings for parents and under 5s. Programme for parents includes cooking, arts and crafts and discussions. *Creche* provided. All activities are FREE. Also run a well stocked toy library, cafe and Wed pm clothes rail.

National Women's Register
9 Bank Plain, Norwich, Norfolk NR2 4SL
01603 765392

Local groups in Edinburgh and all over Scotland, which meet for conversation and discussion. Make new friends. Phone Ruby Kerr 0141 884 8821 for details of nearest group. Conference in Edinburgh, Oct 1995 phone for details.

Northfield/Willowbrae Community Education Centre
Northfield Rd
661 5723

Tues 10-11.30 Women's Group; Thurs 10-11.30 aerobics. *Creche*.

Parent's Room
Niddrie Primary School
Niddrie Mains Rd
669 1658 Margaret Smith

Informal set-up for parents to drop in Mon-Fri 9-3.15. Toddlers (must be walking) group for those who have a link with the school (awaiting entry or sibling at the school), outings.

No 20 Women and Children's Centre
20/1 Muirhouse Pk
336 4804 Phyllis McGowan

Community project for local women and children. Support, information, counselling and a variety of groups. Also offers pregnancy testing and counselling. Well equipped playroom and 2 play workers.

Ratho Community Centre
See Sports and Leisure p172.

Roundabout Centre (YWCA)
4b Gayfield Pl
556 1168/557 4695 Susan England

Mon-Thur 9-5, Fri 9-4 *Creche* (under 5s) 9.30-12.30, 1-3.30. Punjabi/Urdu speaking women's group Wed 12.30-2.30 (cooking, sewing, discussions). Fri 1-3 drop in for black and minority ethnic women. Young Women's Forum Wed 5.30-7.30. Volunteer opportunities in anti-racist and multicultural creche and summer playscheme.

St Bride's Community Centre
See Sports and Leisure p172.

South Side Community Centre
See Centres Offering a Variety of Activities p157.

Stepping Stones for Young Parents
126 Crewe Rd N
551 1632 Cathy Carstairs/ Pat Haitner

Mon-Fri 9.30-4. A chance for young parents to meet together and participate in various activities. Large well-staffed and equipped playroom for under 5s. Thrift shop, baby equipment loan, home visits, welfare advice and support.

Tollcross Community Centre
See Centres Offering a Variety of Activities p157.

WAND (Women and New Directions)

See Sources of Information on Adult Classes and Training Courses p161.

Wester Hailes Opportunities Trust (WHOT)

See Adult Classes and Training Courses p165.

Womanzone

Well Woman Project
49/2 Greendykes Rd
652 0182

Discussion groups, counselling, self help, support groups. Chiropractor. Drop in. Various activities. *Creche* and *Cafe*.

SOURCES OF INFORMATION ON ADULT CLASSES AND TRAINING

The following organisations offer information and advice on how to find a class or training course to suit you. Not all courses will have creche facilities but if child care is a problem, consider an open learning course. You can then study at home with only occasional meetings with your tutor and fellow learners. Colleges may also offer part-time courses or a shorter college day if you ask.

See Adult Classes and Training p160 for organisations which offer courses. Colleges and universities send out prospectuses and sometimes adults may join local high school classes. Courses may also be advertised in local newspapers.

Employment Service Jobcentre

See Adult Classes and Training Courses p162.

JIIG-CAL Careers Research Centre

University of Edinburgh,
5 Buccleuch Pl

650 4309 Elaine Turner/Isobel Miller
Regular short courses for anyone considering career change. Computer assisted guidance is used to help identify occupational interests and provide job suggestions. Other activities, group discussion and individual counselling help people to make a plan for the future.

Linking Education and Disability (LEAD)

Queen Margaret College,
Clerwood Ter
317 3439 Kate Russel

Advice on classes or leisure activities for adults who are disabled.

Lothian Region Dept of Education (LRDE)

40 Torphichen St
229 916

LRDE Community Education Service (Ext 2124) Information about all courses in the Community Education Programme. Full list published in local newspapers in mid-Aug, also available from local libraries.

LRDE Further Education (Ext 2160) Details of how to obtain a bursary for full-time study. (Contact individual colleges for information about funding for other courses.)

LRDE Careers Service, South Bridge Careers Office, Infirmary St
556 4110
Appointments for careers guidance for adults.

Lothian TAP Agency

8 St Mary's St
557 5822

TAP (Training Access Points). Training Information Services supply comprehensive, accurate and up to date information on training opportunities via easy-to-use computers at TAP Information Points in libraries, job centres and colleges throughout the Lothians.

Open Learning Consultancy Services (OLCS)
South Campus, Edinburgh's Telford College, Crewe Toll
343 1280

Information on 100s of open learning courses allowing you to work at a time and place to suit yourself. A wide range of subjects available. Small children welcome at appointments to discuss options.

SACRO Lothian
Epworth Halls, Nicolson Sq
668 1091

Advice on training, opportunities and sources of funding, primarily for offenders but also for others. Drop-in facility, cafe, small play area. Various keep fit activities/classes. Phone for details.

Scottish Wider Access Programme
East of Scotland Consortium, Stevenson College of Further Education, Bankhead Ave
458 5468/9

Access courses for adults who do not have the standard entrance qualifications for study in higher education. See Adult Classes and Training p164.

Single Parents' Guide to Further Education
See One Parent Families Scotland in Sources of Information p206.

Training 2000
Dalian House
350 St Vincent St, Glasgow
0141 248 4486

An organisation set up to promote and support women's training in Scotland. Quarterly magazine. Events in Edinburgh and elsewhere.

WAND (Women and New Directions)
Craigroyston Community High School, Pennywell Rd
332 5541

Welcomes women living in Greater Pilton area. Advice and information on educational, training and work opportunities. Individual plans for study and training, guidance and counselling on career issues. Childcare compilments all services available.

Wester Hailes Opportunities Trust (WHOT Shop)
Unit 20D, Wester Hailes Shopping Centre
442 4252

Information for local residents. See Adult Classes and Training Courses p165.

ADULT CLASSES AND TRAINING COURSES

Edinburgh offers a huge variety of education, training and 'new direction' courses. If a venue has a *creche* available this is always mentioned in the entry.

Adult Basic Education
Tollcross Community Education Centre
See Centres Offering A Variety of Activities p157.

Adult Learning Project
184 Dalry Rd
337 5442 Stan Reeves/Joan Bree/ Vernon Galloway

Courses, programmes, projects and

events. Variety of courses in Scottish culture. **Creche** (day classes).

Centre for Continuing Education
University of Edinburgh,
11 Buccleuch Pl
650 4400

Returning to learning programme. Courses specifically designed for adults; 'New Horizons','Return to Work or Study', 'Access' and 'Stepping Stones'. For more information contact RTL secretary at the above address.

Craigmillar Opportunities Trust (COT)
57 Peffer Pl
661 8888 Susan Carr

Courses for local residents, customised to individual needs.

Craigmount Community Centre
English class for Japanese people.

See Centres Offering a Variety of Activities p155.

Edinburgh District Council
Training Scheme
78 West Granton
551 3664 Alec Strachan

Training for unemployed people. Courses in joinery, bricklaying, general building. Also in administration, clerical, finance and horticulture.

Employment Service Jobcentre
Jobcentre
Torphicen St
229 9321 Eileen Thomson

Primarily for individuals with health problems (emotional, mental or physical) who may need specialist help. Courses in assessment, personal development, work prepara tion and office skills to suit client's needs. Help available under 'Access to Work'.

Edinburgh Women's Training Centre
5 Hillside Cres
557 1139 Margaret Collins

Full-time courses in computing and electronics for unemployed women With low or no qualifications.. Training allowance and childcare costs paid.

Foundation for Community Leadership Development
54 Manor Pl
220 4103 Doreen Nisbet

Wide range of training courses in people skills and personal development for both paid project workers and volunteers involved in community-based organisations.

Heriot-Watt University
Riccarton Campus
Currie

449 5111 Public Relations Office

Degree and post-graduate courses in technology, engineering, science, computing, energy resources, maths, accountancy, business and languages. MBA by distance learning. *Creche* (birth - 5yrs).

College of Art
(part of Heriot Watt University),
Lauriston Pl
229 9311

Courses in architecture, town planning, Art and Design.

Moray House Institute of Education
(part of Heriot Watt University),
Holyrood Rd
556 8455
Cramond Rd N
312 6001

Courses leading to qualifications in social work, teaching, recreation and leisure, and community education. *See* also Activities for Children p147, Annual Events p201.

National Centre for Play
Moray House Institute of Education,
Cramond Rd N
312 6001

Mon-Fri 9.30-4.30. Training, information and research facilities for groups and individuals who have an interest in play and play-related subjects. *See* also Pre-school Play and Education p120.

Lothian Coalition of Disabled People
8 Lochend Rd
551 2151 Barbara Howie

Courses for women with disabilities returning to work.

Jewel and Esk Valley College
Milton Rd Centre, 24 Milton Rd E
657 7287

Eskbank Centre, Newbattle Rd, Dalkeith
654 5204 (24hrs)

Very wide range of educational, vocational and leisure courses. Scottish Wider Access Programmes for mature students moving on to higher education. *Creche* ($2^1/_2$-5 yrs) at both sites — early booking advisable. Swimming pool, gymnasium and planetarium at Milton Rd.

Judith Warren Associates
125 Grange Loan
667 5570 Judith Warren

20 week courses for women returning to paid employment or further training by flexible study at home, linked to 4 full day workshops and a work placement. Suitable for women with or without previous qualifications who seek direction. Courses are FREE under the LEEL Training for Work scheme and lead to a nationally recognised qualification.

Microbeacon Computer Project
23 Hardwell Close
662 0545 Margaret Durie

Introduction to computers and other support and training for the unemployed and disabled.

Napier University
219 Colinton Rd
444 226

Full and part-time prospectuses from the Information Office. Contact Advisors of Studies for each of 4 Faculties — Applied Arts, Business School, Engineering and Science. Flexible learning through Credit Accumulation and Transfer Scheme (CATS), open learning facilities and courses. Nursery at Craiglockhart campus 8.30-5.30. *See* Pre-school Play and Education p113.

The Number Shop
188-190 Pleasance
668 4787

FREE one-to-one tuition for adults in numeracy and maths. Tuition times Mon-Thur 11-2 and 5-8.

Open Learning Consultancy Services
See Sources of Information on Adult Classes and Training p161.

The Open University in Scotland
10 Drumsheugh Gdns
226 3851

Open learning courses in wide range of subjects, including BA/BSc degree, postgraduate qualifications, professional updating, management and health and social welfare.There are also study packs for general interest in leisure topics, community issues, childcare and parenting.

Queen Margaret College
Clerwood Ter
317 3000

Admissions 317 3247 Alan Butchart Full-time degree courses in health care, theatre arts, business, management and information studies, hospitality studies.

Leith campus, Duke St

QMC Business Development Centre
38b Drumsheugh Gdns
539 7095 Kate Ellam

Business start-up course and business training for unemployed women over 25.

The Roundabout Centre

English classes for women from overseas. Home tuition on individual basis. *Creche*. See Women's Groups and Parent's Centres p159.

Scottish Pre-School Play Association (SPPA)
Courses in association with Stevenson College leading to SCOTVEC and other awards for playleaders. Also shorter courses offering training for playleaders and playgroup workers; parents very welcome. See Pre-school Play and Education p119.

Scottish Wider Access Programme (SWAP)
c/o University of Edinburgh
57 George Sq.
650 6861 (24hrs)

Wide range of access courses to prepare adults (over 21) who do not have the standard entrance qualifications for study in higher education. Successful completion of an access course at an appropriate level guarantees a place at a range of higher education institutes.

Second Chance to Learn
Edinburgh University Settlement
The Old Fire Station, 27 East Norton Pl, London Rd
661 1788

Short FREE courses for adults with little previous education, wanting to return to work or find a new direction to their lives.Courses include SCOTVEC modules in communications, numeracy, introduction to sociology, learning skills and information technology. *Creche* available. Also at Craigmillar, Pilton and Wester Hailes.

Stevenson College of Further Education
College Information Centre,
Bankhead Ave
453 2761

Wide range of courses, full-time, part-time, short intensive, day release, block release, both certificated (eg SCOTVEC, SCE/GCE etc) and non-certificated, day, evening or flexible learning. Nursery offering a range of play activities for pre-school children 2yrs and over, for children of students enrolled on full or part-time courses.

Stevenson College Community-based ESL Section
Leith Adult Education Centre
4 Duncan Pl
554 7144

FREE Community-based classes (held in schools and community centres all over the city) for adults permanently resident in Edinburgh who speak English as a second language. *Creche* (0-5 yrs) for some classes.

Edinburgh's Telford College
Crewe Toll
332 2491
Course Information Officer 332 0127 (24 hrs)

Wide range of courses in general education, vocational skills and general and recreational interest suitable for preparing to go back to work or wishing to maintain skills and interests. 'Access for Women' course with varied programmes which can be arranged to suit family and other needs, Roz Chetwynd Ext 2265. Large open learning programme and a range of other attendance patterns, ask if shorter hrs are possible. Some subject areas (eg computing and office technology) have some 'drop-in' facility which increases flexibility for students. *Creche* (3-5 yrs) with limited places nr main college site, part-time places may be available at short notice.

University of Edinburgh
Old College, South Bridge
650 1000
Admissions Information 650 4037
David Eccles

Special prospectus for mature students. Entrance qualifications for degree courses may differ for mature students. The University has a nursery (6 wks-5 yrs) 667 9584 Mrs Clouston. *See* Pre-School Play and Education p114. See also Centre for Continuing Education p162.

Women and New Directions (WAND)
See Sources of information on Adult Classes and Training p161.

Workers Educational Association (WEA)
Riddles Court, 322 Lawnmarket
226 3456 Barbara Smith

Friendly and informal courses of general interest, return to study, women's studies and for unemployed. Most classes (day or evening) held at Riddles Court. *Creche* available for some courses.

WHOT Shop (Wester Hailes Opportunities Trust)
13a Wester Hailes Centre, Wester Hailes Rd
442 4252

Offer information and advice, guidance and counselling for the people of Wester Hailes on careers, employment and training options. Can arrange short work experience placements in a range of different job types. Runs a number of training courses. FREE *creche* for customers' pre school children.

Women onto Work (WOW)
137 Buccleuch St
662 4514 Shirley Henderson

Courses in Craigmillar, Greater Pilton and Wester Hailes for women who have been out of paid employment to look at options for employment or further study. Also for women from an ethnic minority or with a disability. Childcare facilities available.

SPORT AND LEISURE

We outline below only the centres which offer cheaper membership and regular creches.

A number of the larger hotels with health clubs attached also offer creche facilities eg the Capital and the Carlton Highland Hotels. Membership of these clubs is expensive. See the Yellow Pages under Hotels or Leisure Clubs for addresses and phone nos.

Leisure Access Scheme Edinburgh District Council Recreation Department offer membership of this scheme giving access to a wide range of benefits and discounts at all Recreation Dept outlets including sports and swim centres, museums, theatres and golf courses. Currently, the scheme offers a Leisure Access Card (LAC) £20 and a Super Leisure Access Card (SLAC) £2 for concessionary categories. Children under 18 only need a SLAC if they wish to book facilities in advance otherwise they are automatically eligible for the cheaper SLAC prices. Parents who are LAC/SLAC holders are entitled to use **creche** facilities in EDC Recreation Dept outlets FREE. The cost to non-cardholders is £1.25/child. Application forms are available from all sports or swim centres, local libraries and other EDC outlets or from the Recreation Marketing Unit, 17 Waterloo Pl, 529 7905. There is now a Creche Co-ordinator for all the Recreation Dept's creches. Information on new creche facilities are available from Julie Higgins 661 5350.

All centres have programmes of current activity/coaching sessions which are constantly being changed so it is advisable to check times etc in advance.

The Edinburgh Herald and Post (Edinburgh's free weekly newspaper) is an excellent sources of up-to-date information on leisure and sports activities for all the family.

Ainslie Park Leisure Centre
551 2400

Wide range of coaching and activity classes includes aerobics, aikido, body conditioning and sculpture, circuit training, fitness/weight training, jive dance, judo, step, yoga and swimming lessons for children and adults of all ages and ability. Antenatal, postnatal and aquafit exercise classes. 'Women Only' evening every Mon 6-10. *Cafeteria*. Programme available from Centre.

Creche £1.25 (FREE to LAC/SLAC holders), Mon, Wed, Fri 10-2; Tues 9-1.30; Thurs 9-12.30. Must be booked in advance. Staffed by 3 qualified creche workers.

See Activities for Children p144 & p145, Birthdays and Celebrations p83.

Balerno High School
See Centres Offering A Variety of Activities p155 and Activities for Children p150.

Calton Centre
121 Montgomery St

661 9121

Various exercise classes with **creche**. Baby changing facilities. **Cafeteria** with unsupervised play area.

Contact the Centre for further details. *See* Pre-School Play and Education p94.

Carrickvale Community Education Office

See Centres Offering a Variety of Activities p155.

Corstorphine Leisure Centre
316 4939

Facilities include gymnasium, large fully matted studio, sunbeds and supervised tanning tables, separate men's and women's saunas, children's indoor playcentre, **café/ lounge**. Classes (£3.50) with childcare are operated am on Mon Strech 'n Tone, Tues Women's Aerobics, Thur Step 'n Aerobics and Fri Step class.

Children are supervised by 3 **creche** workers in the **playcentre**, 75p/ child. Phone centre for full details.

Countryside Ranger Service
Hermitage House, Hermitage of Braid,
447 7145

Carol Huston, Senior Countryside Ranger

Visitor centre Winter Mon-Sat 10-Dusk, Sun 11-Dusk; Summer Mon-Sat 10-4, Sun 11-6

Guided Walks and special events programme based on various themes for all the family from Apr-Oct. Information and programme, 447 7145.

Cammo Lodge
Cammo Rd
317 8797

Ranger Station is not always manned, so phone Hermitage to check.

See also Walks and Country Places p220.

Craiglockhart Sports Centre
177 Colinton Rd
443 0101/02
Mon-Thur 9am-11pm; Fri 10am-11pm Sat, Sun 9am-10.30pm

City's main public centre for racquet sports, with indoor tennis, badminton and squash. Coaching in fencing, yoga, aerobics, step, weight-training, keep-fit and trampolining. Well equipped weights gym. Outdoor facilities include tennis courts and boating pond. Summer canoeing coaching courses. Easy access for pushchairs. Programme available from Centre. The tennis facilities are presently being rebuilt to create the Craiglockhart Tennis Centre with 6 indoor courts and eight outdoor with a new 'stadium' main court. Expected to open May 1995, with **creche** facility.

Creche (5 and under) £1.25 (FREE to LAC/SLAC holders), run by qualified staff Tues, Wed, Thurs 9.15-10.45 and 10.45-12.15pm during women's activities classes (step, aerobics, squash, badminton, pulse centre). Must be booked in advance. The class costs £2.55 (£2.05 LAC and £1.15 SLAC).

See also Birthdays and Celebrations p84, Activities for Children p139.

Craigmount Community Centre
Variety of activities. Classes currently include Aerobics/Body Toning Tues, Thurs 9.45-11.15 with **creche**. Yoga

Mon 2-3.30 but no creche available.

See Centres Offering a Variety of Activities p155.

Dalry Swim Centre
Caledonian Cres
313 3964

Range of exercise and aquafit classes and swimming classes. Antenatal class Tues 9-9.40. **Creche** available at times. Programme available from Centre.

See also Activities for Children p145.

Drummond Community High School
556 2651

Variety of classes such as aerobics and step, with creche.

See Centres Offering a Variety of Activities p156, Toy Libraries p132.

Forecourt Leisure
Ashley Pl, Newhaven Rd
555 4533

Facilities for outdoor sports on astroturf surface (with/without floodlights) eg 5-a-side football, hockey and netball, a fitness suite equipped with the latest hi-tech equipment, sauna (M + F), sunbed (M + F), 2 aerobics/seminar/function studios, cafeteria **'The Pitt Stop'** and children's activity area **'Leos'**. Activities include Aikido, karate, kick boxing, tae kwon do, table tennis, compact tennis, carpet bowls and a wide range of fitness classes at all levels eg step, rebound, circuits, 'Bums, Tums and Thighs', aerobics etc. Programme available from Centre.

Membership not necessary but annual membership provides discount prices and privileges. Details from Centre.

Creche (3 mths-12yrs) facilities in

'Leos' (members may book in advance). Mon-Fri 9-4 £1.80/child under 2, £2.60/child 2yrs +; Mon-Fri 4-9, Sat, Sun £2.60/child under 2, £3.50/child 2yrs + 1½hr sessions supervised by qualified staff.

Toilets Gents and toilet for the disabled on ground floor, ladies upstairs. Parent and child changing room on ground floor, 2 separate areas, 1 with comfy cane chair for feeding, other with 2 changing trolleys. This area leads to children's toilets with low toilets, sink and towels adjacent to 'Leos' activity area.

The Pitt Stop
Mon-Fri 9am-9.30pm; Sat 9am-6.30; Sun 9-7.30
Seating 50, licensed, no smoking, self-service, bottles heated, 5 high chairs, own clip-on seats permitted, children's parties hosted

Children's menu, children's portions on daily menu. Burger bar, roll bar, salad bar, health food and continental-style food at very reasonable prices. Child-size cutlery, melamine glasses and plates available. Breastfeeding permitted in nearby Parent and Child Changing Room (see **Toilets** above).

See also Birthdays and Celebrations p85 and Activities for Children p151.

Glenogle Swim Centre
343 6376

Fitness Centre available hosting range of fitness, exercise and aquafit classes. Antenatal classes Mon, Wed 9-9.40am. Aquafit Mon, Wed 10.20-10.50am, Thur 7-8pm. Full range of swimming classes. **Creche** available at certain times. Programme available from Centre.

See Activities for Children p146.

Gracemount Leisure Centre
22 Gracemount Dr
658 1940

Facilities include multi-purpose games hall hosting badminton, basketball, 5-a-side football, volley-ball, gymnastics, trampolining, fencing, indoor hockey, short tennis, table tennis, martial arts; fitness studio; video/audio library; *cafeteria* and bar facilities; *creche*. A wide range of fitness classes for all ages and abilities are available. Women Only evening Wed 6-9. Playschemes during school holidays at reduced prices for low income and unemloyed families. Outdoor play area with 'boat' swings. Programme available from Centre.

Good access with lift and ramps to all floors.

Creche Mon, Wed, Fri 10-12 noon, £1.25 (FREE to LAC/SLAC holders). Must be booked (up to 5 days) in advance.

Cafeteria
Mon-Fri 10-10; Sat, Sun 10-5.30
High chair (1), bottles heated, no smoking, breastfeeding permitted, children's parties hosted (Centre or own catering), nappy changing facilities
Self-service. Children's portions.

See also Activities for Children p139, Birthdays and Celebrations p83, and Playgrounds and Parks p214.

Inch Community Centre
255 Gilmerton Rd
664 4710

Range of activities. Currently keep-fit/aerobics sessions Thurs 2-3 with FREE *creche*.

Infirmary St Swim Centre
557 3973

Special swimming sessions include aquafit classes and Women Only sessions. No *creche* facilities at present. Programme available from Centre.

See Activities for Children p146.

Jack Kane Sports Centre
669 0404

Facilities for badminton, judo, keep-fit, football, basketball, weights, hockey, tennis and step/aerobics; beginners especially welcome at all coaching sessions.

Creche FREE for children of parents attending keep-fit classes Mon, Wed, Fri 9.30-12. Also available to parents who are using other facilities at these times.

Programme available from Centre.

See also Activities for Children p139, Birthdays and Celebrations p83.

Jewel and Esk Valley College
See Adult Classes and Training Courses p163.

Kicks
552 7613 Carole Robertson
Stretch, tone and dance classes

(Goldenacre and Stockbridge) Wed, Thurs, for all ages. Choice of 3 classes per week. Young children may attend if happy in prams or pushchairs during day classes. Course of classes must be booked and paid for in advance. Initial class pay on the day.

Lasswade High School Centre
Eskdale Dr, Bonnyrigg
663 7171 (Community Education Worker)
660 1933 (Sports Centre)
Mon-Fri 9am-10pm; Sat, Sun 9.30-9.30

Facilities include main sports hall, 2

squash courts, weight training room, hi-tech gallery fitness machines, activities studio, gym-nasium, games room, cafeteria, outdoor facilities, indoor football, rugby and hockey, grass and all-weather area, Sports Injury Clinic. Also variety of daytime/evening classes for adults. **Creche** Mon-Fri 9-4, staffed by qualified nursery nurses, 70p/session. Phone or visit to book. Information leaflets from Centre.

See also Women's Groups and Parents' Centres p158.

Leisure Management Unit
Meadowbank Sports Centre
London Rd
652 2178

Run by Edinburgh District Council, the Unit co-ordinates and develops a wide programme of sport and leisure activities. Many courses are specifically geared to women only and include climbing, golf, aromatherapy, keep-fit, yoga etc. **Creche** usually provided to coincide with day classes. Contact Unit for Programme.

Leith Community Education Resource Centre
554 1509 (9.30-1.30)

See Centres Offering a Variety of Activities p156.

Leith Waterworld
555 6000

'Community Programme' every wkday 9-12 offering aquafit, Parent and Child sessions, ante/postnatal, adults only and sessions for people with disabilities. Women Only sessions Wed 7-9.30pm. **Creche** Mon, Wed, Fri 9-12; Tues, Thurs 10-12. Booking (up to 6 days in advance) advisable. Held in very well equipped and purpose built

room with self-contained toilet and nappy changing facilities. Run by experienced creche workers. £1.25 (FREE to LAC/SLAC holders).

See Activities for Children p146.

Longstone Community Education Centre
Redhall Gr
444 0706

Step/aerobic classes Tues, Thurs 9.30-11.30. **Creche** 50p/child or £1 for 3 or more children, supervised by 1 creche worker assisted by mothers attending classes if necessary.

McLeod Street Sports Centre

22 McLeod St
337 3252
Mon-Sat 9-6 (plus some evenings); Sun 11-7; (Staffed only when classes are on)

Independent sports centre. Activities include football, keep-fit for men and women, basketball, mixed circuit training, step classes, women's' badminton, aerobics, Shotokan karate, short tennis and table tennis. **Creche** (under 3s) during morning classes, FREE. Run on a rota basis by mothers attending classes. Women's Activities sessions Mon 9.30-12; Keep-Fit for women Thurs 9.30-10.30 and Step classes Mon 7.15-8.30. **Cafeteria** sells tea, coffee, sweets and crisps.

Marcos
55 Grove St
228 2141

Leisure centre offering squash, snooker, sunbeds, 2 hi-tech fitness suites, Little Marco's children's fun-place, beautician and hairdressers. Wide programme of aerobic, step and fitness classes for all abilities. **Creche** in Little Marcos supervised by qualified staff Mon-Fri 10-7. Must be booked in advance. £2/child (non-members) 1½ hr session. Discount rates for members.

See also Activities for Children p152, Birthdays and Celebrations p85.

Meadowbank Sports Centre
139 London Rd
661 5351

✔

Tues-Sun 9am-10.30pm, Mon 9.30am-10.30pm (last booking 9.30pm)

Excellent centre on 3 floors built for the 1970 Commonwealth Games. Facilities for over 30 sports including badminton, squash, yoga, aerobics, step, fitness centre and running track. Ramped access and automatic doors wide enough for a double buggy. Lift for disabled and parents with small children. **Toilets** on all floors, at least 1 equipped with chair for feeding and nappy changing facilities. Programme available from Centre.

Creche £1.25 (FREE to LAC/SLAC holders). In Hall 4 Mon-Fri 9.15-12, 1.45-4. Good range of toys in spacious area. At least 2 qualified creche workers on duty at all times. Booking advisable.

Cafeteria

Mon-Fri 10-8; Sat, Sun 10-6

£, High chairs(5), breast feeding permitted, bottles heated, nappy changing facilities, children parties hosted, seating 80

Self-service cafe serving light meals, snacks and ices. Children welcome with plenty of room for pushchairs. Staff request that parents prevent children from running around in temptingly large entrance. **Toilets** close by. 25% discount for LAC/SLAC holders on weekdays.

See also Activities for Children p152

and Birthdays and Celebrations p85.

Moray House College
Cramond Rd N
312 6506

Variety of daytime and evening courses for adults all year. Times and days of basic range of classes vary slightly from term to term. All courses must be booked and paid for in advance. Adult fitness courses suitable for all abilities includes aerobics, step, and circuit training. Swim fitness and aquafit activities. No *creche*. Phone for details.

See Activities for Children p147, Adult Classes and Training Courses p163 and Annual Events p201.

Murrayfield Ice Rink
See Activities for Children p142.

Musselburgh Sports Centre
Newbigging
653 6367

Modern leisure centre offering squash, multi-purpose sports hall, body conditioning room, meeting room, dance studio and lounge area. Wide range of activities includes hockey, volleyball, badmin-ton, squash, table tennis, basketball, trampolining, judo and fitness classes (including step, aerobics and body conditioning). *Creche* Mon 1-2.30; Tues, Thurs 10-12 coinciding with step and aerobic classes although parents can use any facilities at these times. 75p/child. Advisable to book up to 7 days in advance. Programme available from Centre.

See also Activities for Children p140.

Pentland Community Centre
Oxgangs Brae
445 2871

Dancercise class Tues 10-11 with **creche**. Phone Zania McKenzie 445 3856 for information.

See also Pre-School Play and Education p104.

Portobello Swim Centre
669 4077

Creche (1 + yrs) £1.25 (FREE to LAC/SLAC holders) Mon-Fri 9-12. Always 2 creche workers experienced with children on duty. During creche times Centre offers adult swimming classes for all abilities and fitness classes (including step and aerobics) for men and women in Fitness Centre. Alternatively you can just go for a swim. Aquafit ante/postnatal classes. Programme available from Centre.

See Activities for Children p147, Birthdays and Celebrations p86 .

Rannoch Centre
6 Rannoch Ter
339 5351

Badminton Tues, Thurs 9.30-12; Aerobics Wed 10.30-11.30 with **creche**; Step Mon 10.15-11.15 with **creche**. Other classes are run on an occasional basis. **Coffee bar** facilities. Programme available from Centre.

Ratho Community Centre
School Wynd
333 1055

Keep-fit Mon 9.30-11, Fri 9.30-11 (£1.50).

Creche (under 5) 75p/child or £1 for 2 or more. Staffed by 2 creche workers. **Coffee bar** facilities available. Centre regularly organises a minibus to take parents and children to nearby Broxburn Pool and Recreation Centre (no organised creche but mothers look after the children on a rota basis). Contact

Elizabeth Brown on 333 1055 for information.

Royal Commonwealth Pool
667 7211

Creche (5 and under) £1.25 (FREE to LAC/SLAC holders) Mon-Fri 9-2. 2 experienced creche workers on duty at all times. Can be booked in advance if you are attending a course of activity/swimming lessons. You can also use creche (if there are spaces available) when using pool or working out in Fitness Room.

'Clambers' for 3yrs + is Edinburgh's biggest multi-level adventure play area, with slides, tubes, ball pit and lots of soft surfaces.

The Pool offers a wide range of activity/swimming sessions with something to suit all the family. Programme available from Centre.

See Activities for Children p148 and Birthdays and Celebrations p86.

St Bride's and Springwell House Centres
10 Orwell Ter and Ardmillan Ter, Dalry
346 1405

These Centres offer something for everyone with a vast programme of activities ranging from Astronomy to Keep-fit classes.

FREE **Creche** (under 5s) at St Bride's during all morning classes with experienced creche workers. **Cafeteria** with play area for children open every afternoon and some mornings. Nappy changing area in ladies' toilet. Annual membership of the Centres £1 and fees for activities/classes vary. Programme available from Centre.

See Pre-School Play and Education p94.

St Thomas of Aquins RC High School

229 8734

Badminton classes Mon 5.30-7. *Creche*. Various classes on offer as part of Adult Education Programme.

See Centres Offering a Variety of Activities p157.

Saughton Sports Complex

Stevenson Dr, Balgreen

444 0422

Sports Complex with outdoor facilities for football, 5-A-Side football, tennis, hockey and running track with floodlights. Women's running sessions Tues 7-8. Run in safety on floodlit running track and meet new training partners. Suitable for all levels and is supervised by a qualified coach. No need to book, just turn up.

South Queensferry Community Centre

331 2113

Stretch and Relax classes Wed 10.30-11.30. No creche. Badminton Tues 9.30-11.30 with FREE creche.

See Centres Offering a Variety of Activities p173.

Stevenson College of Further Education

See Adult Classes and Training Courses p164.

Edinburgh's Telford College

See Adult Classes and Training Courses p165.

Tollcross Community Education Centre

Tollcross Primary School

Fountainbridge

229 8448

Contact Centre for current information.

See Centres Offering a Variety of Activities p157.

Warrender Swim Centre

447 0052

Full range of classes available including aquafit, antenatal, Parent & Child. Fitness class programmes includes step, aerobics, 'Tums, Bums and Thighs', low impact aerobics and stretch n' tone. Masters swimming sessions and swimming lessons also available. *Creche* Mon, Tues, Thur 9-1; Wed 8.45-1; Fri 9-12. Programme available from Centre. *See* Activities for Children p149.

Wester Hailes Education Centre

See Centres Offering a Variety of Activities p157.

Places to Visit

"I'M SURE THERE'S NO NEED FOR THE DIVING SUIT, DEAR."

Places to Visit; including Art Galleries, Museums, Historic Places, Animals in the City and Boats, Trains and Planes.

We are lucky in Edinburgh to have a wealth of historic buildings, museums and art galleries. However many of these, due to their content, physical structure (eg 17th century tenements), or both, are unsuitable for young children. Here we have concentrated on those places which most children enjoy, and that you will therefore also enjoy, because of the intrinsic interest and the relaxed atmosphere. We have also listed a few of the most famous attractions in the city giving an indication of what you may expect to find.

Usually entry to a museum/art gallery is free, although you may have to pay for special exhibitions but this is indicated within the building.

Information, leaflets, etc can be got from Edinburgh Information Centre, Princes St (above the Waverley Shopping Centre), 557 1700.

The police have asked us to remind parents of the importance of supervising young children wherever they are, for their own safety, and emphasise the importance of teaching small children 'not to go with strangers'.

For city centre locations, refer to map.

For further details and ideas on where to go/what's on, *see* Sources of Information p205 and Out of Town Trips p190.

ART GALLERIES

Children can be fascinated by paintings and sculpture, although holding them up to see properly and constantly telling them not to touch can be tiring.

The City Art Centre
2 Market St
225 2424 Ext 6650 ✔
Jun-Sept Mon-Sat 10-6; Oct-May Mon-Sat 10-5; Sun 2-5 during Festival

Admission FREE except for special exhibitions. Temporary exhibitions, often with a very broad appeal, and Scottish art work. Access to all floors by lift and escalator. Friendly, helpful staff. **Toilets** for the disabled on ground floor. Cafe *see* Eating Out p64.

Fruitmarket Gallery
Market St
225 2383
Tues-Sun 10.30-5.30

Scotland's leading international contemporary art gallery. Ground floor cafe/bistro, art bookshop, **toilet** for the disabled and lift to upper floor. Friendly staff.

See also Activities for Children p135.

National Gallery of Scotland
The Mound
556 8921
Mon-Sat 10-5; Sun 2-5. Later during Festival
Admission FREE

Pushchairs have easy access to most of the building. There is an entrance ramp and a lift at the back of the building to the lower ground floor and the back of the 1st floor.

An outstanding collection of paintings, drawings and prints by the most famous artists from the Renaissance to the post-Impressionists. Also holds the national collection of Scottish Art.

Welcomes parties of nursery aged children. Phone the Gallery's Education Department at the number above.

The **toilet** isn't large enough to change a nappy, but there's quite enough space to take a chair in for breastfeeding (if you wanted to!).

Scottish National Gallery of Modern Art
Belford Rd ✔
556 8921
Mon-Sat 10-5; Sun 2-5
Admission FREE, except for special exhibitions.

Gallery, set in its own grounds with a large lawn in front and parking to the rear. Once a school, it has been beautifully converted to house a permanent collection in which most of the major 20th century artists in Europe and America are represented from Matisse to Hockney. Pieces of sculpture in most rooms and outside on the lawn. Special exhibitions.

The whole gallery is easily accessible with a push-chair — ramp to entrance and lifts inside. The staff are very friendly and sympathetic to children. The ladies' toilet is spacious and has a low chair in it. There are also low comfy chairs (suitable for feeding but not very private) in the passage next to the very pleasant cafe. *See also* Walks and Country Places p231. *See also* Eating Out p74.

Scottish National Portrait Gallery
Queen St
556 8921
Mon-Sat 10-5; Sun 2-5
Admission FREE

Large collection of Scottish portraits

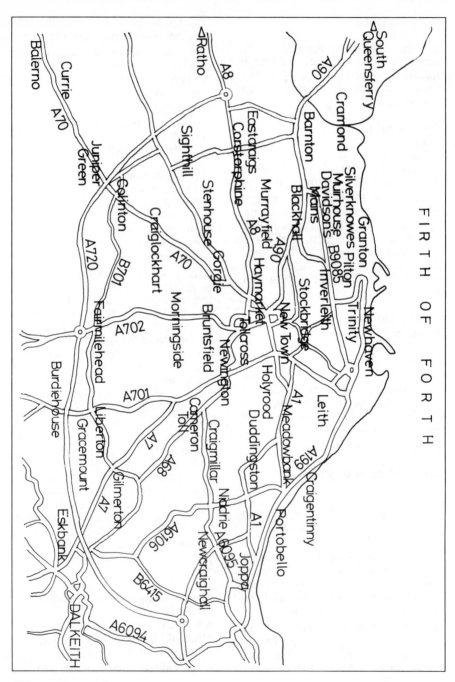

and changing exhibitions. Small toilet at entrance. No facilities for changing or feeding, lift available.

NB: The Royal Museum of Scotland shares this building and includes historic artefacts relating to Scotland. Cafe on ground floor.

MUSEUMS

Camera Obscura
Castle Hill
226 3709
Mon-Sun 9-5 (depending on weather + daylight.)

Under 5s are FREE. 3yrs and above usually get a lot from their visit. Under 3s usually enjoy the hologram exhibition and rooftop terrace more than the camera. This is the oldest purpose built visitor attraction in Edinburgh and is widely regarded as a fun place to visit; both unique and fascinating. Has a narrow staircase which is unsuitable for prams and pushchairs. These may be left in the shop. No special facilities for children or babies but there is a public **toilet** directly across the road.

Huntly House
Canongate, Royal Mile
225 2424
Mon-Sat 10-5, June-Sept 10-6; Sun 2-5 during Festival
Admission FREE

Edinburgh's principal museum of local history with period rooms and reconstructions relating to the city's traditional industries. Also (in display cases) silver, glass, Scottish pottery, shops signs and army relics. It is not possible to install a lift in this restored 16th century mansion and the stairs are steep and winding. Pushchairs may be left at front desk. Small **toilets** on ground floor.

John Knox House
See The Netherbow p187 in Theatres and Cinemas.

Museum of Childhood
42 High St
529 4142

Mon-Sat 10-5; Jun-Sep 10-6; Sun 2-5 during Festival
Admission FREE

A museum devoted to the history of childhood toys, it is of interest to both children and adults. Trains, boats, planes, dolls and many, many more playthings of the past. These are displayed in 5 galleries. Gallery 1 has a few working models including a nickelodeon. Gallery 2 has a children's play table and rocking horse. Gallery 5 has 'Scenes from the Past', a 1930s schoolroom, a nursery, a Victorian street.

Also has different temporary exhibitions throughout the year eg teddies, porcelain dolls.

It is encouraging to see some of the displays at low level, suitable for viewing by small children, but even so, small children may get bored. The museum is partly suitable for pushchairs but there are many steps and it can become very congested. It is requested that pushchairs are left downstairs at the owner's own risk. There is a lift between galleries 1, 2 and 3, ramps to gallery 3, public **toilets** are in gallery 4. They are badly sign-posted. There is a good shop at the entrance, which sells 'old fashioned' small toys/gifts: wooden, tin, paper, posters etc. There are changing and feeding facilities in the **toilet** for the disabled, access with a uniformed attendant by the lift to the basement.

Newhaven Heritage Museum
Pier Pl (adjoining Harry Ramsden's)
551 4165

Mon-Sun 12 noon- 5pm
Admission FREE

The story of the Community of Newhaven is told through reconstructed sets of fishwives and fishermen, displays of objects and photographs, written and spoken accounts. You can look out to the Firth of Forth with binoculars provided and both children and adults can dress up as fisherfolk. There are wooden cut-outs of a fisherman and a fishwife to stick your head into and look at yourself in the mirror opposite. Also two 'feelie' boxes, one with a 'palm' used by sailmakers and one with a buoy; and a tray of shells which can be handled. Small shop selling sea related items, some at pocket money prices. Friendly staff. There are public **toilets** at the end of the fishmarket (near the door of Harry Ramsden's carry-out service)

The People's Story ✔
Canongate Tolbooth, Royal Mile
225 2424
Mon-Sat 10-5, June-Sept 10-6; Sun 2-5 during Festival
Admission FREE

A museum tracing the lives, work and pastimes of the city's ordinary people from late 1700s to present day. The displays include a series of reconstructions — a fishwife, a joiner up a ladder, a servant cleaning a grate, prisoners in a cell, a tea room, a washhouse. These are all enhanced by smells and sounds as well as photographs and displays of everyday objects, which under 5s can appreciate. A 20-min video complements the story line. A lift allows pushchair access to 1st floor but not beyond that. Pushchairs may be left at front desk. Counter selling postcards, pencils, badges etc.

Roomy **toilet** for the disabled may be used for feeding and changing.

The Scotch Whisky Heritage Centre
358 Castlehill, The Royal Mile (beside the castle)
220 0441
Open 7 days 10-5.30 (Extended hrs in summer)
Adults £3.80, children 5-17 £2, under 5s FREE

The 40 min tour starts with an audio-visual sequence illustrating the whisky making processes and regions followed by a walk through the bonded warehouse. New for 1995 is a friendly 'ghost' whose presentation describes the art of the master blender. Upstairs, visitors sit in a barrel for a journey through the history of Scotch whisky with tableaux, sounds, aromas and a commentary in a choice of 8 languages.

The history of whisky will not mean much to under 5s but they will enjoy the barrel ride and the models which include children, hens, cats and dogs. Friendly staff. Group booking advisable. Pushchairs are welcomed (the centre has a lift). Public toilets and spacious toilet for the disabled with nappy changing table.

Royal Museum of Scotland ✔
Chambers St
225 7534
Mon-Sat 10-5; Sun 12-5
Cafe Mon-Sat 10-4.30; Sun 12-4.30
Admission FREE

Don't be put off by the rather imposing entrance, as it opens into a large, glass-roofed building, a wonderful example of Victorian architecture at its best. Here fish ponds (just about toddler proof!), plants and artefacts give the foyer a distinctly Eastern feel. Of most interest to under 5s is the large collection of stuffed animals, from Aardvark to Zebra, and the working model engines, operated by push buttons. Both of these are conveniently situated on the ground floor. Visit the fish exhibition on the first floor where there are more buttons to press — you can hear the mating call of the haddock! The rest of the museum houses on its upper floors most forms of European decorative art and oriental culture as well as a large mineral display and a dinosaur skeleton! It is the largest comprehensive museum in Britain under one roof.

The main entrance involves a long flight of steps, but these can be avoided if you enter from the 'disabled' entrance in Lothian St (rear). Pushchairs are allowed on upper floors, lift available. There is a small museum shop situated on the ground floor. It has a very comprehensive range of books/ toys/gifts catering for all ages (even babies) and all pockets. The ladies' toilet is down a long flight of stairs, but has a table and a chair and plenty of space. The staff are helpful and friendly, and if asked are happy to let you use the parent and baby room (beside the ladies' **toilet**).

Museum Café
Mon-Sat 10-4.30; Sun 2-4.30
£, high chairs, breastfeeding permitted, bottles and baby food heated, no smoking area, parties hosted.

Pleasant, airy, spacious self-service café, selling light snacks and home baking. Small **toilet**.

NB The Royal Museum of Scotland is also situated in Queen St, where it shares a building with the National Portrait Gallery. See p175.

HISTORIC PLACES

Brass Rubbing Centre
Trinity Apse, Chalmer's Close
High St
556 4364
Mon-Sat 10-5, June-Sept 10-6; Sun 12-5 during Festival
Admission FREE

In an old church building tucked away between the High St and Jeffrey St the Brass Rubbing Centre is bright, warm and welcoming within. Of more interest to the over 5s but a mature 4 yr old might enjoy producing a small rubbing. Keep your eyes peeled for the signpost as it is easily missed.

Charge made for each brass rubbing. Materials are provided.

CALTON HILL

Main entrance at Regent Rd. Parking in centre of park at top of hill.

A grassy hill (355') with many famous monuments, and offering wonderful panoramic views over the city, most interesting to children when city landmarks are floodlit over the Christmas season and during the Festival. A popular kite-flying spot. The Nelson Monument (556 2716) may be climbed, but this is not safe for children who are unsteady on their feet. Nowhere to secure pushchairs.

The Time Ball on the top drops at 12 noon GMT (ie 1 pm in summer time) simultaneously with the firing of the cannon at the castle. Every 21 Oct Nelson's famous signal 'England expects that every man will do his duty' is flown to commemorate his victory at Trafalgar. Apr-Sept Mon1-6, Tues-Sat 10-6; Oct-Mar Mon-Sat 10-3. Closed 25/26 Dec, 1/2/3 Jan. Adults £1, under 5s FREE.

See also Annual Events December p204.

At the City Observatory (556 4365), Calton Hill 'Edinburgh in Depth' 3D show 1 Apr-30 Jun and 19 Sep-29 Oct, Mon-Fri 2-5; Sat, Sun 10.30-5. 1 Jul-18 Sep daily 10.30-5. Prices for adults not fixed at publication, please phone, under 5s FREE.

Potted history of Edinburgh from its volcanic beginnings to the present day. Short enough for the attention span of older under 5s who will enjoy wearing the special glasses although the commentary is way above their heads. Keys for **toilets** available from ticket office.

Craigmillar Castle
Craigmillar, off A68
668 8800
Apr-Sept: Mon-Sat 9.30-6.30; Sun 2-6.30; Oct-Mar: Mon-Sat 9.30-4.30; Sun 2-4.30 Closed Thurs pm and Fri
Adults £1.50, children 75p, under 5s FREE. There is a 10% discount for 11 or more persons.

Lovely little castle, dating from the 14th century. It was once the favourite residence of Mary, Queen of Scots. The grounds have plenty of seats and there are attractive little gardens at either side of the castle. Young children need to be closely supervised inside as there are dark staircases, uneven floors and sharp drops from low open windows. Nice place for a picnic. One small **toilet**.

Dalmeny House and Estate
See Walks and Country Places p223 and Annual Events p200.

Edinburgh Castle
Top of the Royal Mile
225 9846
Oct-Mar: 7 days 9.30-4.15; Apr-Sept:

7 days 9.30-5.15. Times given are for last tickets. Closing time about 45 mins later

Adults £5, children £1.90, under 5s FREE (these prices will change 1 Apr 1995). There are good views of the city from the esplanade and no charge for access. The castle itself houses St Margaret's Chapel (built in 1073) and the Scottish Crown Jewels, the National War Museum and military museums and regalia. Not recommended for toddlers or pushchairs as there are steep cobbled paths. The famous cannon, Mons Meg, has been moved indoors and is accompanied by an audio visual display. An old prison cell has been reproduced with wax tableaux of former inmates. Over 3s would enjoy a short visit. Well-stocked shop with many items suitable for children. Note that visitors going only to the National War Memorial can enter free, ask at the ticket office. This right should not be abused.

Free educational visits can be arranged but not in Jun, July or Aug, 244 3087 for further details.

Toilet facilities with a feeding and changing room.

The Military Tattoo is held on the esplanade during the Festival. *See* Annual Events, August p203.

Greyfriars Tolbooth and Highland Kirk
Greyfriars Pl (Top of Candlemaker Row)
225 1900
Sun services 11, Gaelic 12.30
Kirkyard open Mon-Fri 8-6, Sat 10-4
Kirk open Easter-Oct: Mon-Fri 10.30-4.30; Sat 10.30-2.30.

Edinburgh Burgh Church, Scotland's finest collection of monumental sculpture in kirkyard. Covenanters are buried here. A secluded and peaceful spot in the city centre much used for picnics at' lunch time as there are sandwich bars in the vicinity.

Greyfriars Bobby Statue situated opposite the kirk gates, junction of Candlemaker Row and George IV Bridge. The story of the faithful dog is always popular. His master is buried in the churchyard.

Hopetoun House and Estate

See Out of Town Trips p194.

Lauriston Castle

2 Cramond Rd S
336 2060
Castle (guided tours only) Apr-Oct: daily (except Fri) 11-1, 2-4.20 (last tour)
Nov-Mar: Sat, Sun only 2-3.20 (last tour)
Adult £2, children over 6 £1
Grounds 9-dusk all yr, FREE

The house has remained unchanged since 1926 and has a secret room and a notable collection of Blue John ware. Guided tours only, lasting about 40 mins, and not really suitable for young children as once inside the castle you cannot leave until the tour is finished.

There are pleasant walks, suitable with a pushchair, in the peaceful and extensively wooded grounds with fine views over the Forth estuary to Fife. They are particularly lovely in spring when the daffodils are out and the pond is full of tadpoles. There are usually ponies in the fields.

The district council organises some activities in the grounds to coincide with school holidays, see Annual Events p201. Ball games may not be played in the glade. There is a picnic area with tables and arrangements can be made for large parties (apply

to the Recreation Dept, 27 York Pl).

Toilets have a convenient bench seat for feeding or changing. There is also a **toilet** for the disabled. For the nearby Lauriston Farm Restaurant, see Eating Out p80.

The Netherbow

See Theatres and Cinemas p187.

Open Top Buses

See the historic sites of Edinburgh from an open top bus

See Boats, Planes and Trains p185.

Palace of Holyrood House

Queen's Park, foot of the Royal Mile
556 1096
Apr-Sept: Mon-Sat 9.30-5.15; Sun 10.30-4.30
Nov-Mar: Mon-Sat 9.30-3.45; Sun 10-3.45

The Palace is open to the public throughout the yr except when the Queen or her Commissioner is in residence in late May and also in late June. Closed occasionally at other times at short notice.

Adults £3.50, over 60 £3, children (5-16 inc) £1.80, family (2 adults and 2 children) £9, under 5s FREE.

The Palace is the Queen's official residence in Scotland and the part open to the public is fairly small. Guided tours not really suitable for toddlers. Pushchairs are not allowed but backpacks are OK. The ropes dividing the exhibits from the tour are rather too easy for small children to negotiate. The ruins of Holyrood Abbey dating back to the 11th century can also be visited and would provide children with an opportunity to run about.

Toilets have no special facilities but staff very helpful. Public **toilets** at foot of the Royal Mile have nappy changing room. There is a souvenir shop at the Palace gates. *See also* Walks and Country Places p224.

Tearoom above shop at Palace gates open all yr, hrs as for Palace. Tea, coffee, juice, homebaking. **Toilet** is down a steep circular staircase. No special facilities.

St Giles' Cathedral
High St
225 4363
Mon-Sat 9-5 (9-7 in summer); Sun all day. Services Mon-Sat at mid-day, Sun 8, 10, 11.30 am and 8 pm. Musical recital at 6. FREE, Thistle Chapel adults £1.

A landmark on the Mile and probably Edinburgh's most imposing church. Many historical connections. Thistle Chapel visited from within the cathedral. Souvenir shop. Pleasant 'Lower Aisle Restaurant'.

See Eating Out p85.

Scott Monument
See Playgrounds and Parks, Princes St Gardens p210.

Telling the Time
A cannon is fired from the castle at 1 o'clock every day and can be heard from a considerable distance. The floral clock in Princes St Gardens West, at the foot of the Mound is very popular with children, who love waiting for the bird to pop out on the hour; Spring-late Autumn.

Frasers, West End has a clock outside the building, with soldiers and a castle.

ANIMALS IN THE CITY

Birds of Prey — *see* Out of Town Trips — The Deer Centre p196, Lasswade p192.

Butterflies — *see* Out of Town Trips — Lasswade p192.

Deer — *see* Out of Town Trips, Country Park — Beecraigs p193, Hopetoun House p194, The Deer Centre p196, Jedforest Deer and Farm Park p195.

The Edinburgh Dog and Cat Home
26 Seafield Rd E
669 5331
Mon-Sat 9-4
FREE

Used to showing visitors around — if asked in advance they will cater for groups ranging from toddlers to adults. Puppies and kittens feature highly in the under 5s tour, the children usually being allowed to handle them under supervision. Older groups are given a talk and film show after their guided tour.

Edinburgh Zoo
Corstorphine Rd
334 9171
Apr-Sep: Mon-Sat 9-6; Sun 9.30-6
Oct and Mar: Mon-Sat 9-5; Sun 9.30-5
Nov-Feb: Mon-Sat 9-4.30; Sun 9.30-4.30
Adults £5.50, Children 3-14 yrs £2.80, Family ticket £14.90, under 3s FREE
20% discount for groups booked in advance (min 10). Car park £1.
Pushchairs may be hired at entrance for £3 + £12 deposit

If you are a regular visitor it is worth considering membership (annual or life). This entitles holders to unlimited entry to Edinburgh Zoo and the Highland Wildlife Park (nr Aviemore), free parking and the use of the Member's House.

A great day out for families. One of the most naturally beautiful Zoo sites in the world which, although on a slope, provides stunning views. Over 150 species of animals, from giraffes to gorillas, rhinos to red pandas and big cats to tiny poison arrow frogs. Constantly upgrading and improving enclosures, the Zoo aims to provide a more natural and stimulating environment for all the animals. It is also home of the world's largest penguin enclosure, complete with underwater viewing and video surveillance of nesting sites. The famous penguin parade takes place at 2pm from Mar-Oct. Even in wet weather, there is much to see in the primate and reptile houses. At various times through the day, the animals are fed, which is always exciting for children. There are also informative talks throughout the day in the summer months by the education staff, with keepers on hand to answer any questions.

During Easter and Summer holidays there are activities to interest older children, eg brass rubbing and animal handling sessions (min age 3) when you can have close encounters with a variety of small mammals and reptiles. Opening in Summer 1995 is the Darwin Centre, marvellous tortoise shaped maze and covered picnic area. Several other picnic sites, self-service restaurants and numerous kiosks (ice cream,confectionary, soft drinks) are situated throughout the Zoo. Most kiosks are closed outside of the summer months. There are 2 gift shops selling toys, gifts and books with an animal theme. *See* Arkadia, Toy Shops p27.

Access is generally good for pushchairs although the push to the top of the Zoo should be taken in easy stages. There is a Members' entrance from the car park which can save some pushing as it is higher than the main entrance.

There are several toilets throughout the area as well as in restaurants. Nappy changing facilities available.

The Den
Summer only, Mon-Sun 10.30-5.45.
£, High chairs (3), breastfeeding permitted, bottles heated, nappy changing surface, seats 200, licensed, children's menu.

Self-service snack bar. Range of light meals and snacks. May be used for picnics. Chair suitable for feeding in the Ladies.

The Penguins' Pantry
Summer Mon-Sun 10.30-5.45
Winter Mon-Sun 10.30-in line with Zoo closure
£, High chairs (6), breastfeeding permitted, bottles heated, nappy changing surface, seats 120, licensed, children's menu

Large self-service restaurant serving a variety of hot meals and snacks all day. No pushchairs inside but covered area to secure outside. Chair suitable for feeding in Ladies.

Members' House
Mon-Sun 10-5. Winter closing in line with Zoo closure
£££, Highchairs (6), breastfeeding permitted, nappy changing surface, parties hosted, licensed, children's menu and half portions, seats 90

Light meals and full luncheon facilities; tables can be reserved by phone or at reception in the Members' House. No smoking in restaurant or coffee lounge.

See also Birthdays and Celebrations p84.

Farm animals — *see* Out of Town Trips p193.

Fish — *see* Out of Town Trips p193.

Gorgie City Farm
51 Gorgie Rd
337 4202
Mon-Sun 9.30-4.30
Admission FREE, (donation box)

Guided tours can be arranged in advance for a modest charge. Contact the Farm for details.

Especially suitable for visits by small children, this community farm is on a 1 hectare site which used to be the main refuse collection point for the city. There is a wide range of animals including sheep, goats, a Jersey cow, Shetland ponies, pigs, ducks, hens, rabbits, guinea pigs, bantams and pheasants. Also a large organic vegetable garden, a herb garden and a wildlife garden. There is a new Interpretive Centre and an excellent cafe which offers snacks and meals. A children's play area with adjacent picnic area. The farm was established 10 yrs ago as a community project and it is now one of the best in Britain. The animals are all very quiet and friendly and provide an ideal opportunity for children to see farm animals at close range in a suitable environment. Special events and activities are organised at different times.

Good access for pushchairs. FREE parking. **Toilet** for the disabled and nappy changing facilities.

Jemima's Pantry
Mon-Sat 9.30-4-30; Sun 10.30-4.30

Morning coffee, lunches, afternoon teas, snacks. Highchairs (2). Parties are hosted upstairs.

See also Birthdays and Celebrations p84.

Horses — *see* Out of Town Trips p199.

Gorgie City Farm

Come to the Farm in the centre of the City and meet all the friendly animals. See the new Discovery Room and the model farm. Visit Jemima's Pantry which is open every day for coffee, snacks, lunches and teas.

Admission is free and the Farm is open seven days a week from 9.30 am to 4.30 pm March to October and 9.30 am to 4.00 pm November to February

51 Gorgie Road, Edinburgh EH11 2LA
0131-337 4202

Lothian and Borders Police Stables and Dog-handlers

Apply to: Police Headquarters
Fettes Ave
311 3131
Nov-May: Tues 2-4

Entry is at discretion of Police Headquarters. Services include talks and tour. Photos and videos can be taken. Summer visits are restricted to groups with special needs.

Royal Highland Show

See Annual Events, June p202.

Sealife — see Out of Town Trips p297.

Wildlife — see Out of Town Trips p196.

BOATS, PLANES AND TRAINS

More Ideas for Places to Visit

For more details of what you will find at these places, as well as tips for journeys, see Travel and Transport p233.

Edinburgh Airport

Off the A8.
333 1000
Admission FREE but the car park is expensive.

There is a viewing gallery and you can also see the planes from the cafeteria. There are high chairs in the cafeteria. A baby changing room provides a sink, changing surface, comfortable seats and a machine dispensing nappies. There are miles of corridors to explore, shops with toys, books etc. Plenty to entertain children here. See Travel and Transport p242.

Edinburgh Canal Centre

Ratho, Midlothian
333 1320/1251
Prices vary

Two deluxe cruising canalboat restaurants operate from the Bridge Inn, Ratho: 'Pride of the Union' and 'Pride of Belhaven'.

Individual bookings can be made for evening meals during the wk, wkends and on Sun lunch-times. Educational trips are available on wkday mornings with a video available on request and worksheets to accompany the outing — £2.50/head. Self-hire boats available for £3.50/hr with oars and £7/hr with small engine. There is a duck and goose nature reserve, children's play park and a putting green.

See Eating Out p79 Children's parties, see Birthdays and Celebrations p86, see also Walks and Country Places p230. 'Santa Cruises', see Annual Events, December p204.

Inverleith Pond

Inverleith Park, Inverleith Pl

Super pond for sailing model boats, especially radio-controlled ones. Most activity to be seen wkends in the summer, see Playgrounds and Parks p212.

Newhaven Harbour

552 1355

Peaceful and attractive harbour, and the village of Newhaven is worth a look too. There is a fishmarket here on Thurs starting about 6.30 am.

Open Top Buses

Both Lothian Region Transport and Guide Friday operate open top buses which tour the central area — the Edinburgh Classic tour and the Edinburgh Tour respectively. Great for

185

a special outing but quite expensive if you feel an hour is too long for your toddler. The ticket is valid all day, however, so you can get off to visit somewhere and get back on again later. The tours start from Waverley Bridge and do a tour of the Old and New Towns but you can begin your journey at any of the stops en route. Buses run every 15 min May to Sept (Oct for Guide Friday) and then every 30 min LRT and 45 min Guide Friday.

Prices are LRT Adults £4.50, child £1, under 5s FREE; Guide Friday Adults £5.50, child £1.50, under 5s FREE.

The ticket price also includes a discount on admission to some attractions. No need to book — tickets can be bought from the driver.

LRT also operate a 'Sea, City and Hills' tour — with open top buses if weather suitable. These depart from Waverley Bridge once/day.

Guide Friday are at Platform 10 Waverley Station, 556 2244, 9-5.30 daily. LRT are at Waverley Bridge, 220 4111 or 554 4494.

Waverley Station
556 2477

FREE tours are only for older children (8 and over) but younger children will enjoy the atmosphere of bustle and expectancy. The central hall is a nice big area for letting off steam and the notice boards are an attraction too. There is plenty to see but as there is open access to platforms toddlers must be closely supervised. For details of facilities see Travel and Transport p?.

Two recommended short journeys are return trips to Haymarket, and across the Forth Bridge to North Queensferry (or Aberdour and down the Hill to the beach).

THEATRES AND CINEMAS

A regular look at the local press and 'The List' reveals that there's a lot on offer for young children in Edinburgh's theatres and cinemas. Also available from the Tourist Information Centre, Waverley Market is 'Edinburgh for Children' and 'Day-by-Day' a leaflet which is published fortnightly. 'Schools Out' details events during the summer holidays and is obtainable from public libraries.

See Sources of Information p205.

In general, theatres are not well designed for a visit with toddlers - pushchairs are not allowed in the auditorium (although they can usually be left in the cloakrooms) and toilet facilities are usually cramped, with no breastfeeding or nappy changing areas. Some theatres have restrictions on admitting babies and under 3s so it's best to check beforehand what the situation is, and also to find out the duration of the show — some family pantomimes have a horrible habit of going on far too long. Refreshments, when available, may not be suitable for children eg coffee or coke. If you have a particularly lively child it may be advisable to make sure that you are not sitting too near a parapet.

Cinemas tend to have spacious toilets, often with anterooms equipped with armchairs. Check press for details of the many film matinees suitable for the under 5s (Certificate U). Of course, the list of venues and events expands enormously during the Edinburgh Festival.

See Annual Events, August p203.

Various theatre brochures and Festival publications give information on facilities for the disabled including access, wheelchair spaces, parking, toilets, guide dogs and induction loops. Also available from the Tourist Information Centre is a leaflet 'Arts Access for Disabled' which gives similar information.

Assembly Rooms
54 George St
Ticketline 220 4349
Administration 220 4348

Occasional children's shows, mostly during the Edinburgh Fling in May. Lift to 1st floor and to **toilets**.

Brunton Theatre
Ladywell Way, Musselburgh
665 2240

Tickets also available from The Ticket Centre, Waverley Bridge (225 8616). Situated on main road into Musselburgh from Edinburgh. Many shows suitable for young children. Every seat has a view. Pantomime season. **Toilet** for the disabled on ground floor. Bar open and coffee available when there are performances.

Church Hill Theatre
Morningside Rd
447 7597

Mixed programme of musicals, drama, and dance school shows. Occasional shows for children. Ramped main entrance. Staicase to main theatre. Limited parking. **Toilet** for the disabled with nappy changing facilities on ground floor.

George Square Theatre
George Sq
650 1000 ext 8401

Modern venue often used during University holidays for children's shows. It is used as a lecture theatre and has fairly steep steps.

Edinburgh Festival Theatre
13-29 Nicholson St
Box office 529 6000

Occasional children's shows for 3 and over. Level access. The 'Cafe Lucia' is not licensed for children.

King's Theatre
2 Leven St
Ticketline 220 4349

Tickets can also be booked at the Assembly Rooms and the Usher Hall. Occasional children's shows, some specifically aimed at under 5s. Some shows with special low price tickets. Book early for a good seat. Ice cream and refreshments available. **Toilet** for the disabled on the ground floor.

The Thomas Morton Hall
28 Ferry Rd
554 1408

Children's shows held during the school holidays. Level access. **Toilets**.

The Netherbow
43-45 High St
556 9579
Mon-Sat 10-4.30

The Netherbow is incorporated with John Knox House into a cultural and community centre for the Old Town. Children's theatre events eg a puppet festival every Easter and a storytelling festival each Oct. Small intimate theatre, every seat has a view. Workshops including some for under 5s. Exhibitions on theatre themes. Lift to theatre for wheelchair users. Cafe. Nappy changing on ground floor near reception.

See also Activities for Children p135, Birthdays and Celebrations p86, Annual Events p201.

Playhouse Theatre
18-21 Greenside Pl
557 2590

A wide variety of shows including opera, musicals, ballet and rock concerts. Occasional children's shows. **Toilets** on ground floor.

The Queens Hall
37 Clerk St
668 2019

Some concerts and events for children, including puppet shows, but a long term programme of events is being developed. Bar and Cafe. Breastfeeding permitted. **Toilet** for disabled. *See* Eating Out p77.

Ross Open Air Theatre
Princes St Gdns West

Occasional children's shows during school holidays. For information about future events contact Eileen Rae 529 4048.

Royal Lyceum Theatre
30 Grindlay St
229 9697

Christmas shows for young children. Lifts to all levels. **Toilets** for the disabled on ground floor. Bars and Phipps' Theatre Restaurant, 229 8663. Bookings can be made at A T Mays, the Queen's Hall and at the Ticket Centre, Waverley Bridge, 225 8616.

St Bride's Centre
10 Orwell Ter
Haymarket
346 1405

Children's shows mainly in the school holidays and popular films shown on Sat mornings and school holidays. Cafe with large, enclosed play area. Nappy changing facilities. **Toilet** for the disabled on ground floor. *See also* Activities for Parents p172 and Pre-school Play and Education p94.

Theatre Workshop
34 Hamilton Pl
Stockbridge
226 5425

Many shows geared for school children and occasionally under 5s. Also exhibitions and classes. Concession rates apply to children's tickets. **Toilet** for the disabled.

Cafe *see* Eating Out p75.

Traverse Theatre
10 Cambridge St
228 1404

Occasional Christmas shows and holiday workshops for children. Bar and cafe. Lift to eating area and **toilets**. *See* Eating Out p71.

Cinemas

MGM Film Centre
Lothian Rd
Box Office 228 1638
Programme Information 229 3030

Cameo Cinema
38 Home St
228 4141

Dominion Cinema
18 Newbattle Ter
Morningside
Box Office and Credit Card Bookings 447 4771
Information Lines 447 2660/8450

As visited by Maisie. the Cat and illustrated by Aileen Paterson in 'Maisie Comes to Morningside'! Cafe (some seats downstairs). **Toilets** on ground floor and basement level.

Filmhouse
88 Lothian Rd
228 2688

Sat Cinema for children. Must be 3+ yrs to be admitted to cinema but younger children allowed in cafe. Full facilities for the disabled.

Odeon Film Centre
7 Clerk St
667 7331/2
Credit Card Hotline 668 2101

UCI Cinemas
7 Kinnaird Park, Newcraighall Rd
Credit Card Hotline FREEPHONE
0800 88 89 55

Programme Information 669 0711
Twelve Cinema American owned complex. Children's ticket £2.20. No babies in arms. No smoking in cinemas. Light snacks available and there is a children's menu and child-size portions. Delicious 'Baskin Robbins' ice cream is on sale in the foyer as well as the usual popcorn, hot and cold drinks etc. Also cater for children's parties, *see also* Shopping p8.

Out of Town Trips

There are many interesting places to visit within easy reach of Edinburgh. This is a selection of places which have been tried and tested with under 5s. It has been limited to the East of Scotland, Glasgow and the surrounding area would require a separate book. *See* Sources of Information p207 for some recommended guides to other areas.

EAST LOTHIAN

Aberlady
Myreton Motor Museum
01875 870288
Daily 10-6; closed Christmas Day
Adults £1.50, under 16s 50p

An interesting collection of cars, motor cycles, World War II military vehicles, other vehicles, posters and toy cars.

John Muir Country Park
01620 824161

Leave Edinburgh along A1 before Dunbar turn along A1087 for 1 mile. Adventure playground on grass with bark chips at Linkfield Car Park. The Country Park is large with a lovely beach; Clifftop Trail, Dunbar; and woodland walk. Not always suitable for a pushchair — take a sling or backpack. Picnic sites at Linkfield Car Park and Shore Road Car Park. Barbecues for hire. **Toilets**.

Dirleton
Castle Inn

Bar lunches served in a small section of the bar reserved for families. Lovely afternoon teas in the dining-room on Sun 3-5 during the summer. Very friendly staff. High chair. Plenty of space in Ladies' room to change nappies.

Yellowcraig: Drive through Dirleton and turn left just before you leave the village. Paying car park (Easter-Sept). Beautiful beach and nature trail through the woods. Difficult with a pushchair. Take a sling or backpack.

Dunbar
Dunbar 'Splash' Leisure Pool
Castlepark
01368 865456
Special features include a wave machine, beach area, flume and other exciting water features. It also has a health suite with sauna, steam-room, solarium, body conditioning room and poolside cafeteria. **Creche** and baby changing/dressing facilities.

East Fortune

East Fortune Market: Sun 10-4. Similar to Ingliston Market see Shopping p8 but smaller. Lots of stalls with cheap and cheerful baby and children's clothes. Stall which sells adult and children's seconds and Clarks shoes, often at half price.

Museum of Flight
01620 01088 308
April to end Sept; Daily 10.30-5.00. Admission £2 adults, £1 children, £5 family
Fascinating collection of aircraft, engines and rockets etc. Children can sit in the cockpit of a trainer plane. Guard rails are low. Friendly cafe. **Toilets**.

Gullane

Beach 40 mins from Edinburgh. The beach is easy to find. Turn left (into a paying car park) off main road from Edinburgh as you go into the village. Pleasant beach with grassy area in front. Play area nearby with toilets.

Haddington

Delightful town with walks along the river.

Waterside Bistro
1/5 Waterside, Nungate
0162 082 5674
High chairs (3), breastfeeding permitted
Tables outside in summer. Often swans to feed but supervision needed as river banks are not safe. Creche at weekends

North Berwick
Tourist Information 01620 2197
Safe beaches, paddling pool, open air heated pool (summer only).
The Lodge car park with crazy golf, swings, trampolines, aviary and adventure-type playground. Toilets.

Seacliff Beach East of North Berwick on A198. Private beach, £1 coin/car for barrier. Beautiful bay, cleaned regularly. Tiny harbour. Car park. Toilets.

Stenton
Stenton Fruit Farm
013685 321
Wkends only. Take A1 to East Linton, stay on by-pass then 2nd right after Q8 Garage. Pick your own fruit. Ring to find out which fruit is ready. Play area with slide and climbing apparatus. Ducks, horses, picnic area and farm walk. Toilets.

Tranent
Windygoul Farm
01875 614050/614052
Daily 12-2.30, 5.30-9.30; Sat, Sun all day
Friendly staff, junior menu. Children welcome at all times. Outside adventure fort and climbing frame. Inside bouncy castle and ball pool. Special events throughout yr. Advisable to book in advance for meals. Available for parties, with resident nanny.

See also Birthdays and Celebrations p87.

MIDLOTHIAN

Bonnyrigg
Swimming Pool
See Activities for Children p145.

Dalkeith
Country Park
663 5684
Apr-Oct 10-6
Under 5s FREE
Nature trails, woodland walks, picnic benches and large children's adventure playground with supervisor.

Flotterstone
Flotterstone Inn on A702 (Biggar road) nr Penicuik
01968 73717
Country pub which welcomes children at lunchtime. Tarmac road behind which goes up hill to reservoir. Good for pram/pushchair walks.
See also Walks and Country Places p225.

Lasswade
Edinburgh Bird of Prey Centre ✔
Dobbie's Garden Centre, on A7, outside Dalkeith
654 1720
Mon-Sun 10-5.30
Large groups only by prior arrangement 01875 20347
A selection of birds of prey; owls, falcons and hawks, some in aviaries and some tethered. Opportunities for handling these beautiful birds safely. Posters and postcards for sale. The Garden Tearoom (see below) and adventure playground situated in

Garden Centre. **Toilets** in car park (no nappy changing facilities).

Edinburgh Butterfly and Insect World: ✔
Dobbies Gardening World, on the A7 nr Dalkeith
663 4932
Mar-Jan: Mon-Sun 10-5.30
Adults £3.30, children £2.10, under 5s FREE; Family Ticket (2 adults, 4 children) £9.80; Season Tickets: adults £17.00, children £10.00, family £35.00. Group rates; guided tours and talks available.
Europe's largest butterfly farm. A popular attraction with a min of 500 free-flying butterflies (which can escalate to 1200 at times) on display, in a landscape of tropical plants surrounding little waterfalls and pools, which contain fish and terrapins. Indidividual displays of other creatures — bees, spiders, beetles, stick insects etc. Also life cycles of butterflies and insects and habitats on display. Entrance is through the shop, a good selection of books and gifts. The Garden Tearoom (see below) and adventure playground situated in Garden Centre. **Toilets** (see below)

The Garden Tearoom
Dobbies Garden Centre
663 0009
Mon-Fri 10-5; Sat, Sun 10.30-5
£, high chairs, breastfeeding permitted, baby food heated, seats 80
Bright, spacious self-service cafe overlooking Garden Centre and next to adventure playground. Small menu of hot dishes, chips available with everything, sandwiches and light snacks. Delicious home baking. Pushchairs can be brought in. Toilets nearby with chair suitable for feeding and a nappy changing surface.

See also Lasswade High School Centre in Activities for Parents p158.

Pathhead
Vogrie Estate and Country Park

12 miles south of Edinburgh, signposted beyond Dalkeith, just before Pathhead. Open all yr. Admission FREE. *See also* Parks and Playgrounds p218.

WEST LOTHIAN

Broxburn
Swimming Pool
01506 854723

Easy to find on the main street. There is a beautifully warm baby pool (too deep for toddlers to stand in) with playpens and baby changing areas at side of pool and in changing room. Pleasant spectators area overlooking the pool.

Linlithgow
Forth Valley Tourist Board
Annet House, High St
01506 843306

Special events held throughout yr such as jousting tournaments, Fairs and riding the marches.

Town Centre: Lochside walk to feed the ducks and geese accessible down several side roads. Car park and new playground (modern equipment and bark chips) at bottom of Water Yett.

Beecraigs Country Park
01506 844516

Woodland walks, deer farm, reservoir and pond. Trout farm (to help feed the fish phone for feeding times). Barbecue areas for hire, £13 includes charcoal. Restaurant open all day for refreshments as well as bar meals

and evening meals. Breastfeeding permitted. Shop selling ice cream, books, gifts and outdoor wear. **Toilets**, changing area in toilet for disabled.

Linlithgow Palace
01506 842896

Ruins of castle where Mary Queen of Scots was imprisoned. Pleasant grounds with grassy banks for picnicking.

Livingston
Almond Valley Heritage Centre Millfield. Take A705 to Mill roundabout then 1st left B7015. The farm is signposted
01506 414957

Open all yr, 10-5 (cafe 11-4). Adults £2.20, children £1.10, under 3s FREE

A restored 18th Century water mill and farm. Ususal range of farm animals, including Clydesdale horses, cattle, sheep, goats, donkeys, and a range of ducks, geese and chickens. Milking demonstrations twice daily and in spring baby animals to feed. Tractor drawn trailer rides around the farm operating throughout summer. A play tractor course, exclusively for the under 5's just completed. The 'Oilshale Adventure Zone' provides imaginative indoor adventure playground for the 4-12 year olds. Country-side walks and nature trail. Picnic tables and play area with bark chips. Small, pleasant cafe.

Broxburn
Almondell and Calderwood Country Park
Visitor Centre 01506 882254

Almondell North car park (closes at sunset) is nearest to Visitor Centre. Signposted off A89, the entrance is 2 miles south of Broxburn. People with walking difficulties can park in disabled car park next to the Visitor Centre, phone in advance to make sure the North gate is open.

Country park in the grounds of an old estate. Well-made paths suitable for pushchairs. Picnic tables and barbecue site (book in advance). Walks along the River Almond. Visitor Centre Sun-Thurs (closed 12-1) has aquarium, displays and seasonal exhibitions. Refreshments available — hot drinks and confectionery. Enclosed 'tea garden' behind the Centre with plenty of seating. Two full-time Rangers arrange a series of FREE activities and family events throughout yr.

Calderwood It is possible to walk from Almondell (see above) to Calderwood along the River Almond though this involves passing the Mid Calder sewage works; by road from East Calder follow B7015 for a further mile and then turn onto B8046 Pumpherston/Uphall rd. Car park is 200 yds along on right.

Calderwood has been left as a natural area to encourage wildlife. The paths are rough tracks and there are no facilities unlike Almondell.

South Queensferry
Boat trips to Inchcolm Island
24hr Sailings enquiry service
331 4857

Sailings from Hawes Pier. Adults £6.25, children £3.25, under 4s FREE, family £16. Cruise under the Forth Rail Bridge to Inchcolm Island, wildlife, seabirds and 100% seal sighting record. Boat seats 225. Snack bar with sandwiches on board. Sailing time 30 mins each way with 1½ hrs ashore to explore the 12th century abbey, sandy beach and wartime gun emplacements, Picnic area and visitor centre. Toilets on boat and island.

Boat trips to Deep Sea World
24hr sailings enquiry service
331 4857

50 person passenger ferry between North and South Queensferry, sails alongside the Forth Rail Bridge every half hour. The best way to get to Deep Sea World. Adult £2, children £1, under 4's FREE

Hopetoun House
On A904 from S Queensferry, 12 miles from Edinburgh
331 2451
Daily end Apr-Sept 10-5.30
House and grounds adults £3.50, children £1.70, under 5s FREE. Grounds only, £1.80 and 50p respectively

The House is 'Scotland's finest

stately home' with a magnificent art collection. Plenty for children without visiting the house. The gardens are extensive with plenty of room for ball games and running about. Picnic area, nature trails, deer park and a stable exhibition about 'Horse and Man in Lowland Scotland'. Self-service restaurant and gift shop. Toilets with nappy changing surface.

Also the Walled Garden Centre at entrance to Hopetoun House. Tiny cafe with toilets, no changing surface.

BORDERS REGION

Country Houses

There are numerous old houses of interest in this area, all easily found on most maps. Most have extensive gardens for walks, games or picnics as well as tearoom or restaurant. As opening times vary between houses and seasonally it would be advisable to telephone first. More popular houses are listed below:

Abbotsford (Galashiels) 01896 82043

Floors (Kelso) 01573 223 333

Manderstone (Duns) 01361 883450

Mellerstain (nr Melrose) 01573 881292

Thirlestane (Lauder) 01578 82430

Traquair (Innerleithen) 01896 830 323

Duns

Crumstane Farm: Take A6105 from Duns east towards Berwick, 1½ miles along the farm is signposted.
01361 883268
Adults £1.70, children £1, under 3s FREE

Over 60 varieties of farm animals and poultry to see. Feeding of animals possible. Easy walking between enclosures.

Jedburgh
Jedforest Deer and Farm Park
Follow A68 south, 5 miles from Jedburgh, signposted on main rd, turn off and travel ¼ mile to 1st farm you come to
01835 840364
May-Aug 10-5.30; Sept-Oct 11-4.30
Adults £2.50, children £1.50, under 3s FREE

Farm not only includes deer but also many rare varieties of most farm animals. There is a 'clapping' area where children can touch animals and help bottle feed animals who need it. Walks in wooded area following colour-coded signs lasting ½-1½ hrs. Large adventure playground. Rides on trailers pulled by tractors. Barbecues for hire, picnic area, cafe with high chair and shop.

Peebles
Tourist Information 01721 20138

Busy market town with museum, cafes and some interesting shops. Walks and playground area by the River Tweed.

Hay Lodge Park: Follow the path beyond the *swimming pool* (with toddler pool) along the river's edge to this large play park (2 small flights of step along path). Annual Bear Fair, early Aug, 01896 830833 for information. Music, theatre, puppets, jugglers, face-painting, stalls, refreshments.

Kailzie Gardens: Take B7062 2 miles out of Peebles
01721 20007
Daily 11-5.30
Adults £1 (Jun-Aug £1.50), under 5s FREE

Woodland walks, adventure playground, **tearoom** and shop.

CENTRAL REGION

Bo'ness
Bo'ness and Kinneil Railway
Bo'ness Station, Union St, Bo'ness.
01506 822298
Sat, Sun, Easter-Oct; daily Jul and Aug
Adults £3, children £1.50, under 5s FREE

Steam train trips. A very pleasant outing for both children and parents. Special events are very popular eg Teddy Bears' Picnic in Jun; Thomas the Tank Engine weekend in Aug; Santa train trips in Dec. Details from Railway Preservation Society 333 1281. *See also* Annual Events p204.

Stirling
Tourist Information 01786 79901

Beechwood and Bike Park: off St Ninian's Rd, Stirling

Bikes of all sizes for hire. Plenty of play equipment and walks.

Blairdrummond Safari and Leisure Park: Leave M9 at Junction 10 and travel west from about 3 miles
01786 841456
Mar-Oct. Adults £5, under 3s FREE. Price includes most attractions

Wild animals — lions, monkeys etc (drive through park takes ½ hr, this may be uncomfortable on a hot day with the windows closed), farm animals in field through which you can walk and touch animals eg sheep, pigs, llamas, performing sea lions and adventure playground, plus other fun activities. **Restaurant** with high chairs, picnic and barbecue area.

Stirling Castle: Apr-end Sept: Mon-Sat 9.30-6; Sun 10.30-5.30;
Oct-Mar: Mon-Sat 9.30-5; Sun 12.30-4.30

Very impressive views from the castle walls with plenty to look at. Museum and **coffee shop**.

FIFE

Aberdour
Tourist Information Centre 01383 720999

Silver Sands: Lovely beach with play area and **toilets**. Trips in small boat (max 12) to Inchcolm *see* South Queensferry p194. Take waterproofs.

Burntisland
Tourist Information Centre 01592 872667

Swings, mini-golf, trampolines, paddling pool, lovely beach, fun fair in summer.

Cupar
The Deer Centre
2 miles west of Cupar on A91
01337 481391
Visitor centre May-Oct: 10-5, Restaurant 10-6
Adults £3.50, children £2.20, under 3s FREE

Deer farm walk (to meet the deer), nature trail, picnic area, animal pens (usually abandoned pets children can touch). Daily falconry displays. Aerial walkway. Covered all-weather adventure barn. Superb outside adventure playground and maze. Restaurant and snack kiosk.

Lochore
Lochore Meadows Country Park
01592 860086/860261
Cross Forth Bridge and follow M90.

At Junction 3 take Kirkcaldy turn off. Take Lochgelly exit from this road, then B920 to Crosshill. Signpost for park on left. Adventure playground/ beach/BBQ.

North Queensferry
Deep Sea World
Close to Forth Road Bridge
01383 411411
9.30-6 daily

A diver's 'eye view' of thousands of fish through an amazing underwater viewing tunnel featuring the first pirate exhibition in Scotland. Free face painting, rock pool, 200 seat **cafe**, baby changing facilities, ramp access everywhere. Free car parking. Special educational nursery programme by arrangement. Adults £4.60, Children £3.35, Under 4's FREE, Family £13.95

St Andrews
Tourist information 01334 4720221

Two really lovely beaches, both sandy although sea very cold.

Craigtoun Park
2 miles sw of St Andrews on B65
01334 473666
Over 5s £1.50, under 5s 75p
Facilities open in summer 10.30-5.30 grounds open FREE outwith these hours.

Plenty to do: mini-steam train for rides, boating lake, putting and crazy golf, trampolines, bouncy castles, pets corner, aviary, Dutch village, gardens and open-air theatre. Adventure playground with special area for under 10s. Visitor centre with excellent nature displays and activities for children. Restaurant and snack kiosk. 3 **toilet** blocks.

East Sands Leisure Centre
01334 476506

Swimming pool. Adults £1.50, children £1.10, under 4s FREE
Flume 10p/ride (12 for £1)

Lovely warm toddler pool with toys. Baby changing tables and playpens in special area in mixed changing room.

Janettas: East end of South St. Very special ice-cream, extensive range of flavours.

Sea Life Centre: The Scores
01334 474786
Open all yr, 7 days, 10-6
Adults £4.25, children £2.95, under 4s FREE

Fascinating display of sea creatures native to Britain, some of which can be touched. Quiz trail throughout centre and outside pool with excellent viewing. Giant blackboard so budding artists can watch and draw. Services for the younger guests include nappy changing facilities, childrens meals in the restaurant and a FREE back-pack loan service as there are some stairs as well as some tanks being at waist height. **Coffee shop** and gift shop. Birthday parties arranged.

STRATHCLYDE

Biggar
Tourist Information 01899 21066

An easy to find adventure-type playground by the river. Grass and bark chip although supervision is essential as river runs through the middle.

Gasworks Museum
Royal Museum of Scotland 225 7534
Turn right off the High St
Jun-end Sept: 2-5 daily

Gladstone Court Museum
01899 21050
Go through the gate nr the Chocolate
Box and follow signs
Easter to end Oct: 10-12.30, 2-5; Sun
2-5
Adults £1.20, children 50p, under 5s
FREE

Purves Puppets
Broughton Rd
01899 20631
Mon-Sat 10-5 (closed Wed); Sun 2-5
Adults £4, children £3

Puppet theatre and Museum. Shows
(1½ hrs with 15 min interval) and
guided tours.

Tearoom, outdoor games, souvenir
shop, attractive gardens. Will do
parties either at Broughton St or by
arrangement at a local venue. Car
park and **toilets**.

Coatbridge
The Time Capsule
02364 449572

'Half ice/half water, a whole lot of
fun for time travellers of all ages'.
Swim through warm dinosaur
infested primeval swamps, paddle in
the spaceship bubble and enjoy the
many rides and slides. Skate across
the frozen loch under the watchful
eye of a giant woolly mammoth. Bob
skates are available for young
adventurers.

Lanark
New Lanark Visitor Centre
Less than 1 hr from Edinburgh along
Lanark Rd. Signposted on all major
routes
01555 661345
11-5 daily

Famous cotton mill village. Journey
round historical exhibition in travel
car. Learn about spinning and
weaving. Games for children. Visit

Falls of Clyde (a nature reserve).
Adventure playground, outdoor
picnic areas, craft shops and Scottish
Wildlife Centre. Gift shop and cafe for
meals and snacks. **Toilets**. Visitor
Centre pushchair friendly.

Motherwell
M & Ds Fun Park:
01698 51720

Easy to find, adjacent to M74. Set in
Strathclyde Park there is something
for everybody. Dodgems, Flying
Carpet, Ghost Train and Scotland's
only looping roller coaster and many
children's rides.

TAYSIDE

Crook of Devon Fish Farm
01577 840297
Open daily late Mar to end of Oct,
then wkends to Christmas

Working fish farm. Children can feed
fish. Farm food bar and adventure
playground.

Dundee
RRS Discovery: moored in Victoria Dock
01382 201245
Open all yr, 7 days 10-5 (4 Nov-Mar)
Adults £2, concessions £1.50

Superb visitor attraction built
alongside Captain Scott's ship RRS
Discovery. Winner of Scottish
Tourism Oscar and Scottish Museum
of the Year. Parking, cafe, disabled
access and toilets, parent and baby
rooms, gift shop.

Perth
Leisure Pool

Easy to find. Leave M90 following
signs to Perth, look out for the left
turn with sign to Leisure Pool

01738 630535
10-10 daily
Under 5s FREE

Leisure pool and new 'Toddler Interactive Water Playground'. Children's pool and slide in tropical setting. Tunnel to outdoor pool and wild water channel. A wide variety of other activities available. Family changing cubicles with baby changing shelf. *Cafe* for meals and snacks.

Fairways Heavy Horse Centre
Newton Farm, Glencarse, Perth (5 miles from Perth on A90 Dundee road)

01738 632561
Open all yr 10-6

Clydesdales, wagon rides, farm implements, video, *cafe*. Facilities for disabled.

Scone Palace
01738 652300
Adults £4.50, under 5s FREE, Family £13.

An impressive tour round the house with plenty of interesting items. The grounds are well kept and very spacious. Picnic area, ball games allowed. Adventure playground. *Tea/snack room* with high chairs.

199

Annual Events

"A CHOCOLATE FESTIVAL OR A SWEETIE FAIR, NOW THAT WOULD BE SOMETHING!"

JANUARY

Pantomimes and plays at King's Theatre; Royal Lyceum; Theatre Workshop and other venues.
See press for details and Places to Visit p186 for addresses and facilities.

FEBRUARY

Snowdrops at Cammo Park and Dalmeny House, South Queensferry, where gardens open one Sun for charity. Lots of space to work off excess energy.
See Walks and Country Places p221 and p224.

EASTER

Animal handling sessions at Edinburgh Zoo.
See Places to Visit p182.

Easter Egg Rolling in West Princes St Gardens on Easter Sun. Also puppet shows and horse and cart rides. Egg rolling at Dunsapie Loch in Holyrood Park.
See also Playgrounds and Parks p210.

Named Easter Eggs
Casey's, 52 St Mary's St, cnr Easter Rd/London Rd and Thorntons, St James Centre and Gyle Centre and within Hallmark, Cameron Toll Shopping Centre, see Shopping p7 sell decorated and named Easter Eggs from about one mth before Easter. Best to shop early to avoid queues, eggs are named 'on the spot'.

Play session at Meadowbank Sports Centre. Organised activities with emphasis on fun and play. Soft play, inflatable castle, general games. See Activities for Children p152.

Playscheme at Moray House College, Cramond Campus, various activities including music and movement, art and craft, quizzes, games. 3-5s morning or afternoon sessions. Approximately £18.20 / child / wk. Application form from Community Activities, Moray House College, Cramond Rd N, 312 6506.
See Activities for Children p147 and Activities for Parents p163.
Puppet and Animation Festival, The Netherbow, 43 High St, 556 9579.
See Places to Visit p187.

Edinburgh International Science Festival. Hands on events for all the family.
Easter bunny hands out eggs on Bo'ness and Kinneil trains throughout Easter w/e. *See* Out of town trips p196.
Almond Valley Heritage Centre: Chicks and other baby animals on show. *See* Out of town trips p193.

APRIL

Funfair in Meadows at end of wk. Stalls, sideshows, music, face painting.
See also Playgrounds and Parks p213.

Student Charities Week. Procession of floats along Princes St on last Sat of wk at end of April, 225 4061 for details.

MAY

Lauriston Castle Edwardian Extravaganza — Brass bands, puppets shows, kites, pony rides, mini trains to ride etc in spectacular setting. FREE admission.
See also Places to Visit p181.

Scottish International Children's Festival, Inverleith Park. A variety of shows and workshops for children. Creche and mother's room. Some activities FREE. Shop. Phone 554 6297. *See* also Playgrounds and Parks p212.

Spring Fling. Community Arts Festival organised by District Council. Music, dance, theatre, children's events and exhibition. Many shows FREE, otherwise low priced. *Creche* at many events. Programme from libraries or Arts Outreach Team, 12 Nicolson St, 529 4875.

Festival of the Environment organised by the District Council. Music, clean-ups, open days and fun for kids. Many events FREE.

JUNE

Corstorphine Fair. Community fair at St Margaret's Park. C. Kelso 334 2388.
See also Playgrounds and Parks p216.

Craigmillar Festival. Concerts, puppets, music. Craigmillar Festival Society 661 2202 or see press.

Gorgie/Dalry Festival. Puppet shows, children's entertainers, clowns, theatre for children. Most shows FREE or small charge. See press or contact Gorgie/Dalry Festival Office, 258 Dalry Rd, 346 8422.

Leith Gala Day. Children's events, stalls, teas. Contact Leith Community Centre 554 4750. *See also* Parks and Playgrounds p212.

Meadows Festival. Sat and Sun beginning June. Lots of stalls, jumble

to home baking. Many organised by charities. Sideshows, funfair, puppets, face painting, live music, fancy dress, mime. A lively place for a picnic if weather fine. Feeding and changing tent organised by National Childbirth Trust. See press or call Tollcross Community Centre, Tollcross 229 0321.
See also Parks and Playgrounds p213.

Northfield/Willowbrae Gala Day. Children's events, stalls. Northfield/Willowbrae Community Centre 661 5723.

Old Town Gala. Stalls, entertainment in closes of old town. The Netherbow 556 9579.

Oxgangs Gala Day, Colinton Mains Park. Parade, fair, stalls. Pentland Community Centre 445 2871.
See also Playgrounds and Parks p214.

Portobello Community Festival. Float parade in High St, children's events, Lynne Aitchison 669 1108

Prestonfield Gala. Prestonfield School Playground and Park. Entertainments, Linda Wright 667 9005.

Ratho Children's Gala. Parade to playing fields, entertainment, Norwood Community Wing 333 1021.

Royal Highland Show. Thur-Sun 3rd wk June. Ingliston Showground, Newbridge. Lots of animals to look at, tractors to climb on. Creche. Daily arena events — gymkhanas to marching bands. Playground in Forestry area. Snackbars and cafes. Adults about £12, 5-16 half price.

Under 5s FREE. Reduced prices for adults after 4 pm and cheaper family tickets on Sun. Special buses from Edinburgh. See press or contact Royal Highland and Agriculture Society of Scotland, 333 2444.

Scotland Yard Summer Festival. King George V Park, Canonmills. Family Festival with stalls, activities and music, 557 8199. *See also* Playgrounds and Parks p218.

Scottish Miners' Gala. The Meadows. Children's entertainment, funfair, bands. STUC 0141-332 4946.
See also Playgrounds and Parks p213.

JULY

Most Edinburgh schools break up for the summer around the 1st wk.

Animal Handling Sessions and other events during summer at Edinburgh Zoo. .
See Places to Visit p182.

Soft fruit picking, Stenton Fruit Farm, *see* Out of Town Trips p191.

Play Session at Meadowbank Sports Centre.
See Easter and Activities for Children p152.

Recreation Department, Edinburgh District Council organises a programme of children's summer holiday activities and entertainment. For brochures contact EDC Marketing Unit, 529 7902/3/5
See also Walks and Country Places p221.

Stockbridge Festival. Many events throughout Stockbridge including dance, puppet shows, Ken Hyde 557 1925.

Summer Playscheme at Moray House College, Cramond Campus. Details as in Easter Playscheme entry. Runs for 6/7 wks in Jul/Aug. Also dance and games for over 4s. *See* Activities for Children p147.

AUGUST

The city centre burst into activity this month. (A bad time to try and shop in Princes St — just enjoy yourself!). Apart from official and fringe events, street entertainers are a great attraction too. Best places to find them are outside the Fringe Office in the High St and in 'Festival Place' (at the bottom of the Mound beside the Galleries), although the crowds here can be so thick that movement with pushchair is impossible and toddlers are in real danger of getting lost or being trampled underfoot.

Book Festival. Charlotte Sq. Biennial event in 'odd' years, ie '95, '97. Children's Book Tent, storytelling by authors, visits from characters from books etc. Shona Munro 228 5444. *Creche.*

Edinburgh Highland Games. Meadowbank Stadium. Traditional Scottish field events, Dave Farrer 062 081 408.
Schools and Playgroups generally re-open mid-month for a new academic yr.

Edinburgh International Festival. Details from Festival Office, 21 Market St, 226 4001. Programme available end May. Some performances for children eg foreign circuses and puppets. Bargain ticket booth at foot of the Mound selling half price tickets for shows that day.

Festival Cavalcade. Procession of floats, pipe bands etc on 1st Sun of Festival. A must! See 'Evening News' for route map and get your pushchair parked beside the kerb early to beat the crush and ensure a good view.

Festival Fringe. The many children's Fringe shows are an ideal introduction to the Arts for little ones — performances are short and less formal, with smaller audiences in smaller venues. Programmes available from Fringe Office, 180 High St, 226 5257. Included in children's section are circuses, puppets, drama, music etc.
See also Places to Visit, Theatres and Cinemas p186 for information on venues.

Fringe Sunday. Lots of FREE performances in Holyrood Park 2nd Sun of Festival 12-4, very popular.

Grassmarket Fair. Sats during Festival. Lots of market stalls, junk, home-baking, plants, live music (pipe bands to buskers), bustle and excitement.

Jazz Festival. FREE shows in Princes St Gdns on a Sun afternoon and venues throughout town.

Military Tattoo. Pipes, drums and marching bands on the Castle Esplanade after dark, but a few early evening shows on Sats. You will be confined on high and cold seats on terraces. So if you think your child can cope, take blankets and refreshments. Cushions can be hired. Tickets half price at dress rehearsal.

203

SEPTEMBER

Union Canal Society, Harrison Park. Water based events on canal. Information from local shops and by the boat house, Ashley Terr.

AUTUMN

NCT Edinburgh South Nearly New Sale. Bargains in nursery equipment, children's clothes, maternity wear and toys. A small percentage of money from goods sold goes to NCT, the rest to the seller. Contact local secretary. Other NCT branches may also hold sales in Autumn. Phone NCT office for details see Health Care Facilities p256.

OCTOBER

Children's Book Week. Competitions and readings organised in several bookshops.

Half-Term Holiday Highlights organised by District Council. Puppet shows, special events at sports centres and swimming centres. Exhibitions at museums and art galleries. Programme from libraries or Recreation Marketing Unit, 557 2480 or venues.

Scottish Book Fortnight — includes a Storytelling Festival at the Netherbow see Places to Visit p187. Events in bookshops and libraries, some suitable for under 5s. Scottish Book Marketing Group, 228 6866.

NOVEMBER

Charities Hypermarket. Assembly Rooms, George St. Craft stalls, gifts, Christmas cards, second hand toys, clothing, home-baking. Creche. *See* Shopping p7.

Fireworks at Meadowbank Stadium. Large well organised display. Entry around £1. There are also several smaller local firework events around town, eg Portobello Beach (bottom of Brunstane Rd) FREE; Balerno Round Table Fireworks Display on Currie playing fields.

DECEMBER

Calton Hill to view Christmas lights on Princes St and George St. See Places to Visit p180.

Pantomimes and Children's Shows. *See* January p200.

Santa in residence at various department stores — Jenners, Debenhams and Menzies are well decorated.

Santa Barge Trips on the Union Canal from Ratho, The Bridge Inn 333 1320. Adults and children £4.50. Book in advance. Trip to secret island lasts over an hr. Snacks provided and a present for each child.
See also Places to Visit p185 and Birthdays & Celebrations p86.

Santa Steam Trains Trips from Bo'ness Station.
See also Out of Town Trips p196.

Shoppers Christmas Creche organised by EDC Women's Unit. Usually in the St. James Centre Mon-Sat, and Sun pm £1.25/hr/child.

Hogmanay Celebrations around Princes St, fairs, street entertainment, fireworks. Organised by EDC.

Sources of Information

MAGAZINES

What's On
Published monthly. Cinemas, theatres, shops and restaurant guide. Art galleries and exhibitions. Distributed FREE, available at Tourist Office and many other public places.

The List
Published fortnightly and includes a section 'Kid's List' providing information about events in and around Edinburgh and Glasgow. Available at newsagents.

NEWSPAPERS

The Scotsman, Evening News and Scotland on Sunday
20 North Bridge
225 2468

The Scotsman
Daily morning paper, birth announcements, details of exhibitions, theatres, art galleries, etc especially on Mon. Church Service information on Sat. Back page has list of events.

Evening News
Daily afternoon and evening paper full of local news. Full details of cinema programmes daily. Theatres, sales, fetes, etc, especially on Fri.

Scotland on Sunday
Scottish Sunday paper. Has events page.

Edinburgh Herald and Post
Atlantic House
38 Gardner's Cres
228 5042

Published every Thurs and delivered FREE to most homes in Edinburgh. Details of sales, fetes, etc. Large 'For Sale' columns.

RADIO

Radio Forth
'What's On'
Max AM
Forth House, Forth St
556 9255

TOURISM AND TRAVEL

Edinburgh Information Centre
(formerly Tourist Board)
3 Princes St
557 1700
What's on 0891 775703
Where to take children 0891 775711

Scottish Tourist Board
23 Ravelston Ter EH4 3TP
332 2433

Tourist information for the whole of Scotland. Phone calls and letters only.

Grapevine
Lothian Disability Information Service
8 Lochend Rd
555 4200
Mon-Fri 9-5

Provides information on all aspects of disability including access.

Traveline
24 St Giles St
225 3858
Mon-Fri 8.30-4.30

A 'one-stop' information service covering all public transport in Lothian.
See also Travel and Transport p238.

MISCELLANEOUS

One Parent Families Scotland (formerly Scottish Council for Single Parents)
13 Gayfield Sq
556 3899/4563

Booklet *'Holidays'* and guides to leisure in Lothian. *See also* Welfare p247.

Arts Outreach Team
Edinburgh District Council,
12 Nicolson St
529 4875/4829

Advice and assistance on a wide range of arts activities, produce a Gala directory FREE,which lists entertainers etc.

Leisure Management Unit
Edinburgh District Council,
Meadowbank Sports Centre
141 London Rd
652 2178

Community Information Officer
Community Services Division
Edinburgh District Council
249 High St
529 4272

A-Z of Council services

BOOKS

Guides to Edinburgh
All District Council libraries have files of useful information for reference purposes. These include:
1. Community Information sub-divided into Advice, Education, Government, Health and Leisure.

2. Citizens' Advice published by Citizens Advice Bureau.
3. Edinburgh Information Pack including information on child-care and nursery education; local and regional councillors; local churches, etc.
4. Child Friendly Edinburgh published by Edinburgh District Council Women's Committee. Available FREE.
5. Local Clubs and Organisations.

Capital Information Point
Most libraries have a computer based information system listing Edinburgh District Council and Health services. Also available at E.D.C. sites such as the City Chambers and Royal Commonwealth Pool. *See* Libraries p127.

The Red Book: Lothian Directory of Local Services.
Available from libraries and contains details of voluntary and statutory organisations in the fields of health, social work, community and allied services,
See Welfare p246.

CFUF (Committee For Under Fives)
Booklet detailing facilities for under 5s in Balerno, Currie and Juniper Green. Contact Nursery Teachers, Curriehill Primary School, 210 Lanark Rd W. for copies.

Lothian Childcare Guide covers childcare options in the region. Copies from One Parent Families Scotland (formally Scottish Council for Single Parents), 13 Gayfield Sq EH1 3NX, 556 3899, price £2.50 (£1.50 single parents) *See also* Welfare p247.

Guides to other areas

Kirkcaldy — First Steps in Kirkcaldy and District. A joint National Childbirth Trust and District Council

booklet. Available FREE from Tourist and Council offices.

Stirling with Kids available from Stirling District Council Women's Unit 0786 79000.

Playgrounds & Parks

There are over 150 playgrounds in Edinburgh, ranging from small, housing estate play areas to larger city park playgrounds. Edinburgh District Council is now in its 3rd year of its 6 year programme (ending 97/98) committed to developing and improving the playgrounds in the city. The funding available allows for two playgrounds to be established in new areas and also the upgrading of 14 existing playgrounds.

The movement promoting safer and more stimulating play, has come from parental pressure throughout Britain which has prompted local authority action for all playgrounds to meet specific safety standards. These include the removal of outdated and unacceptable equipment and the use of safer surfacing to reduce the impact of any fall. While these factors do undoubtedly increase safety, parental or adult supervision will always be the most important safety precaution, as young children absorbed in their play cannot be on the lookout for potential dangers happening around them.

In order to have some consistency and guidance in the upgrading of playgrounds, EDC Recreation Dept now employ a Play Development Officer. It is her responsibility to consult with the community to develop and design, the playground most suited to its needs. This involves visiting schools and community groups to discuss ideas before a playground is upgraded, and then liaising with the Technical Officers and Design Team in the District Council to create the most appropriate layout. Obviously, budget will act as the inevitable limit to ideas, but the main objective is to give each community a playground that children will feel involved with and be responsible for.

The new playgrounds nearly always have bright, colourful multiplay units which ingeniously incorporate a variety of activities using every possible space. Several children can enjoy them simultaneously and new friends are often made and new games invented. EDC are also keen to encourage imaginative play through thematic playgrounds with static equipment such as trains and boats. These have proved very popular and the Play Station in Corstorphine Park is excellent (although they do seem to be targets for graffitti). Other new features are the ground level panels with bells, chimes, spinning spirals, beads and noughts and crosses. These can be enjoyed by children of all abilities and although there is generally no specialised equipment for children with special needs in the playgrounds, a number of playgrounds do have low decks, ramps and handrails as well as ground level activities. (See also Scotland Yard Adventure Playground).

The Play Development Officer has now been in position for over four years, and is receiving favourable feedback to playgrounds developed in this way. She goes back to visit children once the project has been completed to discuss its success, strengths or weaknesses which will help in the planning of future developments. The Recreation Dept are keen to advertise their achievements and have produced a colourful leaflet introducing three symbols; a teddy, a sun and a kite which indicate the age for which the playground is most suitable. These are being used on both the apparatus itself (as at Raeburn) and in the safety surfacing (Fauldburn).

Priorities for redeveloped playgrounds include: fenced-off area with self-closing gates or dog grid; safer surfacing under all play equipment, either bark-chips, rubber tiles or more recently in Kirkliston, sand; if playground includes equipment for a variety of age groups, then toddler play equipment should be grouped together. Other improvements include putting in notices displaying the name of the playground and a contact number to report any damage, increased inspection of playgrounds by council representatives. The Play Development Officer always welcomes feedback on playgrounds, good or bad (529 4131).

Lack of nearby toilets are still a problem at many playgrounds, and, while the Recreation Department can upgrade play facilities, they have no say in the allocation of public toilets. It would appear that when playgrounds are situated near toilets, it is more by chance than by design. Clearly to have no toilet facilities is a serious drawback for people entertaining young children, especially if a trip to a playground is part of a day's outing or a picnic. Perhaps this lack of facility is where we need to concentrate our campaign for improvement in the future.

Listed below are some of the most popular playgrounds in the city, including new and recently upgraded ones. Despite the supply of litter bins, litter, broken glass and graffiti are still evident in many playgrounds. With an increase in the number of areas now fenced off, dog fouling is less of a problem.

CENTRE

Princes Street Gardens

The city's most famous park runs alongside Princes Street under the lee of the Castle. The park is a useful rest point for weary parents, mid-shopping, as there are plenty of seats. It also provides an open space for toddlers to let off steam after the confines of a pushchair in the nearby department stores. The area was originally known as the Nor Loch but was drained during construction of the New Town area to the south. There are lawns, flower beds and many statues of interest to parents. Look out for the tree with a hole right through it, near the gardener's lodge in the West Gardens. The Park's Patrol officers will be pleased to point this out, or help you with any other questions or problems. The gardens are locked at sunset or 10 pm (11 pm during the Festival *see* Annual Events, August p203). Please note that dogs must be kept on a lead.

The park is divided into two by the Mound. Access to the **East Gardens** is from the Mound and Waverley Bridge and gates off Princes Street between the two. The **Scott Monument,** a Victorian, Gothic spire and landmark can be climbed for an admission fee. The stairs are very

steep near the top and may not be enjoyed by small children or mothers-to-be! A nine hole **pitch and putt** golf course is open from mid-April to mid-September. Trains can be viewed from the bank beneath the National Gallery. Near the Scott Monument is a kiosk selling ices, sweets, hot and cold drinks to take away, (open spring and autumn: 10-6; summer 8 am-10 pm). There are plenty of pigeons, sparrows and squirrels to feed, and some of the kiosks sell nuts and pigeon food.

Nearest **toilets** (open 8 am-10 pm) are by the Mound, ladies and disabled to the east side, gents down steps on the west side of the Mound, near the floral clock.

The **West Gardens** can be accessed from the Mound, Princes St, Johnstone Ter and Kings Stables Rd. The famous **floral clock,** next to the steps down to the park at the junction of Princes St and the Mound is a delight for parents and children. The clock is composed of up to 35,000 small plants and functions from Spring to late Autumn. A cuckoo emerges from a wooden house every quarter hour, when the clock is in operation. It was the original idea of an Edinburgh clockmaker in 1903 and there are now copies all over the world including one in Napier, New Zealand. (*see also* Places to Visit p182)

In summer there is often entertainment in the **Ross Bandstand,** children's events during the school holidays by the Norwegian Stone, and a carousel operates near the Ross Fountain. (*see* Annual Events p202 and Sources of Information p205).

Over the railway, the south side of the Gardens is less formal, with a steep grassy slope leading up to the Castle. The slope is covered with daffodils in spring. There is a gate into the Castle esplanade via a zig-zag path, but the gate can be locked at times (especially during the Edinburgh Military Tattoo). There is level entrance to the Gardens from Kings Stables Rd, opposite the multi-storey car park, and a sloped entrance from Johnstone Ter, round the side of the Castle. These paths join up and cross a railway footbridge into the Gardens near the playpark. A path also leads from the bridge, behind the railway to another bridge that bring you to the Ross Bandstand. Further along is another bridge, the path here coming out near the Gardener's lodge and leading up to the floral clock.

Playground

The nearest entrance is from Princes St, down the second gate from the west end, as the first gate has a long flight of steps. Also level access from Kings Stable Rd or through St Cuthberts churchyard.

Although the playground is unfenced, dogs in the gardens are supposed to be kept on leads and it is relatively clean. Plenty of seating for parents but younger children will need to be watched closely, especially when the equipment is crowded. The multiplay unit is loosely based on a castle theme, with ramps, slides and walkways suitable for toddlers, eventually leading up to a high tower with enclosed slide, interesting for older children. A new feature is the octagon of low-level panels with bells, perspex drums, chimes and crazy mirrors accessed by a low ramp on wooden boards suitable for wheelchairs. Other activities include a 'television', noughts and crosses and an abacus.

The presence of the railway line in the Gardens is a bonus, especially the bridge behind the Ross Bandstand from which children can safely and easily see the trains coming and going and the drivers usually oblige with a wave!

Toilets near the playground with nappy changing facilities. The key can be obtained from the attendant on duty from 10-10 (except from 3-4 when they are closed for cleaning). NP there is no ramp up to Princes St from these toilets. Also at the Ross Bandstand.

The Gardens are a good place for a picnic: many of the Princes St stores sell sandwiches, yoghurt, fruit, etc. Ice cream kiosks are dotted around the park.

Piazza Open Air Café
W Princes St Gardens
225 5533
£, bottles heated, 160 seats
7 days. Apr, May: 11-6; June-Aug: 9.30-9.30; Sep-Oct: 11-5; Nov-Mar closed.

An outdoor café with self-service fast food, snacks, etc. Close to the playground. Children's groups can be catered for by arrangement with the management.

NORTH

Beaverbank Playground
Broughton Rd

Fenced and stepped down from the busy main road, the playground has been upgraded and all equipment is on soft slabs. Equipment mainly suitable for younger children.

Dalmeny Street Park
Nr Leith Walk. Entrances Dalmeny St; Iona St; Sloan St.

Fenced off 2-acre park with

equipment mainly for toddlers, all surrounded by rubber matting. Also a hard surfaced area suitable for tricycles and wheeled toys.

Inverleith Park
Arboretum Pl, opp Royal Botanical Gardens

61 acres of playing fields and allotments as well as a rose garden and pond. Playground is in the SW corner and is unusual in that it incorporates a large wooden 'ship' - the 'HMS Edinburgh'. There are 2 low slides, and as children climb up vertical ladders inside the ship and slide into the 'sea' adults desperately try to be on both sides at once. Also in the ship is a climbing frame and fireman's pole. There are 6 animal swings, very popular but dangerously heavy. Equipment is surrounded by safety surface. Dog-free zone. See also Annual Events p201.

Leith Links

50 acres of parkland dominated by hillocks which are 16th century gun emplacements and great for toddler mountaineering. Paths suitable for pushchairs and tricycles. Dog-free zone.

Fenced area subdivided in 2, one part for toddlers and one for 4-10 yrs. Both areas include climbing activities and swings, toddlers may be tempted to venture into the older children's area, and would require stricter supervision, especially when the playground is busy. Toddler equipment on safety surface, Junior equipment on bark.

Separate area on sand to stretch older children's dexterity, is a net Eiffel Tower. A very tall rope structure on a mast, which children can climb. Wonderful for older brothers and sisters, and too high for toddlers even to start climbing. Also in the sand area, a 'Stompa' wooden gymnastic structure, designed to exercise balance and controlled movement. Picnic Table.

Leith Links is an excellent destination for a family outing, marred only by the lack of open toilets.

Montgomery Street
Large playground with separate toddler area partially divided from main playground. Good range of play equipment for both toddlers and older children, all on safety surfacing, but spoiled by graffiti and litter, despite bins. Adjoining asphalt area with goal posts suitable for football or tricycling and an additional fun ball game.

Muirhouse Park
Muirhouse Medway

Brightly coloured enclosed playground set well away from the road. A low fence separates toddler equipment from a very large activity climbing frame.

Pennywell Gardens (Muirhouse End)
A new, enclosed playground just for toddlers with low level multiplay activity area, cradle springs and springy horse.

Pennywell Road
A brand new playground, again just for younger children, set back from road between Pennywell Grove and Pennywell Gdns. Enclosed with attractive low brick wall and fence with colourful multiplay unit and two springy motorbikes which will no doubt be very popular.

Pilrig Park

In this 2 acre park there are football pitches and two playgrounds, one next to Pilgrig St (East side) and the other at end of Balfour St, close to school. Surprisingly neither are fenced. The Eastern playground is set on bark chips with commando slide, small, brightly coloured wooden tower with bench and seat inside but only grass underneath and one or two rubber mats. Picnic tables but a lot of broken glass around when visited.

The playground near the school has much newer equipment and an elaborate slide with small shelter underneath and roof on top. Good safety surfacing, incorporating coloured shapes but a wooden, log walkway with no side protection could be dangerous for young children.

Pilton Park West

An enclosed playground near the Primary School with separate toddler and junior areas, each with its own multiplay units, the junior one incorporating an aeroplane and the low-level toddler one includes an inviting tube to crawl through. Also 3 cradle swings and 4 junior swings.

Victoria Park

Between Newhaven Rd and Craighall Rd, Trinity

18-acre park with fenced-off toddler playground. Some equipment is on rubber matting. Centre-piece is a climbing frame house with a low double width slide, which gives more scope for sociable play.

Elsewhere in the park is a wooden climbing frame incorporating a bridge and a low slide. Also a tyre tower and wobbly wooden platform, all on bark-chips.

SOUTH

Bruntsfield Links and The Meadows

An extensive area of flat grassland and paved walks. Areas suitable for ball games, picnics, a putting green, and pathways excellent for tricycles. Surrounded by busy roads, but the 3 playgrounds are fenced off.

Meadows West

Corner of Leven Ter and Melville Dr

Fenced off, with self-closing gates and all equipment is surrounded by brightly coloured sponge matting. Popular playground for young children, with an imaginative climbing frame, incorporating bridges, tunnel, fireman's pole and rope ladders as well as swings and roundabout. Extended fenced off grassy area for safe ball games and popular during the summer.

Meadows Toddlers

Towards the east end of Melville Dr, next to the tennis courts, this grassy playground is ideal if your toddler is always tempted to more adventurous play equipment designed for older children. Fenced off and dog-free, with new equipment on protective rubber mats; climbing frames, slides etc. particularly suitable for under 5s. However, the old, concrete paddling pool was retained although to date it has been kept empty.

Meadows East

Corner of Buccleuch St and Melville Dr

Playground designed for older children with Helter Skelter slide and climbing frame for more challenging play. Area fenced with self-closing gates, all equipment on safety surfacing. **Toilets** nearby.

Dog Free Zone, Whitehouse Loan

This clean patch of grass opposite Edinburgh Bicycle Co-op with seats and small hills, great for toddlers and young children to have a run. No ball games allowed.

Buckstone Park

Enclosed playground well back from the road in a large grassy area. General surface is bark-chips with soft slabs under most of the equipment. Play designed mainly for younger children, except for the high see-saw.

Colinton Mains Park
Oxgangs Rd N, Firrhill

This upgraded playground provides play for a wide age range of children. Toddler area partitioned off from junior play area.

Gracemount Leisure Centre
Off Captain's Rd

At the side of the centre just visible from the car park there is a small playground set in a stockade with bark-chip surfaces. Centre-piece is a large wooden boat which incorporates a rope ladder, fireman's pole and double-width slide. Particularly suitable for young children.

See also Activities for Children p139.

Falcon Gardens
Nr St Peter's School, Morningside

Recently upgraded, this small park is safe from roads with an adjacent grassy area. Equipment includes a 'multiplay unit' suitable for children up to 10, all set on safety surfacing.

Harrison Park East
West Bryson Rd, Watson Cres

At the north end of Harrison Pk,

fenced off from the road, this playground is more suitable for older children. Surface is asphalt with soft surfaces under equipment.

Glenvarloch Crescent

A brand new playground due to be completed April '95 designed after close consultation with local school children.

Liberton Recreation Ground
Entrances from Liberton Gdns and Alnwickhill Rd

In the middle of the park and well away from traffic, this brightly coloured playground looks very attractive from a distance, but on closer examination the surfaces are very uneven, tripping up many unsuspecting toddlers. There is often broken glass, and no litter bins for rubbish. The equipment is set on grass, gravel and rubber matting in poor condition. Equipment mainly suitable for over 5s; one slide has a drop at the bottom. Area is not fenced off and park is a popular dog-walking area.

Morningside Park
Enter Balcarres St and Morningside Dr

Bright new playground, partly funded by the Morningside Association. Toddler play equipment partially separated by fence and includes climbing frame with slide. Toddler bucket swings located in one corner with safety barriers to help prevent children running in front of moving swings. Centre-piece for older children is a large climbing activity area with a big platform on top, good for accommodating the large number of children playing when the park is busy.

Park is fenced off and was clean and

tidy when visited, but no self-closing gates. Old tennis court adjoining playground ideal tricycling area. A very popular and attractive park.

EAST

Craigmillar 'The Station'
Niddrie House Sq

Toddler playground, upgraded and includes an 'activity train' with coaches, table and seats. Very popular and well-used.

Dumbiedykes Road
Faces on to Queens Pk

Large colourful playground. Equipment, all on safety surfacing, suits a wide age-range of children. A picnic table is an added attraction. *See* Walks and Country Places p224.

Joppa Quarry Park
Off S Morton St, Portobello

Adjacent to large grassy area and football pitch where dogs are walked. Recently upgraded, the playground is fenced in and has safety surfaces under all play equipment. Play to suit a wide age range of children, including a popular helter skelter.

Lochend Park
To the SW of Lochend Rd

23-acre park with small playground. Play equipment more suited to older children apart from the 'buck-abouts'. Some safety surfaces. Path on one side of the loch, and you can sometimes feed ducks through gaps in the wiremesh fence!

Meadowfields

Due to be completed in 1995, this playground has been designed after consultation with local school children and is intended to reflect the work they have done with the Countryside Rangers on the environment. Built of natural materials, it is to be landscaped into the hillside and will include trails and other interesting features.

Mount Lodge Park
Mount Lodge Pl, off Windsor Pl, Portobello

Large playground recently refurbished providing play for wide age range of children. Large coloured 'puddles' of safety surfacing under all equipment.

Northfield Broadway
Next to Northfield Community Centre

Recently built toddler playground, colourful and very popular. Centrepiece is a 'Pirate Ship' activity providing imaginative play. All equipment on safety surfacing. Plenty of seats for parents.

Prestonfield Park
Prestonfield Road

An excellent, stylish and safe playground showing just what can and should be achieved in all playgrounds. Enclosed, with separate toddler and junior sections all on bright, themed safety surfaces. Toddler equipment includes 3 cradle swings, a low level multiplay unit which manages to include 2 slides, curved ladder, rope ladder, tunnel, fireman's pole, an abacus and naughts and crosses, all above an attractive surface depicting a pond with fishes and flowers. The junior section has modern atrium type decorations and platforms of a tough rubber/plastic with walkways, climbing structures, bright helta-skelter slide and a hand slide over the crocodile river! Well thought-out providing plenty of scope for imaginative play. Also features good old-fashioned hop-skotch!

Rosefield Pl, Portobello

Small recently built playground for toddlers with popular equipment all on safety surfacing. Play area is fenced in with self-closing gates. The rest of Rosefield Park is quiet and pretty for walks, but beware of Figgate Burn running through the park, which is not fenced.

Straighton Place
Portobello

Small toddler playground with a 'boat' activity.

WEST

Carrick Knowe, Corstorphine Park
The Play Station

A highly imaginative and popular new playground with plenty of scope to enact 'Thomas' stories. Based on the theme of a station with painted railway tracks on the ground leading to a static train with coaches, signals and a road that runs around 'Playtown' (multiplay unit). Interesting low level panels; coloured spirals and a maze.

Clermiston Park
Clermiston Gdns

Recently upgraded, this fenced playground has an attractive view over the city towards Fife. Probably more suitable for older children, although equipment includes bucket swings and 'buckabouts' with all equipment completely surrounded by soft slabs.

Fauldburn Park
East Craigs

Well away from roads, this small, new enclosed playground has one

multiplay unit with walkway, tube and slide suitable for toddlers one end and more adventurous activities the other. Also springy animals, all on safety surfacing incorporating the EDC's playground symbols of teddies, sun and kite (see intro).

Haugh Park
Brae Park Rd, Barnton

This playground is attractively situated in a dell close to the River Almond Walkway see also Walks and Country Places p223. There is a paddock close by in which horses are sometimes kept. The play equipment is mostly wooden, all set on bark-chips. Picnic tables and benches.

Ravelston
Craigcrook Rd

Recently rebuilt toddler playground with all equipment on safety surfacing.

St Margaret's Park
Corstorphine High St

An attractive and clean wooded and grassy park, with some cradle swings and spring animals.

Fort Saughton, Saughton Park
Entrances on Gorgie Rd; Balgreen Rd; Stevenson Dr

The 47 acre park is mostly given over to football pitches and a putting green. Two features worth mentioning, both accessed from Balgreen Rd. Saughton Gardens have been developed especially for the blind, with an emphasis on scented plants. They are attractive and well paved.

Fort Saughton, probably still Edinburgh's most exciting children's playground, which is well set back from the road and very popular. The equipment, all of which is on bark-chips, is divided so that older and younger children are at different ends of the well-fenced playground. Excellent range of play equipment including wooden climbing frames and 'commando' slide for older children. Benches and picnic tables.

Winter Gardens

Attractive heated greenhouse with tropical plants and pool (fenced) with fish. Benches and cafeteria area (irregular hrs) selling home baking, drinks etc. **Toilets.**

Roseburn
Roseburn Cres

New playground in the shadow of Murrayfield Stadium. Easy parking on waste ground at end of Roseburn Cres. A long multiplay unit with 5 towers, graded from toddler end, shown by red teddy symbol, to junior section (sun). Well thought-out with seating under towers to play 'house' and an interesting detail; the ladder at junior end has no lower rung to deter overambitious toddlers. Seating for parents. Situated at the edge of open playing fields, it is surprising the playground is unfenced.

Sighthill Park
Broomhouse Rd

Large enclosed playground within Sighthill Park, well set back from the road and very popular. Play equipment to suit wide age range, all on safety surfacing. No dogs allowed.

Wester Hailes

This area has very few playgrounds, but Edinburgh District Council has a New Play Programme for Wester Hailes, to be put into operation over the next few years. Currently there is a new toddler playground in Westburn Grove which is fenced and has a colourful range of equipment, all on safety surfacing. Future planning for another 2 in 1995.

White Park
Gorgie Rd

Recently upgraded with ramp access. An interesting playground to visit as it has some unusual play activities including an elephant slide and a net climbing structure. Picnic table. Fenced with self closing gate. Ramp access.

Also on Gorgie Rd directly opposite the City Farm is a recently built small playground. Set a little back from the busy road, but only low fencing and no gates, so have to keep a close eye on toddlers. Interesting play equipment for younger children, all set on safety surfacing.

Juniper Green
Bloomiehall Public Park

4 coloured cradle swings, slide and metal sphere roundabout are set along edge of an open field and although there are attractive views over to Fife, it feels quite exposed to the elements and wind! A large new playground for all 3 age groups to be built April 1995.

Balerno

Dean Park

New playground just completed in Dean Park, next to Primary School with separate bright, colourful multiplay units for toddlers and juniors. The toddler equipment is packed full of interesting and challenging ideas, slides, ladders etc. Also 2 springy animals.

ADVENTURE PLAYGROUNDS

Adventure playgrounds are less formal than the playgrounds described above, and offer greater opportunities for creative play, making them harder work for parents. Some adventure playgrounds are really only suitable for older children, but two with facilities for toddlers are worth a mention here.

Scotland Yard
King George V Park, Eyre Pl

This award-winning play area includes a playground for toddlers as well as facilities for older children. The toddler area is separated from the main play area and all equipment is on deep bark chips. The rest of the park has been attractively landscaped, has a football area, paths for tricycling and a separate grassed area for picnics and games. It also aims to provide exciting, challenging and adventurous play for children and young people with a wide range of special needs. The Centre is staffed Monday to Friday 9am-5pm and Saturdays 10am to 12.30pm and can be used by special schools, groups and families — brothers, sisters and friends are also welcome. It is important to phone the playground before visiting; Theresa Casey, Scotland Yard Adventure Centre, 70 Eyre Place, Edinburgh EH3 5EJ Tel: 557 8199 for further information.

Vogrie Estate and Country Park
Nr Gorebridge, approx 10 miles SE of Edinburgh

Adventure playground may be used from toddling upwards, as long as parents are prepared to clamber around too. All equipment is on deep bark chips, which can become messy if it has been raining, so wellies would be a good idea. As well as the playground the park has barbecue sites, grassy areas suitable for games, woodland walks, tea room and nature trails. Toilets. See also Out of Town Trips p193.

Playbus

The EDC Recreation Dept is to share with other depts. in the Council ie. Countryside Rangers, Library, Arts, Sports etc, a converted double decker bus which can be used as a creche facility during the day and after school activities and workshops for older children. It is hoped that the Playbus will be fully operational by May 1995.

Walks & Country Places

"IT'S O.K. DAD, I THINK I CAN SEE THE TOP NOW!"

Edinburgh has a wealth of open places where children and adults can relax or let off steam, without having to travel miles out into the country. The walks in this section include carefully tended parks and wild open hillsides. We have tried to give some indication of the terrain in terms of accessibility for pushchairs and small bikes (of course children can also be carried in a backpack or sling). Obviously conditions may vary on non-surfaced paths, particularly after rain.

More detailed information and maps may be found in Edinburgh City Libraries and local bookshops. In particular a map of city cyclepaths published by 'Spokes' (the cyclists' organisation) is useful for walks where pushchair accessibility is important. *See* Travel and Transport p235. Another useful guide is Bartholomew's 'Walking in Edinburgh and the Pentlands' which grades the walks listed according to degrees of difficulty.

Happy Tramping!

THE BRAIDS

A golf course, grassy slopes and hills, good for kites, walking and sledging. Access and parking at the entrance to the Braids Hills (Public) Golf Course on Braids Hill Approach and along Braids Hill Dr. There are horses to be seen in fields nearby at Liberton Tower Farm.

THE HERMITAGE OF BRAID AND BLACKFORD HILL

Car park at the Royal Observatory. Good car parking on Braid Rd and Midmar Dr, limited on-street parking at Cluny Gdns (for the pond), and at

219

Glen Rd, Liberton. Maps of walks at the entrances.

An extensive and attractive wildlife and conservation area within the city, comprising the **Blackford Hill** (540 ft) and an area of woodland along Braid Burn. Walks at lower levels negotiable with wheels and at higher levels with determination. Beware of the cliffs at the old quarry. Several picnic sites, sledging in winter and popular for kite flying. Unfortunately the area is badly fouled by dogs, especially around the Observatory and at entrances.

The beautifully situated **Blackford Pond**, to your right as you enter from Cluny Gdns, contains some of Edinburgh's best fed ducks, moorhens, geese, coots and swans. The swans can be very enthusiastic so keep children behind the low rail on the path. Sometimes there are squirrels to be seen too. There is a shelter on a landscaped patch to the east side of the pond. Dogs are not allowed around the pond. **Toilets** are near the entrance.

The Hermitage of Braid is one of Edinburgh's best areas for bird and wild life. A good flat entrance from Braid Rd (south of the mini roundabout) leads through a wooded valley along the Braid Burn. The road leads to Hermitage House, a ranger centre with maps and leaflets. The centre is open 7 days a week, all day in summer; winter 10-4 Mon-Sat and 11-6 Sun; but is only manned by one ranger so phone first to check if the ranger is in. **Toilets** inside the house or outside (although these are best only used in an emergency). Picnic tables on a flat grassy area in the front of the house. There is a tearoom now open inside Hermitage House. If you take the right fork past the house, on the right there are a

few steps up to an old ice house, used to store ice in bygone days. The path follows on over bridges — excellent for 'Pooh sticks' — to the Lang Linn Bridge (can be muddy). Here you can continue along to Blackford Glen Rd and eventually the foot of Liberton Brae. This path has recently been resurfaced and is a nice walk for pushchairs. There are often cows in the fields across the burn and lots of bird life.

From the bridge there are steps with a gate that might be tricky for pushchairs and a stony path up to your left which will take you around the side of Blackford Hill to the pond. It is well worth the effort. The Hermitage is riddled with steep twisty paths and is wonderful to explore if you are not restricted with a pushchair. Bluebells in spring, bird boxes hidden in trees and inquisitive squirrels are all easy for tots to spot. The centre often organises 'interest walks' for families, women (creche provided) and can take playgroups and nurseries at quiet times. Phone the Countryside Ranger for details, Carol Huston 447 7145.

See Activities for Parents p167.

Royal Observatory Visitor Centre
668 8405
Open 7 days a week
Apr-Sept: 12 - 5.30, Oct-Mar1 - 5 (9pm Fri)
Public telescopes open on clear weeknights (7-9), please phone after 4pm to book for that night (except Fridays).
Adult £2.00, concession £1.25 under 5s FREE. Car park

Access by Bus: 40 & 41 from the Mound, City Centre; alight Blackford Station. 38, 41 & 24 from Cluny Gardens, Morningside; alight Blackford Avenue. Note: it can be quite a pull up Observatory Rd.

The Visitor Centre comprises two of Scotland's largest telescopes, several exhibitions and a Inter-Active Discovery Room as well as an astronomy shop. It is probably more interesting for the older child (and parents) but younger ones may enjoy a 'peep' through the telescope. Excellent views of the city. The building is floodlight over The Festival and at Christmas. Many steps so not suitable for pushchairs (which can be left at the desk). Clean, spacious cloakroom. Talks and tours can be arranged to suit individual groups, please phone for details. Evening Lectures for the General Public start at 7.30 pm.

Outside there is a fairly easy walk, for pushchairs, to the top of Blackford Hill, from the Observatory.

BRAIDBURN VALLEY PARK
Pentland Ter.

A stream, hilly slopes and walks, no play equipment. There is a 'fairy ring' made from trees and shrubs, good fun for picnics. It is also used by the Recreation Dept of Edinburgh District Council, see Annual Events, July, p202. The stream is suitable for fishing for tiddlers and is shallow enough for supervised paddlers near the 'fairy ring'.

BRUNTSFIELD LINKS AND THE MEADOWS
See Playgrounds and Parks p213.

CALTON HILL
See Places to Visit p179.

CAMMO ESTATE
Main gate and Visitor Centre at Cammo Rd, Barnton
Ranger Service 447 7145 (based at the Hermitage of Braid)

Cammo House has all but disappeared, but its 100 acres of wildlife habitats in woodlands, meadows and marshes leave a city park of unusual character. There are often cows in the nearby field, snowdrops in spring and lots of butterflies in summer. Look out for nest boxes and their inhabitants in spring. The ruined remains are good for clambering over and playing hide and seek. There is also a walled garden. Most paths are accessible for pushchairs but can get quite muddy after rain

The estate was left to the National Trust for Scotland in 1975. They made the house safe and feued the estate to the City of Edinburgh District Council. It is now managed to enhance the plant and wildlife environment, for use as a teaching resource and by the general public.

The Visitor Centre in the Lodge has **toilets** (including disabled, but no nappy changing surface), maps and leaflets about the park and displays (including an aquarium and touch table). The Centre is open for groups by arrangement with the Ranger Service, and sporadically at other times. See also Annual Events p200.

CAMMO AND THE RIVER ALMOND
Cammo Rd, Barnton.

The paths along the River Almond can be joined from Cammo. These routes are not really suitable for pushchairs as they are narrow, uneven and overgrown.

Start the walk along Cammo Rd, just past the last house. A gate on the right and a rough wide path lead down to the river. Here the riverbank is very steep. The path continues to follow the river upstream towards the airport. It can be very overgrown here. There are stepping-stones about half way along. OR turn up that path to the left near the bridge and you will eventually rejoin Cammo Rd again. Along this path you pass Craigiehill Temple — a locked tower. Good for holly picking. OR turn right over Grotto Bridge. The river is very narrow here and looks quite spectacular after rain as it thunders underneath. Just over the bridge is a cattle grid, which has been known to capture clambering youngsters! The path follows the river downstream and can be rough with some steep drops down to the water. It ends near the Crammond Brig Hotel (see Eating Out p79). For a walk further downstream, see Crammond, South: The River Almond Walkway p223. This area is also covered by the Cammo Park leaflet mentioned above.

CEMETERIES

There are several overgrown cemeteries in the city which are now almost nature reserves. Do be careful if you explore them; the headstones may not be secure and there have been tragedies.

COLINTON DELL

See Water of Leith Walkway p231.

CORSTORPHINE HILL

Panoramic views of the city and beyond are offered at the 530' summit. The terrain is varied; with a rocky and steep section — which includes a flooded quarry — between the Queensferry Rd and Clermiston Rd entrances, and large areas of woodland. Flora and fauna include conkers, acorns and pine cones, squirrels, badgers and foxes. Good for raspberry and blackberry picking. There is also Clermiston Tower, built in 1851 to commemorate the centenary of Scott's birth. It is sometimes floodlit but can no longer be climbed.

There are several routes to the summit of the hill: Clermiston Rd (3 paths: the one near the Capital Moat House is rough and steep); Queensferry Rd (steep and rugged); Craigcrook Rd (a long push, between new houses, up a fairly steep gradient, but a reasonably smooth path); Ravelston Dykes Rd (near Mary Erskine School and about 200 yards north of Murrayfield Golf Clubhouse); a one way revolving gate (out!) of Edinburgh Zoo and from Cairnmuir Rd, at the junction with Kaimes Rd. This latter route is easiest for pushchairs (although muddy after rain) and there is car parking. There is a grassy slope with picnic tables on the left near this entrance (also good for sledging). The path to the summit follows the edge of the zoo (where some animals may be seen) and it then joins the paths from the Ravelston Dykes and Craigcrook entrances.

CRAIGLOCKHART DELL

See Water of Leith Walkway p231.

CRAIGMILLAR CASTLE AND GROUNDS

See Places to visit p180.

CRAMOND

The village is situated at the mouth of the River Almond. Walks radiate in all directions from the yachting centre. There is a large car park on Cramond Glebe Rd, below Cramond Kirk and above the Cramond Inn. A ramp leads down to the esplanade. Below the Inn are public toilets.

North: To Cramond Island

There is a rough causeway across the tidal mudflats out to Cramond Island, which is negotiable at low tide. Tide charts are pinned up at the start of the causeway monthly but often get torn down. The 'Inn Step' sweet and gift shop (on Cramond Glebe Rd) and 'The Maltings' (on the quay) often display the times too, as does the tearoom (see below, East: the Esplanade). Take a picnic to your own small uninhabited island. Good views of the Forth Bridges, but keep an eye on your watch for returning.

South: The River Almond

About 1½ miles, the walkway starts on the esplanade, near the yachting centre, and follows the river upstream on a wooded path. No cycling. The path is wide and on the level but can be muddy. The river is tidal up to Cockle Mill Cottages, where the path opens out onto to a grassy area. There is also a small car park (access from Whitehouse Rd via School Brae). The path continues to Fair-a-Far Mill where there is a waterfall and a fish ladder. The mill is now a ruin and children will enjoy running through the arches and up a few steps. The river is railed at this point but toddlers can get underneath quite easily. People throw pennies into the water at the top of the fall (and boys collect them later!). The path continues to the Cramond Brig Hotel (see Eating Out p79) and Haugh Park (see Playgrounds and Parks p216), but there is a steep flight of steps and pushchairs would have to be carried. See also Cammo and the River Almond p221, for a description of the route further upstream.

East: The Esplanade

A broad paved footpath runs for 2 miles from Cramond through Silverknowes to Granton Point (West Shore Rd). An attractive area for promenading with the pram, cycling or roller-skating. Plenty of seats and shelters. Superb views across to Fife on clear days. Suitable for picnics on the grassy banks at Silverknowes where there is parking along Marine Dr (steps down the slope at the west end, a road at the east). **Toilets** here too and a tearoom which also has a takeaway drinks and snacks service. Tide charts available for reference in summer. Also ice cream vans, pipe bands and entertainments over some summer weekends. The beach itself is sandy at Cramond and stony elsewhere. It can be oily and there are often pollution warnings out about collecting shellfish. The beach is gently sloped but the tide can come in fast and could maroon you on a sandbank — prepare to paddle!

West: Across the River Almond

There is no bridge across the Almond at Cramond, but it may be crossed by foot passenger ferry. This small boat operates Apr-Sept 9-7; Oct- Mar 10-4. Closed 1-2 and Fri. Adults 50p, children 10p. Folding pushchairs allowed but no dogs, prams, picnic baskets or large cases. There are plenty of swans and boats on the water. The land to the west of the river belongs to the Dalmeny Estate (see below). There is a path to Dalmeny House (approx. 2 miles) but it is not negotiable with a pushchair. Better for pushchairs is the 4½ mile shore walk to South Queensferry along a woodland path (see below: Dalmeny House and Estate).

DALMENY HOUSE AND ESTATE
A90 and then B924
Administrator 331 1888

House and estate open 1 May to 30 Sept: Sun (1-5.30), Mon & Tues (12-5.30); last admission 5. Guided tours of the house are not of great interest to young children.

The estate is pleasant to walk around — fields, shore and woodland, with cows, sheep, pheasants and a statue of a horse. There is a sheltered woodland walk through the rhododendrons and azaleas of the garden valley. No dogs allowed. Picnics only by prior arrangement. No fires.

As well as the walks above (West: Across the River Almond), the house may be reached on a walk from Long Craig Gate, South Queensferry (2½ miles). This walk is negotiable with a pushchair. Gate closes 9 pm summer, 6 pm winter.

There is a bus service from St Andrew Square to Chapel Gate, 1 mile from the house.

See also Annual Events p224.

FIGGATE PARK

Entrances at Duddingston Rd and Hamilton Dr behind Portobello High School.

A strip of parkland with trees and grassy slopes along the Figgate Burn in Duddingston. Easily negotiated paths but the park is popular with dogs and the burn is littered with cans and old tyres. On Figgate pond there are plenty of tame wildfowl to be fed. On raised ground to the north-east of the pond, there is a children's playground (a slide set in a bank, four wobbly buckabouts, a roundabout on rubber matting and three climbing frames, but no swings). Next to the Burn are the Craigentinny Carriage sidings, off the main railway line, and which can be interesting for junior trainspotters, particularly when shunting is in progress.

HOLYROOD PARK

Car parks at Dunsapie Loch and near the entrances at Duddingston Loch, Holyrood Palace and Meadowbank Ter.

A rugged park, including Arthur's Seat (823ft) and Salisbury Crags, and three small lochs. A surfaced road (Queen's Dr.) runs around the park (approximately three miles). Apart from a small stretch of surfaced path from the Holyrood House entrance up Haggis Knowe towards St Anthony's Chapel (about 200 yds), all the other routes are rocky or on grass. The climb to Arthur's Seat is a steep one for youngsters (shortest route from Dunsapie Loch) but there is an excellent view at the top with a Trig point indicating surrounding sites of interest. Lower down there are good views from Dunsapie Hill (523 ft) — not quite a climb. It is possible to walk round St Margaret's Loch with a pushchair and there are ducks and geese to be fed here. Rowing boats can be hired in the summer. In the south east of the park is **Duddingston Loch**, a bird sanctuary, where the geese and swans can be quite aggressive. The Scottish Wildlife Trust have produced a booklet describing a nature trail in the park and can arrange walks (approx 2 hrs). Contact them at 16 Cramond Glebe Rd, or phone 312 7765.

The northern area of the park is the venue for 'Fringe Sunday' during the Festival see Annual Events, August p203. There is a fenced and surfaced children's playground at **Dumbie-dykes**, near Holyrood Gate, with swings, climbing frames, buckabouts and roundabouts. Flat access from the park itself or down steps from Dumbiedykes Rd. **No toilets** nearby.

Leaving Queen's Dr, below Salisbury Crags and to the south-east of the Pollock Halls is a cycle track and footpath, suitable for prams, known as the **Innocent Railway** (*see* Railway Paths and Cycle Tracks p228).

See also Places to visit p181.

HOPETOUN HOUSE AND ESTATE
See Out of Town Trips p194.

INCH PARK
Old Dalkeith Rd, near the Cameron Toll Shopping Centre

A large area of grass land, with playing fields, deciduous trees, slopes for sliding down, paved paths for prams and learning to ride a bike. No play equipment. Edinburgh District Council Nurseries are situated here, and during the school holidays entertainments are sometimes organised.

LAURISTON CASTLE
See Places to visit p181, Annual Events p201, and Eating Out p80.

THE PENTLAND HILLS
Regional Park HQ 445 3383

A beautiful range of hills spreading along Edinburgh's southern edge. Managed by Lothian Regional Council, The Pentland Hills Regional Park consists of country parks, reservoirs (no swimming permitted), nature reserves and other private areas. Within the Regional Park there are several areas of interest to parents with young children.

Bonaly
Where Bonaly Rd crosses the City By-pass, there is a fork in the road. The right turn, Torduff Road (public vehicle access for only a few hundred yards and limited parking at the end) leads up to Torduff Reservoir and is surfaced but a long push for prams and small cyclists. At the reservoir, you can turn left for a walk across to Bonaly Country Park (*see below*) — steps and a grassy path, but good views over the city. For pushchairs, a better walk is to follow the west side of the reservoir along to the end where there is a short push up to Clubbiedean Reservoir ($\frac{3}{4}$ mile). Here there is more space for picnics and there are sometimes anglers in boats to watch. The path alongside Clubbiedean is rougher for pushchairs but energetic parents with backpacks may like to continue on to Currie (one and a half miles).

Following Bonaly Rd, from the City By-pass as far as it will go, brings you to a car park. This area is known as Bonaly Country Park and from here you can walk up into the hills. There is an information board with maps, and a picnic area. **Toilets** are further up but not always open. Of the three paths up from here, the left is too steep for youngsters, the right takes you over to Torduff Reservoir (*see above*) and up into the heather. The middle path (possible with pushchairs and reasonable walkers) leads up through a plantation of fir trees to Bonaly Reservoir.

Glencorse Reservoir
A702(T) Biggar Rd, $7\frac{1}{2}$ miles from the city centre; turn right at the Flotterstone Inn.

A Rangers Office with displays and maps in the car park. The road up to Glencorse Reservoir is closed to public vehicles. Ideal for prams and cyclists. As you leave the car park, on your left next to the burn, is a BBQ and children's area (no dogs). There are some wooden animals to climb and sit on and some wooden 'stepping stones' in the burn. Further along, off to the left across a footbridge, is a wooded picnic area, and another up the hill in woods on the right. Several paths fork off across fields and up into the hills. At the reservoir, anglers in boats can often be seen. It is possible to follow the northern edge along to the end on a surfaced road. The water is fenced or walled off. Paths branch off to the right at intervals up to Castlelaw firing range and across the hills to Harlaw (unsuitable for youngsters). Lambs can be seen over the fences in spring.

Harlaw and Threipmuir Reservoirs

Harlaw Reservoir car park is reached by leaving Currie on Kirkgate or Balerno on Harlaw Rd; turn off at Harlaw Farm. There is an information board here. At the gate, turn right and follow a surfaced road about 100 yards to the reservoir. It is possible to walk all the way around with a pushchair but the south side is bumpy with tree roots and can be muddy. On the north side is a track (occasionally used by council vehicles) which can be reached by a small metal bridge or across the overflow itself in summer — fun for paddlers. The track (with paths off through the trees to explore) continues to the end of Harlaw Reservoir where it joins up with Threipmuir Reservoir by way of another overflow. To continue on around Harlaw, cross the footbridge here and turn left through the gap in the wall. The track follows the wall and over the bank on your right is Threipmuir Reservoir (not fenced). Turn left at the end of the wall to continue on around the south side of Harlaw. Those without pushchairs may like to negotiate the stiles further on for a walk back to the car park, along a lane across the fields.

It is possible to walk along Threipmuir from the overflow (keep to the right and do not cross the footbridge). This is an easy walk for pushchairs but you cannot link up with the car park at Red Moss (see below) as there are a series of kissing gates at the other end. It is not possible to walk all the way around Threipmuir Reservoir. A variety of birds can often be seen on this walk, keep your eyes peeled for herons and cormorants.

Hillend Country Park

Follow the Biggar Rd out just beyond Lothianburn Golf Course on the right and turn up to Hillend. The No 4 bus from St Andrew Square stops on the main road and there is a long path up to the ski centre. Some picnic tables and a Ranger Centre near the foot. There is a noticeboard with maps, general information on the Pentland Regional Park and the rangers often put up nature notes to suit the time of year. At the top of the road there is the Hillend Ski Centre and a large car park. A chairlift at the artificial ski-slope here may be used by non-skiers. It is open 7 days a week during daylight hours. Adults £1.50, under 15s £1, family (2 adults, 2 juniors) £4; generally children taking a seat pay. No pushchairs. There are several bench type seats so you can tuck tots in between adults, a bar comes down to lap and foot height and keeps you safely in. Very active toddlers should not use the chairlift. There is a stop half way up to get off if a child was frightened. The ride up to the top is exhilarating, sailing over skiers and golfers below. At the top there is a viewfinder on a cairn and there are paths through the heather which energetic tots (or parents with backpacks) could cope with. The weather can change quickly though so don't stray too far from the chairlift. At the top of the lift are cameras and a tannoy so that the operators can check everybody is safely in before moving. **Toilets** and refreshments at Ski Centre Lodge which also has a viewing terrace to watch skiers coming down the slopes (gracefully!)

Inn on the Hill
Next door to the Ski Centre.
Mon- Sat 9am-9pm , Sun 9am-8pm.
Steps up to front door. Patio and picnic tables around the back. 'Elephant's Sufficiency' (children's menu) available from noon. For speciality evenings, children under 12 enjoy a 50% discount when accompanied by the equivalent number of adults. Children's parties arranged. Phone 445 5552 for details.

Red Moss Wildlife Reserve and Bavelaw Bird Reserve, Balerno
Follow the signs to Marchbank from Balerno. At the site of the Marchbank Hotel (closed), turn left and park in the Threipmuir car park. There is a picnic table here and an information board with maps. A short footpath (unsuitable for pushchairs) leads down to Threipmuir reservoir and along to Harlaw (see above section). With a pushchair the best route is to turn left out of the car park and follow the road along towards a bridge. On your right is the Red Moss Nature Reserve. This area is boggy so keep to the wooden planks laid out for you. Continue over the bridge and up a steep, tree-lined hill. Bavelaw Bird Reserve is on your right and there is a bird hide on the shore, over a fence and along a narrow boggy path. Note: the key is held at Balerno Post Office.

A signpost at the top of the hill gives walking options. Only the left continues to be suitable for pushchairs until you reach the stile opening onto the Pentland Hills. This walk is exposed and can be cold but worth it on a clear day for the views. There are sheep and cattle in the fields, waterfowl and fishermen on the reservoir below. Good for sledging.

Swanston Village Farm
Access from Oxgangs Rd, by Swanston Rd over the City By-pass.

A small picturesque village at the foot of the Pentlands (near Fairmilehead). R.L. Stevenson lived at Swanston Cottage from 1867 to 1880. There is a mid-19th century farm and steadings and the whitewashed, thatched cottages of old Swanston village, dating from the 17th Century. Beyond the village are grassy slopes with sheep grazing and lambs in springtime. Higher up is rougher ground. It is possible to walk over to Hillend but not with a pushchair. Nice for picnics.

PORTOBELLO BEACH AND PROMENADE
The paved promenade runs for 1³/₄ miles from Seafield Rd to Morton St in Joppa. The 'busy' west end of the beach is reached from Bath St. Here you will find donkeys on good days in summer, an indoor amusement arcade, open all yr, with some children's rides including a carousel as well as the usual take-away snacks. Portobello Fun Fair can also be reached down Bath St then turn left at end, or down Pipe St. *See also* Activities for Children p147. Down John St there is a paddling pool which is filled in the summer. The quiet end of the beach is reached through Portobello and down

227

Brunstane Rd. The beach is sandy and the District Council do clean it regularly; a no dog policy is usually adhered to in the summer. There is a summer beach programme of entertainments and events for all ages. Parking in local streets. *See also* Annual Events June and August p201, p202, Playgrounds and Parks p216, Birthdays and Celebrations p86 and Activities for Children p147.

PRINCES STREET GARDENS
See Playgrounds and Parks p210.

RAILWAY PATHS AND CYCLE TRACKS

Railways were developed throughout Edinburgh by rival companies. All that remains now are flat routes which are gradually being developed into a network of cycle and footpaths. The paths although flat have often been redeveloped and are no longer straight (and boring!), but meander between birch trees, rowans and brambles. 'Spokes' (the cyclist's organisation) publishes a map which shows them all. *See* Travel and Transport p235. They include parts of the Water of Leith Walkway (*see below*) and the Innocent Railway. This is so-called because the carriages were initially pulled by horses, not steam engines. It runs from Holyrood Park (south-east of the Pollock Halls) to Craigmillar, walled between Prestonfield Golf Course and Duddingston Loch Nature Reserve; then on through Bingham to Musselburgh, following the main East Coast railway line (approx. 6 miles). Another ex-railway cycle track starts from Roseburn Ter in Murrayfield (access from Balbirnie Pl where there is a map of the route). This metalled track crosses the Water of Leith with steps down to

join the Walkway and continues north to the old Barnton Railway junction at Craigleith, where it divides. One branch goes to Davidson's Mains and the other passes the Western and Northern General Hospitals before branching again to Leith and Pilton.

RIVER ALMOND
See Cammo p228 and Cramond p222.

ROYAL BOTANIC GARDEN
East gate on Inverleith Row and West Gate on Arboretum Pl where there is also car parking.
552 7171
Daily, except 25 Dec and 1 Jan.
Nov-Feb: 10-4
Mar-Apr, Sept-Oct: 10-6
May-Aug: 10-8
Admission Free

A beautifully landscaped and well sign-posted garden, clean and pleasant, perhaps because no dogs or picnics are allowed (Note: also no wheeled toys, ball games or sledges). Tarred paths, grassy slopes and a pond where you can feed the ducks. Also tame squirrels. Themed gardens — alpine, cryptogamic (!) and, new for 1995, a Chinese garden — will interest the older child and parents.

The Glasshouse Experience
Daily
Mar-Oct: 10-5
Nov-Feb: 10-3.45
Voluntary donation of £1.50 suggested

You may be daunted by the large suggested donation if you are a regular visitor or one who only spends a few minutes in here looking at the fish. Staff stress that any donation is voluntary. There is only one entrance into the glasshouses — all other doors are exit only. Leaflets are available. Pushchairs can be left at the cash desk as the displays are on two levels and some paths between plants are quite narrow. Some ponds have no railings so hold on to active youngsters. There are old and new glasshouses, at various temperatures and humidities, and a small aquarium.

Inverleith House, in the centre of the Garden, houses a botanical art gallery with a programme of historical and contemporary exhibitions. No pushchairs or prams allowed.

Botanic Garden education staff lead guided tours and provide resource material for school parties. They are willing to give advice to Playgroup and Nursery teachers and to adapt their materials to suit parties of younger children. Phone 552 7175. The shop, at the West Gate, has a range of goods suitable for younger children starting to learn about the environment. **Toilets** at the glasshouses, Inverleith House and the West Gate. Nappy change and feeding facility at the East Gate; ask the Park constabulary there to give you a key. There is a snack bar (Dills) open May-Aug 11-4 and often an ice cream van at the West Gate and there are two cafes:

The Terrace Cafe
552 0616
Nov-Feb 10-3.30 Summer 10-5
££, High chairs (7), breastfeeding permitted, bottles heated, nappy change surface (Disabled&F), licensed, seats 150 (extra on terrace)

Beside Inverleith House, this is a popular meeting place for parents and tots. The menu includes hot and cold meals and snacks. Tables not suitable for clip-ons. Children's portions. You can reserve tables for a group and sit outside in the warmer weather. Pushchairs allowed in the cafe but it is courtesy to leave them just inside the door when it is very busy. **Toilets** and toilet for the disabled.

Rachel's Tearoom
7 Inverleith Row 557 4465
Situated at the East Gate.
Mon-Fri 11-4.30, closed Thur; Sat, Sun 11-5.30
£, High chair (1), breastfeeding permitted, bottles heated, no smoking, seats 48

This is a pleasant tearoom serving snacks and light meals. Steps down to the door make access slightly difficult, but the staff will help with pushchairs. Pushchairs should be left in the corridor to the seating area as space is limited. **Toilet**.

SAUGHTON GARDENS
See Saughton Park, in Playgrounds and Parks p216.

SWANSTON VILLAGE FARM
See Pentland Hills p227.

THE UNION CANAL
The Union Canal runs, with obstructions, from the Lochrin Basin in Edinburgh's West End (access from Gilmore Park and Leamington Rd) to Falkirk. The towpath is on the north bank. Obviously children need close supervision. From the centre of the city and industrial buildings (but where swans sometimes nest) the canal passes suburban gardens and parks and eventually into woods and open countryside. The canal is carried by aqueducts over the Water of Leith by the 12 arch Slateford Aqueduct (you can join up with the Water of Leith Walk here, *see below*), over the River Almond beyond Ratho and again by the Avon Aqueduct, Scotland's largest and tallest

aqueduct over the River Avon. It disappears for a mile into culverts beneath Wester Hailes and is cut through again by the M8 between Broxburn and Ratho. The canal offers an easy (although you may have to negotiate steps to reach it) and delightful walk through countryside alive with flora and wildlife. The original mile posts can still be seen at the side of the tow path.

Two canal boats — 'Pride of The Union' and 'Pride of Belhaven' operate from the Edinburgh Canal Centre at The Bridge Inn, Ratho, see Places to visit p185, Annual Events, December p204 and Eating Out p79. An annual canal jump is held here in mid-June. There are also boats to hire from the Canal Museum, Linlithgow, see Out of Town Trips p193. Entrance to the museum is free. A Ranger operates from here. She is keen to encourage children to use the canal and can arrange talks, guides, walks and help with other activities related to the canal.

VOGRIE ESTATE COUNTRY PARK
nr. Gorebridge.

A beautiful country park with walks and nature trails, a ranger centre and map boards. **Toilets.** Adventure playground.

See Playgrounds and Parks p218.

THE WATER OF LEITH WALKWAY

The Water of Leith rises in the Pentland Hills, to the west of the City and runs through Balerno to the New Town and on to Leith docks where it flows into the Firth of Forth. In its 23 miles it flows through wooded dells, past abandoned mills, elegant Georgian terraces and new housing developments, before opening up into a broad river surrounded by the dignified commercial buildings of Leith docks.

The walkway runs along most of the river in the City and most parts are negotiable with a pushchair. Unfortunately access is not always so easy and we have tried to list alternatives to steps, where they exist. Some sections are well used by dogs too. Keep an eye on young cyclists as the banks can be steep and there are not always railings. Parents, please watch out for more exuberant cyclists racing ahead; pedestrians and dogs are not always aware of bikes behind them, and this leads to collisions and tumbles.

The brown water is due to peat and although safe for paddling, there is always the possibility of pollution from sewage, pesticides or industrial waste so warn tots not to drink it. Giant hogweed, a large umbelliferous plant, has established itself on several stretches. Touching this plant or blowing through sections of its hollow stem may cause an allergic reaction and photosensitivity of the skin. These plants are routinely treated with weedkiller and hacked down but return each year. Along stretches of the river are raspberries and blackberries which should be safe to eat, but remember that dogs may have been there before you.

Leaflets giving maps and details of some parts of the 'walkway' are available free from the City of Edinburgh District Council, Planning Dept, 1 Cockburn St, EH1 1BP, 529 3595 and in some libraries and places of interest. Edinburgh City Libraries stock a good selection of books on the Water of Leith.

Balerno-Currie

The walkway begins to the north side of Balerno High School, Bridge

Rd and follows the track of an old railway. The path is wide and has recently been resurfaced with grit; ideal for pushchairs and budding cyclists except in winter when it can still become rutted and muddy. There is talk of upgrading this section to tarmac in future to encourage more cyclists. There are a number of access points along the route to Currie; easiest for pushchairs is Waulkmill Loan. At Currie Kirkgate, there are steps up to the walkway, next to the bridge. Here, it is better for pushchairs if you continue under the bridge and up the road to Currie Baptist Church where there is access to the walkway via an old goods yard (you can park here too).

Currie to Juniper Green

The walkway continues along the old railway track for approx. 1½ miles to Juniper Green. Easiest access is at Kinleith Mill, through the industrial estate, off Blinkbonny Rd (off Lanark Rd W, nr Veitch's Garden Centre). There are also steps up from the walkway to Blinkbonny Rd bridge. There is a section here where a 20 foot wall drops sharply down to the river below, with no railings or bushes at the top, so hold onto wandering tots. The path then crosses to the north side of the river again. Access here is from Baberton Loan, a steep path and steps down from Juniper Green Post Office. Best to continue on to Woodhall Millbrae, if you have a pushchair, and rejoin the Lanark Rd just before the City By-Pass. Look out for kingfishers and herons around here.

Juniper Green to Slateford
(Inc Craiglockhart Dell), leaflet available

Along this attractive and peaceful section of the river, the walkway

continues on the old railway, passing under the City By-Pass and into a wooded dell, crossing the river several times. Good access off West Mill Rd, Gillespie Rd (by the bridge) or through Spylaw Park, Colinton (there is a good play area here). Continuing on, the walkway enters an old railway tunnel (about ¼ mile, usually dimly lit — freephone CLARENCE if it is not) and emerges way above the river with other paths below. From Dell Rd, Colinton (down past the church), the walkway runs through Colinton and Craiglockhart Dells, the latter in the wooded estate of Craiglockhart House. Access points include Katesmill Rd, at Redhall Mill and behind the "Tickled Trout", on Lanark Rd at Slateford.

The Walkway crosses Lanark Rd at Slateford and it is possible to join up with the Union Canal here (*see above section*).

Slateford to Belford Rd

There is no walkway or river path along much of this section, although you will be able to follow the river with the aid of a street map, as it passes through Saughton and Roseburn Parks, and around the ice rink and rugby ground at Murrayfield. From Roseburn, the path is accessed from W Coates Ter. (okay for pushchairs). Recently upgraded, it is easy to follow to Belford Bridge. There are steps at the bridge so it is easier to leave the path by the back of the Hilton Hotel, *See* Eating Out p74. There is also access to the Gallery of Modern Art, *See* Eating Out p74 via a bridge and steep zig-zag path, and to W Coates Pl.

Dean Bank Footpath
Leaflet available

This is a picturesque section along

231

the north side of the Water of Leith, following a slow moving loop running in a deep hidden and wooded glen from Belford Bridge to Dean Path. The path has now been surfaced and is ideal for pushchairs. The track runs on the riverbank, a precarious few feet above the water. Some sections have handrail about 3 ft high — useful for adults but small children can slip underneath quite easily. Access is from Dean Path (steps a little way up the hill from Dean Village) and Belford Bridge (see above). For pushchairs a better option is at the footbridge along from Sunbury Mews in a modern housing development or the bridge at Haythorn Bank which leads up to Dean Path where it crosses over the river.

Dean Path to Stockbridge St Bernard's Path

This established, well railed and paved section runs along the south bank from Miller Row in Dean, to Saunders St in Stockbridge. As the river gushes beneath the dramatic Dean Bridge, it is hard to imagine the urban bustle only 10 mins walk away at the West End of Princes St. The depth of the steep wooded valley is emphasised by the views of the backs of Moray and Ainslie Pl. St Bernard's Well (a Georgian statue and temple) is half way along the path; and there are several flights of steps down to paddling and fishing spots. There are upper and lower routes between St Bernard's Well and the bridge at Saunder's St. You will find fewer steps on the higher path.

Deanhaugh Footpath, Stockbridge
Leaflet available

A very short stretch (¼ mile) in Stockbridge. There are steps down near the TSB on Raeburn Pl or ramps at Falshaw Bridge and Haugh St. Although it is a useful, secluded spot to remember when you are feeling harassed in the nearby shops, unfortunately it is well used by dogs. There may be ducks to feed. No guard rail.

Rocheid Path

An attractive, established section running between Stockbridge and Canonmills. Trees and slopes provide seclusion from nearby houses. Sledging in winter. Access from Arboretum Rd in Stockbridge, over a wooden bridge that is the continuation of the road between Glenogle Pl and Bell Pl in the Stockbridge Colonies, and from Inverleith Ter Lane, off Howard Pl in Canonmills. Suitable for pushchairs.

Warriston to Coberg St
Leaflet available

This section of the Water of Leith runs from Warriston Cres into Leith (¾ mls), following the line of the former North British Railway. The path is flat and metalled so is ideal for prams and bikes. Unfortunately it is also well used by dogs and there is an excess of litter. The path is often within high stone walls and buildings but there are some views of the city. The river itself is not much in evidence until you reach Leith. There is a children's playground at St Mark's Park on Warriston Rd. It is tucked behind a hedge and you may not spot it until you are on your way back. Although it has not been upgraded to current standards, the Recreation Dept intend to do so during the next round of such work.

Travel & Transport

Venturing out in Edinburgh with small children can be exhausting, particularly if you have to travel by public transport. Edinburgh's bus services were once regarded as the best in Britain because of the cheap fares and high frequencies, but 'deregulation' in 1986 put an end to that. Despite competition between Lothian Region Transport and SMT fares are higher and off-peak services much poorer. Buses are never easy when you're carting children and pushchairs around, and the days of the conductor helping you on and off are only a dim memory now!

Many cities have a suburban rail system as an alternative to the bus but in Edinburgh that too is a dim memory. The only suburban station to survive was Slateford, although more recently new stations have been provided at Wester Hailes, S Gyle, Musselburgh and Wallyford, and Kingsknowe and Curriehill have been reopened.

Proposals are well advanced for a new metro system to serve the city, running from Wester Hailes to Leith and from Muirhouse to Liberton, intersecting at Waverley, but the estimated cost is enormous and it is likely to be many years before the money can be found to build the system.

With the metro still some years away, your choice for the moment is between walking, cycling, or taking a car, bus, taxi or train. The following

233

sections provide details of each option.

ON FOOT

Edinburgh is not the easiest city for pedestrians to negotiate, especially with pushchairs and young children in tow. Crossing the street is probably the hardest thing to do, with George St and St Andrew Square the worst places to cross in Edinburgh. Be wary at the George St junctions of helpful drivers stopping for you to cross only to be over- or under-taken by another car in the other lane.

If you have experienced problems, whether in the City Centre or in your own area, then it is worth trying to do something about it. Write, and encourage friends to write, to your Regional Councillor, pointing out the dangers you and your children face and putting forward your preferred solution. Whatever your views phone Lothian Regional Headquarters on 229 9292 or ask at your local library for the name of your local councillor and write c/o Lothian Regional Council, George IV Bridge.

Road Safety

Road accidents are the major cause of death and injury to children and they are most at risk when on foot and when alone. Most under 5s are accompanied by adults and we as adults should take advantage of this supervision to give our children guidance and training by setting a good example and by beginning to teach them the skills they will need to cope safely when they are older.

The Tufty Club teaches children the following basic rules of road safety:

— Never go out without an adult
— Always hold an adult's hand
— Stop, look, listen before you cross the road

Playgroups, nurseries, etc can join the Tufty Club. Group membership is free. There is no individual membership but the Club will send out free leaflets to individuals if requested. Members receive leaflets and advice, a newsletter 3 times yr.

Write to: The Tufty Club Office, RoSPA, Cannon House, The Priory, Queensway, Birmingham B4 6BS 0121 200 2461 (RoSPA also publish easy-to-read leaflets on all aspects of safety — in the home, in the water, camping and caravanning, etc). New traffic clubs are appearing nationwide, developed by TRRL (Transport and Road Research Laboratory) based on Scandinavian experience. One such is the Children's Traffic Club which now operates in Lothian, sponsored by Lothian Regional Council, Lothian Health and Lothian and Borders Police. The Council provides FREE membership for all children whose 3rd birthday falls on or after 1 April 1994. Eligible children are identified by Lothian Health and automatically receive an invitation to join. Once the child is registered they receive a Traffic Club pack every 6 months until they are 5. Other pre-school children, born too early for the FREE scheme can register with the national scheme by contacting: The Children's Traffic Club, 267 Kentern Rd, Harrow, HA3 0HQ, 0181 909 3626, who will send an introductory pack and information on the cost per child (currently £9.95). Further information on the Lothian scheme from the helpline 0131 311 3066.

CYCLING

When you get fed up walking one step forward and two back with your toddler, you may be inspired to dust off your bike, buy a child-seat and get pedalling. If so, we suggest you bear in mind a few basic guidelines. Firstly, get your bike checked over at a specialist shop and keep it well maintained, especially the brakes. Next, buy the best child-seat and all the safety equipment you can afford. (See Bicycle Shops p31 for details.) Then you will need to practise on quiet side streets or cycle paths until you have mastered the art of balancing a bike with a heavy, wriggling child on the back. Motorists often do not see cyclists, so dress brightly, preferably with fluorescent strips and belts. Watch out for car doors opening carelessly. It is important to recognise the dangers of bicycle travel, especially on the busier or faster roads.

Spokes

St Martin's Church, 232 Dalry Rd
313 2114

Lothian cycle group, campaigning for better facilities for cyclists. Spokes City Cycle map shows alternative routes to your destination along cycle tracks made from disused railway lines, river valleys, minor roads etc avoiding busy and cobbled roads. Available from bike shops, bookshops or £3 post-free from Spokes. For further information and recent FREE leaflets send sae to Spokes.

CTC

Cotterell House, 69 Meadrow, Godalming, Surrey GU7 3HS
0148 341 7217

The Cyclist's Touring Club is Britain's largest national cycling organisation.

It campaigns for all cyclists regardless of age, ability or type of bike. If you become a member you receive a range of services, such as a very informative bi-monthly magazine, touring information, technical advice, mail order, handbook, FREE legal aid and third party insurance in case you are involved in an accident, bike insurance, information on national and local events. There are 200 local groups, many having family sections. There are concessionary membership rates for families and school children.

British Rail

Trains used to accommodate bikes, but in recent times their policy seems to have changed. If you are planning on using the train service on your outing, phone first to make sure the train will actually have a carriage that will carry bikes. There are restrictions and extra charges on many routes. See Travel by Train p240.

Child Safety

It is not advisable to allow children under 9 into traffic. Older children should first be trained under RoSPA's National Cycling Proficiency Scheme. Boys, rather than girls, are more likely to be killed in a cycling accident, so training should start now, and safety always enforced. Make sure bikes are well maintained, tyres are checked regularly, brakes work properly, and helmets are worn at all times. See also Bicycle Shops p33.

TRAVEL BY CAR

Parking in town

Parking is not easy in the town

centre — try Market St, Regent Rd, Heriot Row/Abercrombie Pl, Rutland Sq, Kings Stables Rd, all of which are a tolerable walk for children to Princes St. There are multistorey parks at Castle Ter, St James Centre and Greenside Pl. On-street parking is prohibited (other than in metered bays) on most central streets and in many suburban shopping centres during working hrs Mon-Fri and on Sat mornings. Restrictions are eased on Sat afternoons and Sun when meters are FREE and many yellow lines cease to have effect.

Park and ride
See also Travel by Rail p240.
Free car parks are provided at the following stations: Dalmeny, Curriehill, Musselburgh, South Gyle and Wester Hailes. On Mon-Sat trains run ½ hrly from Dalmeny and South Gyle and hrly from Curriehill, Wester Hailes, Musselburgh and Wallyford, with increased frequencies during peak periods. On Sun a reduced service operates except from Curriehill and Wester Hailes which are closed.

Safety
Statistics show that hundreds of children are injured each year because they are not properly secured while travelling in cars. Since September 1989, if seat belts or child restraints are fitted in the rear of a car, it is the driver's legal responsibility to see that children under 14 yrs use them.

How to protect your child
Various types of child restraint are available, and all safe ones carry the British 'Kitemark' or European 'E' to show they meet recommended standards.
0-9 mths

● rearward-facing baby carrier (up to 10 kg) can sit on the front or back seats, held in place by adult seat belt (back is safest, but distracting for a lone driver trying to keep an eye on a very young baby, therefore probably better in front).

● two-way child seat which begins as a rearward facing baby seat then turns round to fit child until around 4 yrs.

● a carrycot restrained with a harness. It is safer to clip the baby into the carrycot with a harness, as the baby can be tossed out.

6 mths-4 yrs

● child seats are the best idea. Most fix on to existing rear seat belts or you can use an anchorage kit and possibly a special bar for fixing, depending on car. A weight limit for each child seat will be specified by the manufacturer. Another way of assessing when a child is too big for a seat is when child's eyes are level with top of seat back.

● special child harnesses are also available.

● booster cushion or booster seat can be used in conjunction with adult seat belt.

For further information on child car safety and the new seat belt law write to: Scottish Office, Room 3/98A, Roads Directorate, New St Andrew's House.

Local shops which sell the equipment outlined above include Argos *see* Shopping p2, Mothercare *see* Shopping p6, John Lewis *see* Shopping p4, Halfords *see* Shopping p34 and many baby equipment shops. *See also* Shopping p25, and Hiring p57.

Car seat fitting
Some garages will fit seats for you

(for seats that do not have rear seat belts or if you prefer to have fixed anchorage). The following have been recommended for service and/or price:

T C Juner and Son
16a Royston Ter, Goldenacre
552 3769

Supply and fit the full range of Kangol cheaply. Will drill holes to fit seats.

Heriothill Garage
18 Manderston St
553 1012

Only fit to Volkswagens. They successfully fitted a child seat to the back seat of a VW caravanette without removing the engine, which was advised by other garages. The fitter is experienced and familiar with all safety requirements.

Kwik-fit

Specialist fitting centres throughout Edinburgh — child safety seats suitable from birth to 4yrs (18kg). Supplied and fitted for £39.90 with a £20 refund in Kwik-fit vouchers when seat returned after child's 4th birthday. Can only fit a child safety seat to cars with existing rear seat belt anchorage points.

Car Hire and Child Seats

Most local rental firms seem to offer car seats for 9 mths-4 yrs, but costs and further facilities vary enormously.

Alamo Rent A Car
Arrivals Concourse,
Edinburgh Airport
333 5100

Rearward facing baby seat available for £2.95/day. It is best to book in advance.

Arnold Clark Hire Drive
Lochrin Pl, Tollcross
228 4747

Baby seat, toddler seat and booster seat all available at no charge. The seats are supplied but are not fitted for insurance reasons. It is best to give as much notice as possible.

Hertz Rent-a-Car
10 Picardy Pl
556 8311
Also Airport
333 1019 and
Waverley Station
557 5272

Baby seat and toddler seat available at a charge of £3/day

Kenning Car Rental
Newbridge Self Service
11 Edinburgh Rd
333 4555
Toddler seat and booster seats available for £5 for duration of rental. One day's notice required.

Melvilles Motors
9 Clifton Ter
337 5333

Toddler seat available for £10 — 2-3 day's notice is advisable. Roofrack also available at £10.

Turner Hire Drive
51 West Harbour Rd,
Granton
552 0341/557 0304

Baby seat, toddler seat and booster seat available for £25 returnable deposit. One week's notice required. *see also* Hiring Equipment p57.

BUS TRANSPORT

The majority of bus services in and around Edinburgh are provided by two companies: Lothian Regional Transport (maroon and white buses) and SMT (green buses — formerly Eastern Scottish). There are also city tour buses run in competition with LRT by Guide Friday *see also* Boats, Planes and Trains in Places to Visit p185 and there are a few other independent operators such as Edinburgh Transport.

In general LRT has a more modern fleet of buses than SMT, but there is little to choose between them when it comes to boarding and alighting with small children and pushchairs, which is always difficult. SMT's mini-buses (City Sprinters) are particularly cramped and have little space to stow pushchairs.

INFORMATION OFFICES

Lothian Region Traveline Information:

The regional council operates an information service at St Giles St which provides a 'one-stop' information service covering all bus and train services, 225 3858.

See also Sources and Information p206.

Lothian Region Transport

Waverley Bridge Ticket Centre
220 4111
Summer Mon-Sat 8-7; Sun 9-4.15
Winter Mon-Fri 9-4.30
Office
27 Hanover St
554 4494 (Admin)
220 4111 (24hr enquiry service)
Mon- Sat 8.30-6

Both offices deal with general phone enquiries and sell travel cards, bus maps, tokens and publications. In addition Waverley Bridge handles tours, while Hanover St deals with OAP tickets, scholars passes and all postal enquiries. Tickets and information can also be obtained from a network of agents throughout the city.

Lost Property Office Shrubhill; Mon-Fri 10-1.30

SMT

Bus Station
St Andrew Sq
558 1616

Enquiries: Bus Shop (next to Platform A) for local services. Bus Shop is open 8.40-5 (Wed 9.10am).

Lost Property Office within Bus Shop. Left luggage lockers Mon-Sun 6.30-10pm (Platform A)

Snack Bar (next to Platform A) Mon-Sat 7 am - 8 pm; Sun 9-7

Self-service cafe, very smokey and not recommended for children.

The bus stops for city buses are not in the Bus Station itself, but on St Andrew Sq.

Rules for under 5s

Both LRT and SMT have the same rules as regards fares. Under 5s travel free on the understanding that they give up their seats for fare-paying passengers. An adult can be accompanied by up to 2 children travelling FREE. The standard child fare must be paid for more than 2 under 5s.

Fares

The fares charged by both companies are almost the same for the same journey. A journey of 2 miles costs around 55p depending on route. 5 + yrs pay reduced fares.

On LRT buses you must provide the

exact fare (or more), because no change is given. Pound coins are preferred to notes. On SMT the driver will usually give change. Neither company operates a through-fare system, so you have to pay again each time you change buses (this is particularly annoying during evenings and on Sun when fewer through-services operate).

Frequencies

A 15-min interval is usual on most main routes on wk days 7-7 pm, so you can usually rely on a bus every few mins on roads served by several routes. SMT's City Sprinter services operate a 5-10 min frequency.

After 7 pm and on Suns, bus services are reduced very severely in most parts of the city. Many routes stop altogether, others only run on part of the route, and frequencies are reduced to ½ hrly or even less (except City Sprinters which maintain 10-15 min frequencies on some routes). At these off-peak times you are strongly advised to consult a timetable (available free from LRT and SMT offices or from Lothian Regional Council Traveline office in St Giles St) BEFORE going off to a bus stop with children, because you could be in for a very long wait.

Cheap Tickets
LR

Ridacards can be bought giving unlimited travel on LRT services in and around Edinburgh (including Balerno, Riccarton, Dalkeith, etc).

The **Edinburgh Freedom Ticket** gives one day's unlimited travel. The **Touristcard** gives visitors unlimited travel, reductions on coach tours, plus concessions at various shops, restaurants, theatres and museums. All these tickets are competitively

priced — please ask for details. You will need a passport-sized photo for your Ridacard, but both offices have booths.

SMT

SMT offers various cheap tickets along similar lines to LRT.

Where to buy tickets

Some tickets can be purchased from the driver, others from some local post offices or newsagents or at the Bus Station.

Longer Distance Buses

Scottish Citylink and Stagecoach both operate services to many parts of Scotland, and also run services to London and other parts of England. Although fares are lower than those for comparable rail journeys, a long-distance coach trip can be arduous, particularly with small children. The gap between coach and rail fares to London has been narrowed with the introduction of Apex rail fares.

TAXIS

There are a number of radio-cab companies in Edinburgh: **Central** 229 2468, **City** 228 1211, **Radio-Cab** 225 9000 and **Castle** 228 2555 are just a few, see Yellow Pages.

Charges have increased a lot in recent yrs. All black taxis charge the same rates: there is no extra charge for 1 under 5. 2 children under 12 count as one passenger. For further information contact Edinburgh Cab Office, 455 7986.

The seat belt law exempts children from using rear restraints if they are travelling in a licensed taxi or hire car where the rear seats are separated from the driver by a fixed partition. It is, of course, safer to use a seat belt if there is one available. The newer taxis do have them, and when phoning to order a taxi, you could request one with rear seat belts but may face a longer wait. Most taxis have automatic door locks (a red light illuminates on the door when the lock is operating) but in older taxis keep children away from the doors and windows. Some taxi drivers will allow you on board with your child strapped into a pushchair, which does make for an easier journey.

TRAVEL BY TRAIN

Enquiries
Waverley Station
Enquiry Office
Mon-Sat 8 am-11 pm; Sun 9 am-11 pm

Passenger train enquiries 556 2451 (24hrs) (calls are answered in rotation, so be prepared for a wait at peak hrs)
Sleepers 556 5633
All other enquiries 556 2477
See Phone Book under British Rail for numbers of other information services.

Stations

Because of the lack of suburban services, trains are of limited use in Edinburgh. There are currently 10 stations in the Edinburgh area: Waverley and Haymarket in the city centre, and Dalmeny, South Gyle, Curriehill, Wester Hailes, Kingsknowe, Slateford, Musselburgh and Wallyford.

Waverley is a major station in the rail network. Trains run from here all over Scotland (Glasgow, Aberdeen, Inverness, Oban) and there are busy local services to Fife and the Lothians. Main line trains also run south on the east and west coasts, and these are now all-electric.

The best entrance for pushchairs is from Waverley Bridge. Avoid Waverley Steps from Princes St at all costs. The Market St entrance has a short flight of steps to the overhead walkway through the station, and then a lift down to platform level (by Platform 11).

Waverley Station provides many amenities on one level: the travel centre is inside the large airy Victorian waiting hall — great for restless children to charge around in, but beware the automatic doors which allow easy exit. This is surrounded by the ticket and reservation counters, **toilets** ('Superloo'), self-service food court and a bar. Elsewhere in the station there are snack kiosks, a bookshop, newsagent, and photo booths. Hertz Car Hire is on Platform 11, and Guide Friday is on Platform 19.

The **superloos** cost 20p to enter, are clean and have many facilities. The Ladies have toilets, showers and a comfy waiting area, a long well-lit mirror and a small separate **mothers' room** with chair, sink, nappy changing surface and bin — perfect for feeding baby in private. Ask the attendant if you wish to use this room as it is kept locked.

The Food Court
Mon-Sat 6 am-12 pm; Sun 7 am-12 pm
£, *High chair (1), breastfeeding permitted, Bottles heated, no smoking area*

Self-service cafeteria selling meals and snacks. There are 4 counters. Burger King serves burgers, bacon rolls, French fries, etc. *Upper Crust* serves cakes, filled French bread etc. Also Pizza Hut and Cafe Select. All serve drinks. Cold drinks come in lidded cups with straws. Carry out food is served. There is room for pushchairs. No toilets in Food Court but station **superloos** not far away.

Haymarket serves all points west and north. Lots of steps to platforms. The short trip between Waverley and Haymarket is popular with playgroups as an outing. Snack bar Platform 4, waiting room. Mon-Fri 6.30 am-5.30 pm. Light snacks, hot and cold drinks. Babies' bottles and foods can be heated.

South Gyle is a suburban halt serving all Fife trains. Tickets are obtained from a machine on the Edinburgh-bound platform approach, or from the train conductor. Large car park on the south side, but quite a walk from here to the Edinburgh platform. Trains run ½ hrly to Waverley, with extra trains during peak periods. Reduced service on Sun.

Slateford, Wester Hailes, Kingsknowe, Curriehill are served by hrly services to/from Glasgow Central via Shotts. No Sun services.

Musselburgh is served by services to/from North Berwick — trains approx every hr. Reduced service on Sun.

The Trains

Most local services in Edinburgh and the Lothians are provided by modern diesel trains known as 'Sprinters'. All Sprinters have push-button door controls and wide-opening sliding doors, so boarding with pushchairs is easy. There are some corners or spaces available where you can park a pushchair, although the conductor/guard may ask you to fold it up if the train is busy (Sprinters are usually only 2-coach trains and can be very busy at peak periods).

On longer-distance services the most common type of train is the 'Express' diesel unit, which operates to Glasgow Queen St, Perth, Inverness and Aberdeen. Also known as the '158', these also have push-button sliding doors externally and internally, useful spaces for luggage and pushchairs and on-board telephones. Only 2 **toilets** per 2-coach train, one of which is spacious and well-designed with a fold-up nappy-changing table (although the table is on the short side at only 2 ft). The children will like the fact that almost everything works by pushing buttons!

If you are venturing south of the border, your Inter-City train will usually have automatic internal doors and good luggage space, but only on the new East Coast electric trains will you have the added benefits of external push-button sliding doors and **toilets** with nappy-changing facilities.

Train Catering

One of the best ways to keep children happy on a longer train journey is to feed them. Most internal Scottish services now carry a buffet-trolley operated by private catering firms, offering hot and cold drinks, crisps and other confectionery, and sandwiches. There are no buffet cars, except on Inter-City trains to/from England; they offer hot as well as cold snacks, and the steward will usually help out by heating bottles in the buffet micro-wave. It goes without saying that it's far cheaper to buy your train provisions in the local supermarket before you travel.

Fares and Rules

As a general rule under 5s travel FREE, on the understanding that they give up their seats to fare-paying passengers. An adult can be accompanied by up to 4 FREE under 5s. Return fares are usually twice the single fare.

Cheap Day Returns

Cheap day returns are valid on day of purchase only, and are available from Edinburgh to many Scottish destinations. They can be used on any train at wkends but there are restrictions on wkday peak-period travel; details from the Enquiry Office.

Fares for Longer Journeys

When travelling on longer journeys for example south to England on Inter-City trains, remember that 'Saver' tickets are usually available for return journeys and are cheaper than 2 single tickets, and that travelling Sun-Thurs is cheaper than Fri all yr and Sat in summer. For big savings, book an Apex ticket one wk or more in advance, but you must specify your choice of train both ways.

Railcards

The family railcard costs £20 and is valid for one yr from date of purchase. These can be excellent value if you expect to make more than one or two long-distance family trips, and entitle you to a reduction of between 20% and 33% off the adult fare, provided at least one adult travels and is accompanied by between 1 and 4 children each paying a £2 flat fare (**all** children between 5 and 16 must have a £2 ticket, and children under 5 must have a £2 ticket if you want to reserve a seat). The railcard is issued to 2 named adults both of whom must be over 17. If both holders travel, they can take up to two additional adults paying the reduced fare, as well as the accompanied children. The adults and children need not be related to each other.

Seat Reservations

On many longer distance trains, seat reservations are compulsory, and if you are travelling with children they are always strongly recommended. £1 will reserve up to 4 standard class seats if the reservations are made at the time of ticket purchase.

AIR TRAVEL

Edinburgh Airport

A8, 4 miles west of Edinburgh (near Ingliston showground)
333 1000

Reservations: British Airways 0345 222111; Air UK 0345 666777; British Midland 0345 554554. For full details of all airline numbers, see Phone Book under BAA or individual airlines.

The airport terminal is modern, spacious and clean.

Snack bar, restaurant, shop, bureau de change, bar, spectators' gallery and most of the information desks. The external doors are automatic or revolving and lots of luggage trolleys are available. Lifts at Gates 3 and 5. There are **toilets** everywhere, and doors are wider than average making easy access for pushchairs.

Many toilets have a nappy-changing unit, including Gents.

Spectators' Gallery

Reached by the lift at Gate 5, the gallery is open during daylight hrs.

The best time for viewing if you want to see lots of planes is during the summer, especially Sat and Sun and Mon-Fri 12-12.30. In winter the airport is much quieter.

Baby Room

Located at Gate 6 the room is excellent if a bit small. It has comfortable chairs, play-pen, sinks, nappy-changing surface, large bin, nappy-and-wipe machine (50p for 1) and an en-suite toilet. The **toilet** has larger than normal floor-space and a door that opens outwards, so that (for once!) you don't trap your toddler in the door as you enter. There is also a pull-cord for medical assistance which summons one of the enquiry desk staff, some of whom are trained nurses. Fathers may use the room also. Unfortunately the room is only sign-posted once you get to it, so it is easy to miss.

Books Plus

The shop sells books (including a reasonable range for the under 5s), magazines, story tapes, colouring books and toys. In addition it carries everything from travel packs of baby wipes and baby lotion to sewing kits, luggage labels, straps and souvenirs.

Ginghams Coffee Shop

6 am-9 pm daily
££, High chairs (3), FREE baby food, bottles heated, breastfeeding permitted, child's menu, no smoking area, licensed, seating 200

A self-service restaurant in an open area off the main ground-floor concourse. Quick meals and snacks available including dish-of-the-day and vegetarian meals. Child's menu and child-size portions available;

FREE baby food. Prams and pushchairs are allowed.
Mother and baby room nearby. Good view of planes and runway.

Uppercrust and Bar

6.30 am-10 pm daily.
££, No high chairs, bottles heated, breastfeeding permitted, no smoking area, licensed, seating 40

Counter-service café and bar on the ground floor. Light snacks available. Pushchairs allowed, carpeted floor with view of aircraft from seating area. Parent and Baby Room nearby.

Cafe Select and Bar

Open during peak travel periods
£, Bottles heated, no smoking area, licensed, seating 175

Counter-service café and bar on 1st floor (access by lift or escalator). Serves hot and cold snacks. Pushchairs are allowed. **Toilets** nearby, Parent and Baby Room on ground floor.

Which Airline is Best?

All airlines like to know **in advance** that you are travelling with babies and children.

On short flights you may not require much by way of help. Most airlines seem to offer similar services: families are boarded before the other passengers; cabin staff will heat or cool bottles and baby food as required. In addition, Air UK say they give parents an extra seat to spread out into, if there is room. Air UK mentioned that on certain aircraft families are seated in a section of the lane which has extra emergency oxygen masks, to allow for children sitting on parents' knees. If you need help to board the plane, be sure to ask when you check in.

Most airlines are happy for you to

use car seats when you pay for the seat for your children. CAA regulations allow the use of a 'suitable' type of seat — defined in Air Navigation Order 1989, which states that the aircraft seatbelt must anchor the car seat without passing over the lap of the child, or the Carechair which is specifically for use on aircraft. This is currently offered only by Virgin Atlantic Airlines. Air UK (at the time of writing, March 1995) specify only one make of car seat (no longer in production) that they accept as suitable, so check before you book. On longer flights many airlines offer extra services to parents, in addition to the above. British Airways (BA) provide 'skycots' (similar to carry-cots) for babies up to 9 mths. (It is worth asking for one even for a toddler, as sleeping in a cot curled up or with feet over the edge may be better than sleeping on the floor.) These are attached to the bulkheads on long-haul aircraft and are not available on routes within the UK. BA, and most other international carriers, try to seat families in the bulkhead to give them more room. They supply special meals for babies and children if requested at time of booking .

Some airlines allow you to bring your pushchair into the cabin if they are not too full, so that you can wheel your child from the departure lounge on to the plane. If there is no room, most airlines will at least stow the pushchair in the hold last, so that it is first off. You can request that your pushchair be brought to you as soon as you leave the plane. Some airlines have special amusement packs for children with hat, sweets and colouring book. Although geared to school-age children they can be useful to distract younger children.

Pregnancy and Air Travel

Flying is unlikely to be harmful in a normal pregnancy, but airlines will not, as a rule, carry women after the 35th wk. Some airlines require a note from your GP as to your fitness after 28 wks. Anyone who has had a previous miscarriage or premature baby is advised not to embark on long jet flights during pregnancy.

Nappy-changing on Board the Plane

Facilities vary with each aircraft. In the toilet of the larger transatlantic planes there is a changing surface which folds down. The similar planes used on European routes may not have this facility. Ask the steward for help.

Getting to the Airport

The airport is easily accessible by car, just off the A8 dual carriageway to the west of Gogar roundabout (the end of the city by-pass). Watch for the slip road, which is not well signposted.

There is a large long-stay car park, but this is fairly full most of the time and you may have to walk quite a way to the terminal building. You must use the car park unless you are only stopping briefly to pick up and set down passengers. Take care when crossing the road from the car park to the terminal. Look in Yellow Pages for off-airport car park-and-ride facilities.

Bus Services

Both LRT and Guide Friday operate bus services from Waverley Bridge to the airport. Single fare is £3 (LRT) or £3.20 (GF). Both charge £5.00 return but LRT also offer a family day return of £6.60 after 9 am, which can be used by 2 adults and 1-3 children. Journey time is approximately 25 mins and both services run ½ hrly during the working day with reduced frequency at other times.

Taxis
The airport taxis are saloon or estate cars and cost more than the black cabs (approx £13 from the airport to the city centre, or more if there are traffic hold-ups).

Welfare

If you have a problem or a query relating to welfare benefits, tax, divorce, housing, or are seeking counselling or legal advice the following organisations may be of some help:

The Lothian Directory of Local Services

The 'Red Book' is a useful reference book giving the names and addresses of all local government departments, churches, schools, libraries, police stations, etc. This should be available in libraries. *See* Sources of Information p206.

INFORMATION AND ADVICE

Citizens Advice Bureaux

Apart from giving general advice and information on all topics, most branches have an evening clinic once a week where a qualified lawyer can be seen by appointment to give free advice. Local branches:

Edinburgh Central Office
58 Dundas St
557 1500
Mon, Tues, Thurs, Fri 9.30-4; Wed 9.30-12.30, 6.30-8 (legal advice appointments).

Gorgie/Dalry
268 Gorgie Rd
337 6353
Mon-Fri 9.30-12; Mon, Wed, Thurs 1.30-4; Tues 5.30-7 (legal advice appointments).

Leith
166 Gt Junction St
554 8144
Mon, Tues, Thurs, Fri 9.30-3.30; Wed

9.30-12; Thur 6-7.30 (legal advice appointments).

Pilton
661 Ferry Rd
332 9434
Mon, Tues, Thurs, Fri 9.30-12.30, 1-4; Wed 9.30-12.30.

Portobello
191 Portobello High St
669 7138
Mon, Tues, Wed, Fri 9.30-3.30; Wed 6.30-8.

Wester Hailes
1 Murrayburn Gate
442 2424
Mon, Tues, Thurs, Fri 9.30-3.30; Wed 9.30-11.30, 5.30-7.

Citizens Rights Office
Epworth Halls
25 Nicholson Sq
668 1091
Mon 10-12, 2-4.

FREE and independent advice on benefits, housing, employment, debt, immigration etc.

Department of Social Security
Social Security Freeline 0800 666 555

General information and advice about social security benefits.
Local offices of the Benefit Agency:-

Edinburgh South
160 Causewayside
EH9 1QJ

Edinburgh East
Phoenix House
275 Portobello High St
EH15 2AQ

Edinburgh City
38 Castle Ter
EH3 9SJ

Edinburgh North
199 Commercial St
EH6 6QP

Edinburgh West
8 Clifton Ter
EH12 5EX

**Gingerbread Edinburgh and
Lothians Project Ltd**
Gingerbread House
19 Chester St
220 1585
Mon-Fri 10-4

Information/advice service. Legal/counselling service.

Granton Information Centre
134-136 West Granton Rd
551 2459
(24 hrs)

Information and advice on benefits, debt, housing employment etc. Also available for development of local self-help/support groups. Youth and disability rights.

Grapevine

Disability information service.
See Sources of Information p205.

Legal Aid Dispensary
Old College -
Edinburgh University
South Bridge
Wed 6.30-7.45

Free legal advice organised by the Law Faculty. In the Old College Common Room.

Lothian Regional Council
The Advice Shop
86-87 South Bridge
225 1255
Phoneline Mon-Thur 8.30-4.40; Fri 8.30-3.0
Drop-in service Mon-Thur 9.30-4; Fri 9.30-3.30

Welfare benefit information and advice including representation at tribunals, confidential debt counselling service, specialist consumer advice.

**Lothian Interpreting and
Translating Service Trust Ltd**
557 4591

Provides interpreters in Chinese. Urdu, Bengali, Punjabi and many other languages.

**One Parent Families
Scotland (Formerly Scottish
Council for Single Parents)**
13 Gayfield Sq
556 3899/4563

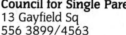

Help and counselling for individuals. Publishes bookets including 'Holidays' and guides to childcare, leisure and further education in Lothian. Send for free list. Working to improve care for school age children.

Scottish Cry-Sis Society
21 Falkland Gdns
Pauline Peat
334 5317

Telephone help for parents with persistently crying babies, difficult toddlers, non-sleeping children. Practical support and medical back-up is available.

SOCIAL WORK

Lothian Regional Council
Department of Social Work
Shrubhill House
Shrub Pl
554 4301
North West Edinburgh District

Covers Granton, Muirhouse, Pilton, Telford, Cramond, Parkgrove, Blackhall, Queensferry, Kirkliston,

SW, SE, NW and NE Corstorphine, Murrayfield, Dean, Stockbridge and New Town.

District Office: Westfield House, 5 Kirk Loan
334 9933

Social Work Centres: 34 Muirhouse Cres
343 1911
40 Ferry Rd Ave
343 3181

South West Edinburgh District

Covers Balerno, Baberton, North Hailes, South Hailes, Sighthill, Longstone, Moat, Stenhouse, Dalry, Shandon, Colinton, Firrhill, Braidburn, Fairmilehead.

District Office: Springwell House
1 Gorgie Rd
313 6785

Social Work Centres: 4 Oxgangs Path
445 4451
5 Murrayburn Gate
442 4131
Springwell House
1 Gorgie Rd
313 3366

North East Edinburgh District

Covers Trinity, Newhaven, Fort, Broughton, Inverleith, Lorne, Harbour, Calton, Lochend, Links, Craigentinny, Willowbrae, Mountcastle, Portobello, Milton.

District Office: Shrubhill House, Shrub Pl
554 4301
Social Work Centres: 9-11 Giles St
553 2121
Loaning Rd
661 8291
163 Leith Walk
554 4017

South East Edinburgh District

Covers Haymarket, Tollcross, St Giles, Holyrood, Merchiston, Morningside, Sciennes, Marchmont, Prestonfield, Mayfield, Alnwickhill, Kaimes, Inch, Gilmerton, Niddrie and Craigmillar.

District Office: Balmwell House, 29 Balmwell Ter
666 2585
1 Victoria St
226 6731
12 Newtoft St
664 6481
182 Greendykes Rd
669 9121

Emergency Duty Team
554 4301

Supported Accommodation Team
20-24 Albany St
For young mothers who have been in care.

HELP WITH PERSONAL/FAMILY PROBLEMS

AlAnon
St Anne's Community Centre
Cowgate
557 2974

Aims to provide help and support for friends and partners of problem drinkers. Regular group meetings.

Association for All Speech Impaired Children (AFASIC)
347 Central Markets
Smithfield
London EC1A 9NH
0171-236 3632/6487

Association of Separated and Divorced Catholics
c/o St Gabriel's Presbytery
83 Merrylee Rd
Glasgow G43 2QY

National co-ordinator: Annette Gray
0141 637 7400

Birthlink
Adoption Counselling Service
21 Castle St
225 6441

Counselling and advice for adopted people, birth parents and adoptive parents.

Children First (RSSPCC)
Melville House
Family Resource Centre
41A Polwarth Ter
337 8539/0 Day (Night 337 4891)

Help and advice to parents and families.

Church of Scotland Counselling Service
21 Rutland Sq
221 9377

Offers individual and group counselling to anyone experiencing a personal difficulty. By appointment (day/evening).

The Compassionate Friends
Margaret McDonald
657 2106

A self-help group for parents who have suffered the loss of a child of any age. Lending library and link scheme available.

Comprehensive Accredited Lawyer Mediators (CALM)
Professional lawyers who offer a mediation service to couples facing divorce.

List available from The Law Society, 26 Drumsheugh Gdns, 226 7411.

Contact a Family
170 Tottenham Court Road
London W1P 0HA
0171 383 3555
Mon-Fri 9.30-5.30
Mon-Fri 10.30-2.30

Introduces and links families whose children have special needs through local mutual support and self-help groups. Offers nationwide support and links individual parents of children with very rare handicaps.

Cruse Bereavement Care
3 Rutland Sq
229 6275 (Answerphone out of office hrs)
Weekdays 10-12.30; Wed 10-3.30 or by appointment.

In addition to counselling, advisory services and social groups Cruse has a Family Group on 2nd and 4th Sat of each month for children up to 12 yrs, looked after by a leader while parents meet informally.

Disability Scotland
5 Shandwick Pl
229 8632

Enquiries can be answered on all aspects of disability (except the purely medical). 26 information directories available. Books and publications in library.

Epilepsy Association of Scotland
Lothian Branch, 13 Guthrie St
226 5458

Edinburgh and Lothian Cot Death Support Group
10 Derby St
551 1094 Mrs Lorna Hayward

Gives personal support to bereaved families by letter, telephone and leaflets and puts parents in touch with other bereaved parents.

Family Fund
Joseph Rowntree Memorial Trust
PO Box 50
York YO1 2ZX
01904 621115

The Fund gives grants and services to families caring for a severely disabled child under 16. Help given must be related to the special care of the child. Help includes: laundry equipment, holidays, outings, clothing, bedding and recreation items. The fund cannot help with things which are the responsibility of statutory services.

Family Mediation Scotland
127 Rose St S Lane
220 1610

Helps separating and divorced parents make arrangements for the future care of their children. Also runs several 'Access Centres' where children can spend time with the parent who does not live with them.

Holiday Care Service
1 Old Bank Chambers
Station Rd
Horley
Surrey RH6 9HW
01293 774535
Fax 01293 774535

FREE information and advice on holidays for people with special needs eg physical disability, learning disability, one parent families.

Homelink
Irene Hannah
664 9880 or 226 31525
or c/o Gilmerton Centre
664 2335

Individual one-to-one support for isolated mothers

Lothian Children (affiliated to AFASIC)
Local contact — Lorraine Dilworth
01875 615898
Fax 01875 615423

Support and campaigning group for families with children with special education needs specialising in children with speech and language disorders. Help for parents in working through the record-of-needs system.

Lothian Marriage Counselling Service
9a Dundas St
556 1527
Mon-Thurs 10-9; Fri 10-6; Sat 10-1

Confidential counselling service for those who are experiencing disharmony and tension in their marriage or personal relationships. Appointment only.

Lothian Victim Support Scheme
15 Calton Hill
556 1718

Mon-Fri 9-4 (Answerphone out of office hrs)

Support and practical help for individuals and families who have experienced loss, distress and inconvenience caused by crime.

The Miscarriage Association
c/o Clayton Hospital
Northgate
Wakefield
Yorks
01924 200799
Local Contact:
Morag 334 8883

Mothers of Sexually Abused Children (MOSAC)
PO Box 1008
EH8 7TH

A self-help group offering friendship and support. Meetings held on a regular basis in the evenings.

Nucleus
39 Broughton Place
556 8066

Support services for families of children with special needs. Counselling, information support groups and informal contact. Curiosity Club on Sat am for siblings and Drop-in at the Engine Shed (See Eating Out p76)

Parents Forever (Scotland)
333 1166
Meetings, 226 McLeod St
1st Mon and 3rd Thur each month, 7.30-9.30

A self-help group providing advice, information and support to non-custodial parents having difficulty in maintaining contact with their children.

The Pastoral Foundation
12 Chamberlain Rd
447 0876

Counselling is available for individuals and couples on a wide range of problems and difficulties. Open to all, irrespective of beliefs on an ability-to-pay basis.

Prisoners' Wives and Families Society
254 Caledonian Rd
London W1
0171-278 3981

Scottish Down's Syndrome Association
158/160 Balgreen Rd
313 4225
467 1172 Linda Scott

Aims to make contact with parents of children with Down's Syndrome as soon as possible after birth, to offer help and encouragement, particularly through the early years. Organises a parent and toddler group and provides information on research, facilities, meetings, etc.

Scottish Society for Autistic Children
Chief Executive Donald J Liddell
Hilton House
Alloa Business Centre
The Whins
Alloa
Clackmannanshire
FK10 3SA
0259 720044

Stepfamilies of Scotland
01383 622109 24hr helpline

Offers support and advice for parents and step-parents.

Simpson House Drug Project
52 Queen St
225 1054

Mon-Fri 9-5 appointment only.

FREE and confidential counselling service to drug users, friends and families.

Wellspring
13 Smith's Pl
5536660

Provides psychotherapy and counselling service. Fees payable on sliding scale according to circumstances.

WOMEN'S AID ORGANISATIONS

Edinburgh Women's Aid
97 Morrison St
229 1419

Offers information, counselling and refuge to women and their children.

Rape Crisis Centre
PO Box 120
MLO Brunswick Rd EH7 5EX
556 9437 (Answerphone out of office hrs)

Information and support for women who have been raped or sexually assaulted. Run by women for women.

Scottish Women's Aid
National Office
13/9 North Bank St
225 3321

Shakti Women's Aid
12 Picardy Pl
557 4010
10-4

Offers advice, support and safe accommodation to black women and their children who are being maltreated by their partners/husbands and/or families.

Health Care Facilities

This chapter describes resources available in Edinburgh for family health care; maternity and paediatric hospital facilities; and lists contacts for advice and assistance with specific problems. We have checked as well as we could that all the organisations mentioned, many of which are charities with volunteer staff, are active and, wherever possible, we have given a local address and phone number.

EMERGENCIES

If your child is in need of medical attention you should contact your local GP's surgery.

GP Phone Number

....

If you feel it is urgent dial 999 or go straight to

Royal Hospital for Sick Children
Sciennes Rd
Hospital Phone Number 536 0000

Useful addresses:

Lothian Health Board
148 Pleasance
536 9000

Lothian Health Council
21 Torphichen St
229 6605

GENERAL PRACTITIONER (GP) SERVICES

If you are new to Edinburgh and wish to register with a doctor, you can receive a list of names and addresses from Lothian Health Board or Lothian Health Council (numbers given previously). The information is also available at Capital Information Points, *see* Sources of Information p206.

If you wish to **change your doctor**, you may do so simply by registering with your prospective doctor. If you do not have your medical card, you will be given a form to complete. If you have difficulty in finding a doctor to accept you as a patient, contact the Health Board which has an obligation to find you a GP.

ALTERNATIVE MEDICINE

Most of these services are offered privately by individual practitioners who charge a fee for consultations and treatment. Your GP may be able to refer you to an alternative medicine specialist or you can approach one yourself. Some contacts are listed below. If you should decide to see a practitioner we would strongly recommend that you check that they are registered with an appropriate professional body and that they adhere to their code of practice.

British Reflexology Association
Monks Orchard
Whitbourne

Worcestershire WRG 5RB
01886 21207

Council for Acupuncture
179 Gloucester Pl
London NW1 6DX
0171 724 5756

Council for Complementary and Alternative Medicine
179 Gloucester Pl
London NW1 6DX
0171 724 9103

List of associations holding registers of practitioners in acupuncture, chiropractic, homoeopathy, medical herbalism, naturopathy and osteopathy. Send ú1 and SAE.

Edinburgh Natural Health Centre
11 Western Ter
313 5434
Mon-Sat 9-6

Acupuncture, Chinese Herbal Medicine, Aromatherapy, Counselling for Adults and Children, Homoeopathy, Nutrition, Osteopathy, Reflexology, Shiatsu. FREE initial consultation for guidance if requested. Courses and Lectures. Consultation by appointment.

General Council and Register of Naturopaths
Frazer House
6 Netherhall Gdns
Camden NW3 5AR
0181 531 0055

General Council and Register of Osteopaths
56 London St
Reading
Berkshire RG1 4SQ
01734 576585

Glovers Pharmacy
18 West Maitland St
225 3161

Mon-Fri 8-5.30; Sat 9-1

Homoeopathic consultations and remedies available. Also mail order service.

Glasgow Homoeopathic Hospital
1000 Great Western Rd
Glasgow
0141 339 0382
Outpatient referrals to above address
0141-334 9800
Homoeopathic treatment is available on the NHS here. You must be referred to the hospital by a letter from your own GP and you will then be sent an appointment.

British Homoeopathic Association
27a Devonshire St
London W1N 1RJ
0171-935 2163

Supplies lists of medical doctors practising homoeopathy (send SAE). Publishes and sells books, bi-monthly magazine.

Society of Homoeopaths
2 Artizan Rd
Northampton NN1 4HU
01604 21400

Publishes 'Register of Homoeopaths', a list of qualified and experienced homoeopaths who are not medical practitioners. All have taken at least a 4 yr part-time course in homoeopathy.

Napier D & Sons
18 Bristo Pl
225 5542, 220 3981
Mon 10-5.30; Tues-Sat 9-5.30

Herbal remedies, health food supplies, vitamins etc in shop. Consultations in herbal medicine, osteopathy, acupuncture, aroma-therapy, homoeopathy and psychology.

Homoeopathic Baby/Children's

Clinic Wed 9-11. No appointment necessary. £5/consultation.

Maternity Units

This section is intended to be a general guide to facilities available in Edinburgh; for more detailed information or if you have a complaint contact the Lothian Health Council, who will be happy to discuss any aspect of hospital facilities.

There are 3 local maternity units:

Eastern General Hospital
Seafield St
536 7000

Simpson Memorial Maternity Pavilion
Lauriston Pl
536 1000

St John's Hospital at Howden
Howden Rd W
Livingston
01506 419666

Antenatal Care

As soon as you think you are pregnant you should visit your GP. Usually you will be asked to choose where you would like to have your baby. Basic facts to bear in mind are your preference and comfort, closeness to home, your medical history, the consultants' policies, hospital facilities and the size of the maternity unit. The Eastern General is a smaller unit than the Simpson or St John's. A mother's requests will be met (circumstances permitting) in all of the units.

Antenatal Appointments

Unfortunately there are sometimes delays at hospital antenatal clinics. During your appointment a *creche* may be available for young children but check with the hospital as times may vary.

Antenatal Classes

You will be offered the opportunity to attend antenatal classes provided free by each hospital. Classes to prepare you for labour are usually held in the later weeks of pregnancy but early pregnancy classes may be available (check at your first antenatal appointment). Parentcraft classes are provided at all hospitals. Local clinics and health centres sometimes offer classes organised by Health Visitors and Community Midwives (sometimes with a *creche*).

Non-NHS classes are also available in Edinburgh from:

Birth Rights
Yvonne Baginsky
2 Forth St
557 0960

Nadine Edwards
Scottish Birth Teachers Association
229 6259

Wkly classes including stretching for active birth, information and discussion. £4/class. Reductions available.

Trisha Harbord
31 Starbank Rd
552 1411

Learning the Alexander Technique can help you take care of your back

255

during and after pregnancy (see 'The Alexander Technique Birth Book' by Ilana Machover and Johnathon Drake). Introductory workshops and individual lessons.

The National Childbirth Trust
Stockbridge Health Centre,
1 India Pl
225 9191
Mon-Fri 9 - 12

Antenatal Classes: Couples Course, £72; Mothers Course, £55; Refresher Course, £30; give parents the chance to discuss and to become informed about all aspects of pregnancy, birth and life with a new baby. Relaxation, breathing techniques, massage and different birth positions are practised and explained enabling parents to approach the birth confidently. Venues vary. Concessionary fee available.

Breastfeeding education is included as part of the antenatal class package and support continues postnatally. Postnatal support groups operate locally where mums can meet for a chat to give and gain support and friendship.
See p258.

Antenatal Exercise Classes
See Activities for Parents p166 for details of centres offering classes.

Antenatal Information

International Active Birth Centre
55 Dartmouth Pk Rd
London N45 1SL
0171 267 3006

Preparation for birth which emphasises self-responsibility, self-help and natural healing. Will provide a list of local teachers if you send a SAE.

Association for Improvements in the Maternity Services (AIMS)
Nadine Edwards
40 Leamington Ter
229 6259

Campaigning group which provides a quarterly journal and leaflets as well as information to parents about all aspects of maternity care including choices in maternity care and home birth.

Maternity Alliance
15 Britannia St
London WC1X 9JN
0171 837 1273

Campaigns for the rights of mothers, fathers and babies. Send SAE for leaflets.

Home Confinement

You may of course choose to have your baby at home instead of in a hospital. However, very few GPs offer home deliveries. If you want a home delivery and your GP is unable to be involved, contact the Nursing Officer in charge of Community Midwifery Services at the Simpson.

Edinburgh and Lothian Homebirth Support Group
Chris
451 5124

Offers information and support for parents considering home birth.

REGISTRATION OF BIRTH

The hospital notifies the Lothian Health Board of the birth of your baby, in addition, a mother or her husband must register your baby's birth with a Registrar of Births,

Marriages and Deaths within 21 days. If you are not married then the baby's mother and father need to register the birth if you want the baby to have the father's surname. The Registrar can advise you on this point. Your hospital, midwife or health visitor will know which office you should contact. You will be given a Birth Certificate for your baby which you may need to produce for various purposes (such as claiming Child Benefit).

POSTNATAL SUPPORT AND NEW BABIES

Community Midwives visit you at home after the birth of your baby (and will attend the delivery if you have a home confinement). If you go home early they will visit every day until the baby is 10 days old (or for longer if there are any problems).

Health Visitors

Health Visitors are Nurses with special training in all aspects of family health, and particularly that of children and older people. Usually they are associated with a GP practice or community clinic but work closely with other health care professonals. Generally they will use their knowledge of child development, behaviour and health to help with any advice or reassurance you need no matter how serious or trivial you may think your problems are. In addition your health visitor should be a valuable source of local knowledge and will be able to provide lists of registered child minders and nurseries; although they cannot reccomend one in particular they may be able to put you in touch with someone using that service. A Health visitor will vist you on the 11th day after the birth of your baby. Regular contact is maintained through home visits, visits to the baby clinic and by telephone during working hours. He or she will monitor your baby's development and growth through developmental assessments, weighing and hearing tests and will also guide you through immunisation. Your Health Visitor will help with problems up until the age of 5 (when the school nurse takes over responsibilty) covering a wider range of areas such as sleep problems, speech therapy referrals, crying babies etc. You do not have to have a health visitor, although one will automatically be assigned to you, but you may need to sign a form confirming it is your wish not to have this help. If you are not happy with the relationship you have with your Health Visitor you can approach another who can advise you on how to change. It is worth mentioning that Health Visitors are also concerned about the health and welfare of parents. Health Visiotors often run clinics and support groups for first-time mothers, breast feeding support, well men, well women, etc.

Sometimes the best support comes from other people in your situation.

Some parent and toddler groups have 'baby groups' attached (see Pre-School Play and Education p91) and the NCT arrange groups for parents to get together (see below for phone no).

The National Childbirth Trust
Edinburgh Office
225 9191
Mon-Fri 9 - 12
Offers extensive postnatal support in

the form of local groups which meet on a regular basis. If you go to NCT antenatal classes your name will be given to your local group representative who should contact you around the time your baby is due, if not before. She will give you details of local meetings and may be able to advise you of who to contact if you have any specific problems. The NCT Office will tell you who your local group representative is if you are not an NCT member. You are welcome to join a Postnatal Support Group, even if you have not been to NCT antenatal classes. Activities include coffee mornings or afternoons, evening talks, fundraising events, working mothers group, picnics, local newsletter etc. Annual membership currently costs £15. Members receive the quarterly magazine 'New Generation'.

See Antenatal Classes p256.

Caesarean Support Network
Sheila Tunstall
2 Hurst Pk Dr
Huyton
Liverpool
L36 1TF
0151-480 1184

Friendly, practical, medical advice. Emotional support to those that have had or may need a caesarean delivery. Factsheets, booklets, newsletters available.

Children First (RSSPCC)
Melville House
Family Resource Centre
41A Polwarth Ter
337 8539/0 Day (Night 337 4891)

Drop in centre for parents with children under 5. A worker facilitated group for women with at least one child under five years. The group aims to alleviate isolation and encourage friendships. Also to look at alternative ways of coping with problems, practical and emotional, encourage growth of confidence and self esteen and help to reduce stress and anxiety.

Tuesdays 12.30-2.30

Homelink
Irene Hannah
664 9880 or 226 31525
or c/o Gilmerton Centre
664 2335

Individual one-to-one support for isolated mothers

MAMA (Meet-a-Mum Association)
Mrs Briony Hallam
14 Willis Rd
Croydon
Surrey
CR0 2XX
0181 665 0357

Self-help groups and one to one contacts throughout the UK for mothers of new babies and small children. Information and support for postnatal depression.Please send SAE for information/local contacts.

Edinburgh Twin Club
Dot Lynch
334 3070

Twin and Multiple Birth Association (TAMBA)
PO Box 30
Little Sutton
South Wirral L66 1TH
0151-348 0020

Supports families with twins, triplets,or more through local Twins Clubs and specialist support groups.

TAMBA Twinline is a confidential listening support and information service Tel: 01732 868000 weekdays 6-11pm; weekends 10am-11pm. It is run by highly trained volunteers who are all parents of twins or triplets.

Parent-Link Scotland

Local contact: Josephine McLeod
332 0893

Parent-Link offers regular meetings for support and new ideas for getting on better with your children. 'We believe that being a parent is the most important job we will ever do and we all need support and encouragement with this task'.

Postnatal Exercise Classes

See Activities for Parents p166.

You should have had your postnatal check up before going to any form of exercise class. If you do see postnatal exercise classes advertised the teacher should be qualified to take such classes or they may be harmful. Community education, health or sports clubs may also offer suitable classes.

The National Childbirth Trust

May be able to offer postnatal exercise classes. Phone to check.

See Antenatal Classes p256.

FEEDING
Breastfeeding

Midwives will encourage and help you to establish breastfeeding before you leave hospital. Ask for any free leaflets available in hospital, they may have reassuring advice when you are on your own at home. The Community Midwife or Health Visitor will help afterwards. The following organisations have a specific interest in helping mothers to breastfeed and will provide mother-to-mother support as well as very good advice.

The National Childbirth Trust

Edinburgh Office
225 9191
Mon-Fri 9 -12

Provides information, support and encouragement through its network of Breastfeeding Counsellors who have all breastfed their own children and been through intensive training. They can also arrange the hire of electric breastpumps. A Breast-feeding Counsellor is usually available at the NCT office each morning. Any mother with a query about breastfeeding can call into the NCT office.

Association of Breastfeeding Mothers

131 Mayow Rd
London SE26
0181 778 4769

Counselling service through support groups offering advice from personal experience.

La Leche League

BM 3424
London WC1N 3XX
0171-242 1278 (24 hrs)

Self-help group providing information and support to women who wish to breastfeed their babies. Compre-hensive literature and discussion groups. Send large SAE for information. No local contact at the moment.

LactAid

Sue Torrance
Health Help for All
22b McLeod Street
346-8495

LactAid is a group of women eager to help and support those who are breastfeeding their babies. They are able to offer support on the phone, by visiting or offering support in a group setting. All counsellors have breastfed their babies and have a variety of experience.

Bottle feeding

Low income families may be eligible for free baby milk. Tokens are given which can be exchanged at health clinics, or, increasingly, at local chemists for baby milk formula. Your health visitor will be able to give you details should you require them.

POSTNATAL DEPRESSION

Conctact your GP, Health Visitor or one of the organisations listed below for support and advice.

Local support groups are occasionally set up for mothers with postnatal depression and your health visitor may be able to advise you.

Association for Postnatal Illness
25 Jerdan Place
Fulham
London SW6 18E
0171 386 0868

Counselling, literature and local support. Send large SAE.

Simpson House Family Counselling Centre
52 Queen St
225 1054/6028

Offers individual counselling to mothers and fathers, and also a weekly group meeting, with *creche* and child care provided, every Mon morning. Phone the centre (Rosemary Dempster) or speak to your GP or health visitor.

See also Welfare p251.

CHILDREN'S HOSPITALS AND WARDS

Royal Hospital for Sick Children
Sciennes Rd
536 0000

Excellent atmosphere and obviously orientated to the needs of children in all areas of the hospital. Clinics, waiting areas, and accident and emergency department are all well stocked with toys and books etc. Extremely understanding staff and excellent reputation.

A resident area is provided for parents wishing to stay with children in hospital. It has 14 beds with sitting room, kitchen and bathroom facilities available. This area is obviously apart from the wards themselves but parents can be contacted at anytime during the day or night to be with a distressed child or for feeding etc. 'Z' beds and reclining chairs can be provided if the parents would prefer to stay beside a child overnight.

No specific visiting hours — parents are welcome at any time. In surgical areas, depending on procedure or operation, the Ward Sister will discuss with the parents what is best for them and the child after the operation. Brothers and sisters are welcome to visit but obviously adequate control and discipline must be exercised. Friends of the child in hospital may also visit, at the discretion of the Ward Sister. Always phone and check.

'Play ladies' are present in all wards except the neonatal ward. Each play lady has a team of volunteers who come on different days to help her.

Playcentre at 11 Millerfield Pl, for children of parents visiting the hospital, is open 9-4.30, Mon-Fri.

RIE NHS Trust

City Hospital
Ward 15 — Children's Ward, in Regional Infectious Diseases Unit
Ward 17 — Out Patient's Clinic, in Regional Infectious Diseases Unit
51 Greenbank Dr
536 6000

Friendly staff. Parents are welcome to stay with their child.A 'Z' bed is provided beside the child's bed for those who stay overnight. There is a parents sitting room beside Ward 15 and parents may use the Visitors' Tearoom or the staff dining room for snacks and meals.

Visiting is open for parents not staying, but no brothers or sisters under the age of 14 may visit because of the risk of cross-infection.

A full-time play co-ordinator, and Hospital Play Specialists play with the chldren all day in Ward 15 and in the mornings in Ward 17. Out patients clinic.

St John's Hospital at Howden
Howden Rd
Livingston
01506 419666

Increasingly, children from the west of Edinburgh are being admitted here. Children whose parents wish to stay with them are accommodated in the single rooms on the ward. Parents are welcome to stay and 'Z' beds are provided.

There is unrestricted visiting for parents. Siblings are welcome to visit but adequate control is appreciated. Visiting times for other relatives and friends are at the discretion of ward sister.

There is a play room in the ward which is staffed by Play Leaders during the wk and is open at the wkend (nursing staff permitting).

There are also paediatric wards or beds at:

Princess Alexandra Eye Pavilion
Chalmers St
536 3899

Princess Margaret Rose Orthopaedic Hospital
41 Frogston Rd W
445 4123

There are paediatric Outpatient and Day Surgery facilities at:

Western General Hospital
Crewe Rd

Support and Information

The Friends of the Sick Children's Hospital
Royal Hospital for Sick Children
Sciennes Rd

Act to further interests of the child health services in the RHSC.

Action for Sick Children (Scotland)
15 Smith's Pl
553 6553

A charity for all children in hospital and for all adults caring for them. Information for parents with babies in Special Care Units. Useful publications for parents of children going into hospital. Hospital playbox for loan to local playgroups which helps parents to prepare children (3-6 yrs) for a hospital visit (includes toys, books, real medical equipment and mini uniforms).

Play in Scottish Hospitals

15 Smith's Pl
553 2189
Mon-Fri 8.30-12.30

Promotes play for children of all ages in hospitals, clinics and health centres. The Group can help you to prepare your child for a planned hospital admission and advise about appropriate toys and books.

SNIP — Special Needs Information Point

Royal Hospital for Sick Children
Sciennes Rd
(c/o Social Work Department)
536 0000
9.15-10, 12.30-2.15 wkdays
Contact: Shirley Young

Operates during clinics in the Out-Patients Dept. Information for parents, carers and professionals about children with special needs.

DENTAL CARE

All dentists providing NHS care can be found on the list held by the Lothian Health Board (see p253), or at your post office or library.

Listen to recommendations by friends and neighbours when choosing a dentist, although what may suit them may not suit you. The majority of children go to a family dentist for treatment but in certain circumstances your child could be treated by the Community Dental Service.

Community dentists have a responsibility to provide dental health education in nurseries and schools. They also monitor the dental health of children through a screening programme.

Mothers are entitled to FREE dental treatment throughout pregnancy and until the baby's 1st birthday.

Children under 18 are also entitled to FREE dental care. It is recommended that the first check up is at about 2 yrs, but of course you may consult a dentist earlier.

The average concentration of fluoride in Lothian's water supply does not exceed 0.2 parts per million, too low an amount to benefit the teeth. Dentists may recommend that children take fluoride drops or tablets which are available FREE from many dentists or at baby clinics. When giving your child fluoride supplements, make sure that only a pea-sized amount of fluoride toothpaste is used on the brush.

Community Dental Service

Duncan St Dental Centre
16 Duncan St
667 7114

Provide information about all aspects of dental health. Happy to provide leaflets and advice for projects at nurseries etc.

British Dental Health Foundation

Eastlands Court
St Peters Rd
Coventry CV21 3QP

Provides excellent information leaflets (for a charge).

PROBLEM SOLVING

Most of us need advice, information or support at some time in the young lives of our children. This list is not exhaustive but may provide a starting point to help solve your problem. Your health visitor may know of local contacts and the

National Centre for Play, 312 6001 (*see* Pre-School Play and Education p120), maintains a comprehensive list of useful addresses for people with special needs.

We have checked as far as possible that all the groups listed here are operational.

See also Welfare p249 and Women's Groups p158.

SNIP — Special Needs Information Point
536 0000 Contact Shirley Young

See Children's Hospitals and Wards p262.

National **Asthma** Campaign
Providence House
Providence Pl
London N1 0NT
0171-226 2260
Helpline: 0345 010203 Mon-Fri 1-9 (charged as local call)

Scottish Development Manager — Pandora Summerfield 0786 449440

Scottish National Federation for the Welfare of the **Blind**
38/39 Ardconnel St
Inverness IV2 3HB
01463 233662

Co-ordinates organisations concerned with blind people in Scotland.

Craigentinny Health Project
Craigentinny Community Centre
Loaning Rd
661 8188 Ann Brown

CHP is a community mental health project for North-East Edinburgh. Runs and supports a variety of groups and courses for people who recognise they have emotional and well-being difficulties. **Creche** always available during group times.

National **Eczema** Society
163 Eversholt St
London NW1 1BU
0171 388 4097

There is no local contact at the moment but the Glasgow co-ordinator is happy to help

Mrs Janette Stafford
0141 942 6092

Health Search Scotland
Lothian Health Promotion Department
Resource Centre
61 Grange Loan
EH9 2ER
662 4661 contact Phil Horne 1-4.30 Mon, Tue-Fri 9.30-4.30

Health Search Scotland is able to provide information about groups relating to specific medical conditions and details of more general services that are available in particular local areas. Information is given direct to enquirers by phone or sent as a print out from the database. Database records can be supplied in a number of formats, and information held is updated regularly.

Health Help for All
22b McLeod Street
346 8495
A local community health project based in the Gorgie/Dalry area. It aims to make health information accessible to the community and to enable people to help themselves in their everyday lives.

The National Childbirth Trust

INFORMED CHOICE

"The National Childbirth Trust offers information and support in pregnancy, childbirth and early parenthood and aims to enable every parent to make informed choices. The NCT is working towards ensuring that it's services, activities and membership are fully accessible to everyone."

Index

A & D Hire & DIY Garden Centre 58
Aberdour 196
Aberlady 190
Abracadabra 89
access programmes see adult education
Action for Sick Children Scotland 261
Active Birth Centre, International 256
activities
 for children 135-153
 for parents 154-173
Acupuncture,Council for 254
Adams Children's Wear 14, 25
Adoption Counselling Service see Birthlink
Adult Basic Education 161
adult education 161-166
Adult Learning Project 161
adventure playgrounds 218
Advice Shop Lothian Regional Council 247
AFASIC see Association for Speech Impaired Children 249
AIMS (Association for Improvements in the Maternity Services) 256
Ainslie Park Leisure Centre 83, 139, 144-145, 166
 Cafeteria 145
airlines 243
airport see Edinburgh Airport
air travel 242-245
 car seats, use of 244
 nappy-changing and 244
 pregnancy and 244
 reservations 242
Aitken & Niven 2, 20, 23
Alamo Rent A Car 237
Al-Anon 249
Allam, Pamela 138
Allan Ltd, G W 45
Allan Cycles, Jocky 33
Almond, River 221-222
Almond Valley Heritage Centre 193
Almondell Country Park 193
alternative medicine 253-255
 Council for Complementary and 254
Amateur Swimming Association 143
animal handling 192, 193, 195, 196, 200, 202
animals in the city 182-185
annual events 200

ante-natal care 255
 appointments 255
 classes 255
 exercise classes see Activities for Parents
 information 256
Applecart Nannies 124
Argos 2, 25, 27, 35
Arkadia 89
Arnold Clark Hire Drive 237
art classes 135
Art, College of 163
art galleries
 City Art Centre 175
 Fruitmarket 135, 175
 Modern Art, Scottish National Gallery of 175
 National Gallery of Scotland 175
 Portrait, Scottish National Portrait 175
Arts Outreach Team 206
Asda 11, 14, 27
Assembly Rooms 7, 187
Association
 of Breastfeeding Mothers 259
 of Cycle Traders 33
 for Improvements in the Maternity Services (AIMS) 256
 for Postnatal Illness 260
 for Speech Impaired Children (AFASIC) 249
 for Separated and Divorced Catholics 249
Asthma Campaign, National 263
Autistic Children, Scottish Society for 251
Babybusters 124
Baby Care (clothes) 53
baby clothes 14
baby equipment see nursery equipment 25
Baby Equipment Hire 58
Baby Shop 15
babysitting circles 125
Baggins 15, 56
Bairnecessities 43
Balerno Children's Book Group 39
Balerno High School 150, 151, 155
Balgreen Library 129
Ball, Ruth 47
ballet classes see dance
Ballet School Supplies 21
Bargain Books 43
barges
 Edinburgh Canal Centre 185
 Pride of Belhaven 86

 Santa trips 204
Barnton Hotel 79
Bauermeisters Booksellers 39
Bavelaw Bird Reserve 227
Bayne and Duckett 23
beaches
 Cramond 223
 Gullane 191
 John Muir Country Park 190
 North Berwick 191
 Portobello 227
 St Andrews 197
 Seacliff 191
 Silver Sands 196
 Yellowcraig 190
Beechwood and Bike Park 196
Beecraigs Country Park 193
Beaverbank Playground 211
Bell Photography 49
Bennets Hire Centre 59
Benetton see United Colors of Benetton
Bereavement Care, Cruse 249
Bewleys 62
BhS 3, 15, 27, 62
 Patio Restaurant 62
bicycle shops 31-36
Biggar 197
bike park, Stirling 196
Bird of Prey Centre, Edinburgh 192
birthday parties 83-90
 at home 87
 catering and cakes 88
 entertainment 89-90
 venue 83
birth
 announcement 49
 certificate 257
 registration 256
Birthlink 249
Birth Rights 255
Birth Teachers Association, Scottish 255
Blackford Hill 220
Blackford Pond 220
Blackhall Library 129
Blairdrummond Safari and Leisure Park 196
Blazing Saddles 34
Bloomiehall Public Park, Juniper Green 217
Blooming Kids 53
Blooming Marvellous 53
Blues 36
boat trips
 canal 185, 204, 230
 Deep Sea World 194
 Inchcolm Island 194
Body Shop 14
Bo'ness and Kinneil Railway 196

House 16
Burdiehouse and Southhouse
    Community Centre 155
Burger King 63, 79
Burntisland 196
bus travel 237-239
    airport 244
    bus station 238
    fares 238
    frequencies 239
    information 238
    open top 185
    rules for under 5's 238
    SMT 238
    tickets 238, 239
    Traveline 238
Butterflies (clothes hire) 57
Butterfly and Insect World,
    Edinburgh 192
Caesarean Support Network
    258
Cafe Rioz 63
Cafe St James 63
Cafe Select and Bar 243
Cake and Chocolate Shop 88
cakes for celebrations 88
Calderwood Country Park 194
Caledonian Hotel 63
Calton Centre 166
Calton Hill 179-180, 204
Camera Obscura 177
Cameo Cinema 188
Cameron House Community
    Centre 133, 155
Cameron Toll Shopping Centre 7
    The Terrace 78
Cammo Estate 221
Campbell and Stillwell 40
Canal, Union
    barge trips 185, 230
    Centre 185
    Society 204
C & A 3, 13, 16, 36
cannon, 1 o'clock 182
Capital Information Point 127,
    206
car
    hire 237
    parking 235-236
    safety 236-237
    seats 236
    seats on aircraft 243-244
Carrickvale Community
    Education Office 155, 167
Cartoon Hire 89
Cash's Name Tapes 55
Castle Inn, Dirleton 190
castles
    Craigmillar 180
    Edinburgh 180
    Holyrood House, The
    Palace of 181
    Lauriston 181, 201

Linlithgow Palace 193
Scone Palace 199
Stirling 196
catering 88
Celebration Books 55
Celebration Cakes 88
cemeteries 222
Central Cycle Hire 57
Central Library 129
Central Region trips 196
Central Scotland Ballet School
    136
Centre for Continuing Education
    162
CFUF 206
Charities Hypermarket 50, 204
Charities Week, Students' 201
charity shops 43
chemists 44-45
childcare
    at home 122
    organisations 123-124
    professional 124
Child Carers Association,
    Lothian 123
Child Friendly Edinburgh viii-ix
Childhood, Museum of 177
childminders 121-122
Childminding, A Parents Guide
    to 122
Childminding Association,
    Scottish 122, 124
Children, Action for Sick 261
Children First (RSSPCC) 249, 258
Children's Book Group
    Edinburgh 39
    Balerno 39
children's
    Book of the Month Club 52
    books 38-43, 52
    Book Week 204
    centres 123
    clothes 14-19
    Festival 201
    Foot Health Register 23
    hospitals and wards 260-
    261
    parties at home 87
    shoes 23-25
    Traffic Club 234
child seats
    bicycle 32
    car 236
    on aircraft 243-244
Child's Garden of Verse, A 39
Child's Play 56
Chiquito 73
Christmas lights 204
Christmas Shoppers' Creches 50
Church of Scotland Counselling
    Service 249
Churchill Theatre 187
cinemas 188-189

Circles Coffee House 63
Citizen's Advice Bureaux 246
Citizen's Rights Office 246
City Art Centre 175
    Cafe 64
City
    Cafe 64
    Cycles 34
    Hospital 261
    Observatory 180
Clambers 151
Clan House 16, 20
Clarks 24
classes
    adult 155-158, 161-166
    children 135-153
Clermiston Park 216
Clermiston Tower 222
clocks see telling the time
Clothkits 52
Cloth Shop, The 22
Cloth Shop Too! The 22
clothes
    children's 14-19
    hiring 57
    mail order 52-54
Clovenstone Community
    Education Centre 155
Coatbridge 198
Colinton Mains Park 214
Colinton Dell 231
College of Art 163
Colorfoto Ltd 49
Committee for Under Fives
    (CFUF) 206
Commodore Hotel, The 79
Commonwealth Pool, Royal 86,
    148, 172
Community
    Care Registration and
    Inspection Service 121
    Dental Service 262
    Information Officer 206
    Leadership Development,
    Foundation for 162
Compassionate Friends 249
Comprehensive Accredited
    Lawyer Mediators CALM
    249
complementary medicine see
    alternative medicine 253-
    255
Conservatory Coffee Shop 75
Contact a Family 249
Contact Point Drop-In Centre
    158
Co-op 6, 12, 25, 27, 35
Cornerstone Cafe, The 64
Corstorphine
    Fair 201
    Hill 222
    Leisure Centre 167
    Park Playground 216

Pram Centre 16, 25
Cosmetics To Go 55
COT see Craigmillar
  Opportunities Trust
Cot Death Support Group,
  Edinburgh and Lothian 250
Cotton-On 52
Council
  for Acupuncture 254
  for Complementary and
  Alternative Medicine 254
  and Register of
  Naturopaths, General 254
  and Register of Osteopaths,
  General 254
Counselling Service
  Church of Scotland 249
  Lothian Marriage 250
Countryside Ranger Service 167
country houses 195
  Dalmeny House 223
  Hopetoun House 194
country parks
  Almondell 193
  Beecraigs 193
  Calderwood 194
  Dalkeith 192
  Hillend 226
  John Muir 190
  Lochore Meadows 196
  Vogrie 193
  Yellowcraig 190
country places 219-232
Craigentinny Health Project 263
Craig, Jimmy 89
Craighead, Nina 141
Craiglockhart Sports Centre 84,
  139, 167
Craiglogan Pharmacy 45
Craigmillar
  Castle 180
  Festival 201
  Library 129
  Opportunities Trust (COT)
  162
  toddler playground 215
Craigmount Community Centre
  155, 167
Craigroyston Community Centre
  156
Craigroyston Community High
  School 133, 156
Craigtoun Park, St Andrews 197
Cramond 222
  Brig 79
  Esplanade 223
  Ferry 223
  Island 222
  River Almond Walkway
  223
  School of Ballet 136
Crannog Seafood Restaurant 64
Crawfords Country Kitchen 64

Creche Co-op, Edinburgh 124
creches while shopping 50
Croft Mill 55
Crook of Devon Fish Farm 198
Cruelty to Children, see Children
  First (RSSPCC)
Crumstane Farm 195
Cruse Bereavement Care 249
Cry-sis Society, Scottish 247
CTC see Cyclists' Touring Club
Cupar 196
Cycles Williamson 34
cycle tracks 228
cycling 235
  safety, child 235
Cyclists' Touring Club 235
Dalkeith Country Park 192
Dalmeny House 223
Dalmeny St Park 211
Dalry Swim Centre 145, 168
Dance Base 138
dance classes, children 135-138
Dancewear 21
dancewear shops 21
Davison Menswear 57
day care 123
day centres 123
Dean Park Playground, Balerno
  217
Debenhams 3-4, 16
  Freebody's Restaurant 65
Deep Pan Pizza Co 73
Deep Sea World 197
Deer Centre 196
Delifrance 65
De Niro's Ristorante 76
dental care 262
Dental
  Service, Community 262
  Health Foundation 262
Department of Social Security
  (DSS) 246
department stores 2-7
depression, postnatal 260
Derwent, Lavinia 39
Digger 27
Dimple Photos 49
Directory of Local Services, The
  Lothian 246
Dirleton 190
Disability Scotland 250
Disabled People, Lothian
  Coalition of 163
Discovery, RRS, Dundee 198
Disney store 16, 27
Dobbies Garden Centre 192
  Garden Tearoom 192
doctors 253
Dog and Cat Home, The
  Edinburgh 182
doll repair 27-31
Dolls' Hospital, Geraldine's of
  Edinburgh 28

Dollycare 53
Dominion Cinema 188
Dorling Kindersley Family
  Library 56
Dorothy Perkins 13
Dowie, Sheana 47
Down's Syndrome Association,
  Scottish 251
Dress Sense 43
dressmaking supplies 21-23
Drummond Community High
  School 151, 156, 168
Drummond Toy Library 132
Duddingston Loch 224
Dumbiedykes Road playground
  215
Dunbar 191
  Splash Leisure Pool 191
Dundee 198
Duns 195
Early Learning Centre 28, 31, 43
  mail order 54
East Fortune 191
  market 191
  Museum of Flight 191
East Lothian trips 190-191
East Sands Leisure Centre 197
Easter eggs 200, 201
Eastern General Hospital 255
eating out 60-82
  birthdays 84
  central Edinburgh 62
  east Edinburgh 73
  north Edinburgh 73
  south Edinburgh 75
  west Edinburgh 79
Eczema Society, National 263
Edge, The 47
Edinburgh Airport 185, 242-243
  baby room 243
  Books Plus 243
  bus services 244
  Cafe Select and Bar 243
  Ginghams Coffee Shop 243
  spectators' gallery 242
  Uppercrust and Bar 243
  taxis 245
Edinburgh
  area map 176
  books about 39
  Bicycle 34
  Bird of Prey Centre 192
  Book Festival 38, 203
  Butterfly and Insect World
  192
  Cab Office 239
  Canal Centre 185
  Capital Story, A 39
  Castle 180
  Central Library 129
  Central Children's Library
  130
  Central Map vi-vii

Children's Book Group 39
Creche Co-op 124
Dance Centre 138
Dog and Cat Home 182
Festival 203
Festival Cavalcade 203
Festival Fringe 203
Festival Theatre 187
Freedom Ticket 239
guides to 206
Herald and Post 205
Highland Games 203
In Depth 3D Show 180
Information Centre 174, 205
Information Pack 206
and Lothian Cot Death Support Group 250
and Lothian Home Birth Support Group 256
Natural Health Centre 254
Sitters 124
Twin Club 258
University see University of Edinburgh
Walking in, and the Pentlands 225
Women's Aid 252
Women's Training Centre 162
Zoo 84, 182-183
Edinburgh District Council
Arts Outreach Team 206
Leisure Management Unit 170
Play Development Officer 209
Recreation Dept 202
Training Scheme 162
Education, pre-school 91-125
Education Dept see Lothian Regional Council
Education, Moray House Institute of 163
Edwards, Nadine 255, 256
Eglinton Hotel, The 82
Egnell breast pump hire 58
Elliott Sports Ski Shop 36, 59
Ellersly House Hotel, The 79, 82
Embroidery Shop, The 22
embroidery supplies, see make your own
emergencies 253
Emergency Mums 125
Employment Service Job Centre 162
Engine Shed Cafe 76
entertainment 89
Epilepsy Association of Scotland 250
Etam 13

Evening News 205
Fairways Heavy Horse Centre 199
Falcon Gardens playground 214
family
doctors 253
Fund 250
MediationScotland 250
Fairs (galas)
Corstorphine 201
Grassmarket 203
farms
Crook of Devon Fish Farm 198
Crumstane 195
Gorgie City 184
Jedforest Deer and Farm Park 195
Fat Sams 65
Fauldburn Park playground 216
Festival
Book 203
Cavalcade 203
Children's 201
Craigmillar 201
Edinburgh International 203
Environment 201
Fringe 203
Fringe Sunday 203, 224
Gorgie/Dalry 201
Jazz 203
Meadows 201
Portobello Community 202
Puppet and Animation 201
Science 201
Scotland Yard 202
Stockbridge 202
Storytelling 204
Theatre 187
Fife trips 196-197
Figgate Park 224
Filling Station 65
Filmhouse 188
Finishing Touch 22, 57, 87
firework displays 204
First Needs 53
Firth Hairdressing, Greig 48
Flight, Museum of 191
floral clock 182
Flotterstone Inn 192
flumes 148
Foam Centre, The 26
food, mail order 54
Foot Health Register, Childrens 23
Forbuoys 28
Forecourt Leisure 168
Leo's 151-152
Pitt Stop, The 168
Fort Community Wing 156
Fort Fun 84
Fort Saughton 216

Forth Valley Tourist Board 193
Foundation for Community Leadership Development 162
Fountainbridge Library 130
Fowler, Julia 141
Francis, Jon 48
Frasers 4, 13, 16
clock 182
restaurant 65
Freebody's Restaurant 65
Freemans 53
French playgroup, La Petit Ecole 99
Friends of the Sick Children's Hospital 261
Frog Hollow 55
Fruitmarket Gallery 135, 175
fun fairs
Meadows Fun 201, 202
Portobello Fun 152
Gaelic Toddlers 97
Gala days
Leith 201
Northfield/Willowbrae 202
Old Town 202
Oxgangs 202
Prestonfield 202
Ratho Children's 202
galleries see art galleries
GAP 16
Garfunkels 65, 84
Garvald Community Enterprises Ltd 132
Gasworks Museum, Biggar 197
General Practioner (GP) Services 253
Gennaro 66
George Hotel 66
George Square Theatre 187
Geraldine's of Edinburgh 28
gifts 27-31
Gilchrist, Sandy 34
Gilmerton
Community Centre 156
Library 130
Gingerbread 247
Ginghams Coffee Shop 243
Giuliano's 73
Gladstone Court Museum, Biggar 198
Glasgow Homoeopathic Hospital 254
Glasshouse Experience 228
Glenogle Swim Centre 146, 168
Glenvarloch Cres. Playpark 214
Glovers Pharmacy 254
Glowworm 40
Good, Fiona 49
Gordon's Magic & Punch and Judy Show 89
Gorgie City Farm 84, 156, 184
Jemimas Pantry 184

268

Gorgie/Dalry Festival 201
GPs 253
Gracemount Leisure Centre 83,
    139, 169
  cafeteria 169
  playground 214
Granary 66
Granton Information Centre 247
Grapevine 205
Grassmarket Fair 203
Greengables Toy Library 132
Green Tree, The 82
Greyfriar's Bobby
  The Tale of 39
  statue 181
Greyfriars Tolbooth and
    Highland Kirk 180-181
GT Books 40
Guide Friday 185
guidebooks 206
Guide to Leisure for Single
    Parents in Lothian 206
Gullane 143, 191
Gyle Shopping Centre 8
  creche 50, 115
  food court 80
Gym Monkeys 139
gymnastics 138-140
Gymsters 139
Haddington 191
hairdressers 46-48
Hairizons 48
half-term 204
Halfords Superstore 34
Hand-in-Hand 43
Happit 16
Harbord, Trisha 255
Harburn Hobbie Ltd 28
Harrison Park East playground
    214
Haugh Park 216
Hawes Inn, The 80, 82
Hawkes, Tracy 137
Hay Lodge Park, Peebles 195
Haymarket Station 241
Health
  Board, Lothian 253
  Centre, Edinburgh Natural
    254
  care 253
  Council, Lothian 253
  Help for All 263
  Search Scotland 263
  visitors 91, 257
health problems 262-263
Heinz Baby Club 55
Helios Fountain 22, 67
helmets, safety 32
Helping Hands 124
Hendersons 67
Herald and Post, Edinburgh 205
Heriot Watt University 162-163
Heriothill Garage 237

Hermitage of Braid, The 219-
    220
Heron Pharmacy 44
Hertz Rent-a-Car 237
Heinz Baby Club 55
Highland
  Games, Edinburgh 203
  Kirk 180
  Laddie 21, 57
  Show, Royal 202
Hillend Country Park 226
  chairlift 226
Hilton National Hotel 74
hiring
  bicycles 57
  cake tins 57
  car, child seats 58
  clothes 57
  equipment 58
  inflatables 58
  skis 59
  toys 132
  video cameras 59
historic places 179-182
Hogmany celebrations 204
Holiday Care Service 250
Holiday Inn (Garden Court) 80,
    82
Holyrood House, The Palace of
    181
Holyrood Park 224
Home Birth Support Group,
    Edinburgh and Lothian 256
home confinement 256
Homelink 250, 258
Homoeopathic
  Association, British 254
  Baby/Children's Clinic 254
  Hospital, Glasgow 254
  Pharmacy 254
Homoeopaths, Society of 254
Hopetoun House 194
Horizons 48
hospitals
  children's 260-261
  dolls' 28
  homoeopathic 254
  maternity 255
  Play in Scottish 262
Huntly House 177
Ice Rink, Murrayfield 142
ice skating see skating
Inchcolm Island 194
Inch Community Centre 156,
    169
Inch Park 225
independent schools 118
infant schools 119
Infilling, The 76
Infirmary St Swim Centre 146,
    169
inflatables, hiring 58-59
information sources 160, 205

Ingliston
  Royal Highland Show 202
  Sunday market 8
Inn on the Hill 227
Innocent Railway Footpath 225,
    228
Institute of Education, Moray
    House 163
International
  Active Birth Centre 256
  Children's Festival, Scottish
    201
  Festival, Edinburgh 203
Inverleith House 229
Inverleith Park
  Playground 212
  pond 185
Iona Hotel 76, 82
Mohammed Iqbal 45
Irene's 17
Jack Kane Sports Centre 83, 139,
    169
James Thin Bookshp Cafe 71
Jane Goulding School of Dancing
    136
Janettas, St Andrews 197
Jarvie, Frances and Gordon
Jazz Festival 203
Jedburgh 195
Jedforest Deer and Farm Park
    195
Jemima's Pantry 184
Jenners 4, 17, 22, 26, 28, 35, 43,
    67, 87
  Rose St Restaurant 67
Jewel and Esk Valley College 163
Jigsaw World 29
JIIG-CAL Careers Research Centre
    160
John Knox House 177
John Muir Country Park 190
Johnston, David 49
Jolly Babies 44
Jolly Giant Superstore 29, 31, 35
Joppa Quarry Park 215
J R's Toys and Cycles 29
Judith Warren Associates 163
Julie's 88
Juner and Son, T C 237
Junior Jenners see Jenners
Kailzie Gardens, Peebles 195
Kane, Jack — Sports Centre see
    Jack Kane Sports Centre
Kaye, Danny 49
Kay's Bookshop 43
Kennilworth, The 67, 82
Kenning Car Rental 237
Kicks 169
Kids' Stuff 53
kilts 20-21
Kindergym 140
Kings Fabrics 23
Kings Theatre 187

Kinnaird Park 8-9
Kirkcaldy, First Steps in 207
Kirkliston Toy Library 133
Klondyke Garden Centre 75
Klownz 48
knitting supplies see make your
    own 21-23
Koko's 84, 151
    snack bar 151
K Shoes 24
Kwik-fit 237
Kwiksave 11
Lact Aid 259
La Leche League 259
LAC/SLAC see Leisure Access
    Scheme
Lady Nairne Hotel 73
Lanark 198
Lasswade 192
Lasswade High School Centre
    158, 169
    creche 170
late night chemists 45
Laura Ashley 15, 21
Lauriston Castle 181, 201
Lauriston Farm Restaurant 80,
    82
Lazarska, Madam H see Madam
    H Lazarska
Lazio Restaurant 68
LEAD (Linking Education and
    Disability) 160
Lefties 55
Legal Aid Dispensary 247
Leisure Access Scheme (LAC)
    166
leisure activities, adult 166-173
Leisure Management Unit 170,
    206
Leith
    Community Centre 156
    Community Education
    Resource Centre 156, 170
    Gala 201
    Links 212
    Toy Library 133
    Water of, Walkway see
    Water of Leith Walkway
Leith Waterworld 84, 146, 170,
    cafeteria 147
    creche 170
Leo's, Forecourt Leisure 85, 151-
    152
Lewis, John 4-5, 13, 17, 20, 21,
    22, 24, 26, 29, 31, 36, 40,
    67, 88
Liberton Recreation Ground 214
Liberty 21
libraries 126
    Balgreen 129
    Blackhall 129
    Craigmillar 129
    Edinburgh Central 129

Edinburgh Central
    Children's 130
    Fountainbridge 130
    Gilmerton 130
    McDonald Road 130
    Moredun 130
    Muirhouse 130
    Newington 131
    Oxgangs 131
    Portobello 131
    Sighthill 131
    South Queensferry 131
    Stockbridge 131
    toy 132-134
library services
    Audio Service 128
    Ethnic Services 128
    mobile 130
    Youth Services Team 129
Lindsay & Gilmour 45
Linking Education and
    Disability (LEAD) 160
Linlithgow 193
    Palace 193
Lintern, Raymond 49
List, The 205
Little Chef 77
Little Marco's 85, 152
    cafe 152
Littlewoods 5, 17, 68
Livingston 193
Lochend Park 215
Lochore Meadows Country Park
    196
Lo-gy Centre 85, 139
Longstone Community
    Education Centre 170
    creche 170
Lorenzo's 68
Lothian
    and Borders Police Stables
    and Dog-handlers 185
    Childcare Guide 206
    Child Carers Association
    123
    Children 250
    Coalition of Disabled People
    163
    Dance Academy 137
    Directory of Local Services
    206, 246
    Guide to Leisure for Single
    Parents 206
    Health Board 253
    Health Council 253
    Interpreting and Translating
    Service Trust Ltd 247
    Marriage Counselling
    Service 250
    Racial Equality Council 158
    TAP Agency 160
    Victim Support Scheme
    250-251

Lothian Regional Council
    Advice Shop 247
    Dept of Education 119, 160
    Dept of Social Work 91,
    247-248
    Special Education Services
    119
Lothian Region Transport 238
    open top buses 185
    Ridacards 239
    Traveline 238
    Waverley Bridge Ticket
    Centre 238
Lovat, Scott 89
Lower Aisle Restaurant 68
Lullaby 44
Lyceum Theatre, Royal 188
M & Ds Fun Park, Motherwell
    198
McCalls of the Royal Mile 57
McDonald's Restaurant 68, 73,
    80, 85
McDonald Rd Library 130
MacDonald Cycles 35
Mackays 17
McKenzie, Peter 50
McLeod Street Sports Centre 83,
    170
    creche 170
Macpherson Ltd, Hugh 21
Madam H. Lazarska 13
magazines 205
Magic Bob 90
Magic Readers 142
mail order shopping 52-56
Maisie Comes to Morningside
    39
make your own 21-23
Malt Shovel 69, 82
MAMA 258
Mamma's American Pizza Co 69
Manor School of Ballet 137
maps
    Central Edinburgh vi-vii
    Edinburgh area 176
Marco's Leisure Centre 170
    creche 170
    Little Marco's 85, 152
    lounge 152
markets 7-10
Marks and Spencer 5, 11, 17
marriage counselling see
    Welfare
Martin, Jack 90
Maternity Alliance 256
maternity units 255
Maternity Services, Association
    for improvements in 256
maternity wear 12-14
    mail order 53-54
MAVA bras 13
Meadowbank Sports Centre 85,
    152, 171

cafeteria 171
creche 171
Leisure Management Unit 170, 206
Meadowfield Playpark 215
Meadows
    Festival 201
    Playgrounds 213
Meet-A-Mum Association (MAMA) 258
Melvilles Motors 237
Merlin, The 77, 82
Menzies, John 6, 29, 43, 69
MGM Film Centre 188
Mhairi Hogg School of Dancing 138
Microbeacon Computer Project 163
Midlothian trips 192-193
midwives, community 257
Military Tattoo 203
Millar Pharmacy 45
Millets 37
Mini Minstrels 141
Miscarriage Association 251
mobile library 130
Mobile Projects Association 120
Monkey Business 59, 87
Montessori Nursery 104
Montgomery St Playground 212
Montrose (UK) Ltd 54
Morag Alexander School of Dancing 136
Moray House
    College 147, 171
    Institute of Education 163
    National Centre for Play 120, 163
    Play Resource Unit see National Centre for Play
Moredun Library 130
Moredun Toy Library 133
Morningside Park 214
Morningside Pharmacy 45
Morton Hall, The Thomas 187
Moss, E 45
mother and toddler groups see parent and toddler groups
Mothercare 6, 13, 17, 26, 29, 36
    Home Shopping 53
Mothers of Sexually Abused Children (MOSAC) 251
mothers' rooms 51
Motherwell 198
Motor Museum, Myreton 190
Mount Lodge Park 215
Mr Boni's 77, 85, 88
Mr Boom 90
Mr Macawz 29
Mr Mario's 80
Muirhouse
    Library 130
    Park 212

Under Twelves and Parent Centre 159
Mulberry Bush, The 29
Murrayfield Ice Rink 142
museums
    Childhood 177
    Flight 191
    Gasworks, Biggar 197
    Gladstone Court, Biggar 198
    Huntly House 177
    John Knox House 177
    Motor 190
    Newhaven Heritage 177-178
    People's Story, The 178
    Royal Museum of Scotland 178
    Scotch Whisky Heritage Centre, The 178
music and movement classes see dance classes
music lessons 141-142
Music School, St Mary's 141
Musselburgh Sports Centre 140, 171
    creche 171
My Adventure Books 52
Myreton Motor Museum 190
nannies see childcare
Napier, D and Sons 254
Napier University 163
Nanny Service, The 125
Nappy Days 26, 55
nappy laundry service 26, 55
National
    Asthma Campaign 263
    Centre for Play 120, 163, 263
    Eczema Society 263
    Gallery of Scotland 175
    Women's Register 159
National Childbirth Trust (NCT) 13, 26, 44, 58, 256, 257-258, 259
    Nearly New Sale 204
    Trading Ltd 54
Naturopaths, General Council and Register of 254
Nature's Best 54
Nature's Gate 54
NCT see National Childbirth Trust
Nelson Monument 179
Netherbow Arts Centre 86, 135, 187
Nevisport 37
New and Junior Profile 13, 17
New Bike Shop 35
New Conceptions 54
Newcraighall see Kinnaird Park
Newhaven
    Harbour 185

Heritage Museum 177-178
New Heights 37
Newington Library 131
Newkirkgate Shopping Centre 9
New Lanark Visitor Centre 198
newspapers 49, 205
Next 18
Next Best 44, 56
Next Directory 53
Night Nannies 125
Nippers 18
North Berwick 191
Northfield Broadway playground 215
Northfield/Willowbrae Community Education Centre 159
    Gala Day 202
North Queensferry 197
Norton Tavern, The 81, 82
No. 20 Women and Children's Centre 159
Number Shop, The 164
Number Two 18
Nucleus 251
nurseries
    independent schools 118
    primary schools 116-118
    private 107-115
    state 116
nursery equipment 25
    repairs 25
Nurseryland 44
nursery nurses 122
nursery schools 116
NWR see National Women's Register
Observatory, Royal 220
odd shoe service 54
Odeon Film Centre 188
Old Bordeaux Coachhouse 77, 82
Old Inn, The 82
Old Town Gala 202
OLCS see Open Learning Consultancy Services
One Parent Families Scotland 206, 247
One Step Ahead 37
Open Door, The 77
Open University in Scotland, The 164
Open Learning Consultancy Services (OLCS) 161
open top buses 185
Orthopaedic Hospital, Princess Margaret Rose 261
Osteopaths, General Council and Register of 254
Outdoors 31
outdoor shops 36
outdoor toys 31
Owl and the Pussycat, The 29

Oxgangs
    Gala Day 202
    Library 131
    Toy Library 133
Palace of Holyrood House 181
Pancake Place 69
pantomimes 200
Parent
    and baby groups 92
    and toddler groups 92-97
Parent-link Scotland 259
parentcraft classes see
    antenatal classes
parents centres 158-160
Parents
    Forever Scotland 251
    Room 159
    at Work 120
park and ride 236
parking 235
parks 208-218
Pathhead 193
parties see birthday parties
party-plan shopping 55
Pastoral Foundation 251
Paterson, Aileen 39
Pauline's of Morningside 14
Peacock Inn 74, 82
Peartree House 82
Peebles 195
Pennywell
    Gdns Playpark 212
    Rd Playpark 212
Pentland Community Centre
    171
Pentland Hills 225-227
    Bonaly 225
    Harlaw and Threipmuir
        Reservoirs 226
    Hillend Country Park 226
    Glencorse Reservoir 225
Peoples' Story, The 178
Perth 198
    Leisure Pool 198
Peter Pan Nannies 125
Peter Pepper 90
photographers 49-50
piano lessons 141
Piazza Open Air Cafe 211
Pierre Victoire 74
Pilrig Park 213
Pilton Toy Library 133
Pilton Park West 213
Pine and Old Lace 18
Ping On 74
Piper, Thomas 35
Pitt Stop, The 168
Pizza Hut 69, 86
Pizzaland 70
Place Pigalle 70
planes see Edinburgh Airport
play
    centres 151-153

Development Officer 209
    grounds 208-218
    organizations 119-120
    schemes 201-203
    sessions 152
    Resource Unit see National
        Centre for Play schemes
playbus 218
playgroups 97-106
    community 97
    home 97
    private 98
Play in Scottish Hospitals 262
Playhouse Theatre 187-188
PMR see Princess Margaret
    Rose
police stables and dog-handlers
    185
Polly Wolly Doodle 30
Portobello
    beach and Promenade 227
    Community Festival 202
    Library 131
    Rosefield Park 216
    Straighton Place
    playground 216
    Toy Library 133
Portobello Fun Fair 84, 152-153
    cafeteria 153
Portobello Swim Centre 147-
    148, 172,
    creche 172
    Refreshment Room 73, 86,
    148
Post House Hotel 81
postnatal
    depression 260
    exercise classes 259
    Illness, Association for 260
    support 257-259
Poundstretcher 18, 30, 36
pregnancy, air travel and 244
pre-school play and education
    91
Presto 11
Prestonfield
    Gala 202
    Park Playground 215
    Toy Library 133
Pride of Belhaven, The 86, 185
Pride of the Union 185
primary schools with nursery
    classes 116-118
Princess Alexandra Eye Pavilion
    261
Princess Margaret Rose
    Orthopaedic Hospital 261
Princes St Gardens 210-211
    floral clock 182, 210
    Piazza Open Air Cafe 211
    playground 211
    Ross Bandstand/Open Air
    Theatre 210

Scott Monument, The 210
Prisoner's Wives' and Families
    Society 251
private nurseries 107-115
    problems, help with 249-252
problem solving 262-263
public toilets 50-51
pubs 81
    Central Edinburgh 82
    North Edinburgh 82
    South Edinburgh 82
    West Edinburgh 82
puppets
    festival 201
    theatre 198
Purves Puppets 198
pushchairs see baby equipment
Quality Mark Wholesale 18
Queen Margaret College 164
Queens Hall, The 77, 188
Rachael's Tearoom 229
Racial Equality Council, Lothian
    158
Radio Forth 205
Radio Rentals 59
Raeburn House Hotel 82
Raeburn Pram Centre 18, 26
railcards 242
railway paths 228
railways see trains
Rainbow Magic 90
Rannoch Centre 172
Rape Crisis Centre 252
Ratho Children's Gala 202
Ratho Community Centre 172
    creche 172
    gym club 140
Ratho Park, The 81, 82
Ravelston playground 216
Raymond 48
reading 142
Recreation Dept see Edinburgh
    District Council
Recycling (bicycle shop) 35
Read Books 43
Real Foods Ltd (Mail Order) 54
Recording the Event 49
Red Book 206, 246
Red House Children's Book Club,
    The 52, 56
    Party Post 55
Red Moss Wildlife Reserve 227
registration of birth 256-257
Reflexology Association, British
    253
Remnant Kings see Kings
    Fabrics
Refreshment Room 73
repairs
    dolls 27-31
    nursery equipment 25-27
restaurants see eating out 60-81
retraining see training

Riccarton Arms Hotel, The 78
Richards Pizzerama 86
Rights Office, Citizen's 246
River Almond 221-222
road safety 234
Roseburn Playpark 217
Rosefield Park 216
Ross Open Air Theatre 188
Roundabout Centre 159, 164
Round Table Restaurant 70
Royal Academy of Dancing 136
Royal Botanic Garden 228-229
    Glasshouse Experience 228
    Rachael's Tearoom 229
    Terrace Cafe 229
Royal Blind Asylum Shop 26
Royal Commonwealth Pool 86,
    148-149, 151, 172
    cafeteria 149
    creche 172
Royal
    Highland Show 202
    Hospital for Sick Children
    260, 261
    Lyceum Theatre 188
    Mile Miniatures 30
Royal Museum of Scotland 178
    Cafe 71, 179
    Shop 43
Royal Observatory Visitor
    Centre 220
Royal Society for the Prevention
    of Accidents RoSPA 234
Royal Scottish Society for the
    Prevention of Cruelty to
    Children 249
RRS Discovery, Dundee 198
Russell and Bromley 24
SACRO Lothian 161
Safari Park, Blair Drummond
    196
safety
    car 236
    car seats 236-237
    child, cycling 235
    equipment, cycling 32-33
    road 234
    Tufty Club 234
Safeway 11-12
    Pharmacy 45
Sainsbury's 12
St Andrew Square Bus Station
    Cafe 238
St Andrews, Fife 197
St Bernard's Toy Library 133
St Brides Community Centre
    172, 188
    creche 172
St Fillan's 'Nearly New'
    Children's Clothes Shop 44
St Giles Cathedral 182
    Lower Aisle Restaurant 85
St James Centre 9

Food Court 62, 71
St John's Hospital 255, 261
St Margaret's Park 216
St Mary's Music School 141
St Thomas of Aquins 157, 173
sand (for sandpits) 31
Santa 204
    barge trips 204
    steam train trips 204
Saughton
    Fort Saughton 216
    Park 216
    Sports Complex 173
Savacentre 12, 18, 30
Scandic Crown Hotel 71
schools
    independent 118
    nursery 116
    primary 116-118
    special 119
    starting 119
school wear 19
Scone Palace 199
Scotch House, The see
    Burberrys and The Scotch
    House
Scotch Whisky Heritage Centre
    178
Scotland on Sunday 205
Scotland Yard
    adventure playground 218
    Summer Festival 202
Scotmid Co-op see Co-op
Scotsman, The 205
Scott Monument 210
Scottish
    Amateur Gymnastics
    Coaching Award 91
    Birth Teachers Association
    255
    Book Fortnight 204
    Childminding Association
    121, 124
    Council for Single Parents
    see One Parent Families
    Scotland
    Cry-Sis Society 247
    Downs Syndrome
    Association 251
    Independent Nurseries
    Association 107
    International Children's
    Festival 201
    Miners' Gala 202
    National Federation for the
    Welfare of the Blind 263
    Pre-School Play Association
    91, 119, 164
    Society for Autistic Children
    251
    Tourist Board 205
    Wider Access Programme
    161, 164

Wildlife Trust 224
Scottish National Gallery of
    Modern Art 175
    cafe 74
Scottish National Portrait
    Gallery 175
sea, swimming in the 143
Seacliff Beach 143, 191
Sea Life Centre, St Andrews 197
Sea World, Deep 197
Second Chance to Learn 164
secondhand goods 43-44
Seconds & Firsts 18
Seeds Cafe 78
Separated and Divorced
    Catholics, Association of
    249
sewing supplies see make your
    own
Shapes Furniture Ltd 26
Sherry's 78
Shetland Connection 19
Shoe City 24
shoes, children's 23
    mail order 54
Shoos 24
Shopping from Home 52-56
shopping centres 7-10
Sick Children, Action for 261
Sick Children's Hospital see
    Royal Hospital for Sick
    Children
Sighthill
    Library 131
    Park 217
    Toy Library 133
Silversands 196
Simpson House Drug Project
    251
Simpson House Family
    Counselling Centre 260
Simpson Memorial Maternity
    Pavilion 255
single parents
    Guide to Leisure in Lothian
    206
    Scottish Council for see One
    Parent Families Scotland
    Guide to Further Education
    161
skating 142
ski shops 36
SMT 238
    bus station 238
SNIP (Special Needs Information
    Point) 262, 263
snowdrops 200
Social Work Dept see Lothian
    Regional Council
Society of Homoeopaths 254
Somerfield 12

Song of Sixpence 44, 56
South Bridge Resource Centre 157
South Queensferry 194
    Community Centre 157, 173
    Library 131
    Toy Library 133
South Side Community Centre 157
    cafeteria 157
Special Effects 48
special needs see SNIP
Special Needs Toy Library 133
special schools 119
Speech Impaired Children, Association for (AFASIC) 249
Spencer, Mary 141
Splash Leisure Pool, Dunbar 191
Spokes 235
sports, adult 166-173
Sports Warehouse 37
SPPA see Scottish Pre-School Play Association
Spring Fling 201
Springwell House Centre 172
Springwell House Toy Library 133
Sprogs 19
Stardust Mobile Children's Disco 90
Startrite - mail order 54
stations
    Haymarket 241
    South Gyle 241
    Waverley 186, 240
Stenton Fruit Farm 191
Stepfamilies of Scotland 251
Stepping Stones for Young Parents 159
Stevenson, R L 39
Stevenson College of FE 164
Stirling 196
    Castle 196
    With Kids 207
Stockbridge
    Bookshop 41
    Festival 202
    Library 131
Stockingfillas Ltd 55
Storytelling Festival 204
Straighton Place playground 216
Strathclyde trips 197-198
Streamers 87
Student Charities Week 201
Studio One 30, 57
Sunday Best 19
Sunday chemists 44-45
supermarkets 10-12
support groups, women's 158-160

Suzuki Institute, British 141
Swanston Village and Farm 227
SWAP (Scottish Wider Access Programme) 161, 164
Swedish Rainwear 56
swimming
    adults 168-173
    children 142-151
    family 143
    pools guide 144-151
    sea 143
swingparks see playgrounds
Sycomore Tree, The 78
Tale of Greyfriars Bobby 39
TAP (Training Access Point) 160
tap dancing see dancing
Tattler, The 74
Tattoo, Military 203
taxis 239
    airport 245
Tayside trips 198-199
Telford Arms 75, 82
Telford College, Edinburgh's 165
Terrace, The 78
Tesco 12
Theatre School of Dance and Drama 138
Theatre Workshop 75, 188
theatres 186-188
Thin, James 41
    Cafe 71
Thistle Chapel see St Giles Cathedral 182
Thomas Morton Hall, The 187
Thomson, George 90
Time Capsule, The 198
time, telling the 182
Tiso, Graham 26, 37
Toddle In 19
toilets, public 50-51
Tollcross Community Education Centre 157, 173
Topsy Turvy 19
tourist board see Edinburgh information Centre
Tourist Board, Scottish 205
touristcard 239
toy libraries 132-134
toys
    mail order 54-55
    outdoor 31
    shops 27-31
Toys Galore 30, 88
Toys R Us 6, 19, 27, 30, 31, 36, 88
Traffic Club, Children's 234
trailers, bicycle 32
training courses 161-166
Training 2000 161
trains 240-242
    Bo'ness and Kinneil Railway 196
    British Rail 240

catering 241
fares and rules 242
railcard 242
reservations 242
Santa trips 204
stations 240-241
travel 240-242
Waverley Station 240
Tranent 191
travel 233-245
Traveline 205, 238
Traverse Theatre 71, 188
Trefoil Holiday & Adventure Centre 86
Tridias 55
Trusthouse Forte Coffee Shop 72
Tryst Crafts 56
Tufty Club 234
Tumbletots 140
Turkington, Marjorie 141
Turner Hire Drive 237
Twins and Multible Birth Association 258
Twin Club, Edinburgh 258
UCI Cinemas 189
Union Canal 229-230
    trips 230
    Society 204
United Colors of Benetton 15
universities
    Edinburgh 165
    Heriot-Watt 162
    Napier 163
    Open, The 164
Uppercrust and Bar 243
Usborne Books 56
Verandah Restaurant 72
Victim Support Scheme, Lothian 250
Victoria Park 213
violin lessons 141
Vogrie Estate and Country Park 193, 230
    adventure playground 218
Walking in Edinburgh and the Pentlands 219
walks 219-232
WAND (Women and New Directions) 161
Warrender Swim Centre 149, 173,
Water of Leith Walkway 230-232
    Balerno-Currie 230
    Currie-Juniper Green 231
    Dean Bank Footpath 231
    Dean Path-Stockbridge 232
    Deanhaugh Footpath 232
    Juniper Green-Slateford 231
    Rocheid Path 232
    Slateford-Belford Road 231
    Warriston-Coburg St 232

Waterside Bistro, Haddington
    191
Waterstone's Bookshop 42
Waverley
    Food Court 72
    Market 9
    Shopping Centre 9-10
    Station 186, 240
    Wharf 72
WEA (Workers' Educational
    Association) 165
Wellspring 252
Well Woman Project,
    Womanzone 160
Wesley Owen Books and Music
    42
West and Wilde Bookshop 42
West Lothian trips 193
Westburn Grove playground
    217
Westbury Hotel 81, 87
Wester Hailes
    Education Centre 87, 140,
    157
    Opportunities Trust (WHOT)
    161, 165
    Playpark 217

Shopping Centre 10
Wester Hailes Swiming Pool
    150, 157
    cafeteria 150
Western General Hospital 261
What Everyone Wants 19, 30
What's On 205
Whisky Heritage Centre, Scotch
    178
White Park 217
WHOT see Wester Hailes
    Opportunities Trust
Wildlife Trust, Scottish 224
Wilson Hairdressing, Gordon 48
Wind Things 31
Windygoul Farm 87, 191
Womanzone 160
Women
    and Children's Centre, No
    20 159
    and New Directions (WAND)
    161
    onto Work (WOW) 166
women's aid 252
    Edinburgh 252
    Scottish 252
    Shakti 252

Women's
    Directory, The 158
    groups 158-160
    Royal Voluntary Service
    132
    Training Centre, Edinburgh
    162
wool shops see make your own
Woolworth 7, 19, 31
Workers' Educational
    Association (WEA) 165
Working Mothers' Association,
    see Parents at Work
WOW see Women onto Work
Wrap 31
Yellowcraig 190
YWCA
    Roundabout Centre 159
Youth Services Team 129
Zoo, Edinburgh 84, 182-183
    animal handling 183, 200
    The Den 183
    The Penguin's Pantry 183
    Members' House 183
    Shop-see Arkadia

Crisis Lines

More details of some of these organisations are provided in the text.

AMBULANCE, POLICE, FIRE 999

CRYSIS for help with persistently crying babies 334 5317

RAPE CRISIS CENTRE 556 9437

ROYAL HOSPITAL FOR SICK CHILDREN 536 0000

THE SAMARITANS .... (24 hrs) 221 9999
25 Torphicen St (9am-10pm)

SHAKTI WOMEN'S AID 557 4010
12 Picardy Place

SOCIAL WORK DEPARTMENT (Lothian Regional Council) .... (24hrs) 554 4301

WESTERN GENERAL HOSPITAL 537 1000

WOMEN'S AID .... (24 hrs) 229 1419

WOMEN AND CHILD SERIOUS SEXUAL CRIMES 662 5785
Mon-Sat 8am-10pm, Sun 10-6. Answer machine outwith these hours
(will call back or visit if required)

LOCAL POLICE STATION ....

GP ....

GP NIGHT CALLS ....

HEALTH VISITOR ....

MATERNITY HOSPITAL/MIDWIFE ....

DENTIST ....

CHEMIST ....

NCT BREAST FEEDING COUNSELLOR ....

....

....